I0821619

Cypress Gardens, America's Tropical Wonderland

UNIVERSITY PRESS OF FLORIDA

Florida A&M University, Tallahassee
Florida Atlantic University, Boca Raton
Florida Gulf Coast University, Ft. Myers
Florida International University, Miami
Florida State University, Tallahassee
New College of Florida, Sarasota
University of Central Florida, Orlando
University of Florida, Gainesville
University of North Florida, Jacksonville
University of South Florida, Tampa
University of West Florida, Pensacola

Cypress Gardens, America's Tropical Wonderland

How Dick Pope Invented Florida

University Press of Florida
Gainesville · Tallahassee · Tampa · Boca Raton · Pensacola · Orlando · Miami · Jacksonville · Ft. Myers · Sarasota

Printed in China on acid-free paper

15 14 13 12 11 10 6 5 4 3 2 1

Library of Congress Cataloging-in-Publication Data
Vickers, Lu.
Cypress Gardens, America's tropical wonderland : how Dick Pope invented Florida / Lu Vickers.
p. cm.
Includes bibliographical references and index.
ISBN 978-0-8130-3499-7
1. Cypress Gardens (Winter Haven, Fla.)—History. 2. Tourism—Florida—History. 3. Winter Haven (Fla.)—History. 4. Pope, Richard Downing, d. 1988. I. Title.
GV1853.3.F62C978 2010
791.06'8759—dc22 2010009770

The University Press of Florida is the scholarly publishing agency for the State University System of Florida, comprising Florida A&M University, Florida Atlantic University, Florida Gulf Coast University, Florida International University, Florida State University, New College of Florida, University of Central Florida, University of Florida, University of North Florida, University of South Florida, and University of West Florida.

University Press of Florida
15 Northwest 15th Street
Gainesville, FL 32611-2079
http://www.upf.com

For the Cypress Gardens family, most especially the family of Dick and Julie Pope

PHOTO COURTESY FLORIDA CYPRESS GARDENS
Florida Sunburst Blosson

Contents

1 Land of Sunshine and Roses

Driving down Highway 27, the old Dixie Highway, from Ocala toward Cypress Gardens, it's possible to get a glimpse of the Ghost of Florida Past. Back when the Orange Blossom Trail, as that section of 27 came to be named, was bordered by fragrant orange groves, it cut right through the "scenic heart of Florida."[1] As one writer colorfully put it, "It's the road that runs up the middle of Florida like the ridge on the back of an alligator."[2] In the 1950s, this ridge, a "remnant of an island that in prehistoric times was all of Florida above the sea," was home to some of Florida's major tourist attractions: Bok Singing Tower, Silver Springs, Highlands Hammock State Park, the Cypress Knee Museum, and the epicenter of modern Florida tourism, Cypress Gardens.[3]

In the 1940s and 1950s, the Orange Blossom Trail was filled with station wagons, sedans, and tour buses crammed with tourists who wanted

In 1927, the Orange Blossom Trail replaced the portion of the Dixie Highway that ran down the center of Florida. Author's collection.

Left: Esther Williams pauses for a photo shoot during the filming of *Easy to Love* in 1953. By permission of Cypress Gardens.

Above: Duke Ellington brought his orchestra to the Gardens in 1969 for an appearance on the *Mike Douglas Show.* Here Duke Ellington and saxophonist Harry Carney wait for their cue. By permission of Cypress Gardens.

to get a look at the real Florida, the one promised to them in glossy brochures: a sun-filled paradise of palms and balmy breezes with a few alligators and parrots tossed in. They wanted to see the eight-hundred-year-old giant laurel oak at Highlands Hammock; they wanted to hear the carillon at Bok Tower. But most of all, they wanted to see Cypress Gardens, "America's Tropical Wonderland," the Technicolor Florida dream fashioned out of a swamp by a man named Dick Pope. And they weren't alone. Carillons and giant oaks were one thing, but Cypress Gardens had flowers *and* "camera models" and Aqua Maids.

By 1941, 20th Century Fox had arrived at the Gardens to film scenes for *Moon over Miami*, a musical about two sisters who head to Florida in search of rich husbands. In one scene, actor Don Ameche asks his costar, Betty Grable, to marry him while they drift through the Gardens' tea-colored canals on an electric boat. By the 1950s, movie star Esther Williams had become the "unofficial goddess" of Cypress Gardens; she couldn't stay away from the place or from Dick Pope, whom she called the "little Napoleon." She made two films and a television "spectacular" at the Gardens, and persuaded Dick Pope to build three swimming pools for her, one shaped like the state of Florida. In the 1960s, Johnny Carson filmed his only off-site television special at Cypress Gardens and wore swim trunks almost the entire time. Daytime talk-show host Mike Douglas filmed his first color show at the Gardens, bringing in Muhammad Ali and a grapefruit-colored elephant. Duke Ellington and his orchestra played "Mood Indigo" beneath the palm trees.

These days, Highway 27 is the road less traveled. Since the heady 1950s and 1960s, the Florida Turnpike, I-75, and Disney have siphoned away the tourists, putting a strain on Florida's scenic heart. What used to be one of Florida's main thoroughfares is now a back road; what used to be Florida's main attractions are now minor ones. But that has only increased their charm. The savvy traveler knows that a trip down Highway 27 toward Cypress Gardens is well worth the effort, if for nothing else, to catch a glimpse of the simple things that used to give us pleasure.

The rattlesnakes that Ross Allen used to milk for fun and profit at his Reptile Institute are gone (as is the anaconda he wrestled underwater for a short film), but Silver Springs will always be there, and at Ocala, a short dogleg off 27 will land you at the attraction, where, after more than 130 years, you can still board a glass-

A swimmer poses underwater for this souvenir postcard foldout from Silver Springs, 1936. Author's collection.

When it was built in 1956, the Citrus Tower in Clermont was surrounded by orange groves. Author's collection.

bottomed boat and get a fish-eye's view of an alligator.

Back on 27, you could swing by the WPA-era Venetian Gardens just outside of Leesburg, or you could forge ahead and drive through the area known as the "Little Everglades," a spot so crowded with lakes that a 1950s tour guide warns drivers to keep an eye out for "deer, wildcats and alligators," soberly noting that "An alligator can ditch a speeding car as readily as a log."[4] These days, you don't need to worry about the wildlife.

South of Leesburg, past the crumbling remains of old motor courts, past the kitschy House of Presidents (Abe Lincoln sits out front; Mount Rushmore stands to the left), you'll come to the Citrus Tower, the "world's biggest monument to an orange."[5] In 1956, when the tower was built in Clermont, it was surrounded by the fragrant orange groves that gave 27 its new name. Back then, people said, from the top of the tower you could see more than a third of the citrus grown in the United States. The tower had its own packing plant, candy factory, and glass blower. After a series of freezes in the 1980s, the trees are gone except for a few patches growing between strip malls and housing developments. Instead of citrus groves, the tower overlooks miles and miles of the "Little Boxes" Malvina Reynolds immortalized in song:

> Little boxes on the hillside,
> Little boxes made of ticky tacky,
> Little boxes on the hillside,
> Little boxes all the same.
> There's a green one and a pink one
> And a blue one and a yellow one,
> And they're all made out of ticky tacky,
> And they all look just the same.[6]

Still, despite the ticky tacky, it's worth a trip to the top of the tower—the elevator is like a time machine, with its hand-painted orange tree. A tiny airplane flies in the sky behind its branches, its banner rippling in the wind: "Thanks for visiting the Grand Citrus Tower." On the observation deck, hand-lettered signs point to nearby attractions: Weeki Wachee. Silver Springs. Cypress Gardens. One sign proclaims that "over 17 million citrus trees" are visible from the deck. That was true in the 1950s, but you can compare black-and-white photographs of yesteryear's orange groves with the full-color reality of what is there now: developments with names like Lost Lake Reserve and Skyridge. The massive retirement community King's Ridge sprouted on what used to be the "showplace grove" of the R. D. Keene Citrus Company.[7] After gazing out at miles and miles of roofs, you can drop a quarter in a slot, press your ear to a pipe in the wall, and wait for the coin to hit the bottom. On your way out, you can buy one of the few remaining Citrus Tower orange mesh bags for a dollar. It's a steal.

Outside of Clermont, at Orange Mountain, the signs nailed on an abandoned roadside fruit stand hint both at the area's citrus history and its demise:

> Welcome to Orange Mountain
> Fresh Fruit Honey
> Indian River Fruit
> For Sale or Rent

As late as 2006, a reporter described stopping at this very spot, where she was offered "a taste of red-fleshed oranges and bittersweet grapefruit."[8] The stand, built in 1948, was owned by Peter and Joan Feitsma, who lived in the adjacent block building that originally served as a store for orange grove workers. Most of the fruit the Feitsmas sold came from area growers, although some of it came from the sixty or so trees growing behind their home. In the mid-1990s, the Feitsmas fended off a developer who wanted their small parcel of land after buying nearly 1,300 acres around them. "At first, they

This living "Hidden Mickey" lies in the woods off Highway 27, just south of Orange Mountain. It can be seen via Google Earth. By permission of Google Earth.

wanted us to leave," Peter told a reporter in 1998. "You can understand—they wanted the whole thing." His wife remembered bartering oranges for a kitchen floor. "We've always lived in orange groves," she said. "We're not getting rich running this stand. But we're paying our bills and hoping to put these two younger kids through college."[9]

The Feitsmas are gone now, but the stand remains, almost like a museum piece, a relic of old Florida situated in the middle of a huge housing development. The bins are still there, empty. Tattered plastic flags flutter in the wind. A few orange trees grow out back.

Ironically, a couple of miles down the road in the woods off 27, untouched, there grows a "hidden Mickey," a giant Mickey Mouse head carved out of a grove of slash pines. It's visible from Google Earth. The origin of the hidden Mickey is unclear—it's a secret, after all—but apparently in the 1980s as a prank, Disney "imagineers" started placing these "hidden Mickeys"—usually the silhouette of the circular head and ears of The Mouse—in their movies, on golf courses, on fruit trays, throughout their theme parks. There are field guides, one written by an emergency-room doctor who relocated his family to Orlando to be closer to Disney World.[10]

The Lake County slash pine Mickey remains a mystery—no one will admit to having planted it. But one thing is certain. That slash pine Mouse head is irrefutable evidence of what the Disney brothers did to Florida: they slipped the Sunshine State a Mickey. A big one.

And yet, Florida's scenic heart beats on. Just down the road from Orange Mountain at Haines City, it is clear that all has not been lost to the Mouse. Atop an asphalt-covered hill, the shiny 1970s-era Orange Ring seduces the traveler with neon orange mesh bags bursting with plastic oranges and grapefruit. The bags hang from the bright orange awning that circles the building, just above tables piled high with pyramids of the real thing. Inside, a wooden Indian sits by the door. Shell sculptures, saltwater taffy, and alligator-shaped ashtrays fill the glass shelves. At the Orange Ring, you can ship boxes of zipper-skin tangerines and Indian River grapefruit to your relatives up North, or you can choose a variety pack of tropical spreads: honeybell, temple orange, and lime marmalades, along with tangerine and orange jellies. Or you can forego the fruit and buy a Florida pinup-girl postcard or a mug shaped like an orange.

South of Haines City, Highway 27 now officially crests the Lake Wales Ridge, the ancient sand dune that forms the highest part of Florida. Two million years ago, the ridge was a series of islands poking up out of the Gulf. Today it is host to more rare and endangered species than anyplace else in the United States. Why? The answer becomes clear as one cruises along the ridge deeper into Polk County. It's the same thing that threatens Florida's original roadside attractions: habitat loss.

The highway winds past miles of clear-cut land bordered by a succession of giant pink and

The Florida pool that juts out into Lake Eloise at Cypress Gardens is one of a kind. By permission of the Winter Haven Historical Museum.

Bette Davis tours the Gardens with the Popes in the 1950s. By permission of Cypress Gardens.

blue and green flags as far as the eye can see. It looks as though the artist Christo has been here and installed a Cracker version of *The Gates*. But no. A developer has just supersized those eye-catching plastic flags that always seem to be flapping at used-car lots.

After passing the few remaining orange groves and scrubland and Western Wear stores, you draw even closer to Cypress Gardens, the epicenter of Florida tourism, literally, the heart of Florida's scenic heart.

Esther Williams's Florida-shaped pool is a made-to-order metaphor for the real thing. The pool is still at the Gardens, still jutting out into the tannic water of Lake Eloise the way the real Florida juts into the Gulf of Mexico. After over a half century, the Florida pool has lost its tile, but it hasn't lost its power to stir the imagination—there's not another one like it in the world. And just like the real Florida, you have to brave the humidity and hike past palm trees and cypress knees to find it. When you do, it's easy to imagine Esther Williams and her costar John Bromfield floating amid a thousand gardenias center-state, right where Cypress Gardens is located. If you are quiet enough, you can almost hear the long-gone violinists who perched on cypress knees around the pool to play their serenade for this very scene in *Easy to Love.*

Dick Pope knew he had a piece of the real Florida in his Gardens—long before he built the Florida pool—and he knew tourists wanted it: *We are going to sell 100,000 of them 25 cents worth of Florida*, he said in the 1930s. And he did. He reeled them in, big and small, got them to hook a right off 27, make the drive in to Cypress Gardens. Moms and pops. Grandmas and grandkids. Uncles and aunts. Stars like Bette Davis, Carol Burnett, Arthur Godfrey. Arthur Godfrey's mother. Aunt Jemima. Tiny Tim. The movie star Joan Crawford was a fan of both the Gardens and the Popes. In a note to "My very dear Julie and Dick," she wrote, "Thank you for all this beauty."

John F. Kennedy dropped in at the Gardens from time to time before he became president, flying up from his compound in Palm Beach. The shah of Iran came to water-ski, prompting Dick Pope to quip, "There's no business like Shah business." King Hussein of Jordan flew up from Palm Beach. The Duke and Duchess of Windsor arrived by train. Willie Hartack, the most famous jockey in 1950s America, won four races at Tropical Park in Miami, climbed down off his last

Tiny Tim visited the Gardens in 1977 when he relocated to Orlando. By permission of Cypress Gardens.

The famous jockey Willie Hartack accepts a wreath of gardenias from a group of southern belles in 1955. By permission of Cypress Gardens.

horse, and said to his manager, "Now, can I fly up to Cypress Gardens and go waterskiing?"[11] Elvis water-skied here on the sly, even though Dick Pope didn't like him one bit. Maybe that explains why there's only one photograph of the King in swim trunks, skiing across Lake Eloise, the wind blowing through his hair. Even Elsie the Borden Milk Cow came and rode on a pontoon boat through the canals.[12]

But how did Dick Pope get people to come? To Imperial Polk County, smack dab in the middle of the state? Like the proverbial Creator, or more accurately, like the folks who drained the Everglades, or like Carl Fisher, who drained and filled wetlands to create Miami Beach, Dick Pope scooped mud out of canals, drained the swamp, and filled the land with brightly colored flowers. But instead of just standing back and admiring his Garden, he whipped out a camera and started taking photographs, and before long he peopled those photos with southern belles and water-skiers, and the tourists came and the newspapers came and the film crews came and they came and they came and they came.

In 1963, Cypress Gardens and the Grand Canyon tied as the number-one tourist attraction in the country. Number One! And the Grand Canyon is 277 miles long, 18 miles wide, and one mile deep. It could hold a thousand Cypress Gardens, and yet in 1972, a year after Disney dropped its Mickey bomb on Florida, author Frank Deford wrote that if he could take a visitor from another country to only one attraction in the United States, he would take them to Cypress Gardens. Not to the Grand Canyon or Disney World. "Cypress Gardens is American to the core," he wrote.[13]

But why? The answer lies in that truly American form of storytelling that reveres the larger-than-life hero. The tall tale. Think Paul Bunyan and Babe the Blue Ox. Johnny Appleseed. Annie Oakley. Pecos Bill. Dick Pope. Dick Pope was a small man, but he believed in outrageous gestures, like claiming he was "born in the middle of an Iowa cyclone," and wearing outlandish suits that looked like they were sewn from drapes. "As you can see," he said, "I'm a short person, so I have to dress noticeably to get attention. If I didn't wear the flashy jackets, people would think I'm just a tall fire hydrant."[14]

One writer called him a "sartorial symphony in lemon slacks, lemon sports shirt and lemon sports jacket."[15] Pope didn't just go for bright colors; his wardrobe included floral-print jackets and white, perforated alligator shoes. "I'm not a funeral director," he said. "I'm a salesman of Sunny Florida, and I like my clothes to match my job." He once chastised the Florida Council of 100 for dressing "like a bunch of morticians,"[16] and bought blue-and-white-striped sports jackets for each one of them.[17] He gave away flowers by the stem *and* the boxload and once planned to blanket the streets of New York City with a million gardenias dumped from a plane. The Civil Aeronautics Board intervened. He famously told Conrad Hilton, the California-based hotelier, "I just *love* your state; I bought my first and only overcoat there."

Dick Pope Sr. poses with Dumbo and a southern belle for the *Mike Douglas Show* in 1968. By permission of Cypress Gardens.

His motto, he told Norman Vincent Peale, was to "Think big about everything." It worked. By 1955, he was expecting to sell a dollar's worth of Florida to over 1 million people. And when he wheeled up to Miami's Hotel Fontainebleau in his brand-new Lincoln, he was swarmed with

Young women engage in a "Florida snowball" fight with gardenias, circa 1930s. By permission of Adrienne Pope Watkins.

"parking lot boys" who wanted to pay him a dollar for the privilege of parking his car.[18]

Thinking big about everything seemed to be the creed of nearly everyone in Polk County. When the folklorist Zora Neale Hurston came home to Florida in the late 1920s, Charlie Jones of Eatonville said that if she wanted to hear some big talk, she needed to head to Polk County:

> Course, Zora, you ain't at de right place to get de bes' lies. Why don't you go down 'round Bartow and Lakeland and 'round in dere—Polk County? Dat's where they really lies up a mess and dat's where dey makes up all de songs and things lak dat. Ain't you never hea'd dat in Polk County de water drink lak cherry wine?[19]

Charlie Jones could've been referring to Dick Pope, who really did convince people that the "water drink lak cherry wine" down in Polk County.

But Dick Pope was just one of a long line of big talkers to come out of Winter Haven, which once billed itself unabashedly as the City of a Hundred Lakes and the Home of a Hundred Millionaires. After meeting a few Havenites, the impression that the water drinks like cherry wine deepens. This is no metaphor, but a reality. Practically everyone that had anything to do with Cypress Gardens appears larger than life. Bob Kehoe, who retired after fifty-two years at the Gardens, runs a farm called Critter Creek where you can find what seems to be the world's biggest horse alongside the smallest. Eighty-year-old Bill Bell can still recite his 1950s-era ski-show spiel without missing a word. Dubie Baxter, who practically lived at the Gardens and whose father died when he was a boy, is brim full with stories

A 1924 aerial view of Winter Haven. Photo by Robert Dahlgren. Author's collection.

of how the African American waiters at Cypress Gardens helped to raise him. *There was a Legion Hall in Florence Villa, the black section of town, and when I was about 15 . . . we went to see James Brown and the Flames, and buddy I had never seen anything like that in my little white life.*

The Polk County tendency toward exaggeration in both life and words is a trait that goes way back. Throughout the 1800s, newspapers referred to Winter Haven as "A Spot on God's Footstool That Is Incomparable," "the Land of Sunshine and Roses," "the Sportsman's Paradise and the Trucker's Eldorado." It was said that visitors could "see pineapples ripening, feast on guavas, drink refreshing lime juice and eat sweet potatoes for dessert."[20] Winter Haven was the "banana capital," "the tomato capital," and the "citrus capital." Legend has it that Hernando de Soto crossed Polk County in 1539, eating Spanish oranges and dropping the seeds along the way. More than 350 years later, in 1898, Teddy Roosevelt and his Rough Riders were said to have passed through Lake Alfred on their way to Cuba for the Spanish American War, and Winter Haven residents gave each man a bag of oranges as a souvenir.[21] They certainly had fruit to spare.

One writer, under the subheading "A Magnificent Paradise That Is Overflowed by Tropical Fruits—A Cordial Invitation to Parties Seeking Investment," described the bounty in Winter Haven:

> We saw the first Kelsey Japan plums, Pear trees of the LaConte, Keefer and Bartlett varieties all fruiting. The quince ladened [*sic*] with its beautiful fruit, persimmons, apples, peaches, cherries, goose berries, guavas, custard apples, while the orange and lemon trees showed many fine fruits.[22]

In 1891 a "Polk County lady" offered the following tale as an explanation for the numerous lakes and fertile lands in Winter Haven:

> The Creator called together his most expert workmen providing each with a fine sifter demanding of them an extra and choice creation. When finished He came down to inspect the work. When from each of his footprints there gushed up a beautiful crystal lake of pure water. . . . About this time old Zero and Jack Frost came nosing around. When with a mighty stamp of his foot he bade them both be gone, never to return to this region. . . . The banishment of old Zero and Jack Frost accounts for the successful growing of all tropical fruits and vegetables in the lake region.[23]

Another Polk County resident observed, "Only God could have created Winter Haven," as if someone had suggested the devil might have had a hand in its creation.[24] Clearly, he hadn't seen the likes of Dick Pope and his creation yet, although one writer seemed to prophesize the coming of Cypress Gardens, which would indeed become famous across the world:

> When automobile and coaching parties have found this natural location for their pleasures, they will throng here . . . then . . . the lake regions will be famous, as are the Lakes of Killarney, the Scottish, Swiss and Italian lakes."[25]

Having a green thumb and bragging about it seemed to be the county's main pastime, one that should have come in handy for Dick Pope in the 1930s, when he began to transform that cypress swamp into what would become Florida's number-one tourist attraction, Cypress Gardens. Despite all that braggadocio about "God's footstool" and gooseberries, when Dick Pope began digging the canals and planting grasses, instead of hailing him as a visionary, the local press called him "Swami of the Swamp," and "Maharaja of the Muck." Little did they know that he would later be known as "The Man Who Invented

Dick Pope Sr. poses as the Swami of the Swamp, circa 1950s. By permission of Cypress Gardens.

Florida," "Mister Florida," "Florida's Human Buzz Saw," and "The Father of Florida Tourism." In 1978, Pope was roasted at an event celebrating the creation of the Dick Pope Institute for Tourism Studies at the University of Central Florida. In 1998, he was named one of the fifty most influential Floridians of the twentieth century.

He came by his larger-than-life personality naturally; his successful father, J. Walker Pope, was also one of a kind. "J. Walker was an amazing man," said Margaret Chase Parry, Dick Pope's niece, "because at sixteen he took off on horseback with his brother to go west, to make his fortune, to find gold." Margaret spent a lot of time with Dick and Julie Pope when she was growing up and is privy to a lot of the Pope family lore. "J. Walker ended up living with the Navajo Indians for a while, finding very little gold, traveling and experiencing the West," she said, "and then he came back."[26]

Julie Pope Dantzler, Dick Pope's granddaughter, possesses a worn leatherbound scrapbook and a bundle of pale blue letters tied with a ribbon, letters J. Walker's wife Lillian wrote him while he was on the road in the early 1900s. "When J. Walker Pope was a travelling salesman," Julie said, "he sold insurance, I guess. He would travel during the week, and Lillian would send him letters to wherever it was that he was going to be General Delivery, or whatever hotel he would be staying in, and she pretty much wrote him nearly every night. And it's funny because in a couple of these she talks about Granddad and what a handful he is, and *what am I going to do with him?*"[27]

The letters also reveal a true love. They begin with, "My Precious Husband," "My Own Dear Love." But then there's this exasperation with *you know who*, although Dick's sister Inez gets called out as well. In one letter, written on a Monday, Lillian writes about "Richard," noting that he is recovering from having accidentally cut himself with a knife. "He tries me so, he wants to play and is not able. *It now seems a long time until the end of the week.* . . . I think Richard has gone to tenth street."[28] In another letter, she writes: "Just now, dear I am having some trouble with the children. I cannot allow them to play with the tenth street children; I have found out Richard and Inez are learning some bad things. It's going to be hard as they are both determined to play there. . . . I suppose it would have been just as well if I had not told you this. I shall do the best I can."[29]

Unfortunately, Lillian died when Dick was still a very young child. His father would remarry

Esther Malcolmson, a Minnesota woman, and would have two more children with her: Malcolm and Louise. "One of the stories my mother used to tell me was the way J. Walker met my grandmother, Esther Malcolmson," said Margaret. "They lived in Minnesota on Loring Park, and Dick was skating and had a little cat . . . but he fell and was crying, and I guess Esther walked up and said, 'What's wrong?' and he said, 'My cat ran away and I don't have a mommy.' Anyway, she walked back with the nanny and Dick to the house, and that's how she met J. Walker. And Dick used to always say he was the only man who'd introduced his father to his mother."[30]

Dick Pope's fondness for coming up with amusing sayings like this one led a reporter to call him the "philosopher Dicapopalis," and to refer to his quips as "Dicapopalisms."[31] Far from being insulted, Dick Pope had cards made up featuring some of his favorite lines: "The world is coming to an end. Pay now so I won't have to look all over hell for you." "Where there's Pope, there's life."

In 1911, after Dick's father, J. Walker, remarried, he moved to Winter Haven with his family. Dick Pope remembered the move years later: "I was 11 years old when I came to Florida, and the first word somebody said to me was 'Are you a damnyankee?'"[32] That comment didn't slow him down one bit. He entered a local Charlie Chaplin look-alike contest and walked away with first prize.[33] Meanwhile, his father, J. Walker, was getting settled in. He hired architect Addison Mizner, who later became famous for launching a Mediterranean-influenced "Florida Renaissance," to design and build his office on Sixth Street and Avenue B Northwest in downtown Winter Haven.[34] The building would go on to become the Hob Nob, a popular Winter Haven bar, and Bill Bell would come to own it. By 1950, the Hob Nob was "the place to be seen in Polk County," even though Polk County was dry at the time, and all the patrons could buy was beer. Willie Hartack, the famous jockey, and comedians Joey Bishop and Carol Burnett stopped in whenever they visited the Gardens. "The owner asked me if I'd like to be the bartender," Bill said. "And I told him I would love to buy this bar. At that time my wife had been the hostess at the Terrace Restaurant at Cypress Gardens for ten years, so Cypress Gardens was always connected with me. The owner of the restaurant there, Lil Shoenthal, loaned us the money to buy the Hob Nob: $15,000. So I bought the Hob Nob and fixed it up a little bit, and Joanne got all the girls from the Gardens to come in. At that time they had an air base out

Dick Pope Sr. won ten dollars in a Charlie Chaplin look-alike contest in the 1920s. By permission of Julie Pope Dantzler.

there where they trained flyers, and the flyers would come in, and this place was so crowded you couldn't get into the door."[35]

A couple of years after J. Walker set up the office in Winter Haven, he set up another one in Lake Wales—the first in that town—and began feverishly selling land.[36] He quickly made a name for himself, according to historian Janice Barnwell Ahl: "Those who knew J. Walker Pope said he was a hustler, a live wire and a man of great vision, boundless energy and unquenchable optimism."[37] She might have been describing his son, Dick Pope. That same year, Dick took his first paying job as "clerk, errand boy, window dresser, janitor and general handyman" at Vic Edwards's clothing store in Winter Haven.[38] He was thirteen years old, and claimed to have sold his first house a couple of years earlier. "My dad was out of town on a business trip," he told a reporter, "and a young couple came in wanting a house. By the time he got back, we already had the deal settled." He earned three hundred dollars.[39]

Reading one of J. Walker Pope's sales brochures, it's easy to see where Dick Pope got his knack for salesmanship:

> Lake Wales, its beauty so entrancing, so tranquil—is the result of thousands of multicolored nightfalls, which have tinted the landscape with a harmony of color painted on nature's own canvas. . . . The undulating hills are covered with a wealth of semi-tropical verdure which mingles with the stately pine forests whose tree tops, waving in the sunlight, cast their shadows and are mirrored in more than a score of beautiful clear-water lakes.[40]

Of course, the image of Florida as a garden, as Margot Ammidown, a Florida history scholar writes, originated during the latter part of the Renaissance and was "based on the Judeo-Christian image of Eden as bountiful and temperate." She notes that Ponce de Leon's famed Fountain of Youth was in fact a sort of marketing tool used "to promote further travel and settlement and thus help [the Spanish] secure the territories."[41]

J. Walker Pope didn't have a Fountain of Youth to entice prospective landowners, but he did have some amazing fruit trees. In a photo postcard designed to sell tourists the promise of citrus-grove riches, he posed with several local businessmen in front of "a three year old grape fruit tree," its branches bent to the ground with globes of fruit.[42] Like his father, Dick Pope would

J. Walker Pope talks on the phone in one of his real-estate offices. Photo by Robert Dahlgren. By permission of Julie Pope Dantzler.

later use photography to sell his own chunk of real estate, but he figured out early on that oranges sold a lot better when a beauty queen picked them. By 1967, the Gardens had been featured on more than three hundred national magazine covers—prompting one reporter to ask: "How does he do it? . . . The answer is girls—girls on water-skis, beautiful girls in colorful old-fashion costumes, girls in spectacular garden scenes."[43]

J. Walker knew that fruit itself wasn't enough to attract potential buyers, but the pinup girl wouldn't come of age until the 1940s, so he worked on improving the cultural offerings of the county. In the summer of 1914, he brought the Whitehair Orchestra to the Hotel Wales—the first live orchestra seen in those parts. J. Walker didn't limit himself to just promoting orange groves or selling real estate. He was a member—soon to be president—of the Polk County Good Roads Association, and he convinced the locals to cast their votes in favor of a

Florida was depicted as a garden on *Florida Facts*, a brochure issued by the Bureau of Immigration, Department of Agriculture in the 1920s. By permission of the P. K. Yonge Library of Florida History, University of Florida.

$1.5 million bond to construct roads connecting every town in Polk County. Up until that point, Polk's roads were little more than cart paths—a drive across the county would take all day. No one else in Florida had ever asked for so much money for roads, but the people voted, and before long, every town in Polk County was connected by asphalt roads.[44]

Another improvement in the area took place in 1915, when workers began construction of the Twenty Lakes Boat Course Canal in Winter Haven to ferry fruit and vegetables and to carry visitor through "Florida's greatest dreamland," making available "some of the most beautiful residence property in the state."[45] This project would later play a role in the development of Cypress Gardens when Dick Pope would engage the Canal Commission to help him dig and drain his little spot of land. But that was yet to come. A year after the Canal Commission began work on the canals, Dick Pope began officially working in his father's real-estate office. He was sixteen.[46]

Soon Dick Pope and his younger brother Malcolm were gaining attention in the press for their stunts on water. Malcolm would become nationally known as a stunt- and speedboater, but in 1917, with his brother Dick, he indulged in America's newest water sport: aquaplaning.

J. Walker Pope (*left*) shows off his grapefruit trees for prospective buyers in the early 1900s. Photo by Robert Dahlgren. By permission of Julie Pope Dantzler.

"Aquaplaning," said Dick Pope, "riding on a square board pulled behind an outboard—was considered quite remarkable in 1917. Seems like this was a time when anything we did got noticed."[47] In fact, on one winter day that year, Dick got noticed in a big way as he careened over the lake, aquaplaning behind an outboard. A newsreel cameraman—one of the first to come to Winter Haven—caught the action on film.

Dick Pope Sr. (*left*), Dick Pope Jr. (*center*), and Malcolm Pope aquaplane in Lake Eloise, circa 1938. By permission of Cypress Gardens.

As Kevin Desmond, author of *The Golden Age of Waterskiing*, wrote, "This was the first film record of the sport and the stunt man's name is worth remembering—Dick Pope.[48]

Aquaplaning caught on across the country. A short clip in the *New York Times* exclaims that New Yorkers could aquaplane in their own backyard: "Oyster Bay society has discovered that it does not have to go to Florida for aquatic sports and that Oyster Bay is peculiarly suited to aquaplaning."[49] A *Los Angeles Times* headline boasted that "Aquaplaning Has Thrills: Sport Is Exhilarating in Watery Lines; Looks Almost Suicidal, But Is Safe and Sane; Anybody from Baby to Grandma Can Do It."[50] If there was any doubt that aquaplaning was now a national sport, that was laid to rest in 1929 when a racehorse named Aquaplane won "debut stakes at Belmont."[51]

Boom and Bust

In the 1920s, Dick Pope's passions for aquaplaning, boating, and selling real estate came together. Winter Haven, like the rest of Florida, experienced a land boom. The boom had been building in Polk County since the early 1900s, when the Popes had arrived in Winter Haven. It was said that from 1912 to 1920, Polk County garnered more "publicity and more development than any other county in the state."[52] Part of the credit for this publicity went directly to J. Walker Pope and his twenty-year-old son Dick. In 1920, a headline in the *Florida Chief* read, "Largest Grove Sale Ever Made in Florida, J. Walker Pope & Son Managed the Deal." The two had brokered a half-million-dollar payment for an orange grove in Winter Haven. This wasn't the first time J. Walker had scored big. Back in 1915, he'd made what was then the state's largest land deal, and although the honor had passed on to other real-estate agents over the intervening years, the paper stated, "the firm of J. Walker Pope and son have brought [the pennant] back to the Good Old Town of A Hundred Lakes. . . . [J. Walker] says if the ribbon for the largest grove sale in the state is taken away from Winter Haven he will try and find time to bring it back."[53] "Our slogan," Dick Pope told a reporter later, using one of his Dicapopolisms, "was, 'Where there's life, there's Pope.'"

According to the *Florida Municipal Record*, 1920s Polk County was "the richest per capita county in the United States" as a result of the "citrus, phosphate and other industries."[54] J. Walker and his twenty-five-year-old son, Dick, were two of Polk County's wealthier inhabitants.

The Hundred Lakes Yacht Club was built on the banks of Lake Eloise in the early 1920s. By permission of Cypress Gardens.

Both were members of the Haven-Villa Investment Company, a real-estate firm that sought to develop property in Winter Haven. To help promote sales, the company built the Hundred Lakes Yacht Club on the banks of Lake Eloise. John Snively, president of Haven-Villa, and owner of one of the largest orange groves in the state, had conceived the idea of the club and provided most of the funds for building. Snively

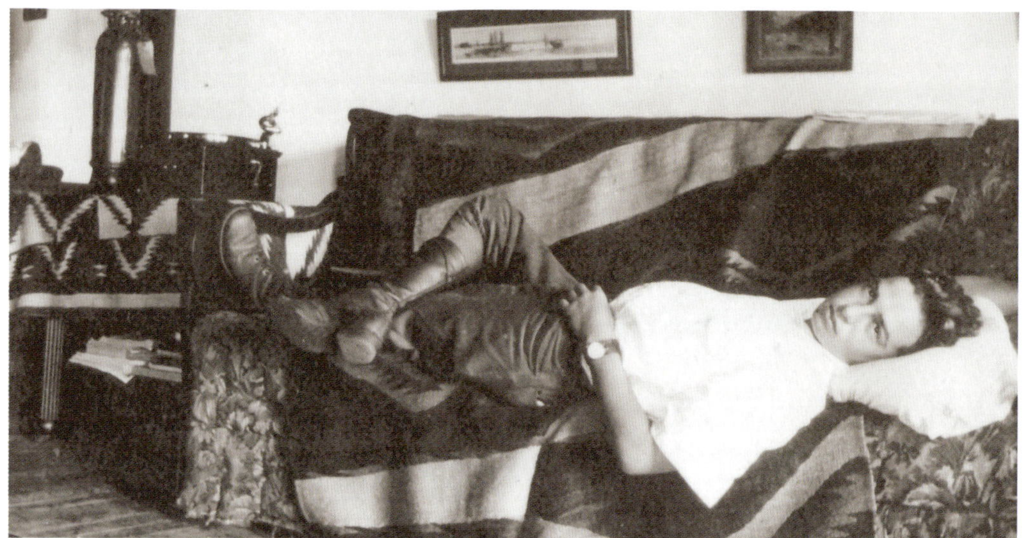

A teenaged Dick Pope reposes in a rare moment of quiet in 1919. By permission of Julie Pope Dantzler.

was the yacht club "commodore," and Dick Pope was "rear commodore." One of Pope's jobs was to help organize speedboat regattas on Lake Eloise.

A March 1925 *Lakeland Evening Register* devoted almost the entire newspaper to the Haven-Villa company and credited J. Walker with "the distinction of having given Winter Haven more publicity through personal advertising and efforts than any other man of the city."[55] Some of the credit for generating that publicity, though, goes to Winter Haven photographer Robert Dahlgren. A native of Sweden, Dahlgren came to Winter Haven in 1911 to look over orange groves for potential buyers; while he was in town, he came across some cameras for sale in a tent. He bought the cameras and the tent and decided to make Winter Haven his home. He got a job with the Haven-Villa company, taking photos the company used to promote its developments.[56] It was Dahlgren who took the photograph of J. Walker with those voluptuous grapefruit trees.

The profile of Dick Pope describes him as the youngest member of the company, "director of the Dundee Fertilizer Company, the manager and secretary of the Ridgeland Avocado Nurseries, Inc., the largest avocado nursery in the state, and a charter member and director of the Lake Region Country Club and former secretary of the Winter Haven Hotel Company." He hoped to make Winter Haven known as the "avocado capital" since he owned the largest avocado farm in the state and was recognized statewide as an authority on the fruit. He was also one of the best golfers in the state, competing and winning in national tournaments.[57] What the profile didn't mention was Dick Pope's daredevil antics with speedboats and skis. In retrospect, it was fairly clear that his future did not lie in avocado farming.

At the height of the boom, mobs of real-estate agents, or "Haven-Villa boys," as they were called, would stand outside of the railroad depot in downtown Winter Haven, waiting for prospective buyers to disembark, while young men who had modified their Model T's played "auto polo" in the streets, brandishing croquet mallets.[58] These potential buyers had been lured to Winter Haven by shout-out-loud ads placed in the *New York Times* and other newspapers, offering eleven-day, one-hundred-dollar round trips to Florida to folks who wanted to get in on the "fabulous profits" being made daily in Florida.

> SEE FLORIDA BEFORE YOU BUY! The most Glorious section of All Florida is the Ridge Section, the center of which is WINTER HAVEN, the city of a hundred lakes, the home of a hundred millionaires. The Haven-Villa Corporation is engaged in broadcasting the suggestion that you go to Winter Haven and see for yourself what opportunities it offers—not only for a winter home, but as a place where you may invest your money with astonishing results.[59]

Harvey Snively, nephew of citrus pioneer John Snively, recalled that the company would often plant people on the trains and buses bringing people to Winter Haven. These "plants" would ooh and aah over a piece of land, only to be told that it had just been snapped up by someone else.[60] As a further incentive, people who made the trip and bought land would have the one-hundred-dollar fee applied to their down payments. Surely Dick Pope escorted a few of these real-estate tourists through the newly dug canals, past the Hundred Lakes Yacht Club, past the swamp that would soon become Cypress Gardens. When he wasn't trying to sell real estate directly to tourists, he and his brother Malcolm staged aquatic feats to attract interest in their father's real-estate offerings. As he wrote in *Water Skiing,* his 1958 book on the sport, "Malcolm and I were known as daredevils, and through the media of newsreels and newspapers, much publicity resulted from our performances at Winter Haven."[61] Of course, as with anything Dick Pope did, it was hard to tell when he was working and when he was just having fun. In January 1925, with Malcolm driving the boat, Dick set out to test an "aquaplane with a wing." A Paramount newsreel cameraman was on hand to film the action. Pope's friend, aviator Harrison Fraser, had constructed the nearly six-meter-square wing, affixing it to an aquaplane.[62]

When Malcolm got the boat up to speed, Dick lifted up off the water and rose into the sky. "[Malcolm] turned around to check how things

Dick Pope Sr. tests out an aquaplane with a wing in 1925. By permission of Cypress Gardens.

were going, but I was nowhere to be found," Pope wrote. "[He] thought I had fallen off, but as his eyes followed the rope, he saw that it went skyward instead of into the water. Sure enough, there I was, thirty or forty feet up in space, having taken the air express powered by a gust of wind to the top floor." Seeing his brother sailing high over the trees, Malcolm got scared and slowed the boat down. Gravity took over. "No matter what it was," Pope wrote about what happened next, "one thing was certain. It caused plenty of action for the cameraman. In aviation vernacular, I did a beautiful Immelmann turn and something resembling a chandelle, and for a finale, a perfect stall. After this, there was nothing left but the crash, but thank goodness there was something left of me."[63]

While Dick Pope and Malcolm were sailing through the air on aquaplanes and jump boats, Edward Bok, a Pulitzer Prize winner, was enticed to buy a house in Mountain Lake, an exclusive neighborhood in Lake Wales that J. Walker Pope helped develop, said Margaret Chase Parry: "My mother used to tell us one of her favorite times in childhood was when her parents, J. Walker and Esther, used to go over and play bridge with Mr. and Mrs. Bok. When they finished the game he would play the organ."[64]

Bok enjoyed walking through the sandhill scrub to the top of Iron Mountain, and while on one of these walks, he conceived the idea of the tower. A local reporter said Bok wanted "to thank the people of Polk County for "all that it has done for him in making him a well man and giving him and his wife the most wonderful months of their lives." But Bok was also dismayed at seeing the trees clear-cut for "mechanically laid out orange groves" and wanted to create "the most beautiful natural park in Florida." Initially, inspired by the way flamingoes had once flown "in flaming clouds" over South Florida, he wanted to create "a great 3,000 acre Flamingo jungle," but the birds had nearly been decimated by 1926. He imported some flamingos from Chile, but they gradually died off.[65]

Above: Malcolm Pope piloted the boat when Dick Pope Sr. test-drove his aquaplane with a wing in 1925. By permission of Cypress Gardens.

Right: President Calvin Coolidge accepts grapefruits from the Citrus Queen at the 1929 dedication of Bok Tower. Courtesy of the State Archives of Florida.

The landscape architect Frederick Law Olmsted Jr. helped Bok modify his plans to include construction of the Singing Tower on Iron Mountain, the highest point in all of Florida, situated on the Lake Wales Ridge. Bok hired his friend, architect Milton Medary, to design the tower. The noted sculptor Lee Lawrie designed the panels, which featured Florida wildlife from cranes to jellyfish. A sixty-bell carillon was installed inside. The neo-gothic/art deco tower was completed in 1929 and was dedicated by President Coolidge, who was given a handful of grapefruit by a Citrus Queen. It was the "single most exotic and intriguing project" at the time in Polk County, a description no doubt aided by the nightingales shipped over from England.

Julie Pope in her wedding gown, 1926. By permission of Adrienne Pope Watkins.

Bok had had to get a special permit to bring the birds to Lake Wales, the first one issued in England in four hundred years. As the press noted: "Early one morning last week, the sweet, golden notes of a nightingale floated through Mountain Lake Sanctuary. It was the first time on record that a nightingale had sung on the North American continent."[66] The local mockingbirds copied their notes, but not for long. The nightingales soon met the same fate as the flamingos, dying off one by one.

Despite the optimism demonstrated by Bok's generous gift, the real-estate boom had begun to fall apart in August 1925 when the Florida East Coast Railway put a halt to shipments going to South Florida. It seems that the flurry of construction was causing delays on the railway. To further exacerbate matters, the word "fraud" was being uttered in regard to Florida real-estate sales. Property values began to fall, and by 1927, the real-estate boom was over.[67]

Somehow, in the middle of all this turmoil, Dick Pope managed to get married to a southern belle from Brewton, Alabama. He'd had no plans to get hitched. "I'm not kidding you," he told a reporter in 1979, "I'd never thought about getting married." But on a trip to Asheville, North Carolina, to give a talk on the then still-booming

Florida real-estate business and to play in a golf tournament, he came across Julie Downing in her "golden looking dress," and quickly changed his mind. "I took her little hand in mine and said 'someday you and I are going to be married.'" Julie wasn't amused by that notion. "Well I can make jokes," she told Dick, "but I don't like to make them like you folks do in Florida." Dick was undaunted, attributing Julie's response to the fact that she was from Alabama: "Of course you know Alabamans, they couldn't put up with the crazy Floridians." That evening he invited her to a party: "I had a piece of cotton nailed to a card . . . and I said I wanted to take her to the cotton-pickin' ball. I just thought it would be funny. Alright, it was."[68] He also told her he was a "great golfer." Julie later told a reporter that she wasn't so sure about that: "When I picked up a newspaper a few days later and saw a headline, 'Dick Pope Wins Golf Tournament,' I thought to myself, maybe he's not as big a liar as I thought he was."[69]

The unlikely couple was married on April 7, 1926, in what the local paper described prophetically as "a wedding of unusual interest throughout the south."[70] That the two were complete opposites was endlessly entertaining to the employees of Cypress Gardens. Walter Doles, whose

Julie and Dick Pope had a perfectly balanced relationship, circa 1980s. By permission of Adrienne Pope Watkins.

father helped dig the canals at the Gardens, and who later became a waiter at the Palm Terrace Restaurant, said: "Dick Pope was something like a comedian; he was always joking. He knew his business, but I don't know where he got the head for it because he'd come in the restaurant, and he always had a joke. I guess he was a tougher man in his office. Among us he was a nice person. If she threw a party, she'd close the bar in fifteen minutes; we had to polish the silver and all this stuff. She was a strict little rich Alabama girl."

After the Florida boom crashed, Julie was able to help Dick, said Walter: "That's where Mr. Pope got his start from; she had the money because her parents ran a lumberyard up in Alabama. When they got married, she had the money, and I think she had some of the brains, too."[71]

Bert Lacey, who worked in public relations, said the two were like night and day: "When Mrs. Pope came in with her red shoes on, you knew you were in deep trouble; you'd better run and hide. She and Mr. Pope were like Walt and Roy Disney. Walt was the dreamer, and Roy was the money man. Mr. Pope was the dreamer; Mrs. Pope kept track of the money. When she didn't like something, it was gone. We spent about $20,000 on new trash cans one year, and she didn't like the looks of them, and they were out of there that night. She had a very strict rule: if you see a piece of paper in the park and you walk by it and don't pick it up, you're fired. So the park was exceptionally clean. Everybody took it upon themselves to keep it that way."[72]

Dubie Baxter's first job at the Gardens was keeping it clean by picking up soda bottles, although he says it was "more babysitting me than anything else" since he was five or six at the time. His grandmother and uncle ran the Palm Terrace Restaurant, and his mother was one of Dick Pope's first secretaries. "Fred Gaffney had a little shack out there where he sold cold drinks and orange juice," said Dubie. "Of course, they were all bottled drinks back then."

The tourists would toss the bottles under the bushes when they were finished, and Dubie would walk around with a little red wagon and pick them up. "I came back with bottle after bottle after bottle, and Fred would pay me a penny apiece, but after about two days, he said, 'Dubie, lemme tell you where they keep the empty bottles; you just go down there and fill your little wagon up.' So we were in cahoots. Fred was a ball of fire, always smiling and laughing."

Dubie was also Julie Pope's godson, and when he was a kid, he went by the Popes' house every morning to pick up fresh flowers Julie had cut for his teachers. She wanted to share the beauty, he said. After the maid escorted him into her bedroom, Julie would ask him how he was, how his dog Rusty was. "She was an entirely different person away from the Gardens," he said. "At the Gardens she was a tyrant—she had red bitch shoes—if she had on those shoes, it was hell to pay."[73]

Julie's red shoes apparently didn't scare Dick Pope. At the time they went on their honeymoon, he was still a millionaire through his real-estate dealings. "We were all innocent bystanders sucked into this maelstrom of profit-making," he told a reporter. However, all those innocents would soon be sucked into the maelstrom of the crash, and by the time his honeymoon was over, he too had lost most of his money when many of Florida's banks closed down.

When the Florida boom came to a halt and selling Florida real estate was no longer possible, Dick Pope turned to his other love—getting attention on the water. The story goes that when he heard Johnson Seahorse Outboard Motors Co. in Chicago wanted to create a new marketing plan to advertise its outboard motors, he wired the company's president, imploring him: "Hold all publicity plans until I get there. Your problems are solved." He was hired at twelve grand a year, and was able to indulge his obsession with racing boats, assuring the company that he would stage at least forty regattas all over the country to promote its outboard motors. He staged quite a few of them in Florida. Over the next three years he was so successful at promotion that he organized the American Outboard Motor Association with offices in New York and Chicago and handled accounts for Champion Spark Plugs, Gulf Oil, Jantzen

Aquaplane clowns joke around on land, circa 1930s. By permission of Cypress Gardens.

Swimsuits, and Johnson Outboard Motors. His brother Malcolm and photographer Robert Dahlgren helped out with his promotions.[74] A quick glance at a 1929 Champion Spark Plug ad reveals how Pope kept one foot firmly in Florida waters, even though by then, he was living on Long Island in New York. The ad depicts Malcolm Pope, outboard motor champion, sitting on a Florida lake in his boat, the *Lookingback Kid*.

Dick Pope wasn't about to let Malcolm have all the fun, so in 1928, he became the first person to jump off a ski ramp, setting a record by soaring 25 feet through the air. He had gotten the skis from his friend Fred Waller, who also worked for Paramount Newsreels. Although skis had been invented in 1922 by Ralph Samuelson, they were reinvented in 1925 by Waller, who patented them as a "twin aquaplane system," and then marketed them as Dolphin Akwa-Skees.[75] (Another man, Don Ibsen, was "inventing" skis about the same time over in Washington. News was slow to get around.) Clara Bow, the 1920s "It" girl, was one of Waller's models; she posed next to the skis in high heels and a bathing suit. Each of Waller's eight-foot-long Akwa-Skees came with a bridle and a rope that was attached to a boat. They also had a rope attached for the skier to hang onto.

Since Waller was well aware of the antics of the Pope brothers, having filmed them in his other life at Paramount Newsreel, he'd sent the Akwa-Skees to Dick, who practiced skiing with Malcolm and Bob Eastman. They put them to good use, most likely in a scheme to promote Johnson Motors: "At Miami Beach in 1928, my brother Malcolm and I were performing some stunts on aquaplanes for the greatest of all publicists, Steve Hannigan."[76] (Hannigan has been credited with originating the "bathing beauty" and for stimulating a "seemingly insatiable desire for the tropics.")[77] "The newsreel cameramen were recording Malcolm's spectacular jumping boat feats. Not to be left out of the act, I had conceived a real humdinger for the movie boys. I went skiing over a long, low slanted ramp, pulled by a fast outboard boat. As I went up and over, I became the first in sports history to jump with a pair of waterskis."[78]

In the end, the Popes put the Akwa-Skees aside and throughout the 1930s, used skis supplied by the Florida Variety Boat Company of Orlando, which later became known as Correct Craft. (Correct Craft quit manufacturing skis in 1950, but would go on to supply Cypress Gardens with boats for more than fifty years.)[79]

Newspapers, newsreel companies, and magazines were tuned into the Popes' daredevil stunts, most of which at this time were staged to promote Dick's publicity accounts with Johnson Motors and Champion Spark Plugs. Malcolm broke the world record for speed in July 1928, covering 6 miles in thirty minutes and six seconds, and he made headlines in February 1929 when he jumped his boat *Sea Horse* during a "water rodeo" staged for the Citrus Festival in Winter Haven.[80] Just two months later, Malcolm revved an outboard up to 35 miles per hour and jumped through a burning hoop of flames. In December, he amped up his performance yet again, attaching thirty-three rockets to his boat in an attempt to set a new outboard motor record—he just wanted to hit 100 miles per hour.[81]

Unfortunately, he wasn't able to overcome technical difficulties, and after three tries, he decided to postpone his attempt. Dick told reporters that—in spite of Malcolm's defeat—rockets "will someday be used to launch airplanes in a limited space," adding that he could "fancy rockets being fired by radio from a remote point."[82] In 1930, Malcolm revisited the rocket boat, finally shooting across Biscayne Bay in his *Dixie Torpedo* at a speed of 55 miles per hour.[83] Both *Popular Mechanics* and *Popular Science* featured

Above: Dick Pope Sr. was the first person to jump off a ski ramp at Miami Beach in 1928. By permission of Cypress Gardens.

Left: The movie star Clara Bow (*left*) poses with a pair of Fred Waller's Akwa-Skees, circa 1926. By permission of the Huntington Historical Society, N.Y.

Above: Malcolm Pope became the first person to make an outboard jump when he came up on a log during a race. Here he jumps through a wall of cardboard bricks for newsreel cameramen, circa 1920s. By permission of Cypress Gardens.

Below: Malcolm Pope jumps his *Sea Horse* through a wall of flames, circa 1929. By permission of Cypress Gardens.

articles on Malcolm; in one, he is shown jumping his *Seahorse* through a wall of flame at Miami Beach; in another, he is pictured demonstrating his "amazing upside down motorboat," the *Baby Grapefruit*, a submarinelike boat he designed.

The coverage of Dick's and Malcolm's antics was just a warm-up for the publicity that was to come. In fact, from the way the Popes were gallivanting around the country—staging a boat race in Miami's McFadden-Deauville swimming pool, jumping over logs in Palatka, jumping boats through fire—it's hard to tell that Dick was actually living in New York, or that it was the middle of the Great Depression.

In April 1930, as president of Outboard Pictorial Services, Inc., he published "Zip It's Motor Boating Time in Auburndale," writing that "Many cities all over the state are now realizing that water sports of every variety are necessary to center the interest of tourists on the lakes and bays." As an example, he cited the Auburndale Thanksgiving Day Regatta, which "resulted in newspaper 'breaks' throughout the nation. . . . When thought is given to the millions of people who read about the regatta under the Auburndale, Florida dateline, the tremendous publicity value of water sports can be realized." On a more lighthearted note, he wrote that the event was "well-planned from a publicity standpoint" because instead of trophies, first-, second-, and third-place winners were awarded a turkey, a duck, and a chicken respectively, in keeping with the nature of the holiday.[84]

In May 1930, *Outboard Motor Boating* published an article titled "Ten Days on Location," featuring photos and descriptions of a film made by Grantland Rice Sportlight with Dick Pope as director. The purpose of the film, as the writer said, was to put "before the public the latest developments in outboard motorboating." One of the developments was a steeplechase in which rubber horses were affixed to the aquaplane and the riders dragged over a series of jumps. Another was a "balloon bursting contest" devised by Pope. The aquaplane riders were given long poles with needles affixed to the ends; they would then try to spear balloons tossed out by the girls in the boats before them. If riding rubber horses attached to aquaplanes wasn't enough, you could always jump your motorboat over a ramp and watch it shatter into splinters as boater Jack Kerr did.[85]

That film would be one of Dick Pope's last efforts as a public-relations man on behalf on Johnson Motors. The Depression finally caught up with him, and in 1930 he found that his

An aquaplane rider attempts to shoot a target for a Grantland Rice newsreel cameraman in 1930. By permission of Adrienne Pope Watkins.

services were no longer in demand. One afternoon, while he and Julie were driving on a Long Island road, she showed him "The Worth of Beauty," a *Good Housekeeping* article about a South Carolina man who opened his garden estate to the public and made $36,000 in three months charging two dollars per person. Later that day, he told Julie he wanted to go home. He was homesick for a Florida he'd never really left. "I never heard of anyone starving in Florida," he told her. "You can make more money here, but look at the way you have to live." He was no longer a damnyankee. The northern weather and the fast-paced city life simply didn't agree with him.[86] In 1931, Julie and Dick decided to head home to the cypress groves of his youth.

The 1930s

The Barnum of Botany

One story has it that he camped on the shores of Lake Eloise as a kid and never forgot the image of the moss-hung cypress trees.[1] Another story, as told by the famous preacher and positive thinker Norman Vincent Peale, goes that one day during the Depression, Pope was walking along the swamps outside of Winter Haven, saw an artist painting "old gnarled cypress trees," and asked him why he "was painting those old trees." The man told him, "Because they are the most beautiful trees I ever saw." The artist opened Dick's eyes to the beauty of those old trees and planted a thought in his head, "Why wouldn't people come from everywhere to get the same inspiration?"[2] A third story, told by Dick Pope himself to the *Saturday Evening Post*, is probably closer to the truth. Once the swamp was drained and shaped, he said, he would take potential real-estate investors on boat rides: "I was going to sell them while they were kind of drunk with beauty."[3]

But before he could get anybody drunk with beauty, the first thing he did when he got back to Florida was go straight to oranges—Winter Haven was the "Citrus Capital of the World,"

Gnarled cypress trees line the edge of the banks of what would become Cypress Gardens. Circa 1900s. By permission of Cypress Gardens.

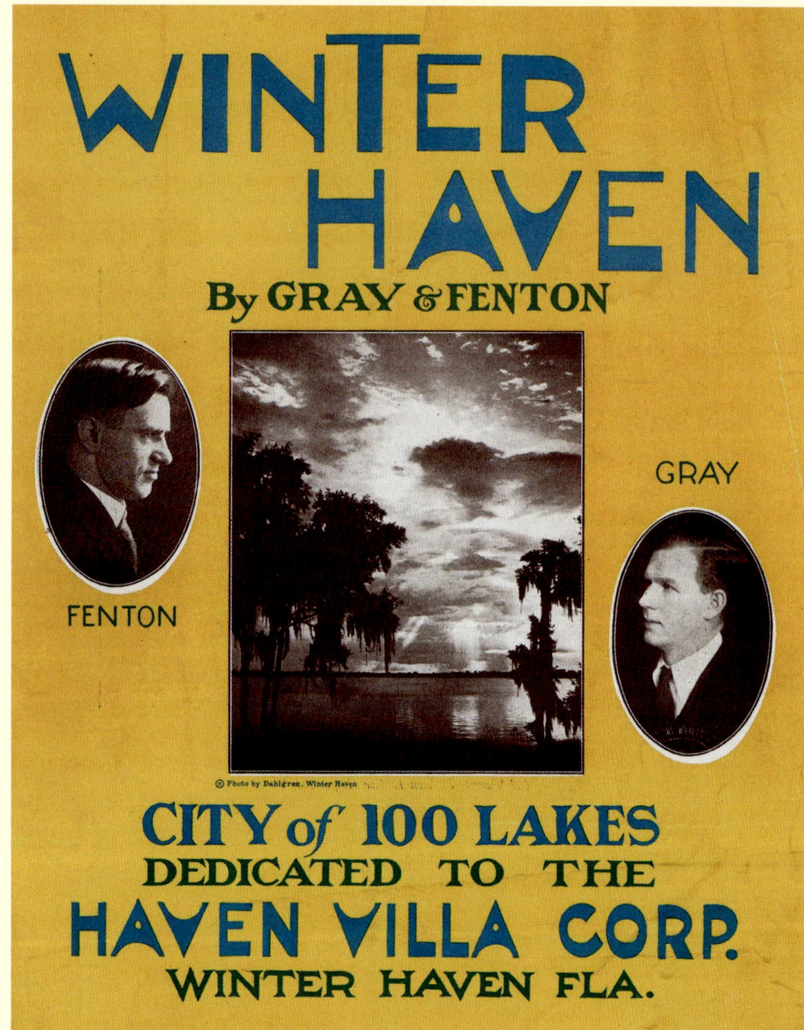

The Haven Villa Corporation advertised Winter Haven's 100 lakes with sheet music by Fenton and Gray. By permission of Tim Myers.

after all. He used his public-relations skills to persuade the citrus industry to adopt a wire-bound orange packing box that would replace an older, bulkier model. Earning a hundred dollars a week, he told a reporter, he was "one of the best paid men in Winter Haven." But he wasn't content with selling orange crates. "The first year, I had no competition," he told a reporter. "The second, there were three of us, and the third year there were going to be 26 competing, so I decided to start something new."[4]

Even though when Pope got home, he discovered that Highway 27 had been slightly rerouted and Winter Haven had been bypassed, he was still dreaming about a way to make Winter Haven a tourist mecca. Winter Haven itself tried to lure visitors with monikers such as "The City of 100 Lakes," as it had done back in the boom, but it was too far off the main roads to tap into Florida's growing tourist industry.[5]

Still, Pope forged ahead. He became chairman of the Winter Haven Canal Commission, which oversaw the construction of canals through the Chain of Lakes. The precursor to the Canal Commission was the Twenty Lakes Boat Club, organized in 1915 to dig canals for moving loads of citrus between the lakes. However, as former Canal Commission member Kenneth Recker pointed out in his history of the commission, even then there was an ulterior motive: stockholders had built their homes on the lakes.[6]

When Dick Pope came along, he took up where the original boat club had left off, except he was more up front about it. He wanted to beautify the canals in the hope of attracting both tourists and real-estate business. "I thought it would be a great way to get back in real estate," he said. "I would take the ladies through the gardens and they would say 'Oh, this is so beautiful and wonderful. If only I could get an acre of land for my husband and me.' And then I would say, 'Well, I just happen to have an acre or so available.'"[7] He bought 12 acres of land and the boarded-up Hundred Lakes Yacht Club from citrus pioneer and former Haven-Villa partner John Snively, then persuaded the Canal Commission to let him "create a community park—Cypress Gardens—in a picturesque area of cypresses and water on the north shore of Lake Eloise."[8]

Lucy Chambliss is a skier-turned-sharpshooter who practically grew up at Cypress Gardens. Both her sisters became full-fledged Aqua Maids, but Lucy preferred pistols. Her parents came to Florida in 1926 and planted 110 acres of orange grove up on River Lake, then moved back to Pennsylvania, where her father flew for Pitcairn Aviation until 1933. "Then we came back to Winter Haven," Lucy said. "My dad was in the citrus business, later on in the real-estate business, and everybody knew Mr. Pope. During the boom, somehow or another, the Snivelys got hold of that whole area. There were some shady land deals that went on during that time, but

Lucy Chambliss and Dick Pope Jr. aquaplane in the 1930s. By permission of Lucy Chambliss.

Mr. Snively stuck it out and kept that Hundred Lakes Yacht Club—and it didn't have a Hundred Lakes and it didn't have a yacht, but anyway it was a beautiful clubhouse, all pecky cypress. It was used for many years as the entrance to the Gardens."[9]

Perhaps Pope convinced the commission he could bring back the golden days, when the Hundred Lakes Yacht Club hosted balls and regattas that were the talk of the town. Or maybe the commission was encouraged by the success of Bok Tower down at Lake Wales, or by Silver Springs over in Ocala, or Sunken Gardens in St. Petersburg. Or perhaps they were encouraged by the 1931 creation in nearby Lake Wales of Chalet Suzanne, a Swiss-style hotel with a world-renowned restaurant. Whatever it was, they got behind him, investing $2,800 in the project. Pope didn't stop there. He also convinced the Federal Emergency Relief Association to help him, much to the chagrin of his lawyer, Hart McKillop. McKillop told a reporter that Pope "wanted to get ahold of a part of the cypress swamp and didn't know where the boundary lines might lie. . . . I went out there with him and we waded

George Turner opened Sunken Gardens to a paying public in 1935. Courtesy of the State Archives of Florida.

down through the cypress swamp and located a concrete marker. . . . Dick asked me to incorporate Cypress Gardens as a non-profit corporation" so he could apply for WPA funds to "finance the building of the dream world," which would include winding paths paved with blocks of cypress.[10]

Ralph Meloon, whose father founded what would become the Correct Craft Boat Company, was hired by Dick Pope to drive him and potential investors through back waterways to Lake Eloise, the current heart of Cypress Gardens. "I was only a teenager," he told James Vincent, author of a history of Correct Craft, "and I didn't realize the significance of those excursions." Some of those passengers were officials from Washington who had come down to see what Pope was up to with the Chain of Lakes.

"Dick Pope would sit in the middle of the boat as we were slowly coasting around the Cypress Gardens area and back into the canal to Lake Summit," said Meloon, "telling his guests what he planned on doing. When he finished his sales pitch, he convinced the WPA to furnish the labor to start the Gardens."[11]

"I sold the WFERA—a branch of the WPA—on the idea that instead of having men raking leaves at a dollar a day," Pope said, "we could beautify and rebuild the canals and chain of lakes. We started with that, and then added a hanging garden on Lake Eloise—and that's what later became Cypress Gardens."[12] The WPA supplied him with workers and paid them a dollar a day to dig the canals, clear the underbrush, and lay the walkways. The men worked in the swamp for five months before the money ran out.[13]

Pope paid Works Progress Administration laborers a dollar a day to clear the land for the Gardens, circa 1932. By permission of Cypress Gardens.

By the time Dick Pope had drained the swamp, Zora Neale Hurston had already made it to Polk County to collect folklore from the labor camps that housed the people who either processed the county's natural resources—citrus, timber, and phosphate—or built the roads to haul them out.[14] It's not unlikely that some of the men she encountered helped build roads under the direction of J. Walker Pope or worked in the groves surrounding Winter Haven. And like them, she was affected by the place, writing that crossing under the arch at the county line reminded her of a blues song:

> How often had I heard "Polk County Blues."
> You don't know Polk County lak Ah do
> Anybody been dere, tell you de same thing
> too.[15]

Her descriptions of Polk County provide a sharp contrast to the "dream world" Dick Pope had in mind, although both saw beauty where others didn't. To Hurston, African American timber cutters were "poets of the swinging blades . . . sweating black bodies, muscled like gods, working to feed the hunger of the great tooth. Polk County!"

The phosphate workers "[bore] witness to the mighty monster of the deep when the Painted Land rose up and did her first dance with the morning sun." Turpentine workers "[bled] trees for gum" to produce "paints . . . perfumes . . . tone for a violin bow and many other things which the black men who bleed the trees never heard about." Orange Grove workers "[scrambled] up ladders into orange trees" where they worked, "singing, laughing, cursing, boasting of last night's love and looking forward to the darkness again."[16]

In Polk County jooks, Hurston danced the "scronch" and the "belly rub," listened to songs about "Ella Wall, the Queen of love," nearly got herself "cut to death" over a man named Slim, and was saved by a woman named "Big Sweet." She didn't make Polk County sound like much of a place for a tourist attraction, but, like Pope, she would use the setting to her advantage. Not only did she write about her experiences in Polk County in *Mules and Men*, her groundbreaking collection of folklore, the setting of her play *Polk County* sounds a lot like Dick Pope's Cypress Gardens:

> the primeval woods of South Central Florida. Huge live oaks, pines, magnolia cypress, "sweet gum" (maple) and the like grow lush. Spanish moss drapes the trees.

Tall cabbage palms tilt their crowns in clusters above the surrounding trees. Scrubby palmettoes make a dense undergrowth.[17]

Like Hurston, Pope saw the appeal of the swamp, although not many others did. Years after the Gardens were built, a reporter asked him why he thought tourists would travel to a swamp in the middle of nowhere in the middle of the Depression to see his creation, Pope said: "Well, I'll tell you. They were packing them in up at Silver Springs and over at Bok Tower, and I just figured they would come here if I could get the word out."[18] However, as historian Stephen Branch points out, Winter Haven was nowhere near the beach and certainly didn't have the sort of glamorous nightlife that drew people to Miami. It's unlikely that the tourists would have made their way to Hurston's sawmill jooks to dance the scronch. Not only that, but Pope had to compete with the "various alligator farms, marine parks, and parrot and monkey jungles dotting the peninsula."[19] At least Silver Springs had Ross Allen's Reptile Institute. Pope could've gotten a few snakes from him if he wanted; they were friends. Pope's daughter, Adrienne Pope Watkins, remembered a day when Ross Allen drove up to her family's house in Winter Haven: "He had a trunk full of snakes, poisonous snakes, and he came in and ate dinner."[20]

Snakes didn't always appeal to tourists, though. Ross Allen helped Lester and Bill Piper found the Bonita Springs Reptile Gardens after they helped him found his institute. However, they soon changed the name to Everglades Reptile Gardens, hoping to attract more tourists with the "Everglades" reference. Then they discovered that the word "reptile" had a negative effect. "Many motorists, especially those vehicles transporting people who were squeamish about snakes, passed without stopping," writes author Charles LeBuff. How the Pipers deduced which cars were transporting the squeamish from watching traffic whizz past isn't clear, but they did change the name again, this time to Everglades Wonder Gardens.[21]

Cypress Gardens wasn't going for the reptile angle or the parrot angle or the monkey angle; that's why it required a master salesman like Dick Pope. By 1932, he'd already managed to get his fledgling Gardens into the movies. His friend Bob Eastman had formed the International Nautical Stunt Team, and they made a movie skiing through the cypress trees where Pope had just begun working.[22] Dick and Malcolm, along with Bob Eastman and Ruth and Dorothy Wirt,

Ross Allen milks a rattlesnake at Silver Springs. Author's collection.

Cypress Gardens aquaplaners cut up for the camera, circa 1930s. Author's collection.

dazzled cameramen by flying over ramps in their jump boats or, in the case of Ruth and Dorothy, aquaplaning through a wall of fire.[23] Robert Dahlgren was always on hand to photograph the daredevils "aquaplaning, tobogganing, and aquagliding." Pope would send the photographs to syndicates, which would then release them all over the country to be used in magazines, newspapers, and on the rotogravure pages popular at that time. As a result of all their efforts, Winter Haven became known as the "water sport center of the United States," and the city "received an incalculable amount of the best publicity." Practically every newsreel company in Hollywood came to Winter Haven at one time or another during this period to catch these Aquabats on film.[24] Pope was well versed in the "value of national publicity in stimulating real estate sales,"[25] and he had this on his mind in a carefully worded article he wrote in 1933 explaining how his project would help the City of Winter Haven with its plans for a series of canals connecting a chain of twenty-two lakes.

> A five-year beautification program has been laid out by the interested civic bodies of Winter Haven in the hope that the many attractions of this beautiful city may be welded together to form something definite which may be advertised to the world at large.[26]

Florida cities had figured out how to sell themselves using their biggest attractions, he wrote: Ocala has Silver Springs, Lake Wales has its Singing Tower, and Sarasota has its Art Museum. Once Winter Haven's "beautification program" is complete, he added:

> It will give Winter Haven a system of canals, with huge lily palms in some lakes and

Young men show off for the newsreels at Cypress Gardens, circa 1940s. By permission of Cypress Gardens.

> a magnificent Cypress Garden, from the heights of which will hang various brilliant-colored flower vines. Out on the north shore of Lake Eloise near the Yacht Club, a building of pure Italian architecture, there is a wonderful grove of cypress trees extending far into the lake. Here, colorful shrubs, such as hibiscus, alamanda and azalea, will be planted along the banks, forming a beautiful contrast to the solemn cypress trees, whose natural beauty will be left untouched. Purple and crimson bougainvillea, flaming bignonia, and the royal blue thumbergia vines will be planted along the shores, and trained up into the lower limbs, so as to hang in this water forest of cypress trees.[27]

Throughout the article, Pope managed to convey the sense that this "hanging garden" was just one beautiful spot on this Chain of Lakes; clearly it wasn't a "private" affair since it would so obviously benefit Winter Haven:

> The noted landscape artist, Charles Ewert Hetherington, recently said of this grove of cypress trees: "The beauty of this inconceivable place, so wonderful and so unearthly, should be in a sense public property, and it is a pity that such a site cannot give pleasure to more people."

Adding a bit of catnip to the mix, he described how numerous "boat-livery companies" were eager to come to Winter Haven, where they would make "the fine new city boathouse their headquarters in return for the concession of taking out visitors to the Cypress Gardens and through those wonderful canals." Pope's ability to merge his own interests with those of Winter Haven and later with those of Florida would come to be a trademark quality of his genius *and* his generosity. As he pointed out, once the project was complete, "Winter Haven can then say to the world in words and pictures: 'Come and see our beautiful Cypress Gardens, and on the way to them, through the chain of lakes, you will pass through marvelous canals that out-Venice, Venice.'"[28]

Despite's Pope's plans to "out-Venice, Venice," it wasn't long before Winter Haven city officials noted that Pope's "hanging gardens" weren't a "public" project, but a "private" venture, and Dick Pope was taunted as the "Swami of the Swamp" and the "Maharaja of Muck." Apparently the name-calling didn't faze him. "Everybody knew Mr. Pope," said Lucy Chambliss. "They'd say, 'here comes the Swami of the Swamp.' They weren't making fun of him; everybody was kidding him about what he was doing out there, and boy, it didn't bother him in the least bit because anything he could do to get the Gardens in the paper, he wanted to do."[29]

Undaunted by the teasing, Pope appealed for more funds, but his request was denied. FERA withdrew its workers, and the Canal Commission withdrew its support. Pope and John Snively repaid the Canal Commission the money it had initially loaned them.[30] "I warned him continuously he was treading on thin ice in using government funds for a private enterprise," his lawyer, Hart McKillop, told a reporter later. "But he was so wrapped up and enthused over the idea that he paid no attention to my apprehensions and went ahead getting one appropriation after another."[31]

After the debacle with FERA and the Canal Commission, Pope said he was so defeated that he thought of backing out. He and Julie tossed a coin to decide whether to move on to Orlando and start fresh, or to take their chances with the swamp. "The coin came up heads," Pope told a reporter. "That meant we'd stay and go ahead with the Gardens on our own."

A 1940s-era linen postcard depicts a Technicolor Cypress Gardens. Author's collection.

John Snively, of Snively Groves, packaged citrus under the Cypress Gardens Brand, 1963. By permission of Cypress Gardens.

He said that all the opposition to his and Julie's idea might have actually spurred him on: "More things are done—great things—just to show people you can do them. I honestly think that if I had had everybody on my side when I started Cypress Gardens, I probably never would have finished the place." And, he added, "most folks were a little bit worried—all except Julie. And I never understood why she wasn't."[32]

The Popes formed the Cypress Gardens Association, Inc., and got back to work. Once they decided to move ahead with the project, John Snively gave the Popes nearly 40 more acres in exchange for a 10 percent interest in the project. Pope hired Vernon Rutter, a gardener from Tennessee, to oversee construction, and Rutter would load his big truck with dozens of men and haul them to work. He got a quarter a day for gas. Julie helped clear the land as well. "[She] worked hours in the hot sun too, overseeing floral plans," Pope said. "She had to. I didn't know an azalea from a carrot then."[33]

Raymond Laughton, Carlos Blake, Joe Joyce, and Jim Doles were some of the many African American workers who helped clear the swamp. Jim Doles's daughters, Betty Doles and Jacqueline Staton, and their brother Walter live in Florence Villa, the "black neighborhood," north of Winter Haven. "Florence Villa was segregated, but I never thought of it being segregated because we had our own things in the black neighborhood, the movie and stores," said Jacqueline. "Florence Villa was named for a white lady who helped build the hotel Florence Villa. They named the park after her husband, Inman."[34]

The "Inman" Jacqueline referred to is Frederick Inman, founder of Florence Villa and "one of the greatest figures who ever trod the stage of Florida affairs."[35] He came to Florida in 1880 and with the help of Dan Laramore, his African American overseer, planted a large orange grove. After a freeze in 1886, Inman and his wife, Florence, decided to open their large home to guests, including the railroad magnate Henry Plant. Inman named the hotel Florence Villa after his wife. Word got out, and by 1893, they had added thirty-six rooms to the original house. The area surrounding the hotel was originally known as Inman's Crossing, but later became known as Florence Villa.[36]

"There were a lot of rich blacks living in this area," said Betty, "but we just had one section we lived in. This whole area was citrus." She points to a pond outside her back door, barely visible from all the green surrounding it. "They call that little pond out there Swann Lake—it was named after one of the rich men too, and all of it was called Swann Groves. Most of the groves were named after whoever owned them; you had Snively Groves and Swann Groves. Some of the blacks actually lived within those groves. They built housing for them, and this is how you were recognized in town—by who you worked for. It was who you worked for that gave you whatever status you had as a black person. If you were one of those that just picked the oranges, then you had no name, no status, no nothing. And really—that was the way it was. Even us. We recognized people by who they worked for. This is the way we looked at each other. You felt if you worked for Snively or if you worked for Pope,

Jim Doles helped clear the land for the Gardens in the early 1930s. By permission of the Doles family.

Workers constructed the Gardens' walkways with blocks of cypress wood, circa 1935. By permission of Cypress Gardens.

then you were a little higher up the status ladder than the average person who did not work for one of them. You know, you were just brainwashed into this kind of stuff."

The Doles siblings recalled their father talking about the Gardens when they were children. "He started there before they actually opened because they were still digging canals," said Betty, "and they were dug by hand with shovels. And they planted all the flowers and they used mules and buggies to haul that stuff out—they didn't have tractors."[37] Jacqueline was only three or four when the Gardens were being built. "My daddy used to say all the time he had a close relationship with Dick Pope. It was nothing for him to ask him to come out there on Palm Sunday because he'd been building the Gardens. They were close."[38] She is referring to the fact that on Palm Sunday in 1942, six years after Cypress Gardens opened, and long before the country desegregated, the Doles would be the first African American family to walk through its gates as the guests of Dick Pope. Betty agreed: "That's the way it was back then. If you worked for someone, you were part of their family life."[39]

The Popes didn't rely only on workers like Jim Doles. They also relied on their friends like photographer Robert Dahlgren. Dick Pope wanted to lay out the walkways and vistas in Cypress Gardens so that a beautiful photograph could be made no matter where the photographer stood.[40] He got Dahlgren to help him. "Cypress Gardens was laid out using a big 8 × 10 studio camera," said Bob Kehoe, who worked at the Gardens for fifty-two years, the last thirty as chief financial officer. "Dick Pope would go around and set up this big tripod and camera and look through it. He'd visualize a scene, then plant various plants with the right height, color, and density to make a good picture. And quite often in the later years, he'd walk around to a gardens area, and put his hands up in a box form, and looking through it, determine if we needed more color on one side or the other to make it look better and more inviting to take pictures."[41]

Apparently their plans worked. As Pope wrote years later, "I truly feel that I built Cypress Gardens with photography."[42] Of course, he built it with plants, too. Lucy Chambliss remembered those days: "He went around to all the people in Winter Haven who had unusual plants; he'd get a camphor tree from this woman, and I forgot what Daddy gave him; it was something that he wanted, and he'd put it down in the Gardens."[43] Pope told one reporter that people weren't

Workers clear the area around the Hundred Lakes Yacht Club, circa 1932. By permission of Cypress Gardens.

Dick Pope Jr. takes a photo in the Gardens, circa 1936. By permission of Lucy Chambliss.

always at home when he helped himself to clippings from their plants.[44]

Billye-Mullins Smith is another Havenite with early ties to the Gardens. In 2007, she was embroiled in her own bit of drama when another teacher suggested that "Where the Orange Blossoms Grow," a song Billye-Mullins says she wrote with her husband, Carroll Smith, "be Florida's new song," apparently without checking with her first. Billye-Mullins simply didn't think the song was appropriate for twenty-first-century Florida. "They are chopping down all the orange trees," she told a reporter in 2007. "I didn't even smell the orange blossoms this year."[45] But she certainly smelled them in 1942, when she came to Florida from New York and met and married Winter Haven native Carroll Smith. His father had long owned a hardware store in Winter Haven. "He was a strong supporter of Dick Pope's farsighted dream of creating 'The Florida Cypress Gardens,'" she wrote in a piece for a local paper, describing how her father-in-law gave Pope tools to begin his work.[46]

Because of a shortage of ready cash to pay his workers, Pope relied on a friend, the local grocer, to help him out. "And when I didn't have the money, I'd call George Jenkins and tell him I was a little short, and could I give out some more (food) chits for $1.25 each, some 25 to 40 of them. He'd say, 'Sure, go ahead—the groceries are just rotting or getting stale on the shelves.'" Pope attempted to repay Jenkins by offering him 25 percent of the stock in the Gardens, but Jenkins declined, saying he'd rather stay in the business he knew best.[47] He did good. George Jenkins, of course, was another of Polk County's larger-than-life characters. The grocery he

An early photo of Cypress Gardens' Wishing Tree, circa 1930s. Photo by Robert Dahlgren. By permission of Adrienne Pope Watkins.

Dick Pope Sr. directs the action for a group of photographers at the Gardens in this 1957 photograph. By permission of Cypress Gardens.

opened in Winter Haven in 1930, stealing the name "Publix" from a local theater, is now a Fortune 500 company with more than nine hundred stores in five southern states.[48] The cigar-puffing Jenkins once drove a car up and down the aisles of one of the stores to demonstrate how roomy they were.[49]

When Dick Pope christened his Gardens, he, like Jenkins, picked an odd namesake. "I actually picked the name 'cypress' from a lumber company whose officers were all millionaires," he said. "I just couldn't resist that bunch of names so I copied their name. I guess I made a good decision."[50] That year, 1933, visitors toured Cypress Gardens for free. On January 24, 1935, the park officially opened, and the Winter Haven officials who had previously snubbed Pope changed their tune, placing an ad in the *Florida Municipal Record* not just praising him, but claiming Cypress Gardens as their own: "Another jewel in Winter Haven's diadem of beauty" that "marks another step in Winter Haven's beautification program."[51] Governor Dave Sholtz came down with his entire cabinet to provide the dedication.[52]

The "formal" opening took place three months later, to the tunes of Homer Mercer and his band. The local paper reported that the old Hundred Lakes Yacht Club had recently been refurbished with cypress by the Southern Cypress Manufacturing Company.[53]

Within a couple of months, Pope was trying to persuade the famous swimming Rawls sisters to come down, and although he hadn't been able to confirm their appearance, the paper reported that "the prospects were bright for getting the renowned mermaids here." He did, however, succeed in getting the Junior Chamber of Commerce to sponsor "an afternoon of water entertainment," including "outboard races in tubs" and "shell races."[54]

Meanwhile, the Gardens were still under construction. Pope opened a sawmill on the premises, and the workers carved up truckloads of pecky cypress blocks that they laid like bricks to create more than a mile of walkways through the Gardens.[55] Even though he must have been busy overseeing the completion of the Gardens, he managed, along with Bob Eastman, to put on a "water carnival" over at Lake Wales to celebrate Armistice Day. The carnival featured Eastman's International Nautical Stunt Team performing stunts such as backward aquaplaning, stilt-planing (riding an aquaplane on twenty-four-inch stilts), and pillow fighting on aquaplanes. Bob Eastman was scheduled to drive his jump boat through a wall of fire.[56] Commodore Dick

Right: The cypress-block walkway winds through the Gardens in this 1930s-era linen postcard. Courtesy of the State Archives of Florida.

Far right: A group of aquaplaners led by Barbara Chambliss, circa mid-1930s. Author's collection.

2023 AQUAPLANING AT THE FLORIDA CYPRESS GARDENS

Pope was on hand to announce the events. Why Pope didn't consider adding "water carnivals" to Cypress Gardens on a regular basis isn't clear, but it might have been that he was still too busy organizing his formal openings to give it a thought.

Creating buzz to get people into the Gardens is something he would do for the rest of his life. Bert Lacey, who has studied the history of Cypress Gardens, said Pope would sometimes get ahead of himself in the buzz department: "In the 1950s, he'd call every newspaper in the state and say, 'You have to be here tomorrow at noon, we have something great going on.' And then he'd call his staff and say, 'I've got every newspaper in the state coming in tomorrow. What are we going to talk about?'"[57] He did the same thing to his children, Dick Jr. and Adrienne. "I remember Daddy calling the people who shot the films and telling them that there was something really special happening at the Gardens," Adrienne told a reporter. "He would get off the phone, look at us two kids and say, 'Well kids, what are we going to do?'"[58]

Pope announced there would be yet another formal opening in December for the "1935–36 winter season" and asked that everyone who'd supplied him with plants or services stop by the clubhouse to "receive their annual passes." The local paper bragged that the Gardens had already achieved national fame with a two-page spread in a booklet for the National Florida exhibit at Rockefeller Center.[59] On the day of the opening, Elizabeth Hull, the Cotton States

A group of young women pillow-fight on aquaplanes for a 1935 newsreel. By permission of Cypress Gardens.

Bob Eastman jumps a boat over a bridge in the Gardens in this 1930s photo. By permission of Cypress Gardens.

Queen, and Betty Runkle, the Florida Orange Festival Queen, clipped a satin ribbon strung across the walkway while being filmed by newsreel cameramen.[60]

Clearly, Dick Pope was on a roll. On January 30, 1936, the governor's wife, Alice May Sholtz, came down to dedicate the park as a bird sanctuary and to point out how important the cypress groves were to the souls of men. For the grand finale of the dedication, Speedy Queen, a champion homing pigeon, and several hundred of her friends were released to "carry the tiny messages tied to their legs telling the story of the dedication of Cypress Gardens as bird sanctuary."[61] One can only wonder if enlisting the pigeons to advertise Cypress Gardens was Dick Pope's idea.

He had certainly hit on a formula for drawing attention to the Gardens: Make something happen. In March 1936, he enlisted the singer Mary Langille to perform at the Gardens; in April, he crowned Eleanor McKay of Tampa as Gardenia Queen to celebrate the "largest known planting of true Gardenias in the world."[62] Eleanor was the first of thousands of queens crowned at Cypress Gardens, a number that caused one reporter to note that, even though Pope may not have invented the beauty queen, "he has done as much as any man to make her an American institution. . . . [T]he most famous of the beauty contests[,] . . . Miss America at Atlantic City[,] issues only one queen a year. Compared to it, Pope is a promotional Henry VIII."[63] Pope's record was crowning nine queens in seven days.

Photographs began to appear almost weekly in the local papers, and almost all were made by Dahlgren: "Snarled Cypress Trees Shown," "Cypress Gardens Bridges," "Bartow Girl Is Festival Maid," "Legend of the Cypress Tree" (the caption explained that anyone making a wish while sitting on this "wishbone" tree would have their wish come true). Commenting on Dahlgren's role in creating the Gardens, one reporter wrote that "he is one of the state's most capable photographers, and all the landscaping and planting has been with a view of supplying backgrounds for comely misses, attractive matrons, dressed in every kind of garb from the latest in bathing suits to 'Gone with the Wind' costumes."[64] The "comely misses" wearing the *Gone with the Wind* costumes should not be confused with the southern belles—they came later. Apparently, Julie came up with the idea of using the "comely misses"

Elizabeth Hull, Cotton States Queen (*left*), and Betty Runkle, Florida Orange Festival Queen, cut the ribbon at the Gardens on the March 1, 1935, opening day. By permission of Cypress Gardens.

The Gardenia Queen poses next to a new car with her court, circa 1930s. By permission of Cypress Gardens.

as "Model-Hostesses," right after the Gardens opened in 1936, not only to greet the visitors but also to pose for them.[65]

The ballerina Gail Armour came down to perform "A Little White Gardenia" during the March 1937 Gardenia Festival. She had previously performed with the Ballet Russe in Paris and was visiting the area before heading to South America. A photo of Armour leaning against the trunk of a cypress tree appeared on Cypress Gardens' first brochure with the caption "Gail Armour, Famous Danseuse as 'The Spirit of Cypress Gardens.'" The accompanying text would have made J. Walker Pope proud:

> No flowers display more brilliant hues than do the fairy-like blossoms of Azaleas. Dazzling shades of pink and rose and red, reflected in the dark water, transform the lagoons into streams of glowing color. . . . The towering trunks of Cypress, rising from fluted and buttressed bases, are covered with huge leaved jungle creepers like the lofty columns of some ancient and forgotten forest temple.

The brochure goes on to entice the visitor with all of the "beauties of this wonderland of tropical and natural beauty: "The Lion's Tail Pine, Rabbit's Foot Fern, the Monkey Puzzle Tree, the Sensitive Plant which droops its leaves when you touch it, The Monstera Deliciosa with its salad fruit which tastes like pineapple, banana, cantaloupe, etc."[66]

Pope loved colorful plant names and even made up a few himself. As he told a reporter in

Far left: The Pope family poses on a bridge at the Gardens, circa 1936. Dick Pope Sr. (*left*) holds Adrienne, while Dick Pope Jr. stands next to Julie. Photo by Robert Dahlgren. By permission of Cypress Gardens.

Left: Dancer Gail Armour poses next to a cypress tree for Cypress Gardens' first brochure. By permission of Cypress Gardens.

Above: Cypress Gardens boat drivers Don "Spider" Bell (*standing*) and Chuck Bryan (*sitting*) wait for tourists in this 1940s-era photograph. By permission of Don "Spider" Bell.

Right: A young woman poses with the *monstera delicioso*, or "fruit salad vine," circa 1940s. Author's collection.

the 1960s: "What kind of romance is there in a flower called *Philodendron eichleri*? I'm gonna call it Sir Ivanhoe's Shield."[67]

Pope's obvious delight in making up colorful names for the plants in the gardens was infectious. Don "Spider" Bell came to Cypress Gardens in 1949 at the suggestion of his brother Bill Bell, who was announcing the ski shows at that

time. "I'd go back out there now and drive boats," he says, and then launches into the spiel he used to give to unwitting tourists: "On the left here is the *Catchiput Malice Malicaluca Rhododendron*—it looks like a palm tree—the leaves stay on, but the bark comes off." He laughs. "Sometimes I'd give them a little Hebrew—this is an *asalocust* plant; sometimes I'd get Jewish people, and they'd say, 'Oh you've got a Jewish plant,' and I'd say, 'we've got a lot of them.' They'd say, 'That was a nice plant.' It was a great job—in the summer we didn't wear our shirts. . . . I took Arthur Godfrey's mother out on a boat, and she gave me a five-dollar tip. That was a lot of money; it cost thirty-five cents to get in the boat. She got in the boat, and Chuck told me, 'This is Arthur Godfrey's mother.' He didn't introduce me so I got in the back, and I was kidding around with her, and I said, 'Have you ever watched the Arthur Godfrey show?' And she said, 'That's my son.'"[68]

Cypress Gardens seems to have bred comics and cut-ups—like its founder, Dick Pope. Dubie Baxter is another one. He began doing canal boat tours in the 1960s, and he carried on the tradition of making up names for plants out of sheer boredom: "You'd go through about fifteen times a day and give the same spiel. Of course, we'd start making up names, playing with the tourists—the *Dickus Popus* plant; the *halitosis hemophilosis*. . . . We named plants after our friends, principals."[69]

In March 1937, Dick Pope announced that Grantland Rice Sportlight was coming to Cypress Gardens to make a film on "outboard motor daredeviltry and aquaplane trickery," featuring Bob Eastman and his International Aquatic Sport Team, fresh from the Chicago World's Fair.[70] Dick Pope would be the director; this would be his 127th film.[71] The film, *Aquabats*, premiered at the Ritz Theater in Winter Haven in early August.[72]

Dubie Baxter remembered the days when Bob Eastman was around: "Mr. Eastman was a very dynamic person, and he kind of brought Mercury into the Gardens; he drove the little hydroplane racing boats and then became head of photography. I used to think Eastman Kodak was named after Bob Eastman."[73] Bob Eastman went on to head the Florida Citrus Commission, and to manage Marine Studios, as Marineland was known in the 1950s.

Besides publicizing the Gardens by using it as a backdrop in films, Dick Pope continued making improvements to his new attraction. Apparently the boat livery concessions he had touted earlier had not come to pass so he hired Col. F. S. Tooey

Grantland Rice Sportlight was one of many newsreel companies drawn to the Gardens by Dick Pope. By permission of Cypress Gardens.

Malcolm Pope owned the electric-boat concession in the Gardens. Author's collection.

of the Jungle Cruise at Silver Springs to bring in "beautiful new electric boats [that] have never been used in the south before." Passengers would pay twenty-five cents for the "thrill of seeing another world" as they glided soundlessly through the canals.[74] Pope's improvements paid off. The 1937–38 edition of the American Automobile Associations travel guide listed the Gardens as one of Florida's "Most Colorful Spots," praising it as a "destination [n]either words nor pictures can adequately describe . . . a wonderland of tropical and natural beauty."[75]

Betty MacCalla appeared in the 1938 Fox Movietone newsreel *What the Well Dressed Aquatic Star Will Wear*. By permission of Cypress Gardens.

Newsreel companies continued coming to Cypress Gardens; in July 1938, Fox Movietone made *What the Well Dressed Aquatic Star Will Wear*, starring Betty MacCalla, who demonstrated aquaplaning. Dick Pope announced that two additional films—one in Technicolor—were being planned for the near future. Even though Cypress Gardens was gaining fame quickly, there was only a cursory mention of the park in the 1939 Federal Writers' Project's *Florida: A Guide to the Southernmost State*. Several paragraphs in the guide describe Winter Haven's citrus industry in detail—down to the "coloring rooms" where an "appetizing hue is given the fruit by the use of ethylene gas." Under the heading "Eloise," the Gardens are described:

> Formerly a wild swamp, the gardens contain native and exotic plantings shaded by huge cypress and oaks, and pierced by quiet log-spanned lagoons. Winding foot trails, paved with pecky-cypress blocks, are marked, as are the majority of the plants.[76]

However, that would soon change. Even though Winter Haven was home to the Florida Orange Festival and considered itself the "Citrus Capital of the World," Cypress Gardens would never take second place to an orange again.

Dick Pope combined his interests—Florida, Cypress Gardens, and citrus—in this postcard created for the Citrus Commission. Photo by Dick Pope Sr. By permission of Cypress Gardens.

3 The 1940s

War, Water Skis, and Belles

In 1945, Dick Pope found himself promoting oranges. And grapefruit. And tangerines. And orange juice. The Florida Citrus Commission picked him to head up their "pictorial publicity program," paying him about twenty grand a year. They got off cheap. In a "statistical report" Pope submitted to the commission, he estimated that the "tangerine" newsreels made by Universal and Fox would be seen by more than 15 million people. An "orange eating sequence" used by Pathe had an audience of 35 million; *Selling the Sun*, a short film made by Paramount featuring the crowning of the Grapefruit Queen, would entertain more than 40 million moviegoers.[1] And each one of these newsreels probably used Cypress Gardens as a backdrop.

He also created a series of postcards for the commission featuring citrus, but he used Cypress Gardens models and Cypress Gardens itself

Postcard created for the Citrus Commission. Photo by Dick Pope Sr. By permission of Cypress Gardens.

as a backdrop. For one card, he created a map of Florida by arranging thousands of oranges and grapefruits on the grass in front of the Hundred Lakes Yacht club. Beautiful Cypress Gardens "maidens" surround the map.

Once, James Clendinen, the clever editor of the *Tampa Tribune,* noticed Pope's knack at combining his interests, and had a field day when he saw an issue of *Collier's* magazine featuring two Cypress Gardens Aquamaids on the cover, with more skiers inside. Next to a two-page spread of "cuties in bathing suits" was a photo of Dick Pope Jr. barefoot skiing. Clendenin wrote Pope an open letter, asking, "What, No Oranges? Florida's Master Publicity Peddler Must Be Slipping."

> Nowhere could we find so much as one orange. Not one teeny, weeny little tangerine. Not even an unobtrusive citrus peel to remind the reader of Florida's great industry. That's why we say you're slipping. . . . What could be more natural than for each girl to carry an attractive gift box of citrus in her free hand? Or maybe a can of grapefruit juice.[2]

All the teasing was done in good spirits. There was hardly anyone in the state who didn't recognize Pope's genius at marketing not just the Gardens, but Florida. In 1940, Pope supplied the World's Fair in New York with a "100 foot length of colored motion picture film" depicting Winter Haven and the Gardens.[3] The promotion paid off; by August 1940, railroad officials reported that trains headed for Florida were carrying record numbers of tourists who'd been enticed to the state by the Florida exhibit. Whether it was the "spectorama of Tarpon fishing" or the "Aquarama" or the smell of orange blossoms piped in through the air ducts that created the

Oranges create the hoop skirt for this tall southern belle, circa 1940s. By permission of Cypress Gardens.

interest, they didn't say.[4] More than 100,000 people visited the Gardens in 1939, and 1940 was looking to be even better. In a letter Pope wrote in the 1930s, he prophesized as much: "For the last 10 years it has been rather hard to sell a visitor $5,000 to $10,000 worth of Florida, so now we are going to sell 100,000 of them 25 [cents] worth."[5] For his efforts, he was recognized as one of the "Men Who Make Florida," as "the fellow

Florida
CYPRESS GARDENS
GUIDE TO
AMERICA'S TROPICAL WONDERLAND
FLORIDA

A late 1940s guide to Cypress Gardens. Author's collection.

The Popes toured the world in search of plants to bring back to the Gardens; here they are in Egypt. By permission of Julie Pope Dantzler.

who made a wonderland out of a cypress swamp, the man who glorified cypress trees and cypress knees, the Floridian who has helped to create what some have termed the world's greatest outdoor studio." Pope shrugged off the compliments, saying of the Gardens, "We never had enough money to spoil the natural beauty."[6]

He and Julie may not have had enough money to spoil the natural beauty of the Gardens, but they both had highly developed senses of detail and design. The Gardens were filled with picturesque plants from around the world. One writer compared Dick Pope to the pharaohs who built the pyramids, and to Shah Jehan, who built the Taj Mahal. "But this time it came to Dick Pope in Florida," he wrote.[7] The Popes took the name of Florida seriously, creating their own "land of flowers" at the edge of the cypress swamp. Visitors could climb aboard the electric boats and "glide around the world" as one writer did:

> The fishtail palm, white jasmine, sugar palm and ardisia from Malaya almost make one feel the surge and beauty of that part of the world. Alocasias of several sorts, forms of elephant ears, come from the jungles of Borneo, while the clerodendrons take one in imagination to Java. The appealing beauty of the orchard trees transports visitors to India; the climbing Easter lily to Mopal; the sky flower, to Bengal, and the coffee plants to Arabia. . . . The famous traveler's tree and the arcca palms transfer us to Madagascar. . . . Traveling through Central and South America, we find the allamandas from Guiana, sisal hemp from Yucatan, tropical sunflowers from Guatemala, and the famous Monstera Deliciosa, or "Mexican fruit salad" plant, a

> fruit bearing vine, with strange perforated leaves from Mexico.[8]

If gazing at all this flora didn't lift your spirits, and "you needed a pick up for your ego," wrote one writer, "the Sensitive Plant offers a novel way of doing this. Just give it a punch or a firm kick to show it you are the boss, and it will meekly drop and fold its leaves in obedience. . . . The large Sensitive Plant . . . is a great delight to visitors who cuff it all day long while the plant with its submissive little leaves and puff-ball pink flowers just takes it."[9]

Pope took one food writer on what he called a "gourmetical tour" through the Gardens, showing her ginger lilies and coconut palms, mango trees and macadamia nut trees, and a "group of pineapple plants labeled 'Pineapple BC.'"—"Before canning," he explained.[10]

Many of these plants were featured on Technicolor linen postcards that must have dazzled their recipients with their otherworldly blues, greens, reds, and yellows. Cypress Gardens wasn't the only Florida attraction to capitalize on the tourists' desire for a Technicolor paradise. St. Petersburg was home to Sunken Gardens, with its traveler's trees and papaya and palm trees. North of Tampa, in Dupree Gardens, 25 acres of flowers were "set to music"; down in West Palm Beach, Rainbow Tropical Gardens were lit up with lights; the Oriental Gardens on the St. Johns River serenaded tourists with "monastery chimes." What each of these gardens had in common was "an intent to organize nature and make it pleasantly accessible and understandable."[11] For Dick Pope in particular, this meant making the Gardens accessible to photographers and filmmakers. He knew what they liked, and he could provide it:

> He insists that he can produce any kind of scenery and background at a moment's notice and the news reel and travel movie editors believe this. If it's a water scene, he can round up some swimmers, a sailboat, kyacks, motorboats, aquaplanes and models almost at the snap of a finger.[12]

Bert Lacey, one of Cypress Gardens' former public-relations directors, explained why the newspapers were so thrilled with Dick Pope's pictures: "When I first came to Florida in 1967, every big city had two newspapers, one in the evening, so they would be clamoring for things to put in, and that helped Mr. Pope get the word out a great deal. Every Thursday they had a mail-out to thousands of newspapers across the country—

Young women pose among the flowers in this 1940s-era postcard of the Gardens. Courtesy of the State Archives of Florida.

every Thursday—a picture of the Gardens or a story."[13]

Hollywood took notice of the lush Florida garden and its beauties depicted in all those newsreels and photos, and in February 1941, Betty Grable and Don Ameche arrived at Cypress Gardens to film a sequence for the 20th Century Fox feature *Moon over Miami*. Grable was two years away from becoming America's pinup girl, a nickname she won with her famous over-the-shoulder photo. But she had already scored her "big break" in her first color film, *Down Argentina Way*, which also debuted the "Brazilian Bombshell," Carmen Miranda.[14]

This would be the first time the Gardens appeared in a full-length feature film. Although the Technicolor film would be primarily shot in Miami, some crucial scenes were filmed at the Gardens. Malcolm Pope piloted one of the speedboats zipping through the cypress trees and leaping over the bridges in the canals. And Don Ameche asked Betty Grable to marry him as they glided through the Gardens in an electric boat. The local paper reported that "All love scenes will be shot through special lenses to create effect of moonlight . . . while other shots will show the stars aquaplaning in the winding waterways."[15] Pope made sure that both Cypress Gardens and

Moon over Miami stars Betty Grable and Robert Cummings pose for a still shot at Cypress Gardens in 1941. By permission of Cypress Gardens.

Winter Haven were given a credit in the finished film.

Local girls found themselves in the spotlight as a result of the increased attention being given Cypress Gardens. One of the directors from Columbia studios requested that Katy Turner, Martha Mitchell, and Alice Bryan be given screen tests to determine whether or not they were star material. Jessie Stough, who doubled for Betty Grable, found herself billed as "the most photographed girl in the world," and featured in a short film titled *Strange Occupations*. Her job, as one paper reported, is "to pose for amateur and professional photographers who throng the botanical gardens. Day in and day out, the cameras click while she assumes various poses suggested by the snap-shooters."[16] When she arrived at Gettysburg College that fall, she was met by a swarm of photographers who wanted to get a shot of the "blonde double."[17]

Lucy Chambliss, sharpshooter, went to the *Moon over Miami* premiere in Winter Haven: "Everybody went down to the Ritz Theater to see it; they had used the electric boats, and they'd sent doubles in, but it was night so you couldn't tell it was the Gardens, but everybody was excited about it."[18]

Cypress Gardens wasn't the only beneficiary of *Moon over Miami*. Both Rainbow Springs and Silver Springs were used as locations, primarily for underwater shoots. Newton Perry, who worked at Silver Springs and who would later found Weeki Wachee, had a bit part in the film. His daughter Delee recalled seeing him on late-night television: "I was flipping channels and saw Don Ameche in *Moon over Miami*, and all of sudden they decided to drive to Silver Springs . . . and there they were on the photo sub, and there was my dad swimming by."[19]

The Advent of the Southern Belle

In February 1940, Winter Haven was hit with a hard freeze that surely would have destroyed the Gardens if it hadn't been for the six thousand gallons of oil burned in the smudge pots among the flowers and foliage. A reporter went out to assess the damage in the Gardens, expecting to find a "soggy remnant of its rare beauty," and found instead a "scorched and begrimed genius, a bit tired but smiling, for Cypress Gardens had been saved." After praising the workers for keeping the fires going, Dick Pope said: "We are all tired but happy and out yonder, among our flowers and trees, you will find our usual quota of visitors. Every one of them congratulated us upon saving our rare plants, palms and vines from destruction."[20] However, it was Julie's genius that got the visitors in the door despite the freeze. Apparently, in their haste to protect the Gardens, they had neglected the signature flame vine next to the ticket office at the Gardens' entrance. Afraid that the frozen plant would scare visitors off, Julie Pope reached deep into her southern belle roots and saved the day. Dick Pope explained:

> [She] had one of the secretaries—Mrs. Jerome Palmer—dress in the old-fashioned costume we used for special pictures, and stand outside to talk to the people, and explain that inside, everything was wonderful. During the day she caused so much comment, and so many pictures were taken of her, that the girls became a fixture."[21]

While other Gardens around the state added parrots or alligators or monkeys to the mix to keep tourists interested, Dick Pope added the southern belle. All it took was for him to see the tourists' response to Mrs. Palmer as she sashayed around the Gardens in her hoop skirt, smiling at the cameras. He later explained to a reporter that as Cypress Gardens was relatively

A southern belle poses with Cypress Gardens famous flame vine, circa 1940s. Author's collection.

After a 1940 freeze, the southern belles became a fixture at the Gardens. Author's collection.

new and lacked a "tradition and background," it had to "furnish its own tradition and the costumes, the hospitality and the beauty of the Old South were modernized and exploited. Not only did the Gardens advertise beautiful girls—it had them out where the people could see them and take pictures."[22]

These days, newspapers aren't clamoring for images of pretty girls in hoop skirts to fill their pages, but the belles are still a fixture at the Gardens. They sit in the grass here and there, skirts fanned out around them, or they stand on bridges clutching parasols, smiling at digital cameras, which make them seem even more anachronistic than they are.

Nancy Zarza Daley oversaw the belles in the late 1970s and 1980s. She's also a former belle and skier herself. In 2008, she was the special contracts coordinator at Cypress Gardens; she's also the former mayor of nearby Lake Alfred. "The belle dress design stayed the same for seventy-two years," she said. "The bottoms of the dresses always have the big hoop skirts, and they can be different designs and colors, but the top of the dress has always been this short ruffled flounce in an off-the-shoulder-kind-of-sexy-but-still-leaving-a-lot-to-the-imagination way. It was a trademark design, the silhouette of the Cypress Gardens southern belle. It's different than the silhouette of the belle you would see in Georgia or Tennessee; it's a certain look, and it's also a certain attitude; it's the friendly hostess who walks up to the guests and asks them if they are having a nice day, if they are finding everything okay."

When Nancy got to Cypress Gardens, Dick Pope Sr. and Julie had just about retired. "Julie didn't really come out very much, but she set the standard," said Nancy. "If you saw her coming, you made sure you looked exactly right: you weren't chewing gum; you weren't talking to your friends."[23]

And if your friend was a sweet-talking skier? Jimmy "Flea" Jackson became a skier in 1957 and performed for the next two decades. "You could only go certain places in the gardens," he told a reporter. "For some reason I was always in the wrong place." One day he had sidled up next to a belle and was giving her an earful when Julie Pope strolled toward them. He knew he was in deep trouble. "I got right underneath [the belle's] skirt because these were big skirts, you know." As Julie walked by, she said hello and kept going. Jimmy thought he had fooled her until he saw her that afternoon. She let him know he didn't.[24]

Dick Pope liked the wholesome image of the belle sitting pretty on the grass, her pastel skirt flared out as if it were a doily and she were a flower. And in a way, the belles *were* stand-ins for flowers. Pope often created postcard tableaus for the belles with headings like "Southern Flowers and Southern Belles Blooming Brightly" or "A Florida Blossom among Grapefruits and Oranges."

"I don't think there'd be one-tenth as many of those pictures taken if they were dressed in bathing suits," he said. But sometimes over the years, the belles *were* dressed in bathing suits prior to donning the belle dress. Some of them doubled as skiers. Nance Stilley Hains learned to water-ski at Cypress Gardens in 1941 before the ski shows actually started. Just a few years later, she became a belle. By then the ski show had begun so she did double and sometimes triple duty: ski, dress up, or sell egg salad sandwiches. "The typical day," she said in an interview, "we'd go out on a Saturday and pick up trash or did whatever. When the tourists started coming, we ran downstairs and put on our gowns and went the back way to the reflecting pool by the bridge. It was a wonderful place to work."[25]

Nance and her little sister, along with Dick Pope Jr. and Adrienne Pope Watkins, were filmed for the newsreel *Waterbabies* early in the

Nance Stilley Hains, a Cypress Gardens skier and southern belle, appeared on the cover of *Life* magazine in 1947. By permission of Cypress Gardens.

1940s. Her photographs appeared quite frequently in the rotogravure sections of newspapers across the country. In one, she's wearing a swimsuit sewn from twenty neckties; in another, she's chomping on a watermelon; in yet another, she feeds an orange to Florida governor Millard Caldwell in her role as the 1947 Citrus Queen. Her biggest photographic coup had to be making the cover of *Life* in February 1947 when she was eighteen. Before the year was out, she moved to New York to work as a model.[26]

Australian native and Cypress Gardens Aqua Maid Brenda Mitchell also doubled as a southern belle between shows. "Under the dress I would be wearing my bathing suit. The bathing suits in those days were made with a very firm shape and so you'd pull the top down and put on a strapless bra and go sit out there. Mostly, you just had to smile and wave at the tourists or they'd come over and stand next to you to have their picture taken." She remembered playing tricks on the tourists: "All the tourists would ask the same type of question, 'What do you have on under there?' 'Where are you from?' One of my friends was from Newburne, North Carolina, and . . . she would say, 'I'm from Mel-bourne, Australia' [in an Australian accent], and I would say, in a southern accent, 'I'm from Newburne, North Carolina.' We'd go crazy."[27]

Tallahassean Judy Miner skied at the Gardens in the 1950s. She remembered "The Falsies Room," a fitting room filled with pieces of foam the skiers tucked into their swimsuits. The skiers wore their tops strapless until a fall revealed that that wasn't such a great idea. When Judy wasn't skiing, she would slip into a hoop skirt and a pair of pantaloons and sit in the Gardens. "Thank heavens we wore pantaloons," she told a reporter. "We'd get bored sometimes and start turning cartwheels." Her friend, Ann Hinson, from nearby Bartow, would tag along, invited by the Popes to "hang around beautifying the grounds for camera buffs."[28]

"In the early days, they would all ski in the show, then come back and be southern belles for the rest of the day," said Nancy Zarza Daley. "There were other times, when the economy was bad, that they would have us skiers put on a belle dress—but when you do that your hair isn't as nice and you don't really have time to take a shower and get dressed up. I remember one time, I had been in the ski show and I was kind of frazzled, and I had combed my hair, and I was sitting out there in the dress in the botanical gardens, and a little boy came by with his mom and he had his camera in his hand, and his mom said, 'Oh take a picture of the girl,' and the little boy looked at me and he said, 'Nahh, I'll wait till we get to a pretty one.'" She laughs. "I don't blame him; you can only do what you can do."[29]

Besides being a belle, Kathy Darlyn performed as "high girl" in the skier's pyramid act, standing on the other girls' shoulders as they zipped across the lake at 30 miles per hour.[30] In 1950, she was crowned Citrus Queen. She had been in Meyer's modeling school over in St. Petersburg when Mr. Meyer decided to enter her in a beauty contest. "But first, he took me to Cypress Gardens and introduced me to Mr. Dick Pope," she told a reporter. "They decided to put me in the Florida Citrus Queen contest at Lake Silver." She decided she wanted to change her name from the unromantic Marion Helzer to something a bit more queenly. "Mr. Meyer told me to go home and write down some names I liked and to practice saying them. I told him I liked Kathy Darlene. Mr. Pope said he always thought of me as a little darling, so he wanted me to change it to that."[31] They settled on the colloquial "Darlyn."

An official photograph of Kathy as Citrus Queen appears on the cover of *Citrus Magazine*; she's wearing her cape and Citrus Queen crown

Kathy Darlyn, a Cypress Gardens skier and southern belle, was also crowned the Citrus Queen in 1950. By permission of Cypress Gardens.

Kathy Darlyn taking a break during her stint as a belle. By permission of Don "Spider" Bell.

(decorated with rhinestone orange slices). The caption inside says she'd been interviewed by national radio star Tom Moore, and told him she wanted to be a model.[32]

Spider Bell has an unofficial photo of Kathy. She is wearing a flowery belle dress and she's sitting on a bench in the sunlight. She's also breaking one of the cardinal rules of belle-dom. "That's Kathy Darlyn there," Spider says, "one of the queens, smoking a cigarette. If Dick Pope saw that picture . . ." He trails off, shaking his head.[33]

If Dick Pope had seen that picture, Kathy might have lost her crown—even though the Gardens had crowned Dorothy Snively as Cigarette Queen back in the 1940s.

Contrary to the strict code of southern belle etiquette that Julie grew up with in Brewton, Alabama, and later enforced at Cypress Gardens, the latter-day belles had to have instruction, some of which might have baffled Julie. "When a new girl came on we gave her tips about how we wanted her to wear her hair," said Nancy Zarza Daley. "There were very strict rules about what kind of jewelry they could wear. They couldn't have any tattoos or body piercing; they had to wear certain kinds of socks and shoes and they had to walk a certain way and sit a certain way; they could only drink water; they couldn't smoke or eat while they were wearing the dresses.

"We didn't have a very strict body type or age group—it was more about personality—the girls didn't have to be real thin. We had one bench in front of where the Gazebo is in the botanical gardens, and the botanical boat cruise would go through there, and that was one place where the girls always had to sit, and they were on half-hour shifts; they weren't allowed to leave until another girl came and took their place. It was a great picture for the tourists and a great advertisement for Cypress Gardens. And there was a little air conditioner under the bench, and they would turn it on and it would help cool them down. That bench is gone now."[34]

The Gazebo turned out to be a favorite spot not just for southern belles desperate for some air-conditioning, but for weddings—by the year 2000, around five hundred couples per year were taking their vows beneath the dome.[35] Pope built the Gazebo in 1947, Bert Lacey said. "That's one of the most photographed places in the park. He bought a used radar dome and four pillars from a burnt-out cigar factory in Tampa, and that's the Gazebo."[36]

OPM Squared: Our Picture Material, Other People's Money

Dick Pope had used photography to sell everything from real estate to citrus and spark plugs to motorboats, but with the southern belles and skiers he was able to take photography to the next level. He even created a formula for his approach: OPM squared—our picture material, other people's money. By the 1940s, cameras belonged to everyone, and a third of the tourists who walked through the Gardens' gates were toting one. If they weren't, they could borrow one. Pope was quick to recognize the advertising potential in amateur photographers; a quarter million tourists would leave Cypress Gardens each year with photographs to show their friends. Gauging that this meant millions of snapshots and miles of home movies, in 1948 he built a shrine to the amateur photographer: a photo pier. He was aware that the "shutterbugs" were being told to "sit down" when they popped up to take photos of the Aqua Maids, so initially he sequestered them on three rows of benches off to the side. When the number of photographers increased, he built the pier, and divided it into three parts: one for stills, one for movies, and one for box cameras. The pier jutted out into the water so the skiers would glide right past it.[37]

Then he hired a photographer to shout out aperture and light directions. "For years, we had the largest single window of Kodak film sales of anybody in the country," said Red McGuire, a former skier and photographer. "Walter Stickler would sit on the pier and tell people when to shoot and what to shoot; he'd go through a roll of film for everybody that was up there and with two hundred people on that photo pier shooting a roll of film on every show—it was quite a lucrative project. Walter Stickler was followed by a guy named Al Adams, but we all used to work on the photo pier. . . . That's just one of the publicity things that built the Gardens. Kodak said that when people went on vacation and shot pictures, they showed them at least three times to other people when they got home. And they're buying the film, and you're helping them shoot it up, which is profitable, but not only that, you're getting a residual when they get home and show it to other people."[38]

Willa McGuire Cook, Cypress Gardens' prima ballerina, remembered when the photo pier was built. "In the beginning they had plastic cushions that they spread out in a natural

The famous Cypress Gardens Gazebo was constructed with recycled materials: a used radar dome and pillars from a burnt-out cigar factory. By permission of Cypress Gardens.

To accommodate all the amateur photographers, Dick Pope built the photo pier in 1948. By permission of Cypress Gardens.

amphitheater on the bank facing the waterskiing circle on the water," she said, "and then it grew and grew, and we got one set of bleachers close to the water-ski circle for photographers, so they would they would take home photographs of us skiing.[39] They also photographed the belles who weren't just posing back then; they, like the rest of the Gardens' employees, were also taught how to help the novice photographers.[40]

Dick Pope built a second pier a few years later. Described as "the largest tinkertoy in the world," and an "octahedron-tetrahedron affair," the second pier was actually constructed between ski shows in about a week and a half by skiers and their boat drivers. Al Adams worked this pier, telling the tourists how to correctly set their camera exposures.[41] Having professionals to assist the amateurs was well worth it to Pope. Besides selling them $300,000 worth of film each year, he charged them twenty-five cents to sit on the photo pier. In exchange, they got a pin that said "Official Guest Photographer, Cypress Gardens, Florida." "Makes 'em feel good," he said, "and they only cost a cent and a half a piece."[42]

Pope didn't just mix the high and the low in the photography department; he really didn't seem to distinguish between the two. Thus in the fall of 1941, he arranged for two of Cypress Gardens'

Ed Carter, one of Cypress Gardens' male models, assists a tourist with her camera, circa 1948. By permission of Cypress Gardens.

Amateur photographers paid a quarter for a pin that made them "Official Guest Photographers." Courtesy of Jennifer Stevens.

The Duke and Duchess of Windsor take a break on the famous Cypress Gardens Wishing Tree during one of their trips to Florida, 1959. By permission of Cypress Gardens.

most recent flower queens to join the Duke and Duchess of Windsor in their private car on the Silver Meteor at the Seaboard station in Winter Haven. Camellia Queen Alice Bryan and Gardenia Queen Martha Mitchell joined the other royals on their way to an event in Sebring. Both of the Cypress Gardens queens were wearing their hoopskirts. "The first thing they asked us," said Martha, "was where Dick Pope was. They knew him because of the gift of gardenias he'd sent them last year. After that they just talked about the Cypress Gardens and our costumes." The queens noted that the duchess was better-looking in person than in photographs, with her "enormous blue eyes and skin like a baby's." They also noted that neither of the royals had southern accents. Surely the queens impressed the duke and duchess with their southern drawls for when it was time to go, the duke said he regretted they couldn't come along for the rest of the trip.[43]

The Duke and Duchess of Windsor weren't the only notable guests who came to Cypress Gardens in the 1940s. Florida was segregated then, so on Palm Sunday in 1942, when Jim Doles and his family arrived at the Gardens dressed to the nines, it was a big deal. Mr. Doles had worked at the Gardens prior to its opening, helping to dig the canals and plant the plants.

Betty Doles explained that after the Gardens opened, her two older brothers would go to work with their father. "Downing (Dick Pope Jr.) was just a little boy running around; they'd play together. They were just out there with my dad; there weren't any babysitters or anything; to keep the kids out of mischief he'd take them to work with him."[44]

Walter Doles laughed at the memory. When asked what he did out at the Gardens those days, he smiled. "Nothing. Trying to stay out of trouble. It was so bad in the 'hood that Daddy had to take us to work. Malcolm Pope was a speedboat driver, and we rode in the electric boats with him. So that kept us out of Daddy's way. He took us all over, through the canals. It wasn't too cool because I was afraid of water. I'd never seen anything as big as Lake Eloise and the canals. After two or three times I got used to it, but starting out I was afraid of it. They had a parrot out there, and I spent more time with the bird than I did anything else."[45]

Betty still has a white linen suit one of her brothers wore that day. "At that time, Florida was all segregated," she said. "Well, we didn't know that; we didn't know what segregation was; we just thought this was someplace we just didn't go, like any other place, like Bok Tower. We just didn't go there because it was whites only. So when they decided to open up to us, it was one day a year, and that was on Palm Sunday, and this is why we were all dressed up in our Easter finery; we were dressed to kill just to go out to Cypress Gardens."[46]

James "Jim" Doles and his family were invited to the Gardens on Palm Sunday, 1942. *Left to right*: Jacqueline, Walter, James Jr., Richard, James Sr., Betty, and Annie Mae. By permission of the Doles family.

Walter Doles worked as a waiter at the Palm Terrace Restaurant at Cypress Gardens. *Seated left to right*: Tom Sanders, Ulysses Lane, Joe Hill, Ted Phyall, Frank Coleman, Ernest Hayward, Richard McCloud, unknown female, Richard Doles, James Williams, Butler Hagen, and Jonathan Faison (*front*); *standing left to right*: Joe Hohlmeyer, James Gurley, Walter Doles, George Lawrence, Charles Campbell, Isaac Fookes, E. J. Adams, Amelia Newland, and Samuel Carter.

Betty's sister Jacqueline was three or four years old at the time. "My daddy said we were the first African Americans there because our family was the only one that went that day. And I think when they were able to go later in life, no black families went, but we went because he worked there." Still, Jacqueline said she believed Dick Pope would have wanted African Americans to visit the Gardens. "He was trying to integrate when he opened the doors on Palm Sunday, letting blacks come in that day," she said. "He was doing it then, letting blacks be exposed to the same thing whites were exposed to."[47]

"I think Mr. Pope had invited our father, said 'please come and bring the kids,'" said Betty, "because he's the one who snapped the picture; we didn't have a camera. I don't know how we got out there that day because we didn't have a car; it had to be a neighbor or friend; it could've been a car he sent for us, I don't know. Whoever took us evidently didn't go in. It was just a garden; there wasn't even a ski show, just the garden and the boat rides. You walked through the gardens, and they had all these beautiful girls with their dresses on, and they stood around, and you snapped the pictures. The only thing I can remember is there was an organ grinder, and people were all gathered around watching him, and there was a parrot out there, and he could say hello and good-bye."

Asked if her parents talked about Cypress Gardens, Betty said: "All the time. My daddy had a close relationship with Dick Pope. It was nothing for him to ask him to come out there because he'd been building the Gardens. They were close." Still, segregation was the law in 1940s Florida. "Even in later years when the restaurant came—they didn't have a restaurant when we went—they used all black waiters and cooks; it was that southern hospitality thing. You couldn't have white waiters in the South, they had to be black; you weren't a prestigious establishment otherwise. There wasn't such a thing as a white waiter or a white cook. My two brothers were there, so we'd always visit them without paying. You just went on through," said Betty. "You were invisible to a point. Nobody paid you any attention because they knew if a black person was there, he was working there. So we'd go through that employee gate with the rest of the guys."[48]

Jacqueline agreed: "We still sat on the terrace where they served lunch and ate lunch right along with all the other guests. And they never said anything to us. It was like we were part of them. That was amazing right there. We didn't know what it was to pay to go in there."[49]

Dubie Baxter's family ran the Palm Terrace Restaurant. He recalled becoming the first white waiter at the restaurant. "It was nepotism," he said. In 1946, his mother became Dick Pope's first executive secretary, and they grew so close that in 1949, when Pope became unhappy with the management of the restaurant, he asked her if she could recommend a new manager. "It was right after the war, and jobs were pretty scarce," Dubie said, "so naturally, she said 'Well, my uncle has a degree in accounting, and my grandmother has a lot of good recipes, and she has a good friend named Amelia Newland, who has even more recipes.'"

"Amelia Newland's pecan pie was some of the best made in the whole world," said Dubie, who added that he used to shell the pecans for her. But his first job at the restaurant was peeling potatoes for fifty cents per trash can. "We thought we were real important and had great jobs, but all they were doing was babysitting us. But they didn't let on."

All that changed when he grew up: "Of all the cousins I was the oldest, so naturally I became the first white waiter, and two or three years later my brother and our first cousin became dual white waiters, dueling white waiters." He added that the "white waiters" were an anomaly. "They didn't really shift to white waiters; they just did that so we could make some money. The other waiters probably resented that because we were taking money out of their babies' mouths, but we didn't think of it that way. We didn't think until later that we might have been out of place—it wasn't our place to go in there and do something they'd be doing. There was probably resentment, but you wouldn't notice it because nobody ever said anything."[50]

Bob Gernert, executive director of the Winter Haven Chamber of Commerce and a Cypress Gardens aficionado, said he believes Dick Pope would have opened all of the Gardens' doors to African Americans if he could have. Bob is certain local blacks understood this: "If there was long-festering resentment, it would still be there. And I've dealt a lot with the African American community because I'm a history buff; I helped them, and they've helped me. And there was a woman who knew I collected Cypress Gardens things, and her family had worked there, and she was proud of the heritage of working at the Gardens. I think the folks that worked there, white or black, were treated very well. Anybody that worked for the Popes says they were like grandparents."[51]

Walter Doles remembered his days at the Palm Terrace Restaurant: "I can remember Tarzan, Johnny Weissmuller, coming across the Chain of Lakes; he swam about twenty lakes, and I had a chance to serve the king of Jordan, got to see quite a few movie stars because we had the pool and the islands." He explained why Cypress Gardens seemed to be more inclusive than other places in the South.

"Cypress Gardens helped the blacks around here because it was a tourist attraction so we didn't have any problems in Winter Haven that much. The Chamber of Commerce and those people depended on the tourist business. They couldn't have sit-ins around here."

"This town was made up of tourists, northerners, and that helped," said Betty.

"We were treated like someone on the job," said Walter. "We didn't have that many problems. We'd go out and get into a little devilment and just tell the law we worked at Cypress Gardens and they'd let us go. That's how high Cypress Gardens was." Walter said that when Dick Pope got wind of their devilment, "he'd make the calls; he'd call and tell them, 'let my boys out.'" Pope also helped his workers in other ways. "The first automobile I owned," said Walter, "I was looking at it; it was a '55 Ford, and he checked me out and said, 'you want it?' And I said 'yes, I want it, but I don't have the money,' so he went to the bank and got about six hundred dollars for me to get the car I wanted. He told the bank to give it to me. That's the kind of man he was. We didn't make that much money, but we didn't have any problems. If you worked for the right person, all you had to do was call their name."[52]

Cypress Gardens Goes to War

In October 1942, a headline in the *Polk County Record* announced: "Cypress Gardens President Becomes Buck Private." "When I enlisted," Pope told a reporter later, "I listed my occupation as a publicity man. Well, they didn't have anything under publicity and the only opening they had under 'p' was for poles; setting them up for telephone and electric lines. So, that's how I spent the war years, digging holes and setting poles."[53]

He didn't quite give publicity up. From the looks of the Pope family album, he must've carried his own photographer to Camp Blanding. There are photos of Dick marching in formation; photos of Dick using a telephone in the field; photos of Dick erecting telephone poles; photos of Dick peeling potatoes. And photos of Dick publicizing Florida. In one photograph, he clings to the top of a telephone pole, a couple of Florida oranges in hand. On the envelope he sent to Julie in Winter Haven, he wrote, "Julie, Maybe the *Sentinel* could use one of these—have a 5 × 7 or 8 × 10 sent them—use something in the caption about Florida oranges are on top—Dick Pope is still publicizing them."[54]

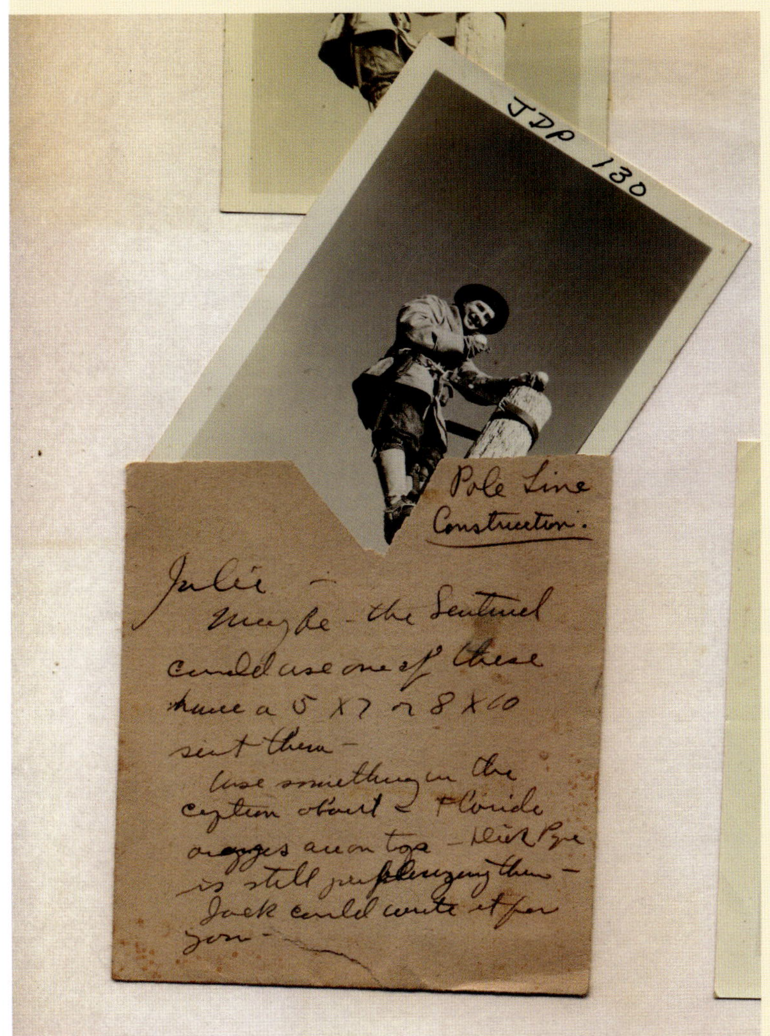

Enlisting in the army did not stop Dick Pope from advertising Florida oranges, circa 1942. By permission of Julie Dantzler Pope.

Pianist Billye-Mullins Smith joined up with Julie Pope to put on shows for the USO, circa 1943. By permission of Billye-Mullins Smith.

While Dick was at Camp Blanding, Julie was left to mind Cypress Gardens on her own. It was tough at first because of war restrictions against travel and gas rationing. "Julie, my wife, had to go it alone practically," Pope told a reporter from *Spray,* a water-ski magazine. "And the people stopped coming to see the Gardens. She sent out pictures, like I had done, and there were covers on magazines about Beautiful Cypress Gardens, but with gasoline rationing and all, we were not allowed to have tourists. So Julie put a story in the paper—*Cypress Gardens now open to the people in the armed services.* And she would go to the military camps. . . . She'd take a piano player, some ladies to sing, and dance, and she'd show pictures of the Gardens. The chaplains thought it was a nice place for boys to come. Well, the servicemen started coming—that's what saved us."[55]

Billye-Mullins Smith, concert pianist, was recruited to play piano and sing: "When Julie called and said, 'I understand you have quite a musical background, let's get some USO shows going,' I got a guitarist; I got a drummer, two adorable girls, June Courson and Connie Hass, and we made a trio. So that was our USO show. So how did we get gasoline? We went out in ambulances and recons and were out until three and four in the morning. I had a wonderful time with them. *Life* magazine even came down and photographed us from way up in the trees because every weekend we would have the show. We put it on out at the Gardens. That's the way we kept the Gardens open."[56]

The war was also responsible for getting the famous Cypress Gardens ski shows started. It's hard to believe that Dick Pope hadn't capitalized on ski shows earlier, given his extensive

The early ski shows at Cypress Gardens were performed by youngsters. *Left to right*: Gene Maratti, Jimmy Gunter, Buster MacCalla, John Dillard, Sandy Reynolds, and Richard Emry. By permission of the American Water Ski Educational Foundation Museum.

background generating press for the crazy stunts he and Malcolm did on water. Lucy Chambliss remembered skiing on the lake before the ski show was formed. "My father had a pair of skis made down at the planing mill here, and Mr. Pope was into the aquaplanes. We lived on a lake, had a little motorboat. The aquaplanes were very hard to stay up on; they didn't have footbinders or anything, but we spent a lot of time on the lake aquaplaning, and my sister learned to ski there."[57] Lucy's sister, Barbara Chambliss, would go on to become a Cypress Gardens skier. In fact, Barbara posed for "Splashing into Matrimony," a "special photo story" Dick Pope concocted before he went away to the army. It seems Barbara decided to "prove . . . that a wedding and a honeymoon on aquaplanes are possible," using herself and Bobby Wheeler as models. The press release notes that "On aquaplanes they bounced along at 40 miles an hour with the throbbing motors out-throbbing their hearts. As the last 'I do' was pronounced they literally plunged in to the literal sea of waves, not matrimony."[58]

It took Julie to come up with the idea of actually putting a daily ski show on. She came up with the idea as a way of dealing with wartime restraints. As Dick Pope explained:

> At that time, soldiers from nearby camps were our only visitors. They seemed to have plenty of time on their hands during these visits, so Julie thought it would be a good idea to have a regular water-ski show every afternoon. Her next step was to write a letter to the editors of the state newspapers enclosing a picture of the skiers, along with the necessary data for a story. Our friend Martin Andersen, publisher of the *Orlando Sentinel*, ran a story in his Monday edition. That same afternoon about three o'clock, a lieutenant, two sergeants, and one corporal passed through the Garden's gates. The group walked up to my wife and asked, "When does the ski show begin that we read about in the *Orlando Sentinel*?"

Julie told the soldiers the show would start in thirty minutes, not mentioning that that's when her children, Adrienne, eight, and Dick Jr., eleven, would get home. That afternoon they, along with Katy Turner, Ruthie Recker, Buddy Boyle, Bill Hatfield, and few other kids, put on Cypress Gardens' first ski show, while fifteen-year-old Trammell Picket drove the boat.[59]

Adrienne Pope Watkins was in the second grade. "I remember getting out of school. She had all these buses of soldiers there, so she gathered us up." Asked if her father put her on skis as soon as she could walk, Adrienne said, "No, actually he put me on an aquaplane. That's the worst thing in the world. An aquaplane would pull back; water skis won't pull back."

She must have done a pretty good job because she got hired: "I remember working on the weekends at the Gardens; we did all kinds of things. My parents paid us fifty cents an hour. You name it, we did it. Later on, in our teens, we got a dollar an hour."[60]

The following weekend, eight hundred soldiers showed up at the Gardens to see the new ski show. Julie managed to get the Gardens declared "an essential industry for entertainment of service men and women in the state,"[61] a designation apparently helped by the filming of newsreels such as *GI Fun*, *GI Joe*, and *Soldiers' Paradise*. The "cameraman's dope sheets" from Movietone News offer a glimpse at a couple of these short films: "Soldiers take things over and crown six flower queens at Cypress Gardens.

Then get the tables turned on them." Another one reads: "A Sgt. Crowns the Orange Festival Queen at Cypress Gardens Fla. The girls have a map of the state made of oranges and grapefruits and the soldiers seem to enjoy eating it."[62]

The soldiers even appeared in Cypress Gardens photos sent out across the nation. In one, labeled "Rounds out His Training," Sgt. Bob Ruccione shows "how he became watermelon-eating champ of Cypress Gardens, Fla." alongside model and skier Tee Matthews.[63] In another, Sgt. Lou Murtha poses with a couple of pelican flowers perched on his hands.[64] Some soldiers even learned to ski. "Because of rationing, we were allowed 15 gallons of gas per week and we taught the soldiers to ski at no cost to them," Dick Pope Jr. told *WaterSki Magazine*. Asked how they managed to stage shows with such a small supply of fuel, he said: "Our shows were very short. And we always carried an extra pair of skis in the boat in case we ran out of gas and had to paddle ourselves back in."[65]

Adrienne remembered those days: "During the war we'd go out and make the sandwiches up for the soldiers. Everything was on shortage. I remember running one of the old washing machines you wring everything out with because we rented the bathing suits and had to

Cypress Gardens was declared an "essential industry" during World War II, and soldiers came en masse to see the ski shows, circa 1940s. By permission of Cypress Gardens.

Both a soldier and a sailor enjoy the attentions of this southern belle, circa 1940s. By permission of Cypress Gardens.

Southern belles wave good-bye to a convoy of soldiers, circa 1940s. By permission of Cypress Gardens.

take them home and wash them every day, wring them out."[66]

Lucy Chambliss remembered when Dick Pope Sr. came home from serving in the army: "My folks gave a dance and he and Mrs. Pope came. Mr. Pope walked in behind Mrs. Pope, and he was very subdued—the army hadn't broken his spirit but it wasn't fun anymore. It took him about six months to snap back. I can see him yet—they cut his hair short."[67]

As soon as he got home, he put his army experience to use in the Gardens. "I had one spot in the Gardens where I really needed some beautiful tall flowers, but I needed something to support them. It dawned on me that what we needed were some of those telephone poles I'd been setting in the army, so we shopped around, found some fairly cheap and planted giant bougainvillea vines. Today that's one of the most beautiful and most photographed spots in the gardens but it wouldn't have been possible without those telephone poles."[68]

He also invited the public out to see the USO show Julie had taken on the road to the soldiers. The show had "been presented 28 times before thousands of soldiers in air fields and camps throughout the state. Airplane hangars, outdoor theaters, reception halls and even chapels have been used for the show." The day's activities would include a "hula-hula dance," a "Georgia Gal number," a "baton twirling exhibition followed by the crowning of the Wistaria Queen," and a performance by the vocal trio Billye-Mullins had put together.[69]

Shortly after Dick Pope returned home, he also asked Billye-Mullins Smith to write a song for Cypress Gardens that he could use in his publicity. "I didn't ski; I didn't want the water in my ears because that's my trade," she said, but she did watch the ski shows. "Dick said one day, 'Well I'm tired of getting all this stuff, beautiful gardenia time in Cypress Gardens, beautiful azalea time in Cypress Gardens; why don't you be the song-testing laboratory for me?'"

The result was "Skiing Is Fun in the Florida Sun." Billye-Mullins sings a few bars from the song bobbing her head and patting her desk top to keep the beat: "You take two boards and you call them skis and you skim across the water with the greatest ease." She pauses, "Now this is Carroll's writing," she says, referring to her late husband, and begins singing again, "Skiing is fun in the Florida sun, there's tan by the ton, your troubles are none in the Florida sun." She pauses again. "I took out the word 'gay.'" And then sings her last line, "A lovely fragrance on the evening breeze."

Much to Billye-Mullins's delight, Dick Pope used the song. She created different versions of the song for different acts including a waltz for the swan act, and a rock 'n' roll version for the jumping act. She recorded the song, and Dick Pope used it as background to the daily shows. She wanted to give the Gardens' previous owners, Brian Philpot and Rob Hardy of Land South Holdings, a copy of another song. She sings: "I want to wake up in the morning where the orange blossoms grow, and the sun comes peeking into where I'm sleeping and the songbirds say hello." If only they would use the song in their

Dick Pope's models landed more magazine covers than anyone else in the country, as this page from a 1940s-era Cypress Gardens newsletter illustrates. By permission of Cypress Gardens.

Life magazine called Cypress Gardens a "cameraman's heaven," adding that Pope had turned the Gardens into an "outdoor studio," complete with props and reflectors. By permission of Cypress Gardens.

ski shows, she said, it would have a restorative effect: "Oh, it is cute, and it would help bring the Gardens back. It's not done for."[70]

Cypress Gardens Cheesecake

The war years in particular were a boon to the young women of Winter Haven and the surrounding area, for this was the era of the pinup. Dick Pope didn't invent the pinup—that distinction goes to Hartzell Spence, founder of *Yank* magazine, who apparently introduced the term first used in *Life* in 1941 as an adjective modifying "girl." *Yank* was the first place where the word was used as a noun. Ralph Stein, author of "The Pinup for 1852 to Now," was a cartoon editor at *Yank* during the war years. He remembered a meeting at which Spence announced, "We've got to have a pinup."

"None of us had ever heard the word," Stein said. "I think Hartzell might have invented it."[71]

Dick Pope's pretty-girl pictures were not as risqué as the pinups making the rounds of the barracks featuring the likes of Norma Jean Baker and Jane Russell. In fact, you might argue that Pope's pictures weren't really pinups. That distinction was mostly reserved for the *Esquire* Vargas Girls and Hollywood stars like Dorothy

Lamour or Betty Grable, who had visited the Gardens in 1941, a month before war was declared, to film scenes for *Moon over Miami*. Dick Pope's success, as one writer put it, is "due to his knack for getting the right kind of girls. He doesn't go in for the *Esquire* type. His girls, most of them from the high schools of surrounding towns, are sweet and attractive: there isn't a sophisticate in the bunch."[72]

Whether or not the young women were sophisticated is arguable, but they did tend to be homegrown. A perfect example of one of Pope's girls would be skier Barbara Chambliss, then nineteen years old. She landed three national magazine covers within two months in 1944.[73] Another would be Tee Matthews. She was selected by a couple of military photographers as "the most photogenic girl" in Florida. The resulting shots got the attention of the editors of *Life* magazine, who sent their most famous photographer, Alfred Eisenstaedt, down to Winter Haven to photograph her for a three-page spread.

After one of Pope's "girls" snagged yet another *Life* magazine cover, a *Winter Haven Herald* reporter wrote that "Dick Pope is nationally recognized as one of America's ace publicity picture men." Russell Kay, secretary of the Florida Press Association, wrote that "thanks to Dick Pope's promotion and showmanship [Cypress Gardens] has become known nationally as the home of the nation's most charming and beautiful girls. . . . [E]ditors of such magazines as *Life, Pic* and *Look* are continually turning to Dick Pope and Cypress Gardens for their pretty-girl pictures."

Taking a more serious tone, he went on to praise Dick Pope for providing a salve to wartime America:

> Picture editors and newsreel officials realize that America is fully conscious of the war, that pictures of dead soldiers, crashed planes and the like have a proper effect on the average American mind, but they know too, that the average American wants a little diversion with his morning war news or in his newsreel and that is where Cypress Gardens enters the picture with pictures.[74]

Amelia Crossland appeared on the cover of *Life* in February 1945, smiling amid sea oats on a sandy white dune. Her photo was clearly "a little diversion." In 2001, Roy Peter Clark deconstructed the magazine, explaining that every image, word and ad in that particular issue of *Life* "speaks of an America at war":

> The 16-year-old girl on the cover does too. St. Petersburg's own Amelia Crossland is what the boys are fighting for, the sweetheart back home, the beach honey with the windswept hair, the Donna Reed smile, the lacy decolletage. She is eternal youth, radiant icon of the home front, resting on a tropical beach, framed by a spray of sea oats and a summery sky. A warm girl for a cold month. Except none of it was real. The beach was nothing more than a sandbox next to a swamp, the sea oats trucked in, the soft sky a cold January illusion.

Clark goes on to point out that inside the pages is a story titled "Murder in the Snow," about a massacre in which over 150 American prisoners were shot by the Nazis. One photograph of a young soldier lying dead in the snow had been retouched to hide his mutilated face. Both the image of Amelia and the image of the dead soldier are "photographic illusions," Clark writes, "one the product of staging, the other of retouching. . . . Cultural mythologies are often constructed upon illusions, and Pope, the pre-Disney, pre–air conditioning genius of Florida escapism, was not about to let World War II get in the way."[75]

Dick Pope caught a lot of heat over this particular layout in 1945 as well, not because he was serving up a bit of palaver to Americans horrified by the atrocities of war, but because the layout was all about *being fake*. He let the audience behind the wizard's curtain to see how he made his photographs. The beach *was* a "sandbox next to a swamp."

Pope had been hired by the City of St. Petersburg in September 1944 to help the city's publicity department beef up their promotions. He was to be paid three grand and given a four-thousand-dollar expense account for five months of part-time work. The *St. Petersburg Times* reported that Pope is "conceded to have obtained more consistent publicity results nationally . . . than any individual or agency in Florida."[76] When the magazine featuring Amelia came out, several city council members criticized the layout because it showed how pictures taken in Cypress Gardens were faked and then sent out as St. Petersburg pictures. They couldn't quite grasp the notion that St. Petersburg was paying for photos made in Cypress Gardens to promote St. Petersburg. One council member defended Pope, saying that the pictures wouldn't have made it into the magazine without Pope's artistic twist and that the city was lucky to have gotten the spread.

In a letter to the editor, a local man made it clear that Dick Pope was getting one over on St. Petersburg: "I think they in Winter Haven chuckle with delight that St. Petersburg is paying Dick Pope for publicity featuring Cypress Gardens and Winter Haven."[77]

Whether Pope's "photographic illusions" were meant to soothe anxious America or get one over on St. Petersburg, the reality is that by 1945, these photos were "old hat" to him. Cypress Gardens itself was conceived as a stage. One of Pope's very first "illusions" was a 1936 image of a little boy holding up a stringer of large fish in front of a cypress tree at the Gardens. The little boy, Roy Clary, had actually caught the fish on Lake Martha, a couple miles west of Cypress Gardens. When Dick Pope heard about it, he got in his Lincoln, picked up the boy, his little sister, and the fish, and drove them over to Lake Eloise, where Robert Dalhgren photographed them and then sent the photo out to the wire services. The photo brought a lot of attention to the fledgling Gardens.[78]

As for Pope's "not letting World War II get in the way," it's important to note that although not officially part of the USO, he and Julie did more than their part to "bring pleasure and happiness to thousands of G.I. tourists" from every state in the union. Of course, the GIs did their part as well. Without the thousands who showed up during the war, the Gardens would not have been able to stay open. So, in addition to putting on boat races and water-ski shows for their entertainment, Dick began the practice of crowning as many as five queens a week. The soldiers loved it. Newspapers did too. Cypress Gardens crowned the Camellia Queen, the Cigarette Queen, the Queen of the Butterfly Lilies, the Wisteria Queen, the Azalea Queen, and the

Dick Pope claimed he once crowned nine queens in one day. During the war, the soldiers got to do the crowning. Circa 1940s. By permission of Cypress Gardens.

Top: Pope often liked to pose his queens with brand-new cars, hoping the photos would get picked up as advertisements. Here he gets a plug in for Marine Studios and the Gardens, circa 1940s. By permission of Cypress Gardens.

Below: Famous ventriloquist Edgar Bergen and his sidekick, Charlie McCarthy, crown a queen in 1952. By permission of Cypress Gardens.

Yellow Aster Queen. For the Holly Queen contest, only red-heads were allowed to compete. Over 1,100 soldiers watched as Laurel Norden was crowned Gardenia Queen; a soldier snapped his own "pinup photo" of Poinsettia Queen Sylvia Chambliss; air force cadets got to pick the Magnolia Queen.

Name a flower, and Pope had a queen. They were crowned by soldiers on stages with cutouts of bombers behind them; they were crowned next to maps of Florida made of oranges and grapefruit. They were crowned next to brand new Buick Roadmasters and Ford Super Deluxe convertibles. If someone in Winter Haven got a new car, Dick Pope would ask them to let him use the cars in shoots, hoping the photographs would get picked up as advertisements.[79] "I remember in 1941 when we got a new Chevrolet," Lucy Chambliss told a reporter, "and Mr. Pope got my father to go down to the Gardens to take pictures. He figured he would send them to Chevrolet as promotional shots. I don't know if he ever did, but that's the way he was always thinking."[80] When the famous ventriloquist Edgar Bergen and his dummy, Charlie McCarthy, vacationed at Cypress Gardens in 1952, they too were enlisted to crown a queen. Not to leave anyone out, Dick Pope also placed several "citrus

Riding a jitterboard while wearing a tutu requires a lot of balance and bravado. Circa late 1940s. Author's collection.

Willa McGuire Cook was the original Cypress Gardens prima ballerina. Here she makes jitterboarding *en pointe* look easy. Circa 1950s. By permission of Cypress Gardens.

queen thrones" around the gardens for tourists who wanted to pretend they were royalty, too.[81]

By November 1945, the war was over, but Pope was just getting started. He hosted famed *Life* photographer Eliot Elisofon at the Gardens where Elisofon—under Pope's direction—snapped photos of the girls posing among the cypress trees, on the bridges that spanned the canals, and against the lake. Then Pope—switching into his other role as director of publicity for both Lakeland and St. Petersburg—took Elisofon over to Lakeland, where he photographed seven college girls in order to, as Pope put it, "depict the pleasant life and privileges . . . that girls from other states enjoy at a modern coeducational college in our Land of Sunshine and Pretty Girls."[82] These girls may have been pretty, as the reporters always liked to point out, but they were also pretty physical, performing the way they did on water.

Katy Turner, one of those pretty girls (and Pope's secretary), demonstrated a "new Aquatic sport" at a "two-hour water rodeo" just a month after Elisofon's visit. The sport was jitterboarding—or balancing on a narrow board without the benefit of a tow rope while the board is "hauled through the water at a high speed by a motorboat." Not only did Katy jitterboard like a pro, she also skied on the first slalom course constructed in the South.[83]

Willa McGuire Cook, the world champion skier from Wisconsin who came to the Gardens in 1948, became an expert on the jitterboard. "It was hard for some people," she said. "It was something that was there when I got there, and I asked what they were, and Dick Pope said, 'Why don't you take one out and try it?' and I did, and it was fun. They're a board that jitters if you're not dead center. Men had a difficult time; they tried to ride jitterboards, and it wasn't easy for them."[84]

Lynn Novakofski, former show director at the Gardens, made it clear that Willa was understating the difficulty of jitterboarding. "There's a photo of Willa in ballet toe shoes *en pointe* on this jitterboard. When I got to the Gardens, I tried to ride the jitterboard and couldn't even get up on the darn thing." He raised his eyebrows: "She was *en pointe.*"[85]

Another Cypress Gardens skier, Nance Stilley Hains, made the cover of *Life* and was then featured inside the magazine posing in a swan pose while going 40 miles per hour on a jitterboard. Clearly, these women were making an incredibly difficult sport look easy, and the male reporters didn't seem to know what to do with them. One referred to the performers as "Jitterboard Janes," adding that "If you have the grace of a ballerina, the body balance of a tight rope walker and the nerve of a motorcycle racer, you can excel in the new thrill sport of jitterboarding as it is done at Cypress Gardens."[86]

Still, despite the athleticism of these young women, the editors couldn't take their eyes off them, and that certainly worked in their favor. At the time the magazine was published, Nance had appeared in "12 movie shorts, 31 newsreels and uncounted thousands of stills." She was also one of Dick Pope's secretaries.[87]

James Clendenin, the editor of the *Tampa Tribune*, commented on Pope's success as a publicist:

> Using the old familiar stand-by, to wit: Beauty-in-bathing-suit, you have sneaked more publicity past the guard of hardboiled editors than any other guy except Steve Hannigan. You are, I believe, the original Three-in-One Guy. . . . You bombarded the press . . . with a picture of beauty-in-a-bathing-suit, picking oranges off a tree, with a lake in the background. That way, you'd get in a plug for Cypress Gardens, the bathing suit manufacturer and the Florida citrus industry all with one shot.[88]

Dick Pope managed to get movie star Esther Williams to promote oranges for the Citrus Commission when she came to Winter Haven in 1948 to film *On an Island with You.* By permission of Cypress Gardens.

Esther Williams poses in Lake Eloise during the filming of *On an Island with You* in 1948. By permission of Cypress Gardens.

Dick Pope was about to work his three-in-one magic on movie star Esther Williams. Along with Cyd Charisse, Peter Lawford, and Ricardo Montalban, actors in the soon-to-be-filmed MGM movie *On an Island with You,* Esther Williams arrived at Cypress Gardens in the summer of 1948 with MGM's sixty-five-member crew and three freight trains worth of equipment. She was already one of MGM's biggest stars at the time. In her autobiography, *The Million Dollar Mermaid,* she claimed that in "its era" her 1944 hit *Bathing Beauty*, with costar Red Skelton, "earned more money internationally than any other picture except for *Gone with the Wind*." It was her first swimming movie, and the first filmed in Technicolor, and it made her a star.[89]

Star or not, within a week of arriving in Florida, Esther found herself standing in the middle of an orange grove, posed with a basket of the juicy fruit, no doubt under duress from Dick Pope.[90] As head of the "pictorial publicity program" for the Florida Citrus Commission, he wasn't shy about promoting Florida's fruit.[91] Any of it. Esther Williams was one more orange to him, albeit a juicy one. She should've considered herself lucky he didn't ask her to do the things his usual models did:

> When they are asked to make pictures which depict the citrus industry . . . these girls shift easily from their swim suits or old-fashioned hoop skirts to straw hats and over-all suits, to climb ladders in the groves and pick oranges; to load the boxes on trucks and haul them away to the packing houses.[92]

On an Island with You was supposed to be set in Hawaii so one of those freight cars that arrived with Esther contained props such as fake waterlilies the crew would suspend in the lake with lead weights. As soon as they arrived, a studio "green man" loaded his rowboat with Spanish moss to fling into the cypress trees to "add more local color to the tropical scenes."[93]

Richard Thorpe, the film's director, said that Florida was chosen as a stand-in for Hawaii because of its sunshine. "One reason we made the picture in Florida is because of its wonderful light," the director said, "the same kind of light that helped make *The Yearling* such an outstanding picture."[94] But the reason they chose to film scenes at Cypress Gardens in particular was because Thorpe had been seduced by the images on one of the Garden's brochures. He had been filming Tarzan movies over at Silver Springs, and had made a side trip to Cypress Gardens.

MGM's cameramen film Esther Williams and Peter Lawford in a scene from *On an Island with You*. By permission of Cypress Gardens.

There he "picked up one of the folders showing cypress trees and knees silhouetted against a colorful sunset" and carried it back to Hollywood. He later showed the brochure to the film's producer, Joe Pasternak, who said: "That's great. That's where we want to make those swimming scenes."[95] Never mind that the fluted bottoms of the moss-hung cypress trees look decidedly un-Hawaiian.

The stars stayed at the Haven Hotel across the street from the Hob Nob, and whenever they walked outside they were mobbed by teenagers toting autograph books.[96] It wasn't long before they "made friends" with the locals. Peter Lawford was invited to dinner by a teenaged girl who then forgot to tell her mother he was coming until minutes before he arrived.[97] After filming all day the whole crew would go swimming in Lake Silver. Esther Williams bought a swimsuit at a Winter Haven boutique even though she was rumored to own fifty-nine already.

Despite her busy film schedule, Dick Pope kept Esther on her toes. At one point he instructed her on how to pose for a publicity still: "I placed her beside a royal palm and asked her to put her arm about her head with her hand against the trunk," he told a reporter years later. "'Now look up at that palm tree as if you just love it.' As I waited, I heard her say in a soft voice that could be heard a mile away, 'Mr. Pope, I don't know how we've been able to make all those movies in Hollywood without you there to direct us.'"[98] Just moments later she made a crack about working in a cypress swamp, and Dick Pope asked her if she was a member of the Actors' Union. When she answered "yes," he said, "Then why in heaven's name don't you just

ACT eight hours a day and the rest of the time be natural?" Their feud tickled the locals who assembled on the shores to watch the action.

The local papers reported the strange stories heard out at the Gardens: "A limb from an old oak tree was being nailed to a cypress tree." "A suction dredge was digging a hole in Lake Eloise to make it deeper at the foot of the tree." "Watch out, there goes the dynamite," cried Dick Pope, as "an explosive was detonated to help the dredge." The stories were sorted out later: the oak limb was nailed to the cypress tree to provide a ledge for Esther to dive from; the hole was dug at the foot of the tree so Esther could "do a gainer into the water without breaking her pretty head."[99] And finally, they published a photo of the dive with the caption "Esther Makes Graceful Dive from Tree." The only thing was, Esther used a double for that daring dive.

In her autobiography, though, she wrote that director Richard Thorpe wasn't beyond pushing her past her limits. "Much to my consternation, Dick Thorpe was directing again," she wrote. "[He] reserved most of his malice for Ricardo [Montalban] who he kept referring to as 'that damned Mexican.' That didn't, however, keep him from trying to kill me." She writes that for one scene she was supposed to fall into a 4-foot-deep hole dug into the jungle and camouflaged with brush, which she did. But Thorpe had failed to line the hole with cushions so she injured her ankle and had to spend the rest of the shoot on crutches.[100]

MGM hired a number of local girls to be "mermaids" in *On an Island with You*. By permission of Cypress Gardens.

Lucy Chambliss was one of the twenty-eight Cypress Gardens Aqua Maids MGM employed to work on the film: "We'd just had graduation the day before, and they needed all these mermaids

Marianne Snively doubled for Cyd Charisse in *On an Island with You*. By permission of Marianne Snively.

out there treading water around the cypress trees, while Esther Williams's double dived out of the top of one of those cypress trees, off a little platform. We were going to get paid forty dollars a day by MGM, which was great. We were put in that very dark makeup and a sarong, and it got heavy when it was wet, but we were all born swimmers so that didn't bother us."[101]

Marianne Schock Snively, now married to Harvey Snively, a nephew of citrus pioneer John Snively, was a high school senior then. She doubled for Cyd Charisse and signed autographs; Bobby Matthews, one of the local boys who worked on the film, doubled for Peter Lawford. The island girls made a strong impression on Esther Williams. After a day of paddling around the cypress trees with her twenty-eight Aqua Maids, listening to their "Southern drawls," she told a reporter, "they'll have to change the name of this picture to ON AN ISLAND WITH YOU ALL."[102]

Still, the star must have been somewhat charmed by the teens because she accepted an invitation to attend the high school graduation dance. After working a sixteen-hour day, she arrived at the gym with the rest of the cast in tow. Both she and her costars danced the entire evening. Esther was attended by a "stag line of enthusiastic students," while Montalban and Lawford were kept in the mix by "similar lines, bobby-sox type." It was an evening few of those attending would forget.[103]

On an Island with You premiered in 1948 at Winter Haven's Ritz Theater, and the *Winter Haven Herald* celebrated the event by publishing an entire newspaper devoted to the film, featuring headlines such as "Esther Lost One Swimsuit," and "Esther Wanted Southern Slant." Florida governor Millard Caldwell sent a note to Frank Sparrow, president of the Winter Haven Merchants Association, thanking him for organizing the local merchants to honor Dick Pope, adding that "Dick Pope is an asset not only to Winter Haven and Polk County but to all of Florida."

And not to be left out of the festivities, Esther Williams placed her own ad, in capital letters, in the *Winter Haven News Chief*:

> I hear Dick, you're going to be away for the premiere of "On an Island with You." Can't see how in the world they're going to have a premiere without you. Seriously, I enjoyed my days in Winter Haven as much as I've ever enjoyed myself anywhere . . . want to say that in spite of all those pleasant raps we took at each other, in my book you're one of the finest examples of a fine Florida.

Sincerely hope we can come back again soon and to renew the friendly skirmishes where we left off.[104]

And why wasn't Dick Pope at the world premiere of *On an Island with You*? He was out in Hollywood trying to convince studio heads to make more feature-length films at Cypress Gardens.[105]

Even though he was in the midst of his biggest publicity coup to date, he found himself in the middle of a minor controversy. Referring to him as the "old maestro of 'cheese-cake'" at the gardens, Dale Wimbrow, editor of the *Indian River News*, wrote that several PR men were calling Pope's photos "corny," and suggesting that "Florida should grow up and get out of the bathing girl classification."[106] These weren't just any PR men; they ran the biggest news outlets in the country. Al Resch, the news-photo editor of the AP wire service, declared a moratorium on Dick Pope's "Florida Cheesecake Pictures." Resch wasn't alone. The travel editors of both the *New York Times* and the *New York Herald Tribune* declared at an editor's convention that they "didn't want to receive descriptive material about a tourist attraction that made heavy use of adjectives like 'beautiful' and 'exotic,'" two of Pope's favorite words.[107]

Dick Pope, however, was unfazed. Despite the ban, more of his photos were being published than ever. To accommodate the demand, a month after the moratorium he was busy building what he called a "fashion wall." The "fashion wall" was essentially a 100-square-foot outdoor set with a series of stages that could be used to advertise automobiles as well as other products, and most importantly, to attract "picture men from big [studios]."[108] If they needed something, Pope could provide it:

> If orange blossoms are not in bloom, he has artificial orange blossoms to stick on. If he needs a fruit picture, he has artificial oranges and grapefruits. If the gardenias are not in bloom, he has them blooming in a jiffy. Dick Pope delivers the goods.[109]

And, he might have added, any photo taken at Gardens will be filed under "B." That stands for Beautiful Cypress Gardens.

Dick Pope Jr. skis barefoot in this 1948 photo. By permission of Cypress Gardens.

Barefooting in the Park

Bill Bell became an electric boat driver at the Gardens in 1949, so he was around when the "picture men" showed up with their movie cameras. "Back then they didn't have television and if you went to the movies you saw newsreels of what was happening around the world, and they would throw in the skiers of Cypress Gardens and pictures of Cypress Gardens in the newsreels."[110]

Dick Pope's daughter, Adrienne Pope Watkins, recalled the swarms of newsreel people that descended on the Pope home: "I remember when they had the Gardens really going, we had houseguests or people eating dinner with us all the time. And I finally asked him, can we ever have a family dinner? But we had to feed the people and take care of them and get them liquor because the county was dry."[111]

Some of the photographers didn't need much wining and dining. The editors of *Life* magazine unabashedly maintained that "two of the surest ways for a pretty girl to get publicity are to become citrus queen and to be photographed on water skis." The water-ski formula worked for the guys as well: in 1947, Dick Pope Jr. coinvented barefoot skiing behind a boat going 60 miles per hour. (Another young man, A. G. Hancock, also claimed to be the first at barefooting.) What isn't in question is who got the word out first. That would be Dick Pope Sr.

After watching his son ski barefoot across the lake, Dick Pope Sr. contacted the press, and Dick Jr. was featured in newspapers and newsreels across the country. He also appeared on Merv Griffin's very first variety show, *Going Places*. The show was sponsored by the City of Miami as a way of attracting tourists, but it only lasted one summer. "That was my first emcee show," said Griffin, "and it was a disaster. On the first show I interviewed this water-skier at Cypress Gardens [in Winter Haven, Florida], Dick Pope Jr. At the end of the interview, I said, 'Ready to go?' and he answered, 'Ready to go, Mirth.' Mirth? What the hell?"[112]

Bill Bell had better luck with the barefooter. When the ski shows started, the boats would shut down until the show was over—not a bad idea since the ski-show announcer also sold tickets for the electric boat rides. The boat drivers would step over to the stadium and watch the shows. "I would sit there and memorize things that I'd say while announcing the show; I'd pick up little things here and there," Bill said. "One day the guy that was supposed to announce the show was ill so they came to me and I started announcing."

"Back then, skiing on your bare feet was really a big thing," he said. "Very few people could do that. Dick Pope Jr. skied on his bare feet. He was attending Rollins College at that time, and he would come home on the weekends. Anyway, this was on a Saturday, and they came to me and said, 'you have to go over and announce the show.'"

When asked if he could remember his spiel, Bill Bell stood up, took a deep breath, and then in a radio-smooth voice, said, "This is the introduction to the barefoot ride":

> And now, ladies and gentlemen, there's a ride coming up that I'm sure will have two effects on you. First, it will give you a tremendous thrill, and second, when you see it, you will have a tendency not to believe it. On the takeoff platform is the world's water-ski champion, Dick Pope Jr., and Dick is going out to ride across the surface of water at an incredible speed of 45 miles per hour, going as far as he can possibly go. Did you notice I said "ride"? I did not say "ski"—he's not going to use skis; he's going to do this on nothing but his bare feet. Now, I know the first question that comes to your mind, "Does the boy use trick soles or preparation on his feet?" I can honestly answer that when I say he does not, for he depends entirely on the angle at which he places his feet on the surface of the water, and his tremendous speed. He takes off on a take-off ski, a small sliver of wood, and over around twelve o'clock, the driver will pick up speed, and if you could see into the cockpit of this boat, you would realize that the driver has removed his right shoe and sock in order that his bare foot on the accelerator may give him a finer control of the delicate speeds that are needed in this amazing sport of waterskiing. There he is! He's on his bare feet. Notice how those little pellets of water are peppering his body like buckshot; he's moving his head from side to side; he never knows when the ride will end. When it does end it's like falling off a twenty-story building. There! He's coming in now. Bingo—he hits the water. And you owe this boy some nice applause after a barefoot ride . . .

Bill ended his performance by laughing. "And the people got up and gave me a standing ovation. And Mr. Pope came down and said, 'you're going to announce the show from now on.' I mean the kid didn't know what was going on; the people were clapping; it'd never happened that way before. That's how I ended up announcing the ski show."

Bill said not everyone fell in love with his act. When *Easy to Love* was being filmed in 1953,

Champion water-skiers Charlie Emry, Connie Der, Butch Rosenberg, and Willa McGuire Cook prepare for the World Water Ski Championship at Cypress Gardens in 1956. By permission of the American Water Ski Educational Foundation Museum.

he got the critique of his life: "I'll never forget, while the ski show was on, the filming would stop and Esther Williams was down on the lakefront. And the first time she heard me do the ski show, after this water-ski act, she came over to me after the show was over, and she said, 'Young Man, you have more bullshit than they have in the Chicago stockyard.'"[113]

Throughout this decade, the Aqua Maids and their male counterparts competed in ski tournaments both at Cypress Gardens and nationwide, winning all sorts of medals and all sorts of press. Glenn Kirkpatrick, who would later go on to be "professor of ski-ology" at Florida Southern College in Lakeland, became ski-show director in 1947, after Dick Pope Sr. discovered him filming a newsreel on Daytona Beach. Glenn was skiing in the surf, towed behind a car cruising along on the shore. "There was no real ski show at that time," he said. "When a busload of tourists would come in, we would drop whatever we were doing and go out and ski for them. I finally decided we needed to get organized, so I set up a schedule. Every day we did a show at 10 am, 2 pm and 4 pm."

Pope hired Glen's wife, Johnette, as well. "We had an awful lot of fun doing the show," she said. "It was like one big happy family. Everyone did everything. I worked in the office writing letters, matching film, then I'd change into my swimsuit at showtime and go out and ski."[114]

The "Ziegfeld of Florida," as one editor referred to Dick Pope, saw that the Cypress Gardens skiers continued to appear in newsreels and on the covers of countless national magazines. One way Pope accomplished this was to establish the annual Dixie Water Ski Championship at Cypress Gardens, attracting both skiers and press from all over the nation. Tom Moore, nationally known for his ABC-affiliated radio show *Ladies Be Seated*, travelled from Chicago to broadcast the 1949 event from the Florida Citrus Exposition in Winter Haven. Over 20 million Americans tuned in. But Dick Pope's biggest coup was the fact that every newsreel company in the nation sent cameramen to Winter Haven to film the event. Harry Walsh, cameraman from the NBC Newsreel Company, wrote Pope a letter to congratulate him on his "grand slam": "I believe this is the first event this year that has made all the major newsreels and television—even President Truman dedicating the Everglades National Park didn't hit all the reels. It is very rarely that a story will be used 100 percent by all the newsreels companies so you should be very proud.[115]

In this undated photograph, Dick Pope tours Roy Disney through Cypress Gardens. Courtesy of Special Collections & University Archives, University of Central Florida Libraries.

Willa McGuire Cook also got some attention—and it wasn't just for being a national water-ski champion. One of her jobs at Cypress Gardens was to design costumes for the ski show. Her "dazzling swimsuits made of metallic cloth" caught the eyes of several cameramen at one tournament, who stuck around just to film her skiing across the lake in one of her "trick suits."[116]

Cypress Gardens skiers Dick Pope Jr. and Willa McGuire Cook also flew to Juan-les-Pins, France, in 1949, for the first international ski championship after the war. "Mr. and Mrs. Pope went with us to world tournaments," said Willa. "It was an unbelievable experience to work at Cypress Gardens with two owners who cared and who were involved with everything that happened there. France was the second world championship, but it was the first one after World War II. An admirer of mine, Doug Fonda, contributed the money for my transportation, and the Popes paid for Downing. We skied in very rough water. You'd approach a jump and instead of sliding up on the jump and springing off of it, you'd hit the crest of a wave, and it'd drop you on the jump, and then you'd go up and over. There were octopus under the dock where we skied, and I'd never seen one before. One evening they had a dinner for everyone, and they had a salad, and it had meat in it, and I thought, 'Ooh, that'll be nice, a salad with meat in it,' and all of a sudden I found a suction cup and I said, 'uh oh' . . . that was the end of that salad."[117] Despite the octopus and the 3-foot waves, Willa walked away with three first-place trophies.

Meanwhile, another visitor arrived at Cypress Gardens in 1949, and that was Roy Disney. Dick Pope had rented some Cinderella props from Disney for the Florida Citrus Festival in Lakeland, and when Roy Disney showed up, Pope told a reporter later, he thought Disney was there to collect his $7,500 rent. But as it turned out, he had other things on his mind, mainly checking out Cypress Gardens. He and his brother Walt were thinking about opening a theme park out in California. "We sat here or walked around," Pope told a reporter later, "and he would ask questions about this part of the business or that part, and finally I took him to the bookkeeper and said 'ask any questions you want, look at any of our figures.'"

After several days of scrutiny, according to Pope, Disney borrowed his telephone and called Walt back in California, telling him, "I'm way up here in the hills of central Florida, 100 miles from nowhere and they're getting from 2,400 to 4,000 people with a waterski show and some flowers."[118] Two months later, the Disney brothers announced their plan to build Disneyland in California.

4 The 1950s

The Man Who Invented Florida (and the Florida-Shaped Pool)

By the end of the 1940s, Dick Pope Sr. was known as "one of America's ace publicity men," but by the 1950s, he was unarguably *the* Ace. National news reports and magazine articles frequently focused not just on the Gardens, but on Pope's ability to generate publicity, concentrating on how many photographs, how many newsreels, how much money he spent on advertising. The *Los Angeles Times* referred to him as "a hinterland Merchant of Venus," noting that his film bill topped $25,000 a year, and that by 1949, he and his staff had made forty thousand photographs—all stored in vaults at the Gardens.[1] A layout in a 1948 *Life* magazine's "Speaking of Pictures" feature appeared under the headline "The Governor of Florida Applauds Promoter's Pictures of Fruit and Girls," followed by this pronouncement: "According to Governor Millard Caldwell of Florida, these pictures represent the

A photo version of this postcard appeared in *Life* magazine's "Speaking of Pictures" centerfold, and prompted the headline "The Governor of Florida Applauds Promoter's Pictures of Fruit and Girls." Author's collection.

'advance echelon' in 'the battle for the tourist trade of the nation.'"[2]

One of the photos, a "huge wheel of girls with a hub of oranges and grapefruit" (with girls' legs as spokes), looks like a homage to legendary choreographer Busby Berkeley's famous geometric dance numbers, but it doubles as a ploy to promote Florida citrus, the job Dick Pope was being paid twenty grand a year to do.

In 1950, *Argosy*, a popular men's magazine, anointed Pope as "The Man Who Invented Florida." The writer noted that "Florida is strictly a state of mind to most Americans—a place populated by almost naked girls, millionaires, surfboard riders, tarpon fishermen and Orange Queens. The man most responsible for creating that alluring image . . . is beaming, bustling Richard Downing Pope." The writer went on to argue that rather than grousing about Pope's publicity machine like the editors at the *New York Times* and the AP wire, most newspapers were happy to "brighten their pages with Pope's brand of sunshine and sex appeal." One photograph alone, of a bathing beauty leaping high off the ground to celebrate leap year, appeared in almost four thousand American newspapers.[3]

If a newspaper editor was squeamish about his "brand of sunshine," Pope simply changed his tactics to get what he wanted. In November 1950, he sent a letter and a pile of photographs to the *Orlando Sentinel* under the auspices of his title as VP of the American Water Ski Association; he was hosting Florida's very first International Ski Tournament at the Gardens. Award-winning teams from eight different countries were coming to Winter Haven to compete. For once, Dick Pope didn't even mention Cypress Gardens, even though it was clear that's where the championship would be held. He wrote:

> Without question, this World Championship is going to ring the bell and it will bring more pictorial publicity to our state than any other athletic event that has ever been held up to this time. Actually, water skiing is definitely Florida's answer to the ski trains of the snow skiing resort centers of the north. It is a safer and more glamorous sport and Florida is definitely heading for the winter sports capital of the nation in water skiing. I think that this angle stressed pictorially and editorially in the papers of the state, will give the people of Florida even more confidence in the future of its tourist attractions.[4]

The *Sentinel* must have agreed because it ran the letter and a half dozen photographs of photogenic skiers beneath the headline "World Water Ski Champs of Eight Nations Come to Florida." The *Sentinel*'s publisher at the time, Martin Andersen, went on to crown Dick Pope, "Mr. Florida," writing: "If ever the state of Florida hits another depression and finds it necessary to close its advertising offices, Florida will continue in the resort picture as long as Dick Pope lives. As long as he lives, he will always be Mr. Florida, the man who has done more to publicize the state than any other."[5]

Dick Pope had always combined Cypress Gardens' interests with the interests of Florida. His handling of the Jantzen swimsuit account was a perfect example of his ability to maximize publicity, as the swimsuits could work with any number of other promotions, a "Fancy Fact" reported in a northern newspaper: "New Products Tie in with Swimsuits Easily." A letter from Marine Studios to Bob Eastman at Cypress Gardens thanks him for the Jantzen swimsuits, noting that "releases have gone out to virtually all of the picture services . . . all major newsreels were represented. . . . In all these pictures the girl riding the surfboard behind the porpoise wears a two-piece Jantzen suit."[6] A short note from "Ray" of WPIX in New York City passed along the news that "We just made a TV story on the two citrus queens in a mound of citrus in two Jantzen bathing suits. . . . Hope you're in New York where you can see it."[7] Pope even used himself on occasion. "Mr. Pope had an appendectomy, and they took a picture of him," said Bert Lacey. "He was laying on the hospital bed in a Jantzen swimsuit; he'd had to have them move the logo because it was on the wrong side. And of course they got a lot of publicity because it was an emergency."[8] To this day, a couple of those 1950s photographs

Its instantly recognizable logo made the Jantzen swimsuit an easy product for Pope to promote. Author's collection.

THE FLAGS OF TEN NATIONS waved over Cypress Gardens as the water ski teams from these countries competed in the big International Tournament there September 11, 12, and 13, and all the competitors agreed again that it was "fair-eef-ic." Some of the teams that came from across the waters were Belgium, French, Australian, English, Italian, and one little lone and lovely but not lonely skier, Marina Dorina, representing Switzerland, who finished second to Willa McGuire in the tournament.

Belgium

Swiss

French

Australian

Danish

Italian

Bahamas

Claude and Guy De-Clercq of Belgium.

Beatrice DeSilva, Olga Jarque, Lucy DeSilva, Amparo Batani, four love skiing stars from Acapulco.

Emilio Zamudio of Cuernavaca, Mexico, does the difficult Side-Slide.

Wild Bill Hatfield.

Marc Flachard of France.

Jr. World Champ Caro Ann Duthie skis with Adrienne Watkins.

U. S. Champions, Leah Marie Rawls, above; and Warren Witherall below.

Radio Star Tom Moore

Toribio Durantes, barely "barefoots" on one.

Cypress Gardens hosted Florida's first International Ski Tournament in 1951. By permission of Cypress Gardens.

Far left: Pope combined a promotion of oranges and Jantzen swimsuits in this photograph of a headless swimmer, circa 1950s. By permission of Cypress Gardens.

Left: Even having an appendectomy did not slow down Dick Pope Sr.'s promotions. He had the Jantzen logo switched to the right side of his swim trunks so it would appear in this photograph. Circa 1950s. By permission of Cypress Gardens.

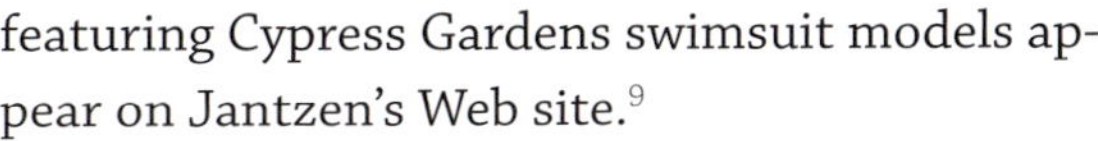

featuring Cypress Gardens swimsuit models appear on Jantzen's Web site.[9]

Before long, it was a given that if a manufacturer came out with a new water gadget, he would send it to Cypress Gardens to be tested out (and photographed and written up). Cypress Gardens skiers rode on motorized skimboards, water toboggans, and plastic boats. In 1951, Dick Pope hosted the annual Cypress Gardens Outboard Steeplechase Race, sponsored by the producer of Mercury outboard motors, who built the boats especially for the race, using the 1931 Century Hurricane as a model. The boats raced through the cypress trees, jumping over ramps and sliding over land. One or two of them ended up in the trees. Dick Pope Jr. won when his boat, *Lightning*, ran aground at the finish line. Of course, newsreel cameras were on hand as were magazine and newspaper reporters. Indeed, someone from Cypress Gardens seemed to be on

Cypress Gardens was the testing ground for all sorts of odd creations: self-propelled surfboards, flivver boats, and large inflatables. Circa 1950s. By permission of Cypress Gardens.

a magazine cover a week, if not more, throughout the 1950s. The skiers appeared in their swimsuits under headlines such as "Model Adds Water Skiing to Her Talents," "Motorized Aquaplaning," "Aquabats in the Cypress Swamps," and "Dancing on the Waves." They were photographed wearing Jantzen swimsuits and drinking Florida orange juice. They appeared on the cover of *Mechanics Illustrated* driving across Lake Eloise on "self-propelled surfboards";[10] they drove flivver boats; and they posed standing next to King Midget Motor Cars.

Photos of the Cypress Gardens water-skiers seemed to be overtaking the crinoline-clad cheesecake photos of the 1940s, when the girls posed with oranges or flowers, but the reality was the models were one and the same. "Most of our skiers come from around the central part of Florida," said Pope, "and work their way up to be top models and skiers by first wearing the old fashioned hoop skirts and then becoming star skiers."[11]

One Cypress Gardens skier was an exception, though, and that was Betty Skelton Erde. Erde was already world-famous for winning the Feminine International Aerobatic Championships in 1948, 1949, and 1950 with her famed Pitts Special aircraft, the *Little Stinker*, which now hangs in the Smithsonian's National Air and Space Museum. She used to give flying lessons at an air base in Bartow and then head over to the Gardens to ski. "The funny part about it," she said, "is I can't swim."

She recalled visiting the Gardens before she moved to Winter Haven, once as a contestant for a beauty contest. "During that visit I met the Popes out at the Gardens, and after I moved to Winter Haven I spent every chance I possibly could out there." The Popes loaned her a boat so she could motor right up to the skiing entrance: "One of the first times I went over there Downing was sitting on the end of the dock, and I went down to meet him, and he said, 'climb up on my shoulders,' and I didn't realize he had a rope in his hand that was tethered to a boat. I don't swim at all, but I climbed up on his shoulders. I thought he was kidding around—we were just about the same age—and he yelled, 'hit it.' And the next thing I knew I was sitting up there on top of him in the middle of a lake. He buzzed around and finally came in and landed, and then I told him I didn't know how to swim. And that was one of the first times I got with Downing and the Popes to any degree. I'd go out there and ski in the show any chance I got. And usually they'd put me up top, because at that time I only weighed about 95 pounds. I had some wonderful, wonderful times at the Gardens."[12]

The world-famous aviator Betty Skelton Erde test-drives a pair of skis at Cypress Gardens, circa 1950s. By permission of Cypress Gardens.

Although she couldn't swim, the "First Lady of Firsts" went on to set numerous records in aviation (flying upside down 10 feet off the ground) and auto racing (driving a jet car across the Bonneville Salt Flats at over 300 mph). Altogether, she has set more aviation

Correct Craft built the "Foto Flat-top" in 1951 to enable photographers to get closer to the skiers. The *Miss Cover Girl* was a later incarnation. By permission of Cypress Gardens.

and automotive records than anyone else in the world and has been inducted into more halls of fame than you can imagine, including the Motorsports Hall of Fame and the National Aviation Hall of Fame.

The more typical water-skier/model was Katy Turner Leifheit, Dick Pope's secretary, who skied, posed in southern belle dresses, and took dictation. Pope explained the shift in his subject material: "Water Skiing today is the most photogenic sport in all the world . . . and it's a paying sport, too." In order to get better shots of these skiers, Pope came up with the "foto flat top," a boat Correct Craft built for the Cypress Gardens photographers. It had a deck like a carrier, and a scaffolding that could hold three or four cameramen at various heights. Portholes allowed photographers to get a "fish-eye's" view. One photographer lamented that the boat could do everything, but "it won't play the Tennessee Waltz."[13]

On the sixtieth anniversary of the Gardens, Dick Pope Jr. recalled driving the photo boat while his father stood on the scaffolding, taking photos: "I cut the engine at the wrong time and poor Dad came crashing down into the boat! A bit stunned, he got right back up and we tried it again."[14]

Cypress Gardens skiers were frequently featured in newsreels churned out by the Gardens; their exploits were seen all over the world. "When I was making newsreels of water skiing, I never dreamed that someday a young Mexican lad in Acapulco would tell me that he had learned to ski from watching the moving pictures made at Cypress Gardens," wrote Dick Pope in his book. "This boy later gave up a bullfighting career to become the world's water ski champion. His name is Alfredo Mendoza."[15] In a 1995 interview, Mendoza said he was just a "beach bum" back then, although he worked at a ski school. He was fourteen years old when Dick Pope invited him to come live at the Gardens. "I wasn't a good skier when I arrived," he said. "But standing on top of the water became easier."[16] He and Willa McGuire Cook were the first of three skiers to be inducted into the International Water Ski and Wakeboard Federation Hall of Fame in 1989.

Dubie Baxter remembered when Alfredo arrived at the Gardens; his first English sentence was, "Up the river without a paddle." The language barrier didn't slow him down. Alfredo soon became one of the first men to jump 100 feet and join what the skiers called the "Century Club."[17]

Alfredo Mendoza makes a long jump in a witch's costume in 1953. By permission of Cypress Gardens.

At that time, the 100-foot jump was like the four-minute mile—it was considered beyond human reach. In 1954, Warren Witherell made the first 100-foot jump; he was quickly followed by Dick Binette, who was nineteen and competing in the 1954 National Water Ski Championship. Of course, after setting the world record, Binette went to work at Cypress Gardens, where he taught jockey Willie Hartack how to ski. Better yet, he said, "Mr. Pope made it a tradition for the new Miss America to come to Cypress Gardens right after she won her crown, and I got to ski with them." He carried them "in his arms . . . on his back . . . on his shoulders."[18]

Binette's world record was broken the next year by Alfredo, who made a 116-foot jump. Apparently when Captain Eddie Rickenbacker heard about it, he compared Alfredo's flight to that of the Wright Brothers. This bit of hyperbole led to a challenge from the chairman of Eastern Airlines: he would award a trophy to the first skier to break the Wright Brothers' record of 120 feet.[19] That honor went to Butch Rosenberg, who jumped 125 feet at a tournament in Lakeland, breaking yet another world's record. "People in street clothes . . . ran out into the water to shake my hand and slap my back," he recalled years later. "Man I was on top of the world. I had shattered the world record. So I retired. My goal was to be the best in the world, to hold the world record. And I did it." When told by a reporter that the 2003 world record was 221 feet, he simply said, "How in the hell do they do that?"[20]

Alfredo and Willa McGuire Cook performed on the *Ed Sullivan Show* in 1957 alongside Gene Kelly and Bert Lancaster. "We skied in a large circular tank with an arm in the center that went around and towed the skiers," said Willa. "They had a winch up in the balcony, and they were having a difficult time controlling the speed of the spar that towed us around. Alfredo was trying to do turnarounds on it to practice, and all of sudden it revved up fast, and he was hanging onto that tow bar, and his body and his skis were straight out, and it finally just slung him out onto the stage. He was okay."[21]

Mendoza was also a professional ice skater with Holiday on Ice. Apparently undaunted by his earlier stint on the *Ed Sullivan Show*, he appeared on the show a few years later as an ice skater. His experiences on ice led to him introducing some new moves to the skiers back at the Gardens. Brenda Mitchell recalled how he created the adagio for the skiers: "Alfredo brought in a lot off the lifts they do in skating. They developed a harness for the male skier to wear so he could then pick up the girl skier and hold her up like the skaters do."[22]

Willa McGuire Cook is Cypress Gardens' prima ballerina, the "Sonja Henie of waterskiing," the woman who brought tutus and tiaras to the Aqua Maids at Cypress Gardens.[23] Willa now owns the Holiday House in Deland, Florida, with her son. She and her second husband opened the restaurant in the late 1950s across from Stetson University. The restaurant still has a distinct 1950s appeal, with its stained-glass windows and mile-high cakes. Willa is also a talented artist, and her paintings hang throughout the dining area, including one self-portrait: the artist as a ballerina on water skis. Her work also hangs in the Water Ski Museum—she painted portraits of each inductee to the Water Ski Hall of Fame, including herself. She was the first woman inducted, in 1982.

Willa learned to ski up in Oswego, Oregon, when she was fourteen. Don Ibsen, one of the "fathers of waterskiing," dropped by her father's marina to sell some water skis and talked them into trying a pair out. "I did not want to do that," Willa said. "I had visions of one leg going one way and the other leg going the other way, and I'd be split in half. But I got up on the skis the first time and went around the lake, and I said, 'this is it.' I knew that was my sport forever."

She went on to become three-time champion of the world overall, eight-time national champion overall, and she competed in tournaments all over the world, skiing over three-foot waves in the Mediterranean, skiing in St. George's Bay off the coast of Lebanon. After she became a national champion, she got a visit from Dick Pope: "He came up to Oregon and asked me if I would come to work at Cypress Gardens. And I went there and stayed on for ten years. Part of the reason I liked working there was I could work in my bare feet."

Dick Pope convinced her that Winter Haven was a hopping cultural center. "I rode down with the Cypress Gardens skiers to Winter Haven," she said. "I had never been very far out of Oregon, maybe California, and we were eating in places where there was no air-conditioning, no screens on the doors, flies on the food—and it was a different kind of food—fried chicken and all this stuff, and I thought, well, when I get to Winter Haven. . . . Dick Pope had painted Winter Haven as a mega–entertainment center: *there was opera*. Well, in Oregon, I went to the opera and to the ballet." She laughs. "Of course, all the streets were paved with gold. The reality was

Cypress Gardens skiers dominated men's distance jumping, setting world records in the 1950s. Author's collection.

not what he had painted: the roads weren't even asphalt—they were just clay. There was no real entertainment; there was a lot of western music on the radio. There was no culture anyplace at all that I could find, but gradually, it got better and better."

One of the reasons it got better was Willa herself. Willa introduced many innovations to show skiing: the back swan, the toe 360, and the swivel swan. Back in Oswego, she had toured with Don Ibsen's ski troupe; her acts had included performing a hula on skis and skiing backward over the water: "I remember up in Oregon, some spectators were watching me on my father's boat dock, and they said, 'why does she ski backward and the guys ski forward—is it easier?' I cracked up over that one."

She also developed the ballet routine, which she introduced to Dick Pope once she got to Cypress Gardens. "I was in charge of the female skiers' schedule and training them, and I came up with some of the choreography for the water-ski show and designed costumes for some of the movie shorts Dick Pope Sr. made and sold. He was happy to let me do anything that caught my fancy at Cypress Gardens. Up in Oswego, we decided to do a ski show, and I wanted to do something that would be an act. I rather idolized Sonja Henie, and I wanted to be an ice skater, but the ice rink was too far away, and I couldn't get to it to take ice-skating lessons. I think a lot of what I did was, 'if she can do that on ice, I can do it on water,' so that was a springboard."[24]

Dick Pope set up a lakeside ballet bar, and Willa and Carma Jean Loucks taught the new skiers ballet moves and routines. Leslie Caron, a ballerina from Paris and star of the film *An American in Paris*, came to Cypress Gardens on her honeymoon and passed along some of the moves she'd picked up in her turn with the Ballets des Champs-Élysées. She also took time out to cook for the water-skiers.[25] Coincidentally (or not), when *An American in Paris* premiered at Hollywood's Egyptian Theater in 1951, the movie was preceded by a newsreel featuring "Beautiful Cypress Gardens," starring Willa and Toribio Durantes of Acapulco.[26]

The American Weekly took notice of the water-skiing ballerinas:

> Skimming over the surface at 35 miles per hour, inhaling the scent of orange blossoms and gasoline exhaust in equal parts, the lovely ladies of the lake do startling things that would seem risky to life and limb on very solid land.

Skiing backward was just one of Willa McGuire Cook's specialties; she could also jump off a ramp backward, circa 1950s. By permission of the American Water Ski Educational Foundation Museum.

The famous Russian ballerina Alexandra Danilova gave the Aqua Maids a few tips. By permission of Cypress Gardens.

The "startling things" these women did included forming a triangle with one ballerina balancing on the shoulders of her two fellow skiers, and doing "ballet steps, along with flip-flops and somersaults," all while wearing tutus and cruising at high speeds over the lake.[27]

Willa was certainly no prima donna when it came to pushing the limits. She might have been the first person in the world to wear a tutu while skiing, but she was also the first person in the world to do a backward jump off a ski ramp. Lynn Novakofski said she did it on a dare: "The guys were kidding her one time that she couldn't be in the jump act unless she learned something new. Well, she went out and did a back jump—the first one ever, male, female, anybody. She was just a natural. Willa was a top female athlete at a time when there were only a handful of female athletes—Babe Zaharias, Sonja Henie, Willa. She's a pretty amazing woman."[28]

Willa said the male skiers resisted asking her how she managed to do that jump: "A sixty-year-old man, Doug Fonda, was one of the original water-ski champions from the very first tournament, prewar, and he was at the Gardens skiing the Senior Men's competition, and I liked him, and I taught him how to jump backward. Well Dick Pope Jr. and some of the guys damn near killed themselves trying to learn to ski over that jump backward. I thought Downing was just going to bust it totally. They didn't ask me to teach them, so I didn't, and this sixty-year-old man won the trick riding over the younger guys."[29]

Cypress Gardens' attention to skiing paid off in a big way in 1952, when director Merian Cooper, famous for creating *King Kong,* came to Cypress Gardens to film the skiers for *This Is Cinerama,* using a revolutionary new camera that could take three different pictures at the same time, creating a "multi-dimensional motion picture." Cinerama was the precursor to the large-screen IMAX familiar to audiences now. Fred Waller, the man who sent Dick Pope a pair of Akwa-Skees back in 1928, had created Cinerama, an invention *Newsweek* pronounced as "the greatest innovation since sound."[30]

Head of Paramount's "trick film department," Waller was no slouch in the invention department. He actually created the Akwa-Skees to provide a support for one of his movie cameras so he could get shots on water. By the time of his death in 1954, he had received patents for over one thousand inventions, including a "Photo-Metric" camera that could measure a man for a suit in a nanosecond.[31]

Waller enlisted two of his friends, the famous newscaster Lowell Thomas and the show producer Mike Todd, to help him launch Cinerama. Dick Pope just happened to be friends with these two men as well. He knew Lowell Thomas from the newsreel days, and he had met Mike Todd in the early 1950s at the Gardens, where he had arranged for Pappy Hallowell to teach Todd how to ski. The cigar-smoking Todd insisted on taking his lesson while puffing away. Pope wrote later that he told Hallowell not to swim back to the Gardens if Mike Todd fell: "Just head for the opposite side of the lake, because we're going to miss you around here." Somehow Todd managed to ski around the lake without falling, then glided ashore like a pro. But at the last minute, he fell forward on his hands and knees, biting into his cigar. He told Dick Pope he was disappointed. "Look," he said, "I put my cigar out."[32]

This Is Cinerama was essentially a travelogue; among other locales, it featured scenes from a

The ballet line at Cypress Gardens became a fixture in the 1950s. Author's collection.

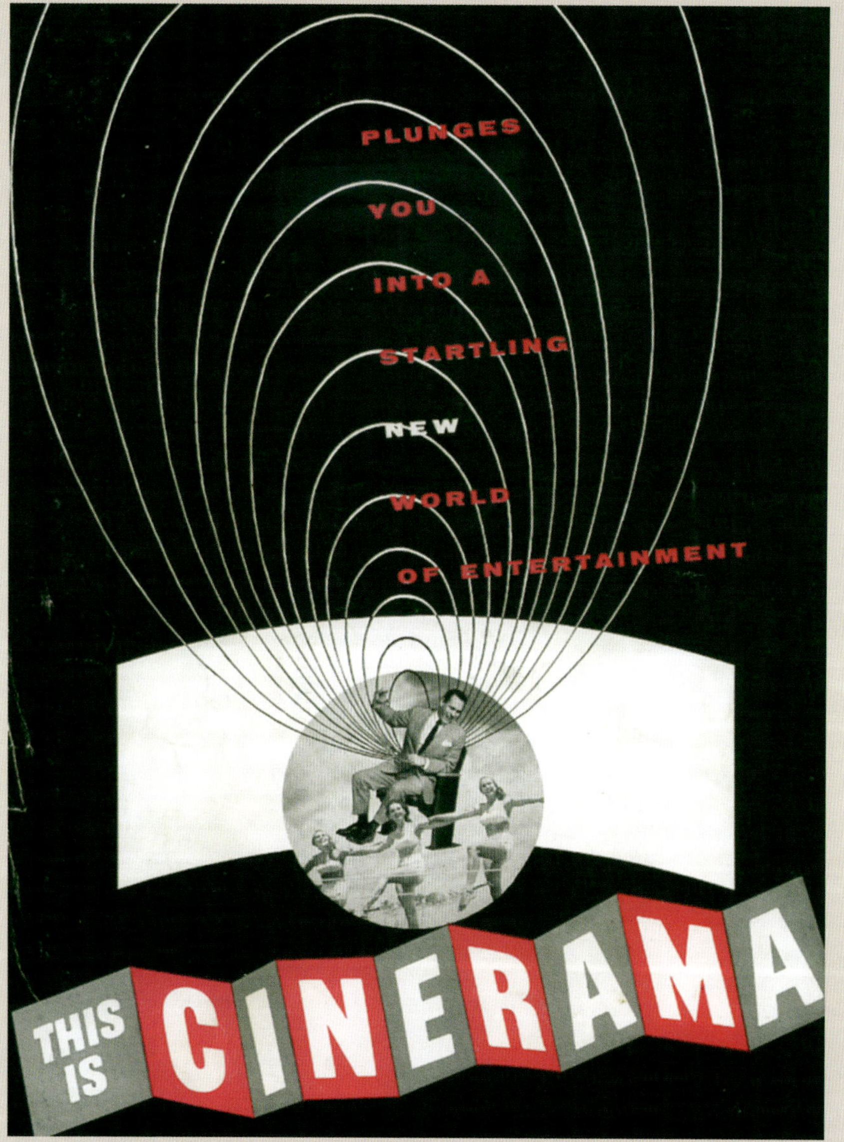

Left: The *This Is Cinerama* program featured Aqua Maids on the cover. Author's collection.

Above: Pappy Hallowell did his best to teach Hollywood icon Mike Todd how to ski. By permission of Cypress Gardens.

ballet at La Scala Theater in Milan, a ride on a rollercoaster, and a helicopter flight over Niagara Falls. The section of film made at the Gardens would focus on the life of a Cypress Gardens Aqua Maid and her boyfriend. Kathy Darlyn and Trammell Pickett landed those roles. Red McGuire was on hand for the filming: "Cinerama was sponsored by Mike Todd and Lowell Thomas, and they actually shot thirty minutes of film and then used twenty-eight minutes of it in the film itself. They did dolly shots through the canals and through the flowers, and we had that big picture boat at the Gardens, and we could mount cameras on that and do high angles, low angles."[33]

With Dick Pope's help (as if he needed any after producing *King Kong* in 1933), Merian Cooper directed the Cypress Gardens segment of the film, concentrating on the "famous water carnival":

> Lashed to the prow of speeding motorboats, the Cinerama camera shot through walls of flame; secured to a platform behind a sawed-off canoe, it languidly explored the romantic cypress-shaded waterlanes. And like thousands of tourists who annually visit Cypress Gardens, Cinerama frequently cast its three eyes in the direction of the lovely Aquabelles as they strolled among the tropical flowers or raced over the lagoon on water skis.[34]

The film also included shots of the famous Cypress Gardens jump boats, one of which was piloted by the first woman jump-boat driver in the world: Betty Skelton Erde. It's a wonder Dick Pope didn't make Betty the star of the show.

When *This Is Cinerama* was finished, it was projected onto a specially made curved screen so that the audience would feel themselves "pulled into the picture." The film premiered at the Broadway Theater in New York City with much fanfare:

Cinerama director Merian Cooper instructs Kathy Darlyn. By permission of Cypress Gardens.

The *Cinerama* crew films jump boats for a scene in the movie. By permission of Cypress Gardens.

> You rise right out of your theatre chair! No longer is a movie screen a flat surface in front of you. Cinerama, the film with a new dimension surrounds you with picture and sound. You'll gasp as you rise high, then grip your chair as you go plunging downward. Images come alive on a sea of screen 6 times the usual size and you're right in the picture. This is your first experience without colored glasses or any viewing gadgets of the most exciting thing that ever happened in a theatre; this is Cinerama.[35]

The Popes went to New York City for the premiere along with Bob Eastman. Other notables in the crowd were Thomas Dewey, the governor of New York; David Sarnoff, chairman of NBC; William Paley, chairman of CBS; and Hollywood big shot Louis Mayer. The Popes' friend Billye-Mullins Smith recalled getting a phone call from Julie in her New York apartment telling her to get ready for the big night: "So Dick arrives, and the driver fetches me from my door. We went to dinner, and we saw the Cinerama with Dick blowing the whistle at the opening—it was the first big screen. Dick was such a marvelous gentleman, just bouncing fun."[36]

Reviewers were equally pleased with the film; *This Is Cinerama* was the first film ever featured on the front page of the *New York Times*, and one critic wrote that the film "bursts on your senses like an aesthetic atomic bomb."[37] Hedda Hopper, the former actress and famous gossip columnist, wrote that she "left the theater convinced that the new medium was the biggest thing to happen to the entertainment world in my time."[38] Cinerama also quickly altered the lexicon. Although it wasn't the first to use the *-rama* suffix, its popularity more than made up for it:

> Immediately after the enthusiastic reception of *Cinerama* by critics and public, the liquor store next door to the theater called its window display a "*liquorama*"; other names followed: *audiorama*, a display of acoustic instruments; *Autorama*, a television show; *colorama*, a color movie; *Dekorama*, an oil paint decal set; *Figurama*, an "amazing new three-dimensional girdle"; . . . *motorama*, an auto-mobile exhibit; *newsorama*, a television news program; *Phonorama*, a new Philco phonograph; *scoutorama*, a meeting of New York State Boy Scouts; *sinerama*, in an advertisement of the jacket of a book called *Jest and Sex*: "Sexplosively Sexational Sinerama of life"; *skinerama*, the headline of a World-Telegram article making fun of baldness concoctions; *smellorama*, the "symphony" of a "smell organ," in an article on experiments in sensory entertainment during the 1920s; *striporama*, a burlesque movie.[39]

As soon as filming for *This Is Cinerama* was completed, Dick Pope took his "ski-borne ballerinas" and "akwa-clowns" to Long Island, New York, where they performed their "Marine Circus" at the Marine Stadium at Jones Beach under the direction of Dick Pope Jr. and Mike Todd Jr. In fact, this show had been the inspiration for Mike Todd Sr. to take a waterskiing lesson at the Gardens in the first place. According to Dick Pope Sr., the director came to the Gardens, and the first thing he said was: "Pope, before we do a water ski show together up at Jones Beach, I want to try out this skiing. Let's see whether it can be done." He found out, of course, that it could be done, and that a person could smoke while doing it.[40]

The "circus" was booked to celebrate the dedication of the Marine Stadium and to warm up the crowd for Mike Todd's lavish production of

Dick Pope Jr. and Mike Todd Jr. produced "The Marine Circus" at Jones Beach Marine Stadium in Long Island, New York. By permission of Cypress Gardens.

A Night in Venice.[41] Red McGuire went along for this show as well: "During the intermission we would do a ski show, enough to encourage people to stay after *Night in Venice* to watch the whole ski show. We'd ski around this island and jump in front of people. Then, in the meantime, we acted as extras in *Night in Venice*—we rowed the gondolas."[42]

Dick Pope remembered Mike Todd and those gondolas. Years later, they served as an inspiration to him:

> We had had some carpenters build some gondolas, six or seven gondolas, and our ski boys were all coming by, skulling these gondolas and [Mike] said, "They look fine. Now that's good for the spear carriers. But what are my stars going to ride in?" "Well can't they ride in one of those?" "Not my stars," he said, "this is a Michael Todd Production and I just simply have to have the best." I said, "Well, you know where a big one is, a real gondola, but it's $4500; Mr. Gimbel owns it over in New Jersey". . . . And this guy went over the next day in the afternoon, when I believe he didn't have 50 bucks in his trousers and nothing in the bank and he went over and talked the man out of it and got that gondola there.[43]

This Is Cinerama and *Night in Venice* were both huge coups for Dick Pope, but an even bigger one was to come in 1953. Joe Pasternak's water romance *Easy to Love,* starring Esther Williams, would bring all of the elements of Pope's life together—the skiing, the Gardens, citrus queens, oranges, and Florida, Florida, Florida.

Not So Easy to Love

Joe Pasternak was no stranger to Esther Williams, Cypress Gardens, or Dick Pope; he'd worked with Esther since 1945, and he'd produced *On an Island with You*. And, according to his autobiography, *Easy the Hard Way*, he periodically made stops at Cypress Gardens to check out the "girls" and visit with his "good friend, Dick Pope, who runs that fabulous tourist establishment":

> Dick puts on a water show at his place that is really a must-see, not only for the intricacies of the aquatic tricks but because of the pretty girls he turns up year after year. Now one of the commodities a producer of musical pictures must have is a good supply of pretty girls, lots of them. Dick knows this and when I stopped by Cypress Gardens last winter he got all his girls together so I might look them over as possibilities for a picture contract.

Apparently none of the girls in the lineup struck Pasternak's fancy, but on the way back to Pope's office, he spotted a girl working at the switchboard. "That's the one I want to sign," he said.[44] That girl turned out to be Joan Fay Brown. Former ski-show announcer Bill Bell remembered her: "Joe Pasternak signed her up; she stayed in Hollywood for a year. He put her up in an apartment, and she'd take dancing lessons and acting lessons, and she kept waiting. He was famous for

Dick Pope Sr. photographs Esther Williams at Cypress Gardens. By permission of Cypress Gardens.

how anytime he saw a beautiful girl in a magazine, he'd sign her up and bring her to Hollywood, and that'd be the end of it. So she got fed up with it after a year and came back."[45]

Given Dick Pope's prodigious output of film, photographs, and advertising, it's not surprising that Pasternak had more than a passing acquaintance with Cypress Gardens and Dick Pope. As Pope wrote:

> There were many reasons for the selection of Cypress Gardens by Joe Pasternak, famous Hollywood producer of MGM, as the setting for this musical epic. . . . During the past quarter of a century, Cypress Gardens has compiled . . . well over a thousand newsreels, 150 movie shorts, and hundreds of movie sequences. Our beautiful Aquamaids and handsome skiing champions . . . have adorned hundreds of magazine covers and newspapers all over the world.[46]

One more factor came into play, and that was money. When it came time to film *Easy to Love*, Pasternak determined that this musical would be too expensive to make on the MGM lot and decided to take the crew to Cypress Gardens.[47] Spider Bell was a boat driver at the time: "The first time Esther came there, Mr. Pope brought her down to the boat dock, and I happened to be in the front boat. Chuck Walters, the director, was with them, and they got in the boat. I didn't give them the spiel or anything. They were looking at locations."[48]

Easy to Love was said to be the story of Dick and Julie, but with generous helpings of fiction, as Adrienne Pope Watkins described it. Esther Williams tried to set the record straight as well with an interviewer. "It's about one of the kids in the ski show," she said. "I am the kid. I fall in love with Van Johnson, who owns Cypress Gardens. Apart from this angle, the story bears no resemblance to Dick Pope's astonishing career."[49] That "the story bears no resemblance to Dick Pope's astonishing career" might've been news to Joe Pasternak, who, Pope said later, "used to kid my wife and say, 'Ve haf found the man who vil play your husband's part. We vil use Lou Costello, yes?' And my wife would scream."[50]

In the film, the Dick Pope character is so driven to publicize the Gardens and its ski shows that he never notices that the Aqua Maid played by Esther is in love with him. She skis for him, types for him, and poses as a southern belle. When he senses another man's interest in her, he hauls her to New York City to sell oranges and grapefruit as Florida's Citrus Queen; then he lines her up to do a lipstick ad. Sounds a lot like Dick Pope.

Even Esther finally had to admit that the real Dick Pope was very much like his character in the film. The two seemed to have picked up where they left off after the filming of *On an Island With You,* when Esther had published a thank-you to Dick Pope saying she hoped they that they could "renew the friendly skirmishes" in the future. And renew them they did. A reporter described one of their first run-ins: "Movie queen Esther Williams wanted to practice her water-skiing. Dick Pope thought she should sit for photographs. This caused Esther to fume a bit at Cypress Gardens last week. Pope, of course, won. 'That guy,' said Esther grouchily, 'is a tyrant. He should go to Hollywood. No movie lot publicity man could fail to learn from him. He's exuberant about his worst ideas and it catches. His best ideas are super-colossal. How could he miss?'"[51]

Although the fictional Dick Pope might have been indifferent to Esther's fictional Aqua Maid, the real Dick Pope was as far from indifferent to Esther Williams as possible. He referred her as "my very favorite movie actress and glamour star," and more importantly, he built her that swimming pool shaped like the state of Florida,

Tourists get a look at construction of the Florida pool that Dick Pope Sr. built for *Easy to Love.* By permission of Cypress Gardens.

Esther Williams christens the Florida pool while a crowd looks on, 1953. By permission of Cypress Gardens.

a swimming pool Busby Berkeley envisioned filling with a chorus of a hundred synchronized swimmers.[52]

"Every time Esther Williams came to the Gardens we built a swimming pool," said Red McGuire. "We built the Florida pool first, and then we built the big pool down in the islands."[53] There was not another pool like the Florida pool in the world. MGM's engineer thought the pool should be built among the cypress trees, extending out into Lake Eloise. "I thought the idea was lousy at first," Pope said, "even when the designer said it would be cheaper and better for the production. Then I began to see what a real genius that movie guy was. Everybody has a pool on land, but who else in the world has a pool in a lake?"[54]

Popular Mechanics thought the Florida pool was unique as well, noting that it was "drawn to scale from a standard road map," and measured almost 90 feet in length from "Key West to the Georgia line." It had to be weighted so it wouldn't float away.[55]

Of course, Dick Pope knew that the film would be one of the biggest publicity stunts he'd ever pulled off, and that the pool would come in handy down the road. "By the way," Bob Kehoe said, "the Florida pool cost $48,000; I happen to remember that. Mr. Pope saw not only was the pool spectacular in terms of promoting Florida—he promoted Florida every chance he got; what's good for Florida's good for us—but he also saw lots of possibilities of how to utilize the pool afterward. For many years, it was a main stopping point: tourists would look at the Florida-shaped pool and take some pictures for the folks back home."

Sometimes Pope would fill the pool with floating oranges and grapefruit for his own photo shoots. "In one of his shots," said Bob, "he has a hundred girls in two-piece bathing suits sitting around the edge of the pool with their feet in it splashing. And I shouldn't tell this, but he came up three girls short, and I don't look good in a two-piece and a cap, but I'm at the top corner with two of the water-skiers; we're in the background. We were just 'one of the girls' that day."[56]

To handle all the tourists who flocked to Cypress Gardens to see the stars, Dick Pope also built a four-hundred-car parking lot around a sinkhole in the middle of what used to be an orange grove. Even this parking lot had a Hollywood touch that would "turn visiting highway engineers green with envy," as the locals reported: "It is a two tiered concentric circle parking lot with a hundred foot lake in the middle. It is built in a natural ravine and will be landscaped in an atmosphere befitting the Gardens," and of course it didn't escape Pope's lens. It, too, was photographed and memorialized on postcards.[57]

Pasternak was so impressed with the finished Florida pool that he decided to forget trying to duplicate the pool in Hollywood as planned and to shoot more scenes at the Gardens.[58] Busby Berkeley, the famous choreographer, was completely "in his element—liquid," as Esther Williams said. She should know; she had worked with him on *Take Me Out to the Ballgame* in 1949 and the year before in *Million Dollar Mermaid,* although that experience had severely tried her. She broke her neck when she dove off a Lucite disk Berkeley had placed on a hydraulic lift for one of her more dramatic scenes. As she rose to a height of 50 feet, she stood encased in a bodysuit studded with fifty thousand gold sequins, a giant gold crown perched atop her head. She was gazing into the fountains shooting up past her when she realized she had lost her equilibrium, the result of burst eardrums. When Berkeley shouted, "We're waiting, Esther! Jump!" she swan-dived, thinking, "Oh Shit," as she realized what was going to happen when that inflexible crown hit the water. She wore a body cast for the next six months. It's surprising that she would work with him again, but then again, the film established her as "America's Swimming Sweetheart." And, as Esther said herself, Busby Berkeley "was one of the most creative individuals in Hollywood, maybe the only true genius I would work with. I knew I needed someone with a real sense of showmanship if my movies were to continue to be successful."

Famous choreographer Busby Berkeley hams it up with Esther Williams on the deck of the Florida pool. By permission of Cypress Gardens.

Berkeley first achieved fame at Warner Brothers in the 1930s with his elaborately choreographed dance scenes and innovative camera angles that transformed his dancers (and swimmers) into kaleidoscopic images. In a series of musicals including *42nd Street*, *Golddiggers of 1933*, and *Footlight Parade,* he employed dancing skyscrapers, neon violins, and a human waterfall. In 1943 at 20th Century Fox, he choreographed *The Gang's All Here*, which featured Carmen Miranda in an outlandish number involving giant bananas, organ grinders, and monkeys.

By the time he got to Florida, he was ready for the Florida pool. True to his vision, "he designed a synchronized swim routine that featured a chorus of a hundred swimmers." In another memorable scene, surrounded by twenty-five thousand floating wax gardenias, Esther swims "romantically" with one of her costars, John Bromfield, while violinists perch on the edges of the cypress trees and serenade them. At one point, the two stars curl together on a slowly rotating platform, Esther swathed in the gardenias because she was pregnant and beginning to show it. She made the announcement shortly after arriving in Winter Haven with her other two children.

The pregnancy didn't slow Esther down. She had never skied before, but as she said, "Waterskiing was wet, so MGM assumed that this was Esther's department and that of course it would be no problem for me to pick up fast."[59] Actually, according to a Cypress Gardens spokesperson, she did pick it up fast: "She goes out daily under the tutelage of Pappy Hallowell. She is doing so well that her doubles (so far consisting of Alys Oglesby, Willa Worthington McGuire, and Diane Van Dusen Jahn) may find themselves out of a job."[60]

Willa McGuire Cook remembered Esther's skiing: "She had never water-skied; it was February, and it was very cold, and she had true grit. She got out there and froze learning to water-ski, just the basics, but she was very devoted to her profession."[61]

Esther's husband at the time, businessman Ben Gage, donned skis as well. During the filming, the ski shows went on, and Gage decided to perform in one, taking his place in the doubles act. A photographer on hand snapped a shot of Esther sitting in the boat while Ben stood on the dock preparing for takeoff. The couple was having marital difficulties at the time, but ever the professional, Esther gave the photographer a big smile, then recorded the event with her own camera.[62]

In private, however, Esther was less than thrilled. "Ben had gained quite a bit of weight and didn't look good in a swimsuit anymore," she wrote in her autobiography. "But there he was in boxer trunks, a big walrus with a girl on his shoulders. Everyone knew he was my husband. I was appalled at this exhibition. . . . [N]ow he was up on water skis in front of a crowd at Cypress Gardens with some show-skier's crotch at the back of his neck and her thighs around his ears."[63]

She must've really kept her feelings under wraps, because Dick Pope wrote that she frequently "summoned her family to the lake front" where they would ski together.[64] The local press loved Esther, referring to her as "Winter Haven's temporary first lady." It was hoped that she would head up the mile-long 1953 Florida Citrus Exposition parade, but MGM officials said the star would be filming on that particular day. The newspaper suggested that if the locals wanted to get a glimpse of the star (who had requested her address not be published), "she can be seen once in a while swimming in the lake that fronts her home."[65]

In spite of how busy Esther was, Dick Pope managed to persuade her to crown Marion Ettie as Citrus Queen for the cover of *Citrus Magazine*. This was a slight reversal for the star, as she herself was going to be crowned "Empress of Citrus" in the film, in a scene featuring loads of Florida oranges, grapefruits, and tangerines.[66] (Ironically, the "Florida" oranges were actually California oranges, as this particular scene was filmed in Hollywood.)

In anticipation of the film's release, Pope also managed to get Esther to pose surrounded by oranges for a series of Florida Citrus Commission ads that would capitalize on the fact that "Florida citrus is so easy to love."[67]

Although "citrus [came] in for a big plug" in the film, the real star of the show was skiing. Esther said that once Busby was "freed from the confines of the pool, he went wild in the wide open spaces of Lake Eloise."[68] The highlight of the film was the eight-minute-long skiing finale that was filmed almost entirely from a helicopter buzzing over the lake. Film critic Ernie Shier said this scene was "Busby Berkeley's crowning achievement. . . . The topper is the big finale when Esther takes to waterskis and leads a whole danged parade of boys and girls, in yellow and black costumes, through a triumphant

Skiers wait behind the scenes to film the grand finale of *Easy to Love*. By permission of Cypress Gardens.

processional that is showier than the recent Coronation and paced faster than a Keystone Cops comedy.[69]

Red McGuire skied at Cypress Gardens for seven years, managing the shows, competing and winning in national ski tournaments before switching over to the photography department for twenty-five years. He also drove one of the boats in the big *V* featuring forty-eight skiers pulled by eight boats, made five of the spectacular jumps, and helped create the first six-man pyramid the skiers performed for the film. "Old Busby Berkeley brought down great things," he said. "He could mash a button and shoot water 50 to 60 feet in the air; we had five ski jumps, five boats, with jumpers going over every one. They had the big *V*. It could just never be duplicated. I mean the guy was really far out when he came up with the idea for that film. It was a difficult stunt. Actually, we hired a bunch of guys who were down here for spring training, and taught them how to ski, and that's where we got fifty people to build that thing with."[70]

Bob Kehoe was on hand for the filming of the climactic scene. The skiers were going to slice through the cypress trees and around geysers that gushed 60 feet into the air. A dozen skiers would fly over jumps simultaneously, and a hundred girls would dot the edge of the Florida-shaped pool. He explained the difficulty of working with eight boats and forty-eight skiers: "We had to have ropes of various lengths to get the skiers placed. You had to plan it out so nobody was riding on top of a wake, or on the side of a wake or in the rough water that forms out on the edges of the wake. You had to coordinate it all at the same time—the skiers getting up, the boats getting together at the right place, and the cameramen at the right place. I think we practiced

Esther Williams leads a pack of skiers through the Cypress trees in a scene from *Easy to Love*. By permission of Cypress Gardens.

it ten or twelve mornings really early when the lake was calm and the wind hadn't picked up yet. A company in Winter Haven had just begun making aluminum irrigation pipes for the orange groves in the 1940s, and they utilized those pipes underwater with hoses and large pumps and created the geysers."[71]

In her autobiography, *Million Dollar Mermaid*, Esther Williams described the danger involved in filming the slalom sequence as a nearsighted pregnant woman. She would be required to ski awfully close to the brass jets that protruded about a half foot out of the lake, shooting up the 60 foot geysers. One morning, after reviewing the layout of the slalom course over and over, Esther strapped on her skis, waited for Busby Berkeley to shoot his starter pistol, and took off with the skiers. The only problem was that Busby Berkeley had filled the photo boat with friends, which caused it to create an enormous wake as it cruised along next to the skiers. As Esther drew closer and closer to the photo boat—to within 10 inches, she writes—she was afraid she would catch a ski in the trough created by the wake and fall into one of the brass jets, endangering herself and her unborn baby. She chose to fall before that happened and made sure she angled her body away from the photo boat. Heading to shore, she swam right past the boat and past a frantic Busby Berkeley, who was shouting, "Why did you ruin the shot?" She later wrote that she wouldn't get on the boat because she was so angry at Busby that she was afraid she'd shoot him with his own pistol.[72]

Ultimately, Esther decided the shot was too dangerous, and Willa McGuire Cook stepped in and doubled for her, skiing the "Avenue of Fountains," as the locals called it:[73] "I did one scene for Busby Berkeley. Esther was supposed to slalom through those geysers, and every time she'd go around one a geyser would shoot up in the air 60 feet." After his run-in with Esther Williams, Busby Berkeley must have considered how dangerous those geysers were. Willa said he told her one thing: "Now when you go around those geysers, don't get your head over the geyser or it will blow your head off."[74]

In spite of his own warnings about the dangers of his elaborate choreography, Esther wrote that Busby persisted in coming up with even more daring acts for her to perform. A few days after the geyser mishap, he was lounging in his bathtub, (where he claimed he got his best ideas), and an over-the-top finale came to him. It was two thirty in the morning, but that didn't stop him from calling Esther to ask her a question about the scene he was concocting: "Can you dive from a swing hanging from a helicopter," he asked, and then explained what he wanted her to do:

> You're skiing along and we drop you the swing from the helicopter. You kick off your skis, and the chopper pulls you up out of the water. You climb onto this trapeze swing, and we fly you over the eight speedboats that're pulling the skiers in V-formation. Then you dive right into the lake and hit right in the center of the V.

Not surprisingly, Esther declined to dive from a trapeze suspended 80 feet in the air from a helicopter, suggesting Busby call Helen Crelinkovich, a friend of hers from L.A. who specialized in platform diving. She told him he needed to pay Helen three thousand dollars for each take since the stunt was so dangerous. He did. And as Esther said, "She made a perfect dive three times from 80 feet and she got herself nine thousand dollars. And I was still alive and safely pregnant."[75]

And Berkeley got his heart-stopping scene. As he described it years later: "I used a helicopter . . . with Esther standing on a trapeze while hanging from the plane, then diving from a height of eighty feet into a V-shaped formation of skiers travelling at thirty-five miles per hour. . . . She then comes up on skis for a furious ride . . . finally hurtling over the heads of the bandsmen, who are merrily playing away."[76]

He didn't mention her double. Although Esther did quite a bit of her own skiing in the film, she didn't "[hurtle] over the heads of the bandsmen." That job fell to another of the Cypress Gardens skiers. Red said when it came time to film the scene where Esther hurtles over the orchestra, Alfredo Mendoza was tapped to double for her, wearing a pink swimsuit. "He did the jump for the pool out in California," said Red. "They shaved his legs."[77]

Red doubled for Van Johnson in one of his boat-driving scenes. Because the two looked so much alike, with the same color hair and facial features, Willa McGuire Cook said she played a joke on Red during the filming: "One day he was down on the beach with the other skiers, and I was up on top of the hill by the clubhouse, and there were a lot of tourists around, and I thought, 'Oh, I'm going to have some fun here,' so I stood up and said, 'Oh look, there's Van Johnson,' pointing to my husband, and they swarmed on him—it was so funny. It took

Cypress Gardens skier Alfredo Mendoza doubled for Esther Williams on the difficult jumps. By permission of Cypress Gardens.

me years and years to let him know who did that to him."[78]

The one star who seemed to have the most encounters with the locals was Esther Williams. Dallas Abercrombie recalled working out at the Gardens in its heyday when he would carry eight or ten gallons of orange juice from Nagles' fruit stand into the Gardens to sell to the tourists: "The orange stand was right down just probably 200 feet after the ticket taker took your ticket, before you got to the little electric boat booth, before you got to the little trail that led over to the photo pier. It was pretty steep, and you had the electric boats, and the canal run through there and the little curved bridges where people could walk. Julie's granddaddy used to come down, and he was a brain; he could hold his fingers like that, like the frame of a 4 × 5 camera, and he'd tell his secretary, Katy Leifheit; he'd say, 'Katy, tell Montey or Dennis—one of the photographers—to get four or five of the girls in hoop skirts and put them over there by that flower bed and take that picture.'"

That advice must've rubbed off on Dallas. During the filming of *Easy to Love*, there's a scene where a hoop-skirted Esther runs up to the phone to take a phone call. Dallas was on hand when the star swooped by. "They'd set up a dummy phone booth right on the grass about 10 to 12 feet from my juice stand. They had a fake phone in there, and they made the phone ring, and they called Esther Williams and said, 'telephone,' and she ran over there and picked up that telephone, and she had that hoop skirt on, and when she did, that skirt flew up, and I had my little box camera, and I took a picture." Unfortunately, he lost the photograph of "Esther's fanny." But he got a consolation prize.

"I've got an Esther Williams swimming pool in my backyard," Abercrombie said. "And Esther Williams swam in it." He found out about the pool when the man who grew up in the house stopped by one day and talked to his wife, telling her the history of the house and the pool: "I'm just surmising that Mr. Pope heard about Esther having her own line of pools and probably got on the phone to California and said, 'where can I find one in Winter Haven?' and they gave him this number, and he brought her out with several of the mermaids and took photos of her swimming in it, probably as a commercial. How many people have Esther Williams swimming pools? How many people have Esther Williams pools that she swam in?"[79]

Dubie Baxter was ten years old when he had his Esther encounter: "It must've been during the summer because I was out at the restaurant during the day, and part of the time we'd wash the silver or work back in the steam room. I used to take all the silver into the employees' dining room. I'd never seen an actress or a movie star before, and I'd heard that we had to clean the people out of the employees' dining room and have it spotless because Esther Williams and

Dick Pope goes Hawaiian at a luau celebrating *Easy to Love*, 1953. By permission of Cypress Gardens.

Dick Pope were going to have a conference in there, so I thought, 'this is my big chance to see what a movie actress looks like.'" He loaded up the silver in a tablecloth and took it into the dining room, where he plopped it onto a table near Esther and Dick Pope Sr. "I was rubbing it down and looking at this movie star, and she looked at me and she says, 'Little boy, can you rattle your silverware somewhere else?' Boy, she was serious, and I mean I shrunk to the size of a four-year-old. That was my first exposure to a movie star."[80]

"I can remember a little about the *Easy to Love* movie," said Betty Doles, "because I worked at the Haven Hotel as an elevator operator. And this was where everybody had to live, all the stars, all the big shots, all the girls that ran for the Citrus Queen. Black people didn't stay at the Haven Hotel, but you felt a part of these things because you saw everything; you saw the stars, and you'd come back and brag that you saw this or that person. Now we had one bellhop there who managed to have a split-second part in that movie, showing Esther coming in and him carrying her bags to the hotel; his name was Simmie MacNeil; he was the bell captain."[81]

Of course, while Esther was in town, Dick Pope took her over to Christy's Sundown, one of the most popular spots in Winter Haven. Nick Christy opened the restaurant in 1948: "There were only three restaurants in Winter Haven, and it was the only tablecloth restaurant in the area where people came in at lunch and for dining at night. When the town went wet, I got a liquor license, and we put in a lounge and had entertainment, and Dick Pope used to bring all the movie stars over: Esther Williams, Carol Burnett, Joey Bishop. He used to bring all of them in here. We were known for our hospitality and good business."[82]

After a couple of weeks of filming, the MGM crew decided to preview all the film they had made up to that point, said Bill Bell: "They hired the Ritz Theater to show the rushes, and I was invited to watch them. I was sitting in the theater, and on the screen comes Esther Williams and Van Johnson and Tony Martin, and then, when it was all over, the lights came on, and all the stars were sitting there, and it was the first time I'd been in a movie house when the lights came on and the stars that were in the movie were sitting in the audience. It felt so strange, and they were all saying goodnight to each other. It was an exciting experience."[83]

At the world premiere of *Easy to Love*, Dick Pope described the film to a reporter: "It's a one hour and 36 minute Technicolor commercial on Florida and Cypress Gardens the like of which has never been seen. It's Florida's first modern picture, no snakes, no swamps or Seminoles," he said.[84] If *This Is Cinerama* put Cypress Gardens and waterskiing on the map, then *Easy to Love* sealed the deal. And it was largely because of Esther Williams, as Dick Pope explained: "When this great woman swimmer donned water skis, it had a significance everywhere. Many thousands took up the sport after Esther had conveyed the grace and beauty of water-skiing to them."[85]

The film premiered at the Radio City Music Hall in New York City a couple of weeks before Christmas in 1953. Florida VIPs ranging from Governor Charley Johns to Citrus Queen Marion Ettie joined the Popes in New York for a three-day whirl of activities. Governor Johns planned to meet with tourism insiders who were predicting that "a billion tourist dollars will fatten Florida cash registers this year," largely as a result of "the shot of adrenalin this interest [in Florida] has received with two motion pictures."

> As *Easy to Love* and *Cinerama* are viewed in additional theaters throughout the land, the yen to come to Florida will bubble and boil. Resulting contagious fever will be cured by

Esther Williams poses for a promotional photograph, 1953. By permission of Cypress Gardens.

map buying, car gassing, train, bus or plane ticket purchasing to cause the greatest jam of visitors the state has ever known.[86]

Life magazine featured Esther Williams and Cypress Gardens in a two-page spread, with Esther skiing across Lake Eloise at the head of the giant *V*, standing atop a fifty-foot platform amid geysers. *Newsweek* hailed the film as a "masterpiece of modern moisture," and found Busby Berkeley's ski scenes "fantastic." Producer Joe Pasternak chimed in that Esther "is clean, wholesome sex. Her pictures have no message. . . . All they do is entertain. If she ever tried to act, she'd be a dead pigeon."[87] The *New Yorker*, surely much to Dick Pope's delight, gave top billing to the Gardens, mentioning that "the piece was filmed at Cypress Gardens, the Florida water hole that is also on view in *Cinerama*. There can be no doubt that the Gardens have a picture-postcard prettiness . . . but I fear there isn't much in the way of water sports that hasn't been exploited by the newsreels."[88] Clearly, that reviewer did not take Busby Berkeley's interpretation of water sports into account, but the *Saturday Review* did:

> An old hand at this business, Berkeley has made a specialty of eye-filling spectacles that are at once absurd, exhibitionistic and wonderfully pure cinema. His camera cavorts with high abandon, zooming and gliding over aquatic designs in flower-filled pools, building rhythmic patterns from fancy high dives. His version of the Cypress Gardens water show is probably the apotheosis of such entertainment—more girls, more music, more tricks, more intricate designs than even the Cinerama cameramen."[89]

Long after the stars were gone, the film left its impact on the ski show at the Gardens. Willa McGuire Cook performed as Corky—one of Esther Williams's roles in *Easy to Love*—in an act that stayed in the ski show for years and years. Willa actually wore the costume that Esther had left behind after making the film, and she performed her clown act four times a day. Eventually, both male and female skiers took turns with the part. Willa remembered one skier who played the part of Corky, skiing on a disc. He'd ski by the dock, slide his arm through the slats on the chair, then place it on the disc and do a handstand. "The skiers weren't too nice to him," she said. "They tied that chair, locked it to that dock, and he went by and almost broke his arm, and it yanked him off his disc. You know, we were not above playing tricks on each other."[90]

"One of our announcers when I first started there," said Richard Johnson, "was Buddy Lee, but he changed his stage name to Bob Collins, and he went on to become sort of the Johnny Carson of radio. He was probably the top DJ in the country in Chicago. While he was at Cypress Gardens, there was a comedy act where there was an exchange between the skiers and the announcer, and they'd have a microphone set up in the cypress trees too so we could take part and ad-lib with him."

In order to shake things up a bit, the skiers would try to get the announcer to start laughing, which was hard, Johnson said, because they did the same act four times a day. One day, Johnson put on his Corky the Clown makeup and prepared to make his entrance sliding from backstage on a cable placed high in a cypress tree when he got hung up about 15 feet off the ground. "Buddy was in the announcer's tower, and I was at about the same height, and I look over and he starts laughing."[91]

Ski-show announcer Mike Markowitz said Corky was often the first act a novice skier would get to perform. Mike came to the Gardens in 1978 as show announcer. "I was a full-time announcer here for twenty-five years, 1978 to 2003. The park closed the day after my twenty-fifth anniversary," he said, referring to the temporary closure of the park in 2003. "They didn't give me my gold watch; I never got my gold watch after twenty-five years; do you believe that? They celebrated by closing the park, putting me out of work." In spite of not getting his gold watch, it's obvious he loves the place. He recalled a day he was in the tower announcing when Dick Pope Sr. walked in and said: "There's a problem with the people in the audience. They don't know how to applaud; there's a proper way to clap. There's a way to acoustically place your hands which gets the most noise." He suggested Mike go downstairs before the ski show "and show people the correct way to clap so they can get that effect."[92]

For a while, Lynn Novakofski, Cypress Gardens' former show director, said, Corky was joined by Dorky, but not for long. "That was a real Dorky act," he said, "but then we tried it with one of the girls, Corkette, and it was an instant hit. Corkette didn't ski as much as the guy clown, but the interaction with the audience was wonderful. She would get tossed in the water, then go into the audience and sit on someone's lap. Well, the old guys just loved that. She'd plant

The water-skiing clowns Corky and Corkette were inspired by *Easy to Love*. Author's collection.

a kiss on their forehead with that red makeup—so Corkette was an instant hit, really a big part of the show."[93]

Stephanie Lenz provided a tourist's-eye view of Corky on her blog under the heading "Embarrassing Photo Night."

> Okay, this bizarre photo is circa 1981 and I am nowhere in it. On the left is my mother and her Giant Handbag and Giant Sunglasses. On the right is my "Aunt" Lois, a friend of my mother's from her HS days. . . . The person in the center is "Corky the Clown"—a water-skier at Cypress Gardens (see ski ramp in background). My mother was obsessed with him. And we all know how much I love clowns. As if "let's go to Cypress Gardens and see Corky!" was some kind of incentive.[94]

Riding on the wave of publicity *Easy to Love* and *Cinerama* brought Cypress Gardens, Pope visited Ben Hibbs, the editor of the *Saturday Evening Post*, to see if he could get the magazine to do a piece on the Gardens. Just like the editors at the AP and the *New York Times* had done, Hibbs refused, saying the *Post* had done way more than its share of Cypress Gardens stories. "So I quit talking about Cypress Gardens," said Dick Pope, "and began telling him about waterskiing, and how thrilling it was, and how beautiful, and how it was sweeping the United States. And before I could get through talking, a reporter had been assigned to do a piece on waterskiing.[95] The resulting article, "Fanciest Frolic on Water," detailed "the most improbable sport ever to muscle in on the American scene." Dick Pope's role in the story was he-who-shall-not-be-named:

> A completely unreliable source—influenced by self-interest and enthusiasm—has estimated that there will be three-quarters of a million American water skiers doing their best to stay water-borne during 1954; even if you halve this generous guess you have a sport which in two decades has passed such ancient and established favorites as croquet, battledore and shuttlecock and walking-in-the-rain-when-you're-properly dressed-for-it.

The writer credits Pope in name for establishing waterskiing as a "branch of show business" with his combination of bathing-suit-clad beauties and speedboats that worked like catnip on photographers and newsreel cameramen and led to the popularization of skiing as a sport.[96]

Cypress Gardens water-skiers helped to popularize the sport. By permission of Cypress Gardens.

Despite *Saturday Evening Post*'s reluctance to do a complete article on the Gardens, in 1954 Pope still managed to land his "pretty-girl" photographs in over a hundred newspapers per day across the country, and nearly 200,000 people per day were watching the Cypress Gardens skiers in *This Is Cinerama*, even though the film had been out for over a year. Pope spent over a half million dollars a year on his photographs, and more than three-quarters of a million people came to the Gardens each year as a result. To deal with the crush, he employed 120 staff members, including five secretaries—some of whom doubled as skiers and models. All this attention must have gone to his head. He decided to try to control the weather.

To this end, he would call the Weather Bureau in Lakeland to complain about the latest weather report: "Oh, Weather Bureau, I thought I was guaranteed you were going to clear up things

Dick Pope Sr. was famous for doing three or four things at a time. Circa 1960s. By permission of Cypress Gardens.

this afternoon and here it's getting cloudy."[97] He was famous for trying to get weather reporters to say it was "mostly sunny" instead of "partly cloudy," inspiring meteorologists and newspaper columnists to tease him with their own versions of weather reports:

> Instead of "severe freeze tonight," make it "extremely bracing invigorating temperatures tonight". . . . Instead of "very hot and humid," make it "bountiful sunshine and moisture-kissed atmosphere."[98]

With so much going on, Pope had built his office without windows to help keep him from getting distracted, but he couldn't stand not being able to see "what was going on out in his bog" so he had a periscope installed in the roof. He also installed a set of buttons on his desk so he could signal the kitchen to bring him orange juice or coffee, but he frequently hit the wrong one, and resorted to shouting out corrections.

Bob Kehoe worked in that office: "The Pope family made everything fun. But you worked. Every day was different. It was never stale, humdrum, or routine. Dick Pope Sr. could talk on the phone, carry on a conversation, dictate a letter, and go through pictures to pick out the next press release, all at the same time and never miss a lick. And he'd call me in with his buzzer, and I'd come in and stand there until he had three seconds to tell me what he wanted, and then he'd go back into his telephone conversation, just as relaxed as he could be."[99]

Pope's office was decorated with larger-than-life photos of Esther Williams, maps of Florida made out of oranges, photos of a southern belle or two. But the manic Pope could not sit still in his office for long. Once, with a reporter in tow, he headed out to the Florida pool, where a shoot was about to take place. He had a fit when he saw leaves strewn across the pool's deck. "Where's a broom for this mess, somebody get a broom," he shouted. When no broom materialized, he found one himself and swept the deck clean.

These "sorties into the sun," as another reporter referred to them, were made even more interesting by Dick Pope's compulsion to match steps with whomever he was walking with. Employees sometimes would throw him off by skipping a step, just to amuse themselves watching him shuffle in an attempt to regain the tempo. While marching along in a lockstep with his companion, he still managed to scoop snippets of paper up off the ground. He once cancelled a particular act in the ski show because he couldn't bear seeing handfuls of confetti fluttering to the ground, knowing he wouldn't be able to resist cleaning it up himself.[100]

Spider Bell and his brother Bill both recalled Dick Pope's attention to the cleanliness of the Gardens. "Bill was saying he saw him pick up candy bar wrappers and stuff," said Spider, "and I saw him one time picking up a Clark Bar wrapper, and I didn't think the same thing Bill thought, that he was just cleaning up the place. I thought he collected candy bar wrappers."[101]

Pope told *Esquire* reporter Arthur Herzog the reason for this particular obsession: "We've tried to make the place an outdoor cathedral, pretty as the cathedrals of Europe. Ruins the effect when there's paper laying around." Herzog noted that this was a cathedral populated by "bathing beauties . . . all holding aloft giant beach balls."[102]

"The botanical gardens is my love," said Bob Kehoe. "I used to go through the gardens every Sunday morning when I was working part-time in college with a pick-up stick and clean up the gardens for Mr. Pope personally so that when people came from church they'd look nice. I would run into Mr. and Mrs. Pope lots of time, walking through the gardens. He always had a big yellow pad to write things on, and a camera, and they'd talk about a new plant here, opening this vista there, and perhaps making repairs or adding signage. They just really enjoyed the gardens. I'm amazed at that."[103]

Kings, Queens, and Television Screens

The Cypress Gardens skiers made their first appearance on the relatively new medium of television on January 16, 1955. They'd already been featured numerous times on radio. In 1948, Ted Malone had paid homage to Pope's flowers,

Edith Wilson, the actress who portrayed Aunt Jemima for Quaker Oats, stopped by Cypress Gardens in 1955. By permission of Cypress Gardens.

In 1955, Willa McGuire Cook skied in the pool at the Fontainebleau Hotel in Miami Beach for an appearance on the *Colgate Comedy Hour*. By permission of Cypress Gardens.

belles, and skiers in his show *Westinghouse Presents*, and Barbara Chambliss had been interviewed on *Breakfast in Hollywood*, at that time "Radio's Top Daytime Show."

Tom Moore, famous for his nationally broadcast radio show *Ladies Fair*, brought a new radio show, *Florida Calling*, to Winter Haven in 1953 at the invitation of the Florida Citrus Commission, the City of Winter Haven, and Dick Pope, although Pope was primarily responsible for persuading Moore to come. These three chipped in to pay Moore's $45,000 tab. In return, his national broadcast boosted the citrus industry, Florida, and waterskiing from a studio inside the Florida Citrus Building. Especially waterskiing—the radio star became so proficient at skiing that he opened the Tom Moore Ski School on Lake Roy, just down the street from Cypress Gardens.[104]

Oddly enough, though, for their first television appearance the Cypress Gardens skiers did not ski on Lake Eloise but in a swimming pool in Miami. "Dick Pope had us booked anyplace he could get us in," Willa McGuire Cook said. "We did the *Colgate Comedy Hour* in the Fontainebleau Hotel pool in Miami." She was accompanied by Dick Pope Jr. and Alfredo Mendoza, and they shared the lineup with Patti Page and Carmen Dragon's Orchestra. "We did whatever we could do on skis," Willa said. "You sit on one end of the pool, and the cable you're attached to winds up on the spool of the winch at a certain speed until you get to the other end and drop the handle and they stop the winch. That was the end of your act." Somehow the skiers managed to do tricks such as turnarounds and helicopter spins. The Orange Bowl Queen was on hand to preside over the show.[105]

A real queen arrived at the Gardens in January 1955, and that was Queen Soraya, wife of the shah of Iran. Of course, the shah came as well; he and the queen had been taking a break from business in Washington, vacationing in

Dick Pope Sr. said the shah of Iran liked to drive fast; here the shah pilots a boat across Lake Eloise at Cypress Gardens, 1955. By permission of Cypress Gardens.

Miami Beach, where they would drive the shah's $25,000 Rolls Royce convertible along the shore. The Sans Souci Hotel in Miami literally rolled out a 40-foot-long red carpet. Because the hotel didn't have a "royal suite," it made one by painting four adjoining rooms in "robin's egg blue," the same color as the shah's Rolls Royce.[106]

Upon their arrival in Winter Haven, the royal couple decided to dispense with the "royal suite" and just act like regular tourists, or, as the local paper put it, they "expressed a desire to live in an American motel." They went by motorcade to the Villa Rosa, a motel right near the center of Winter Haven, but far, far away from the Sans Souci.[107]

Right after they arrived, they headed to Cypress Gardens, where they watched the ski show and skied some themselves. The next day, the shah and an aide met with Governor Leroy Collins and toured some orange groves along with a citrus-packing plant. That afternoon he skied some more, and then he planned to have a pistol-shooting match with twenty-four-year-old Lucy Chambliss. Unlike her sister Barbara, who was a Cypress Gardens ski star, Lucy had gravitated toward pistols and horses. In 1948, her father handed her a single-shot pistol and a box of .22 cartridges, and she proceeded to shoot the hell out of the weapon.

She laughs patiently at the suggestion that she's another Annie Oakley, but she was the national women's pistol champion in 1954, and in 1953 became the first woman in the country to land a spot on the U.S. International Pistol Team. She shot in an indoor studio on *What's My Line?* after she got permission to tote her gun to New York, and she appeared next to Jack Benny on *To Tell the Truth* in 1960. She joined the Winter Haven Police Force as a ballistic expert in 1958. She was still working at the Gardens in 1955 when the shah came, and Dick Pope invited her down one evening for a shooting match.

"It was quite interesting," she said. "General Van Fleet was there, and it was almost dark, February, cold as the dickens. The shah was still in his bathing suit; he loved to ski. So he shot six or seven rounds with my gun, and I shot with his. He was very interested in Colts. There were lots of Secret Service men around. I was kind of proud of that."[108] No one would say who won the informal contest, but one onlooker said, "our Lucy did all right by herself."[109]

The shah felt right at home in Winter Haven. "[He] loved night life," said Dick Pope. "One time we had Lee Meriwether [Miss America] at our house as a guest; he and his group were staying at the motel. When the motel would close, he'd say, 'Now we go to your house.' Every night, four nights in a row, he kept us up dancing til two o'clock."[110]

Although the shah was a proficient skier, he wanted to learn some tricks. The job of teaching him went to Willa McGuire Cook: "He wanted me to teach him to ski on one ski, and okay, here's the shah of Iran; does one touch the shah to keep him from falling when he kicks off the ski or does one let him fall? I was skiing along, thinking, 'oh my gosh, how do I handle this?' and finally I said to myself, 'well I can't let him fall,' and I stuck out my hand and stabilized him when he dropped his ski, and then he did very well; he was up on one ski. He sent me a gold watch after they left, as a thank you. It seems like Pope knew everybody in the whole darn world. He really did."[111]

As a tribute to their Middle Eastern visitor, the Junior Woman's Club of Winter Haven presented the "Follies of 1955" during which they elected Al McFayden "Shah." The gesture was affectionate. After all, the Cypress Gardens ski team had just returned from the World Ski Tournament in Beirut, Lebanon, where they were feted by the president, Camille Chamoun. The Cypress Gardens newsletter gives a rundown of the team's world tour through Paris, Rome, Beirut, Istanbul, and Munich: Dick Jr. taught Queen Soraya how to barefoot; Julie Pope found Kathy Darlyn's photo in a Kodak ad hanging in a store in Jerusalem; Dick Binette and Scotty Scott walked all over Paris trying to rent out scooters; *Easy to Love* was playing in Beirut cinemas; *This Is Cinerama* was playing in both Rome and Milan; Alfredo, Dick Jr., and a couple of the other guys watched a "girly-girly" show in the Quartier Pigalle. Finally, the skiers were pictured back at the Gardens having coffee with Dick and Julie Pope; they were wearing traditional Arab garb, and the caption below the photograph read, "The Arab influence lasts right through coffee time."[112] The Cypress Gardens skiers were anything but xenophobic, having traveled all over the world.

In late January 1955, Dick Pope resigned from his position as vice chairman of the State Advertising Commission, saying he needed to spend more time in the Gardens. He'd been appointed to the nonpaying post in the spring of 1953. "I feel the present commission has extended its operations into the new modern fields of advertising to such an extent that the Florida tourist season is about to become a year round industry," he said. He cited a need for Florida to double its advertising spending from twenty to forty cents per tourist per year, arguing that the money would generate millions in tax dollars. At that time, he was spending more than a half million dollars per year himself just to advertise Cypress Gardens.[113]

The state could have taken some lessons from Dick Pope about advertising. Betty Skelton Erde, the famous aviatrix who'd become the automobile industry's first female test-driver, recalled a stunt she did at the Gardens in 1954 or 1955. "I had gone to work at Chrysler by then, and every time I'd get back to Florida to see my family, I'd go out to the Gardens," she said.

Cypress Gardens skiers wore Arab headdresses to a welcome-home party after competing at the 1955 World Ski Tournament in Beirut, Lebanon. By permission of Cypress Gardens.

Her parents lived on the same lake as the Popes so she would boat back and forth from her house to the Gardens. On one of her visits, she and Dick thought up a publicity stunt: she would launch her jump boat, the *L'il Miss Dodge*, over a brand-new 1955 Custom Royal Lancer at the Gardens: "Dick thought it would be good for Chrysler to see I was doing something interesting over one of their products—that's what

World-famous aviator Betty Skelton Erde jumped a boat over a 1955 Royal Lancer at Cypress Gardens. By permission of Cypress Gardens.

brought that on. We just sat around one day and decided to do it. And we set up the ski jump and the car and got everything ready, and I jumped, and I got hurt on that jump."

When the boat flew over the car, it hit the water so hard that Betty was thrown to the bottom of the boat, injuring her leg and foot so badly she had to go to the hospital. "I had to catch a plane either that night or the next morning to California to do a commercial," she said. "They took me out there and stood me up next to the car, then took the crutches away, and I was leaning against the car, and I was so afraid I was going to fall over before the end of the commercial. It took me quite a while to get over that jump, but it was a lot of fun."[114]

Pope was never afraid to promote another enterprise, especially if he could include Cypress Gardens in the bargain. Sometimes that happened inadvertently. When Silver Springs lost some of its buildings in a fire, he stepped in immediately to see what he could do to help. He enlisted his office workers to mail out eight thousand color postcards to hotels, motels, and travel agencies all over the United States. The cards featured scenes from *Easy to Love*, and Pope had written this message on the back:

> As you have seen in the newspapers and television and heard on the radio, our good friends at world famous Silver Springs have suffered a loss of part of their buildings. This however only interrupted their business momentarily, and we are happy to tell you that their famous glass bottom boats are running along with the photo sub boats and the jungle cruise boats. . . . Believe me, it would

> not be Florida without Silver Springs operating and I trust that you will continue to send them visitors just as you have in the past. A trip to Florida without seeing the famous attraction is like missing half of your life.[115]

Of course, he made the news with such a generous gesture. Silver Springs, was, after all, a major competitor of the Gardens. "It's no news for a guy to blow his own horn," explained one editorial, "but when he goes to a lot of personal expense to blow somebody else's, that makes news—and comments in columns such as these."[116]

It seemed only natural that, a couple of months later, the best-selling author of *The Power of Positive Thinking*, Reverend Norman Vincent Peale, wrote a sermon on Dick Pope for his syndicated column. However, it wasn't Pope's good deeds that caught the reverend's attention. Cypress Gardens was one of his favorite places, and he was intrigued by Pope's ability to "come up with fresh ideas," so he asked him what his secret was. "I always try to think big," Pope told him. "When a thought comes into your mind about business, think big. Think big about your children. Think big about your life. Down here in Florida events always have one queen, an orange queen: I have three queens. If other places start having three, I'll have six."[117]

The column was published in newspapers across the county. And then there were columns about the column. As one editorialist noted about Pope: "The very dynamic gentleman has landed just about everywhere else, and so it was inevitable that he land right in the middle of a sermon."[118] Another one wrote that "While only God can make a tree, only Dick Pope can make people pay to look at one."[119]

Clearly, Pope was able to bridge the sacred and the profane. As Peale pointed out, Dick Pope built the canals through the Gardens "so that people might get close to the natural wonderland." Peale didn't comment on their ability to get close to Pope's numerous queens, southern belles, and Aqua Maids.

Pope was strangely quiet on the subject of Sunshine Springs, an attraction dreamed up in 1955 by another big thinker, a Boston developer named Leonard Tanner. It's clear Tanner got his big idea after he'd seen what Dick Pope had accomplished over in Winter Haven. Unlike Pope, who had to drain his swamp, Tanner had to create one, flooding a pasture southeast of Sarasota to create a manmade lake. Writer Budd Schulberg, on hand opening day to dump three

Leonard Tanner opened Sunshine Springs in 1955 and promptly put Lady the Elephant up on skis. By permission of the Sarasota County History Center.

gallons of orange juice on water-skier Barbara Laney as a sort of christening, said that if Pope was Swami of the Swamp, then Tanner was "Pasha of the Pasture."[120] It's likely that Dick Pope was not amused. Tim Hollis, author of *Glass Bottom Boats and Mermaid Tails*, wrote that "Sunshine Springs . . . more closely resembled Cypress Gardens on steroids than any of the other Florida springs," adding that it has been called "one of the most spectacular failures in Florida tourism history."[121] But in 1957, the *New York Times* reported that "the biggest water spectacles are at Sunshine Springs . . . and Cypress Gardens. . . . The two parks are trying to outdo each other this season in staging strange stunts."

Sunshine Springs' claim to fame, besides imitating Cypress Gardens with its Aquabelles, Aquabeaux, jumping boats, gardens, and electric swan boats, was a water-skiing elephant named Lady who had participated in Dwight Eisenhower's campaign in New York in 1954. She was chained to a couple of pontoons connected with a brace and hauled around the lake with a couple of "comely young women." Baptiste Schreiber, the elephant's trainer, was hoping to have a Himalayan bear up on skis before the end of 1957.[122]

The image of the water-skiing elephant prompted one columnist to speculate on what sort of comeback Pope would have: "Expect some excitement soon. Dick Pope is not going to take that elephant lying down."[123] Dick Pope did not attempt to find another water-skiing elephant, but he did introduce a new stunt: a skier would grab hold of a large kite as he was being towed behind a boat, then rise 50 feet into the sky, hanging on for dear life to the crossbar with his bare hands. One reporter described the crowd's reaction to this new act: "The clicking of tourists' cameras sounds like a thousand crickets on a summer night."[124]

Simon Khoury of Lebanon, Beirut, former world champion skier and show director at the Gardens from 1953 to 1963, recalled the prototype of that kite brought to the Gardens by Doug Leversha in 1956: "I got called to Dick Pope's office, and he said, 'I have a crazy guy from Australia who has a kite, and he wants you guys to take and test it.'" Simon, along with Buster MacCalla and Dick Binette, went down to the show area with Leversha and his kite. "We took the guy up, and he crashed; the kite sunk; and he was crying."[125] A brief news clipping explains why he was crying. He fell about 100 feet when the wind shifted and the kite started darting around. One of his assistants on the boat had gotten scared and released the safety pin that tethered the kite to the boat. When the kite crashed, Leversha hit the water so hard that his skis splintered.[126]

"We took him to a clinic," said Simon, "and Dick Pope said, 'Hey, you have a budget of five hundred dollars, go build a kite for him.' Doug taught us how to build a kite, and we built it and tested it, and that is how the sport started. Dick Pope accepted it," said Simon, "and gave us the possibility to build kites, and this is how kites got going. The flat kite was a dangerous thing and not like the one they fly now, the Delta. The first kite was made of bamboo with a stainless-steel cable, and when you got up to 50 feet in the air you prayed to God that the nose wouldn't collapse on you or you'd fall backward. We had a few kites that broke on us until we found the right way to do it."

"We built the first one at the Gardens; we flew the first ones, and then naturally Ken Tibado came along and learned it and made a profession. He started his own factory, and this was how kite flying started."[127]

Even with the danger involved, Pope's kite flyers apparently were a safer bet than a water-skiing elephant—Sunshine Springs closed in 1959, just four years after it opened.

Leonard Tanner wasn't the only one inspired by Dick Pope's Midas touch. At Pope's suggestion, the producers of NBC's *Wide Wide World* decided to do something that had never been done before on live television: they equipped a 36-foot-long boat with all the equipment they needed to film the show, including a microwave transmitter, generators, and studio cameras. Audiences at home could get an up-close look at Willa McGuire Cook's ski-ballet, the Mercury jumping boats, the human pyramid. The result was so successful that NBC decided to do an "All-

The first kite flyers at Cypress Gardens literally hung on for their lives. Author's collection.

AQUAPLANING, forerunner of water skiing began about 1915, and by 193 there were games of polo played on motorized aquaplanes. Water tobogganing i really fun and even wings were put on an aquaplane as early at 1928 by Dick Pope Sr., who made the first newsreel of aquaplaning back in 1916.

The aquamaids play "Follow the Leader" while on the right Jeff Richards mans the toboggan.

Bob Eastman, Gerald Emry, and Kenneth Recker play thrilling polo for the Grantland Rice Sportlight.

Dick Pope Sr. credited newsreels for helping to create an interest in waterskiing; they started by filming the aquaplane. By permission of Cypress Gardens.

Florida ninety minute telecast" in the future; it would be primarily shot at Cypress Gardens, and would feature, of course, the water-skiers.[128] The skiers went on to perform on Dave Garroway's *Today* show, on Steve Allen's *Tonight* show, and on Garry Moore's *I've Got a Secret*. Moore decided to take up skiing himself, and his first ski attempt was broadcast live during the Florida Citrus Exposition.

Television excited Pope. He must have known it would supplant the newsreels, and he wanted to exploit it. In 1956, after reading an article in *Business Week*, he dashed off a letter to the editor:

> Your special report "Television: The New Cyclops" was terrific . . . and it really opened my eyes to such an extent that I started doing a little planning for my beautiful Cypress Gardens on a ten year basis. . . . It might interest you to know that we spent $14,000 here at Cypress Gardens to get nine minutes on the *Wide Wide World* program . . . and believe me we are going to go after TV more and more in the future.[129]

The article Pope gushed over was far from positive about the impact of television, calling TV a "monster" and worrying that "in less than

10 years TV has become one of the most powerful social forces in the U.S."[130] Perhaps Pope's response was one more example of his unwavering optimism, or perhaps it was because from 1948 to 1955 almost two-thirds of American households purchased televisions.[131]

Newsreels, which had previously been shown exclusively in theaters, were now being beamed into homes via the television. In *A Walk through the 20th Century with Bill Moyers*, a 1984 documentary, Moyers looked back at the fifty-year history of newsreels. "For my generation and our parents," he said, "newsreels were as integral a part of Sunday afternoons as church was of Sunday morning. And far more enticing: the preacher could only tell us of heaven and hell, but newsreels brought us the real thing—Miss America and Adolph Hitler."

Newsreels, the reviewer of Moyers's documentary said, were "imperfect, often frivolous, even fraudulent, [but they] shaped our *Weltanschauung*, defined our purpose and told us who we were."[132] In the first half of the twentieth century, we were water-skiers.

If there was an Academy Award for "creating interest in water skiing," Pope wrote later, it would have to go to newsreels. One writer commented on the newsreels' love affair with skiing after he watched one featuring a beautiful girl aquaplaning over the waters at Cypress Gardens: "As I stared at this girl in the bathing suit . . . I realized that I most certainly had seen her before. Where had I seen her before, and when? In a newsreel—last year. And if truth be told, the year before, and the year before that. I have seen this girl on that aquaplane year in and year out for as long as I have been watching newsreels."[133]

Clearly, television was going to take the place of newsreels—the films would become obsolete by the 1960s—and Dick Pope wanted to be ready for the transition. But he went after a radio station first. Reports surfaced that Pope "would score the state's biggest publicity ten-strike if the Federal Communications Commission grants authority" to move WGTO from Haines City, Florida, "to an orange grove setting overlooking the big nationally-known attraction."[134]

If the move took place, it would make Cypress Gardens the only public attraction in the country with a commercial radio station on-site. However delighted Pope must have been with the prospect of radio waves beaming out of the Gardens, he wasn't about to forget how the Gardens had been immortalized in photographs. And neither was Esther Williams.

In November 1956, the movie star stopped by

To attract more interest from the growing television business, Pope created the "Tropical Isles of Movieland" in 1955. By permission of Cypress Gardens.

the Gardens with her husband, Ben Gage, and children to check out her latest pool. "I talked [Dick Pope] into putting up one of my Esther Williams' backyard pools in a meadow, surrounded by all kinds of tropical flowers," she wrote in her autobiography, "so I could have a beautiful backdrop for all the publicity and advertising stills for my swimming pool business."[135]

She probably didn't have to expend much effort convincing him to build the pool because the deal factored right into "OPM squared." The Esther Williams pool would simply be a part of Pope's "Tropical Isles of Movieland," which had been under construction for the previous year and a half. A 1955 photo in the Cypress Gardens newsletter shows the newly constructed islands recently planted with curvy palm trees, and the caption notes, "This setting will appear in many newsreels, TV shows and ads, and is separate from the Gardens so it won't be cluttered with Yankee Tourists."[136]

For the grand opening of the Isles in the fall of 1956, Carl Kiekhaefer, the president of Mercury Motors, had been enticed by Dick Pope to unveil his new engines before a crowd of more than sixty newspaper editors and writers. More than forty boat manufacturers were on hand to show off the motors. Whoever wrote the press release seemed to forget that Dick Pope had once been called the Swami of the Swamp for sculpturing Cypress Gardens out of its own muck:

> Down thru the centuries many great examples of sculpture have excited the people of the world, and now at Cypress Gardens Dick Pope has brought forth a new art "Sculpturing in Mud," using a 40 foot drag line boom and bucket as a chisel to carve out of a

swamp what will become known as the most beautiful islands in all this world: The Isles of Movieland.

Esther Williams posed for a photo next to her pool, standing on tiptoes, and the newly minted Miss America of 1957, Marian McKnight, flew over the proceedings in a Mercury-powered helicopter. When she emerged from the cockpit and stepped onto the Tropical Isles of Movieland wearing a big smile and a Jantzen swimsuit, it was clear that Dick Pope was ready for prime time.[137] He had never wavered in his belief in the power of beauty, and not just the kind that grew out of the earth. If anything, by 1956 he was more convinced than ever that motors needed models. Pretty ones. The more the better. Before long, Cypress Gardens became known as the "Playground of the Miss Americas."[138]

Sometimes that posed a problem for the diminutive Dick Pope. "He was pretty short," recalled Red McGuire. "When Miss America was in, we'd have to stand him on a block so that he would be somewhat near the same height." The trouble was worth it, Red added. "When the Miss Americas came to the Gardens, that was the only place they were allowed to be photographed in a bathing suit."[139]

"They had a little throne right there when you came in," said Dubie Baxter, discussing Dick Pope's preoccupation with beauty queens. "This is part of the Total Experience: you walk in, and here's a ski show going on, and here's a queen being crowned, and you can stand next to her and get your picture taken. He did that up to probably 1957 or '58 because by 1960 he's bringing in Miss America. Miss America was the biggest thing in the world. He paid me to take them out on the boat. I would've done it for nothing, but he never let anybody do anything for nothing; he'd say, 'Here's fifty bucks, drive her around town; show her Winter Haven; get her a Coke out at Jack and Betty's, but they always had a chaperone and very rarely could you ever get them away from the chaperone. So you'd put on a tie and go somewhere to dinner. There's a picture of me with Debra Barnes—she's reaching over touching a flower, and I've got the canoe. I sent that picture to a friend of mine, and he said, 'that looks like Mark Trail and Jackie Onassis.'"[140]

Actually, the first Miss America to visit the Gardens was Neva Jane Langley, although she hadn't been anointed Miss America yet. She was crowned Tangerine Queen at the Gardens in 1949 before going on to win the national

Dubie Baxter had the honor of taking Miss America Debra Barnes on a canoe ride in 1967. By permission of Dubie Baxter.

competition in 1952. She didn't think those early pageants were any great shakes. "They didn't require any talent," she said. "They required a pretty girl in a pretty dress."[141]

Miss America 1955, Lee Merriwether, was so taken with Cypress Gardens that not only did she dance until the wee hours with the Popes and their guests, she even stopped by on her honeymoon in 1958. When the Miss Americas arrived at Cypress Gardens, they would water-ski, crown lesser queens, and pose as southern belles. Marilyn Debur, Miss America 1958, decided to go whole hog in the Cypress Gardens experience. *Pageantry Magazine* couldn't get over her chutzpa:

> Marilyn was brave enough to try her hand at hang-gliding (yikes!). She also played softball (risky with makeup), and of all things, she went fishing! However, the most unusual (borderline crazy) thing she did was to appear in one of the water-ski shows as a water skier! Do you think the spectators knew that one of the skiers was Miss America?[142]

If they didn't, it's almost certain Dick Pope would have told them. In early March 1957, he strolled into a meeting of the Orlando Jaycees with not one, but four beauty queens in tow. Not surprisingly, it was the biggest gathering of Jaycees for a luncheon in over a year. Who could blame them? These were not ordinary beauty queens. One was the former Miss Sweden, now Miss World; another was Miss Denmark. Then there were the Florida queens: the

Florida Products Festival Queen and the former Camellia Queen. Dick Pope was not there to talk about beauty queens, though. He was there to talk about the Jacksonville-Miami turnpike. He told the Jaycees that the turnpike should have a canal constructed next to it so boaters and skiers could run up and down the state, then "you'd have the biggest tourist attraction of any turnpike in the country." He also made the observation that "Pictures of girls sell everything in the world today," and "By posing for cheesecake pictures, girls become ladies. Only when a girl sits in the hot sun trying to look beautiful when she doesn't feel like it does she become a lady."[143]

Just the month before, Dick Pope had taken some good-humored ribbing about his cheesecake from Mike Morgan, a columnist with the *Tampa Daily Times* who wrote that he went to Cypress Gardens to talk with Dick Pope about "glamour queens and gorgeous skiing gals." An exasperated Pope, said, "Girls! How come you writers come down here and want to talk about girls? Girls are an important part, but just a part of the Gardens. Why don't you write about landscaping and flowers? Do you know that there are more than 4,000 varieties of plants, shrubs, flowers from all over the world on display here? . . . Do you know that there are millions of dollars worth of horticultural exhibits here?" He went on to mention the $300,000 worth of maintenance and the forty-six gardeners.[144]

He was right. Cypress Gardens was a horticultural wonder. And if you visited the Gardens in the early 1950s, you could have purchased a guidebook that "served as an introduction" to America's Tropical Wonderland. The Popes had literally travelled the world in search of exotic plants to bring back to the Gardens: the lipstick tree from the East Indies; the sky flower from Bengal; the reed palm from China. They had visited the Gardens at Versailles and decided tourists "could enjoy sightseeing as the comfort of their feet would permit" so they created "outdoor sitting rooms" such as the Hibiscus Room. It's clear that in all of Pope's crownings of Camellia, Hibiscus and Yellow Aster queens, he was paying homage to the original stars of the gardens: the flowers. As the brochure stated proudly, "Photographic models in old fashioned costumes . . . are always glad to pose and smile or pick a flower and put it in their hair so that the colorful occasion can be preserved for posterity in the camera of the visitor." *Life* magazine called the Gardens "A Photographer's Paradise."[145]

The facing page offered undeniable proof—a checkerboard of eighty-eight magazine covers,

A southern belle poses with the sausage tree, one of the unusual plants found at Cypress Gardens. Author's collection.

each one featuring a Cypress Gardens model. Still, although flowers may have been the original stars of the Garden, it was the combination of queens and flowers that got the tourists in the door.

That was the message of "The King of Beauty Queens," an article in *Esquire* magazine that fawned over Pope's provenance as Florida's publicist and its own Henry VIII. Arthur Herzog wrote that the image of Florida as a tropical garden filled with "beachcake" had been insinuated into American culture by publicists who convinced us that "Ponce de Leon had the wrong century but the right idea." And who was the "grand panjandrum of these specialists in hothouse dreams?" Dick Pope. Herzog picked up the secular thread of Norman Vincent Peale's sermon about Pope's ability to think big, that if the norm was to crown one queen, he'd crown three. Unlike Peale, Herzog noted that as far as beauty queens go, "[Pope] is far more fecund than any of his competitors. From the most famous of the beauty contests, for instance, Miss America at Atlantic City, issues only one queen a year. Compared to it, Pope is a promotional Henry VIII."

Pope confessed to the reporter that the crownings made the tourists feel like they are "in on something big. . . . In the old days, I had a motto, 'A queen a day keeps the Sheriff away.' . . . My record was nine queens in seven days. We're having a crowning today . . . I've got this load of chrysanthemums and I'd better get me a queen before they wilt." He meant that literally. Once, in just under an hour, he found and crowned a Grapefruit Queen to please the director of *Wide Wide World*. To find his Chrysanthemum Queen, he called down to the cottages where the "girls" lived and simply asked who was available. When Bonnie Bradley showed up, he looked her over and said, "Smile for me honey. Great. You're going to be the Chrysanthemum Queen. Shooting's scheduled for three-thirty. We've got Miss America down here for a few days at $500 a day, and she'll do the crowning."[146]

As usual, his promotions didn't just involve homegrown royalty. Earlier that year, in late June, he had hosted King Saud of Saudi Arabia at the Gardens. The king had been the subject of a cover story in *Time* magazine in January, after he decided to accept President Eisenhower's invitation to discuss the U.S. air base at Dhahran and other issues related to the Middle East. Now he had accepted Dick Pope's invitation to watch a ski show. The king arrived in Polk County, landing at the Bartow Air Base with an entourage of about sixty-five people. Apparently he left his

Esquire magazine crowned Dick Pope Sr. the "King of Beauty Queens." Here the queen and her court pose with hotelier Conrad Hilton. By permission of Cypress Gardens.

King Faisal Ibn Saud shakes hands with Jack Watkins Jr., one of Dick Pope Sr.'s grandsons. By permission of Julie Pope Dantzler.

numerous wives at home. When the king and his entourage stepped from the plane, they were serenaded by the Winter Haven High School Band. Once they arrived at Cypress Gardens, they watched the ski show from a huge Arabian-styled tent erected on the banks of Lake Eloise. Simon Khoury served as the king's interpreter.[147]

Since he'd been driving electric boats through the Gardens' canals since he was sixteen, Dubie Baxter had carted loads of royalty around. "I had three kings on my electric boats at different times," he said. "My second king was King Faisal Ibn Saud, the King of Saudi Arabia, big man; I mean, he was about six foot six inches, full gear, robes. We took him through with his entourage, his body guards, his henchmen, and his flunkies. There were fourteen spots, and they filled them, and I gave them the whole spiel, even though I didn't think any of them could speak English. If they knew English, they didn't let on. I was pretty impressed. I was sitting in this electric boat, steering it, and at the end—no one said a word the whole time—at the end, the king stood, and as soon as he acknowledged me, this guy in a black suit pulled out a hundred dollar bill, and they were gone—that was it. My first hundred dollar bill."[148]

It seemed as though Dick Pope was aiming for his own kingdom. Just a month after King Saud left, Pope succeeded in persuading the government to locate a post office in Cypress Gardens, convincing the person in charge that the area around Cypress Gardens constituted a community. This meant that not only would he have "the most glamorous post office in the entire United States postal system," it also meant that the mail would go out stamped "Cypress Gardens, Florida" or, in the case of metered mail, "See Cypress Gardens."[149]

The Gardens was required to construct a post office, and once the building was framed out, Pope put his southern belles to work. Wearing hoop skirts and toting hammers, saws, and 2 × 4s, they climbed ladders and stood on scaffolding while a Cypress Gardens photographer snapped away. A few days later, when the building was nearly completed, Pope had a string of "water-ski maidens" line up inside, as if there to drop off mail. Of course the *Tampa Tribune* gave an entire page to "Postmaster Pope's" first "acts as 'Postmaster.'"[150]

At the same time that the post office was going up, he finally got his radio station. Disc jockey Dale Starkey broadcast his first show while skiing around the lake, "loaded down with a transmitter, several stay-afloat aids, a book of last minute skiing instructions, and a heavy feeling in the pit of his stomach." Cypress Gardens publicity director Al McFayden skied next to him so the DJ could do an "on ski" interview.[151]

Just a couple of weeks later, the Gardens hosted, for the second time, the World Water Ski Championships. More than one hundred skiers from eighteen nations descended on Winter Haven to compete at the three-day event. Governor Leroy Collins declared the entire week to be Water Ski Week, issuing a warm welcome to Cypress Gardens' international visitors. However, the governor's largesse went unremarked just a few months later when his Road Board made the audacious move of taking Cypress Gardens, and other "private attractions," off of the state's road maps. The local press was none too happy and let him know it:

> It's all right for you and your cabinet to go browsing around in the North with big business and big money interests, trying to get them to come to Florida, but why not take care of what is here? . . . When you slap us around with one of our greatest assets—the

A group of southern belles get to work on Cypress Gardens' post office. By permission of the *Tampa Tribune*.

Cypress Gardens—taken off the maps, that's going too far."[152]

To protest the Gardens' exclusion from the map, Dick Pope placed a full-page ad in the *Florida Newspaper News* depicting a tourist eyeing a Florida map with a magnifying glass, looking for Cypress Gardens, reminding the governor that 1 million tourists would make their way to the Gardens whether it was on the map or not. And Dick Pope knew his tourists.

"Before zip codes and zip code surveys," Bob Kehoe said, "I used to walk the parking lot during ski shows with a clipboard and count the number of cars from each state. Mr. Pope would study that to see where the tourists were coming from—Ohio, New York, New Jersey. Then he would know where to take out newspaper ads at certain times of the year. He normally took one out in January in the New York, New Jersey area, because that's when the people were snowbound, and they're looking over their vacation plans early on—*When we get out of here,*

The Cypress Gardens water-skiers were featured in a 1958 *National Geographic* article about the "fastest growing sport in the world." By permission of Cypress Gardens.

here's where we want to go. I had a big clipboard with a form that listed all the states on it. In the early 1950s through '57–'58, once or twice a year, we'd get a group together and put somebody at a major intersection at Haines City or Bartow or Lakeland. Then I would take the entrance to the Gardens' parking lot." They would write down every state tag number, then use the information to determine which roads people used to get to the actual Gardens. "So," Bob said, "if you had pretty good traffic coming from Lake Wales that didn't turn and come to Cypress Gardens, you'd put a billboard there. That was an interesting way of doing that, but it worked."[153] The Road Board finally figured out that even though Cypress Gardens was a private attraction, it had obvious benefits for Florida. The 1958 map included the Gardens.[154]

In August, Dick Pope headed to Europe with Julie to see what he could do to entice foreign tourists to travel to Florida. On his way back he planned to stop in at a "bathing suit manufacturers' convention" in Portland, Oregon, and then end his journey in Atlantic City. He had finally reached the pinnacle of beauty queendom—he was chosen to be a judge at the upcoming Miss America Pageant. He liked that talent was given equal footing with "pulchritude." "Too many beauty contests are just plain cheesecake," he said.[155]

Meanwhile, back at Cypress Gardens, a *National Geographic* reporter arrived to take photographs of the Cypress Gardens ski champions, but couldn't resist putting on a pair of skis himself to see why 3 million Americans had made waterskiing the "fastest growing sport in the world." The resulting twelve-page article, "The Booming Sport of Waterskiing," featured photographs of both young men and women engaged in activities made famous at Cypress Gardens: A male skier soaring over the lake while dangling from a giant kite; a young woman leaping off a floating ramp—in the dark, no less. A skier doing a 360-degree helicopter spin as he comes off a ramp. Igor Benson piloting his Heli-boat over the lake.[156] Dick Pope's enthusiasm for the sport of waterskiing—from strapping on those 1920s Akwa-Skees to hosting national and international tournaments for years—had finally paid off. Waterskiing was finally coming into its own.

Dick Pope Jr. also played a role in popularizing the sport. In addition to his many accomplishments as a skier, in 1956, he bought the Tourney Water Ski factory in Lakeland and moved operations over to Lake Eloise, where he began manufacturing Cypress Gardens–brand

Dick Pope Jr. began manufacturing Cypress Gardens skis in 1956. By permission of Cypress Gardens.

skis. Rick Dantzler, Dick Pope Jr.'s son-in-law, said the Cypress Garden factory "set the standard for the industry for many years."

The skis have become collector's items. Carole Lowe, director of the American Water Ski Educational Foundation and Water Ski Hall of Fame, said: "People would say, 'I've got my Cypress Gardens skis and I'm not taking anything for them.' They are in the homes of many skiers in the U.S. and they treasure them, especially after the Gardens changed its name."[157]

Cypress Gardens sold the ski factory to Bagley Enterprises, Inc. in 1981, and Bagley sold it to ERO Industries two years later.[158] By the 1990s, Cypress Gardens skis had disappeared from retail stores, causing one skier to wonder: "What happened to Cypress Gardens Dick Pope skis? They were the standard, the inventor. This would be like one day going to a bike shop and there weren't any more Schwinns, or no more Wilson tennis racquets."[159] The El Diablos and Dick Pope Jr. skis are still out there—you can find them on eBay, along with Cypress Gardens spoons, salt shakers, tape measures, Viewmaster reels, shot glasses, purses, perfumes, bone china, grapefruit labels, and postcards.

Dick Pope Jr. was more than just the name on a ski. Dick Pope Sr. recounted some of his son's other contributions to the sport in his book, *Water Skiing,* joking that there were times when his son spent more time on water than on land. The practice paid off; Dick Pope Jr. was the U.S. men's champion in 1948, 1949, and 1950. In 1950, he won every major ski title in the world for a "grand slam." When he told his father he wanted to start manufacturing water skis, Dick Pope Sr. said, "Well, I guess it's taken you ten years to decide that barefoot skiing will never replace plain old waterskiing."[160]

Of course, there was no "plain old waterskiing" at Cypress Gardens. As Ed Sullivan wrote in the preface to Pope Sr.'s book, when he was planning his ninth anniversary telecast at Jones Beach Marine Stadium he insisted on having Cypress Gardens' "breathtaking Aquamaids and Aquachamps. . . . Television has never seen anything more stirring than these brilliant stars." Pope's old friend Lowell Thomas, whom he'd known since the newsreel days and from *This Is Cinerama*, wrote the introduction. The book featured some of the earliest photographs made of both skiers and boat racers, including a 1928 photograph of Dick's brother Malcolm flying over a ramp in his "jumping boat," the *Baby Winter Haven III.* It also included early advertisements for Akwa-Skees, created by his friend Fred Waller, whose invention of Cinerama Pope credited with doing "more than any other movie to convey to viewers the real thrill of waterskiing."

Scrolling through the lists of national and international ski stars in the back of the book, it becomes clear that Dick Pope meant it when he wrote that "Through [international tournaments] men and women from many nations are able to find mutual understanding and international friendship in their common love for the great sport of water skiing." As newly appointed chairman of the Advertising and Tourist Development Commission of Florida, Pope went to Hong Kong after the book was released to offer advice on how Hong Kong could increase its numbers of tourists: emphasize the glamour of Hong Kong, he said; use publicity rather than advertising. "You need cinemascope," he told a group at Repulse Bay. "The romance you have here can be perpetuated a little more."[161] After predicting that with the increase of air travel, places like Hong Kong would become more inviting, he ended his talk on a philosophic note:

> People who have visited other countries are friendlier and have more understanding than those who don't, and maybe if more people can be induced to travel we may never have another world war, because more people will have a better understanding of other nationalities and subsequently a better understanding of themselves.[162]

Margaret Chase Parry, Dick Pope's niece, confirmed that not only was he friendly, he was hard to keep up with. While Margaret was studying in Paris, Julie and Dick visited her. She and Julie lost Dick at the Eiffel Tower when they went off to buy kid gloves for the Gardens' female employees. He was supposed to meet them at the midsection for lunch. He never showed up. When forty-five minutes had passed, Margaret suggested they go to the top, but Julie was sure he wouldn't have gone to such a fancy restaurant. They went anyway, and there he was, said Margaret, but not alone; "he had met everyone in the restaurant, including the Count of Lafayette."

Later, Margaret said, they boarded a plane to Geneva, Switzerland, and by the time they landed, she said, "he had not only read two news magazines cover to cover, he had met every single person on the plane and had handed them a card about Florida orange juice—not about Cypress Gardens, but Florida orange juice." When they made it to their hotel in Geneva, Julie decided she needed to buy Margaret a watch for graduation, and Dick decided to check out the hotel. So again they split up. After finding the perfect watch, they went back to the hotel to find Dick. He wasn't there. "Well," said Margaret, "the people at the hotel said: 'Man in the flower coat, he's down on the left; oh yeah, we met the man from Florida in the flower coat.' We went to four places before we finally found him in the lounge. He really didn't drink; he just wanted to visit people. So then we go to this restaurant called the Pearl of the Lake, and we have lunch. Lunch is almost over, and we can't find Uncle Dick. Can't find him. He is in the kitchen talking to the chef, and he's giving him his flower coat. That's just the way he was."[163]

Pope's friendliness must have appealed to the Duke and Duchess of Windsor for they made yet another trip to Winter Haven in 1959. Julie and Dick hosted them at the Gardens, where the couple sat primly on the famous Wishing Tree for a photo. Like the shah of Iran had done when he came to Winter Haven, the duke and duchess decided to go native by staying at the Terra Ceia Court in Winter Haven, their first experience at an American motor lodge. Delighted with the novelty of the motel (the duke had been spotted when he "sauntered from his motel room and stopped to have breakfast at the Cardinal Restaurant"), they generously offered to pose for photos with tourists who "had waited several hours around the lazy-L pool to get brief glimpses of the couple."[164] After finding out that Dick Pope Jr. had married the former Citrus Queen, Frances Layton, and that she had had to abdicate her crown in order to marry him, the Duke told Dick Pope Sr., "That makes your son and myself members of the smallest club in the world."[165]

In spite of rubbing elbows with the rich and the famous, Pope never forgot the people who worked for him, even after they had left the Gardens. Betty Doles, whose father helped dig the canals, said that he'd left the Gardens in the late 1940s to take a job as caretaker at the Winter Haven Moose Lodge. Her sister Jacqueline said that when their father died in 1954, the Popes attended his funeral, along with a lot of Winter Haven's other white citizens: "We even had in the book where they signed, and cards from the flowers they sent—a lot of them were in

A group of tourists watch the 1957 ski show from the first bridge built at Cypress Gardens. By permission of Cypress Gardens.

attendance because they thought very highly of him, the way he carried himself.[166]

Meanwhile, back in New York City, Dick Pope and Cypress Gardens were about to get another boost, and a fitting one. Cypress Gardens skiers were featured in one of the giant Colorama photos in Grand Central Station—right along with the Grand Canyon, Niagara Falls, and some Norman Rockwell–esque scenes of American life—quite appropriate since the Gardens sold more Kodak film than practically anyone else in the country. At 18 × 60 feet, these Colorama transparencies were "The World's Largest Photographs," and they had "refreshed and startled millions" ever since 1950, when Eastman Kodak leased the east balcony from New York Central.[167]

In its introduction to the book *Colorama: The World's Largest Photographs,* the Aperture Foundation explained the importance of these iconic images: "[They] brought photography to the masses with a spectacular display of communicative power. During its forty-year run in Grand Central Terminal in New York City, the Colorama program presented a panoramic photo album of American scenes, lifestyles, and achievements from the second half of the twentieth century."[168]

Cypress Gardens also made it onto a much smaller, but no less iconic canvas. When tourists left Cypress Gardens with their families in tow, they usually found a surprise when they got to their cars: A Florida Cypress Gardens bumper sticker. Dick Pope had three full-time workers doing nothing but gluing Cypress Gardens stickers onto the bumpers of all the parked cars out in his lot. Madison Avenue took notice. A 1959 Volkswagen ad pictured the latest Volkswagen above the caption "We've gone places." Right there on the bumper between stickers for the Alamo and Niagara Falls was a sticker for Florida Cypress Gardens.[169]

Dick Pope must have felt it a sweet revenge against all those newspaper editors who'd poked fun at him over the years when, in December 1959, he was selected by the Florida Public Relations Association to be inducted into Florida's Public Relations Hall of Fame with five other people for their "contributions to the growth and progress of Florida." He was in pretty good company—they also selected Governor Leroy Collins, Henry Flagler, and John Ringling.[170] Not so bad for a man who cleared a swamp.

5 The 1960s

Esther Williams, Mike Douglas, and Johnny Carson Come to Town

In early 1960, a reporter said to Dick Pope: "Esther Williams seems to be the unofficial goddess of Cypress Gardens. How do you feel about her?" Pope explained that they had had "lots of clashes," but that over the years they had come to an understanding that they could each depend on each other to do what they did best. Dick Pope would make sure things like the Florida pool were ready no matter what, and Esther Williams would make sure she did her best Esther Williams.[1]

Despite their clashes, or maybe because of them, when Pat Weaver, head of NBC, suggested Esther film an "Aqua Spectacular" like one she had done in New York a few years earlier, she said they needed to do it at Cypress Gardens because of its "beautiful, exotic location." Also because, as she wrote in her autobiography,

Esther Williams and Dick Pope Sr. check out the Aquarama Pool Dick Pope built for Esther Williams's television special. By permission of Cypress Gardens.

"Dick Pope, that little Napoleon, still ran the place as if he owned not just the land, but the performers as well—me included. . . . [D]oing the special at Cypress Gardens gave me a good chance to make good use of him."[2] She'd already gotten the Esther Williams pool out of him; now she needed a brand-new pool for the show. "Dick Pope likes water people," she told a reporter. "He told me that if I would do one show a year there, he would build me a fabulous pool." She added that she would be doing a "circus spectacular next . . . with trapeze artists diving into the water after their flips and twists."[3]

The new pool would be the Aquarama, and it would feature nine large windows so cameras could film the underwater action. Dick Pope knew that *Esther Williams at Cypress Gardens* would provide one hour's worth of free publicity on nationwide television, and he knew he could lease the pool later for commercials so he agreed to work with Esther one more time, despite her often contentious behavior. Whereas other attraction owners might have balked at building a swimming pool for a one-hour television show, Dick Pope knew its worth.

Now he just needed to convince the State of Florida to kick in some funds. He headed to Tallahassee, where he appeared in front of Florida governor Leroy Collins and his cabinet to plead his case for five thousand dollars to help him pay for the production of Esther Williams's upcoming television show. Because Esther had gone back to Hollywood, he brought along a poster of the star in a swimsuit; for background music he brought along a tape recording of a "catchy tune about Florida," and began his spiel.

"You know the cost of color TV is so much more than black and white," he told the governor and his cabinet, snapping his fingers while the music played. And he reminded them that the film would do more than provide another opportunity for Esther Williams to do an aquamusical; it would publicize the Sunshine State to the whole nation. "Dapper Dick Pope," the *Tampa Tribune* reported, "mentioned a helicopter shot panning down on Esther Williams lying in a swimming pool shaped like Cypress Gardens—oops, like Florida."[4] Governor Collins was impressed, but told him the cabinet didn't have the money; he suggested Pope try the Florida Development Commission. Dick Pope would have to figure out how to get the money out of them because at that time, the commission didn't have a fund for those sorts of expenditures.[5]

Meanwhile, as producer of *Esther Williams at Cypress Gardens*, Esther had to come up with a plotline. At some point she had seen an article about the shah of Iran's visit to Cypress Gardens, and had read that not only was he "dazzled by the place," he also took a turn in a water-ski show, zipping over the lake with a "girl on his shoulders." She decided to take the shah's story, transform him into the "Prince of Persia," and have him arrive at the Gardens with an entourage including eight wives. Since parts of the show would be filmed underwater, she wanted to make sure she had a leading man who could swim so she tapped Fernando Lamas, the former Argentine swimming champion. Plus, Esther wrote, "He was also rather Persian looking," adding that in 1960, studios didn't bother trying to be politically correct.[6]

Lamas acted like royalty too, according to Dick Pope. The actor "boiled over" when he found out that Esther had been provided a "large, luxurious dressing room." To smooth things over, Dick Pope gave him access to the Gardens' houseboat.

When filming began, the Arabian-style tents went up at the Gardens, just as they had when King Saud visited. Comic Joey Bishop played the role of a smart-aleck press agent. Like many of the stars who came to Winter Haven, Joey Bishop stayed at the Haven Hotel right across

Actor Fernando Lamas is surrounded by his harem from the 1960 television special *Esther Williams at Cypress Gardens,* filmed at the Gardens. By permission of Cypress Gardens.

Esther Williams applies her own makeup in preparation for a shoot. By permission of Cypress Gardens.

the street from Bill Bell's Hob Nob. "On the side of the building here I had a big billboard made up," said Bill, "and it said, 'Welcome Joey Bishop, You son of a gun.' I learned a lot from Pope about promoting, you see. So I put that up there, and I knew he would see it since he was staying at the hotel. I finally got in touch with him and asked him if he would come on over, and he said he would. At that time, I had a little trio here, and the place was packed and all, and I got up on stage and said, 'I'm going over to pick up Joey Bishop. Now when he comes in, everybody get up and applaud.' So I went over to the lobby and there he was, and he never said a word walking back over. We walked into the Hob Nob and everybody starts to clap and he turns around to me, and said, 'You son of a bitch. If you're selling tickets, I'll kill you.'"

The two became such good friends that Bishop made a point to come to the Hob Nob each night he was in town. "When he got ready to leave to go back to New York," said Bill, "I took him to the airport. Right before getting on the plane he said, 'On Tuesday night I'm going to be on the *Jack Paar Show*, so listen in.' So Tuesday night, Jack Paar introduces him, and Jack asked him where he's been, and he says: 'I've been down at Cypress Gardens; there's a friend of mine, Bill Bell who owns the Hob Nob. He had a little sign on the bar and it said, 'All beer is ten cents; if Joey Bishop comes in, it's ten cents more.'"[7]

Esther Williams spent one year getting ready to film the production. The show was sponsored by the United Brewers Foundation. Initially the brewers wanted Esther to play a role in the commercials as well. They wanted to sink a refrigerator into the pool and have her dive in, snag a beer, then paddle to the surface and open it. She refused. "There would be no refrigerators at the bottom of my pool," she wrote later. "For 20 years I'd made being underwater glamorous—a place for beautiful languid fanstasies, with coral fans and pearls. I wasn't about to wreck that image."[8] Although she may have been careful with that image, going so far as to cut hopeful actors from the show because she didn't like the way their faces looked underwater, there was little she could do about the commercials, which featured Hugh Downs as a spokesperson. Throughout the show the camera would segue into the black-and-white advertisements so seamlessly, one reviewer described them as "woven so tightly into the plot that when actress Irene Dunne popped up to plug the product, it suddenly seemed that Miss Williams must have an unannounced co-star."[9]

In the show itself, Esther falls for Prince Ahmad from Samal (Lamas spelled backward) and he falls for her (even though he has all those wives). In one strange scene, Esther swims

Comedian Joey Bishop and Dick Pope Sr. check out the tents set up for the show *Esther Williams at Cypress Gardens*. By permission of Cypress Gardens.

Dick Pope Sr. confers with Joey Bishop and Fernando Lamas. By permission of Cypress Gardens.

through a canal past the veiled wives, who then slide into the tea-colored water and join her in a bit of synchronized swimming. Watching, you can't help but wonder, *didn't they worry about alligators?*

The sequences filmed in the pool are pure Busby Berkeley, except they take place underwater, and except for one underwater pole dance Esther indulges herself in. Fernando was able to hold his breath and swim without making funny faces. The show earned a 52 percent share in ratings, which meant that over half the televisions in the country were tuned in to watch Esther.

"Personally," Esther said later, "I think we've brought motion picture quality to television. We took four days to shoot the show in color and I'm sorry there aren't more color TV sets to capture the real beauty of the costumes and background."[10] When a reporter visited Dick Pope after the show had aired, Pope showed him the "stacks and stacks" of reviews from the show, including one "very fat leather-bound book of clippings."

"There are four more just like that," he said.[11] Clearly, as far as Dick Pope was concerned, Cypress Gardens was the true star of the show, even though he, too, had made a cameo appearance. And that's what the *New York Times* television reviewer confirmed: "This aquatic offering . . . was a soggy piece of flotsam designed primarily to advertise the splendors of Cypress Gardens, the Florida resort where it was taped and filmed."[12] The reporter wasn't far off the mark as a *Sports Illustrated* reporter pointed out: "[Pope] feels that people ought to *pay* him to plug his product. Curiously enough, some people do." When the Esther Williams show was finished, Pope began charging a three-hundred-dollar location fee to ad agencies who wanted to use the Aquarama Pool. Not only did they have to pay, but they were required to mention Cypress Gardens in the ad. "We pay Dick Pope $50,000 a year for the privilege of publicizing his own place," one agent said.[13]

Pope also wanted potential advertisers to believe that Cypress Gardens was big enough to have two studios, so he named the one studio at Cypress Gardens "Studio B," said Rick Dantzler. When told they would have to use Studio B, they would assume there was a Studio A.[14]

By the time the 1960s rolled around, Dick Pope himself was as big an attraction as the

Gardens he had so feverishly promoted. Advertisers had already capitalized on his fame. Not only had he been photographed in the hospital wearing a Jantzen swimsuit prior to an appendectomy, he had been photographed in a Champion spark plug ad, as well as a Goodyear tire ad. Just as Malcolm had been tapped to sell Camel cigarettes back in the 1940s, Dick Pope was being tapped to sell cars. "Dick Pope's brother Malcolm was tied to the Ford Motor company through the boat racing championships," said Bob Kehoe. "He was speed king of America, and for a while in the early '50s when they rolled off a new model of Thunderbird, the third or fourth one that came off the line went to Malcolm to use to drive around and show off and use at Cypress Gardens in commercials."

"From 1960 to 1964," Bob said, "Mr. Pope got a new Lincoln Continental, and he parked it outside the entrance where people could see it and take pictures of it. Mr. Pope Sr. got an uncut sheet of ten-dollar bills. Since he always wore flamboyant clothes so people would recognize him, he'd go out front to the car, reach in his pocket, pull that sheet of money out, and dust off the windshield a little bit. You could tell he

Dick Pope Sr. made a cameo appearance in the final scene of *Esther Williams at Cypress Gardens*. By permission of Cypress Gardens.

Sylvester Denmark became a very important person in the Popes' lives. Here he is with Alberta James, the Popes' cook, circa 1950s. By permission of Julie Pope Dantzler.

was having fun. People would ooh and aah, and cameras would come up, and people would talk about him, about the Gardens. About the Continental. He'd promote everything."[15]

One person who benefitted from Dick Pope's Lincoln Continental connection was Sylvester Denmark. Sylvester started working at the Gardens in 1945. He had just gotten out of the army and was sitting on the front porch of his house in Florence Villa when Mrs. Pope showed up to visit with his wife, Annabelle, who worked as a maid at the Pope's house. "I remember just like it was yesterday," Sylvester told a reporter in 1981. "She had me over to plant roses for a few days after that and I've been here ever since. I sure had planned on taking some time off to fish and play golf before starting to work."[16]

"What tickled me about Sylvester Denmark," said Fred "Shack Man" Gaffney, who worked at the Gardens gift shop, "was that he told me he would always pick Dick Pope's cars. I didn't believe him. I wanted to buy a car, and I went over there to Jenkins in Lakeland, and he said, 'Well, Sylvester, what kind you gonna get this time?' and I said, 'I'm not Sylvester; I'm Fred.' He said, 'Oh, I thought you were Sylvester.' And I said, 'I know Sylvester. What does Sylvester do?' And he said, 'Sylvester Denmark picks out all the cars for Dick Pope.' I couldn't believe it. He picked out the Lincoln Continentals. When I came back, I told Sylvester about it. He laughed. He said, 'I know you thought I was lying.' All those cars Dick Pope would get, Sylvester would pick them out. If you had a job working at Cypress Gardens, you had it made."[17]

"Sylvester was going to be seen in those Lincolns," said Dubie Baxter. "He was a very significant cog in the Popes' life."[18] Bob Kehoe agreed: "Sylvester was a very rare person; he could paint well; he could do rough carpentry well; he was Mr. Pope's righthand handyman. If Mr. Pope wanted to take a picture of a certain bush, and horticulture couldn't get around to getting it trimmed up for him, he'd get Sylvester to trim that up for him. That night he'd have Sylvester over at his house, if he had Esther Williams or somebody, to serve drinks. He would be a butler, a chauffeur, a real handyman."[19]

Alvin Denmark, a lieutenant in the Polk County Sheriff's Department, said his father didn't just work at the Gardens, "he slept, he ate Cypress Gardens. Everything that our family benefitted from, most of it derived from my mom's and dad's employment at Cypress Gardens," he said. Every year the Popes bought new vehicles for staff cars, usually station wagons, with the Cypress Gardens seal on the side. "Dad's car they left plain," said Alvin, "and he would use it for personal and family use. This was something that the Popes gave to him." Sylvester passed that largesse on to Florence Villa. When the predominantly black school in

Sylvester Denmark worked directly with the Popes at Cypress Gardens for thirty-six years. By permission of Alvin Denmark.

Florence Villa needed a float, Sylvester would get one from the Gardens, then pull it in the parade. "Dad was very special to the Popes, and the Popes were very special to him and to our family. They called him Sylvester, and I can hear Mr. Pope call him Sylvester this and Sylvester that and Sylvester, Sylvester, Sylvester. And at times they had something special they wanted looking into, and he'd be in Mr. Pope's office, and Mr. Pope would be picking his brain, 'Sylvester, what do you think about this?'"[20]

Sylvester's status as a jack-of-all-trades wasn't just limited to work. "I was the probably the first black in Polk County that learned to ski," Sylvester told a reporter. "That was in the 50s and the skiers in the show taught me. I got up first time. Mr. Pope told me I'd have been a good barefooter because I have such big feet." Sylvester skied with King Hussein, had a bit part as a chauffeur in the movie *Easy to Love,* and played golf with Dick Pope.[21] "Mr. Pope Sr. was an amateur Florida golf champion for several years," said Bob Kehoe. "Lots of times they would go out and play a round, and Sylvester was a real good golfer, and people would come from miles around to play golf with him."[22]

Toward the end of Sylvester's thirty-six-year stint at the Gardens, his main job was to simply be his boss's companion; he'd fix breakfast, then they'd head over to the Gardens in the Popes' Mercedes, swapping it for a golf cart. They'd tool around the Gardens talking about old times. "This guy is monumental," Dick Pope told a reporter in 1981. "He has friends all over the world. When I hear from my friends, they want to know how Sylvester's doing."

"We act like father and son," said Sylvester. "We laugh and we talk; there's never been a hard word between us." When asked to comment, Dick Pope simply said, "Hell, yes."[23]

Pope had become such a monumental figure himself that it was a problem for him at times. In June 1960, the Polk County Commission met with a representative of the Florida Bureau of Public Roads to get the state to include an interchange on a newly constructed section of Interstate Highway 4 that would feed travelers onto a proposed 2.5-mile road that would take them into Winter Haven. Interstate 4 was part of "the greatest era of highway construction in the history of Florida." And it was a direct result of the growing industry of tourism. In 1960, the Florida Development Commission estimated that eight out of ten tourists arrived in Florida in their automobiles. This new highway concerned Dick Pope because it would funnel traffic away from the Gardens. He printed up pamphlets that read "We have two years to live."[24] Much to the consternation of county engineers, reporters kept referring to the 2.5-mile section as "Dick Pope Road" because of his efforts to get the interchange approved. People thought Cypress Gardens was funding the project. Despite the engineers' frustration, the Polk County commissioners voted to complete the "Dick Pope Road"

Dick Pope Sr. lobbied hard to get a Winter Haven spur placed on Interstate Highway 4. Circa 1960. By permission of Cypress Gardens.

Cornelia Ellis arrived at Cypress Gardens in 1961 and became the star of the ski show before marrying John Snively III. After that marriage ended, she married Alabama governor George Wallace. Circa 1962. By permission of Cypress Gardens.

that would connect with the I-4 exchange so that tourists could get to the Gardens.[25]

One person who wasn't upset at naming things after Dick Pope was Florida governor Leroy Collins. On November 25, 1960, Governor Collins proclaimed the following Tuesday would be "Dick Pope Day" in Florida in recognition for his "'service under the sun' promoting the state of Florida as well as his own tourist attraction."[26] It was about time. After all, Florida had been benefitting from his advertising budget for years. Dick Pope had no problem touting his competitors in central Florida because he knew tourists were more likely to visit the region if they could see several attractions instead of just one. He posted a map in the Cypress Gardens gift shop that showed the mileage to places like Parrot Jungle and Monkey Jungle. He had published over 4 million postcards and brochures that also included nearby Bok Tower. And he had "invented a Florida state of mind . . . a place populated by almost naked girls, millionaires, surfboard riders, tarpons fishermen and Orange Queens."[27]

One of those "almost naked girls" was Cornelia Ellis, who later married Alabama governor George Wallace, even though her aunt Ruby Folsom, sister to Big Jim Folsom, Wallace's predecessor, told her "Shoooot, honey, he ain't even titty high."[28] But in 1961, taking her mother's place in a March of Dimes fund-raiser, Cornelia met Mrs. Anna Sawyer, one of Julie Pope's sisters. They got into a conversation about waterskiing—Cornelia had taught herself to ski with instructions from a comic book she'd ordered from the American Waterskiing Association—and before Cornelia left, Mrs. Sawyer decided to make a call to Cypress Gardens to see if they needed any skiers.

Within days, Cornelia got an application in the mail from Cypress Gardens. She sent it in along with a few photographs, and before she knew it she was headed to Winter Haven. She boarded at the home of Mrs. Laura Tucker with six other Aqua Maids, and began skiing at the Gardens under the tutelage of Simon Khoury, director of the ski show. Like many of the Aqua Maids, she did double duty as a southern belle. She took her role so seriously that she made her own dress out of pink organdy, trimmed with pink lace. She even made a pair of matching gloves and found herself a purse, a parasol, and a hat to match. The photographers were so impressed that they asked her if they could keep the dress for promotions. As for her ski career, she was soon the "water-ballet queen," performing the backward swan as the "star act."[29]

Dubie Baxter remembered Cornelia, not just as an Aqua Maid but as a folksinger: "She used to bring her guitar, and she sang with Roy Acuff, the Smoky Mountain Boys. I remember the song she sang that I liked best, 'Black Girl.' She'd play her guitar and sing that song."[30] Her ski career came to an end when she attempted to learn to barefoot without first learning how to fall. She injured her neck and was advised to give up the sport. Luckily, by then she had already met and married her first husband, citrus heir John Snively III.

In 1963, Cypress Gardens and the Grand Canyon tied as the number-one tourist attraction in the country in a travel editors' vote. Just the year before, Dick Pope Jr. had been promoted to president of the Gardens, while Pope Sr. remained in the position of chairman of the board. It seems the transition took a while. Way back in 1954, a reporter noted that "Pretty soon now Dick Jr. will be out of the marines and Dick Sr. plans to turn the management over to his boy, many times water ski champion and inventor of barefoot water skiing." The reporter asked Julie Pope whether Pope Sr. would be able to relinquish control

Velma Breetz sells film to a customer in the Cypress Garden Film Shop located in a corner of the main gift shop. Cypress Gardens was eventually known as the "largest single retail seller of Kodak film in the USA." Throughout the 1950s and 1960s, signs were placed in the Gardens pointing to great picture locations. By permission of Cypress Gardens.

of the Gardens: "Do you think Dick can really keep hands off?"

"Yes," Julie replied, "because we are going around the world next year."[31] The trip must have worked. By the time 1962 rolled around, Pope Sr. seemed settled in his position as CEO. He planned to devote his energy to promoting Florida tourism and development. However, nothing could separate him from the Gardens, so when *Saturday Evening Post* reporter Roy Bongartz showed up to do a piece on the Gardens, the "aquatic Barnum" was clearly the star.

As Bongartz described it in "Superswamp: Florida's Eighteen-Karat Illusion," the trip to Cypress Gardens was well worth it. Cypress Gardens tourists would park in the "award winning Palm Bowl parking lot," deposit their pets in the Mut-tel, and enter a "phony jungle" with "Confederate roses, two-headed palms and monkey puzzle trees." They could buy "seashell handbags, alligator head key chains, stuffed alligators, alligators with conch shells, Cypress Gardens picture towels and Cypress Gardens T-shirts with a bathing beauty whose eyes move."[32] Mimi Pope, Dick's sister-in-law, ran the gift shop. Fred "Shack Man" Gaffney worked at the Gardens for forty-three years, going to work in the dark and getting off in the dark after cleaning the gift shop to earn overtime pay. At eighty, he recalled seeing Esther Williams and other stars when they passed through the Gardens. "They called me Shack Man," he explained, "because when I got out of the army I opened a chicken shack. When I first started to working out there for Mimi Pope, I was working on the orange juice stand, and then after years went along I stopped doing that and started delivering stock to the stock room. Mimi Pope and Julie Pope owned the gift shops, and they worked about thirty people. There were lots of African Americans working there then. That's the only job I ever had. If you had a job working at Cypress Gardens, you were doing good. Otherwise you'd be picking fruit. They didn't pay more than fruit picking, but the job at Cypress Gardens was year round."

"Joe Denmark worked with me doing the same thing I did for about twenty years before he left. We were the only two African Americans working in the gift shop. They didn't have any blacks working in there selling stuff. Selling clothes, film, postcards—that was mostly white girls."[33]

In those days, tourists could get into the Gardens for free if they remembered to bring at least ten labels off cans of Cypress Gardens fruit grown and packaged by Snively Groves.

Tourists were also, wrote Bongartz, "snared into this very small, but very busy bog by a 63 year old talkative troll named Dick Pope, inventor of Cypress Gardens." Despite the clever name-calling, the reporter was obviously taken with his subject, gushing over Pope's success at turning a "patch of muckland into a U.S. tourist shrine." One of those tourists happened to be John F. Kennedy, Pope confided to the reporter. "Jack used to fly up here from Palm Beach . . . and spend the weekend with us. Imagine how I felt when Jack was elected President and we didn't have a single picture of him at the Gardens." Pope himself posed for pictures for the magazine, playing a grand piano attached to a platform towed by a boat, while a skier dressed in a tutu skied backward next to him. When they hit a rogue wave, the whole lot crashed into the water. Victor Borge, the pianist, was supposed to have done the stunt, but his fear of water kept him from following through.[34]

Willa McGuire Cook was wearing the tutu that day. Asked if she remembered the shoot, she replied: "Only too well. I thought, 'Oh, my lord, he's lost it this time. I mean, he's done everything, and this is the living end.' And he's

Fred "Shack Man" Gaffney worked at the Gardens for forty-three years; here he is pictured with the gift shop staff. By permission of Fred Gaffney.

Left: Tourists could get into the Gardens free in the 1960s if they brought in labels from the Cypress Gardens fruit packaged by Snively Groves. By permission of Cypress Gardens.

Above: Dick Pope Sr. and Willa McGuire Cook staged this photo shoot for the *Saturday Evening Post* in 1963. Photo by Red McGuire. By permission of Cypress Gardens.

got them shooting pictures of him on this barge pretending to play the piano, which was gutted, and then he said, 'Willa, come on, I want you to ski beside me,' and I thought, 'Oh come on . . .' So I went out with my tutu and my crown, and I did the ballet as he supposedly played the piano, and what do you know? That was one of the key photographs that they used for decades."[35]

Red McGuire, Willa's first husband, shot the photo. "It was very easy," he said. "Basically, you just put the camera on the arm of that picture boat, and move along beside it, shooting away. When you're ready to quit is when it dies—as long as you're pulling it, it stays up. When they backed off on the boat, that's when it died."[36] The caption beneath the capsizing piano read, "No one was hurt, but the unprecedented accident predictably got the Gardens a splash in the paper."

Dick Pope was legendary for not getting frazzled about accidents. Rick Dantzler said one time a camera crew was filming a movie out on Lake Eloise and somebody dropped a five-thousand-dollar Bell and Howell movie camera into the lake. "I was told that would be like a $75,000 camera today," he said. "But instead of getting mad and firing the poor guy who did it, who was feeling bad enough already, Mr. Pope had them fish the camera out, and then they got another camera, and they had the guy drop the ruined camera into the lake again. They filmed that and worked that into the movie. That became part of the shoot."[37]

"Once in a while we'd have something go wrong, something kind of bad," said Bob Kehoe, "and he'd just think about it a little while and come up with a way to utilize it. A minor fire broke out one time in one of our admin buildings, and it got put out early on, but he immediately put out a press release that said we were still open, the flowers weren't damaged, the ski shows were going on, the world was lovely, bring your camera. Immediately, before anybody could say, 'you have a problem.'"[38]

Not even having hot coffee and pie dumped in his lap could faze him. Dubie Baxter said his brother told him that the Popes had come into the restaurant one day and "ordered peach shortcakes, pecan pies, whipped cream, orange juices, and coffee all around. My brother was nervous as hell, and he takes something off one of the trays, and the whole thing tips over, and the entire coffee, whipped cream, pecan pie, peach shortcake went into Mr. Pope's lap. What did Mr. Pope do? He wouldn't have dared embarrass anyone, never in his life. He just walked to the back, changed clothes and came back out and sat down, and my brother brought new stuff, and he set the tray down and then passed it out."[39]

"Fortunately," wrote William Furlong in "Babes in a Swampland," another love letter to Dick Pope along the lines of Roy Bongartz's "Superswamp," "[Dick Pope] has a gift for turning a disaster into cash, and the one has offset the other in a career liberally sprinkled with hard times." He pointed out the serendipitous turn of events in Pope's life that reporters had trotted out for years: the Florida boom, the crash, the marriage to Julie, the job in New York, the return to Florida, the swamp, the WPA story, the frozen flame vine that gave birth to the southern belles, the soldiers who arrived to see the ski show when there wasn't a ski show. And through it all, Furlong wrote, curiously twisting Pope's optimism into a form of pessimism that begot optimism, "Dick Pope has been able to maintain the melancholy stigmata of the professional promoter: the conviction, though nobody understands it but himself, that sunshine is merely a portent of a total eclipse . . . that at the foot of every rainbow is a pot of burning rubbish."

Furlong couldn't seem to get a fix on Pope—maybe it was Pope's unsettling habit of stooping to pick up bits of paper, or skipping so that they would be in step when they walked. He described Pope as "the apotheosis of press agentry . . . he has the looks of John L. Lewis, the taste of William Randolph Hearst and the restraint of Attila on the March." Later, as Pope sat behind his desk, he looked like "a pouty child adrift on a sea of paper," and when they walked outside and passed a couple of skiers, he became a "*pater familias* laced lightly with Groucho Marx." When Pope is asked by a tourist, "Do you mind if we just sort of 'steal' a cutting to take home with us?" he "beams with all the friendliness of a Jimmy Hoffa on good behavior at an executive Christmas party." Clearly, the writer was overwhelmed by the mercurial little man who handed out cards that read, "Where there's Life, there's Pope." But in the end, he got it: "And behind everybody is the monumental figure of Dick Pope, the man who used a frontal assault to make Cypress Gardens the most successful swamp in America."

The swamp was grossing about $2.5 million by the early 1960s, nearly two bucks a piece for each of the 1.5 million tourists who, as Furlong wrote, "show up each year, their car bumpers thick with stickers, their minds numbed by Disneylands, Storylands, Freedomlands, and Authentic Bad Indian lands, [and] make no complaint about coming all the way to Winter Haven to look at a mock-up for advertising backdrops. They may even think it's real."[40]

Not all the tourists who came to Cypress Gardens were as unsophisticated as Furlong made them out to be. As Dubie Baxter pointed out, some of the Gardens visitors were quite sophisticated: "I spoke probably the best English of any of the boat drivers, which doesn't say much, but in Polk County, if you weren't driving electric boats or skiing, you were working at the ski factory making skis, and you didn't have to have a high school diploma or anything. But I also spoke a little Spanish, because I'd been to military school and had a Venezuelan roommate. So they would call me whenever a Spanish celebrity came through. Or anyone who spoke proper English." The Duke and Duchess of Windsor always made it a point to stop in at the Gardens when they visited Florida. So when they showed up, Dubie was expected to be their guide: "Chuck, the little bandy-legged World War II vet who ran the electric boats, said, 'Dubie, we got a boat for ya.' And of course the duke and duchess got a private boat, and they sat in the middle, and they were very polite, and they asked questions because they were used to English gardens, and now we have a tropical garden."[41]

More than any other royal who visited Cypress Gardens, King Hussein of Jordan loved the roadside attraction best. "I had a relationship with His Majesty King Hussein since the '60s from Lebanon; we used to race cars together," said Simon Khoury, who started working at the Gardens in 1953.[42]

King Hussein first came to the Gardens in 1964, just days after meeting with President Johnson in Washington to discuss Israel's plan to siphon water off the Jordan River, as well as to reassert Jordan's need for U.S. military aid.[43] Jim Ponce, manager of the Colony Hotel in Palm Beach in the 1950s and 1960s, wrote that he remembered when King Hussein decided he needed to take water-ski lessons at Cypress Gardens: "It was 7 a.m. on a Sunday when I received a phone call from Washington D.C. The King required a bathing suit and cash to be able to attend his water-skiing lesson." Ponce had to get the manager of Saks on Worth Avenue to open the store so the king's assistants could pick out a swimsuit for him—they couldn't decide, so they took two whole racks.[44]

The king and his entourage landed in Bartow and headed over to Cypress Gardens, where they sat on the patio and watched a special ski show with "Jordanian accents." After the ski show, the

King Hussein (*left*), Dick Pope Sr., Dick Pope Jr., Julie Pope, and Frances Pope enjoy a moment with Corky the Clown at a ski show. By permission of Cypress Gardens.

king and his crew headed over to the Aquarama to watch the high-diving act. He refused to sit in the "special chair" provided for him, insisting it be given to Dick Pope since it was Pope's sixty-fourth birthday. He even joined in when everyone sang "Happy Birthday" to Dick Pope. After the show, the king got his first ski lesson from Dick Pope Jr. on Lake Eloise.[45]

That trip was just the beginning of a long-term relationship Cypress Gardens had with King Hussein. "He got hooked on waterskiing," said Simon, "and then he pulled all the water-skiing back to Jordan, and we put Aqaba on the map. We did twenty-nine or thirty shows here—the last one was four or five years ago. We might do one this year."[46]

Mark Voisard, a Cypress Gardens skier and kite flyer, recalled King Hussein's love of the sport: "They had us over every year at his birthday in November, and he was an awesome guy. King Hussein personally took us out on his yacht; he partied with us. I met the Empress Farah, the shah of Iran's wife. We taught her son how to ski. They'd take us on trips into the desert, a place called Wadi Rum and to Petra, which was the place where *Indiana Jones* was filmed."[47]

By the late 1960s, as Simon Khoury pointed out, the Gulf of Aqaba was the "center of water sports" in Jordan, a strip of beach lined with palms on the northeast coast of the Red Sea. Until 1967 or so the beach was all but inaccessible, a problem the king rectified by building a 200-mile-long superhighway from Amman to Aqaba allowing travelers to make the drive in just under five hours, rather than the sixteen it took before. "Water skiing has become so popular," King Hussein told a reporter, "that the Cypress Gardens ski team has come here from Florida twice to put on exhibitions that attracted attention throughout the Middle East."[48]

Richard Johnson, who skied and flew kites at the Gardens from 1962 to 1969, also became friends with the king. "He used to come over a couple of times a year. I ended up going to Jordan six different times, doing water-ski shows and vacationing with him. A lot of times he'd come flying in with one of his big military helicopters, and we'd take one of my hang gliders, and we'd strap it onto the side of the helicopter onto the strut and go up into the hills of the Jordan Valley and hunt for a good cliff to foot-launch off, and he'd come and pick me up so I wouldn't have to walk back up. It was pretty awesome. When I first went there, Bethlehem and Jerusalem were occupied by Jordan so we got to tour through Bethlehem and Jerusalem, and a lot of areas they wouldn't normally let tourists. We skied in the Gulf of Aqaba. Simon was from Beirut, Lebanon, and he stayed in Jordan a lot because of skiing in the Gulf of Aqaba on the Red Sea. That was a beautiful beach, somewhat choppy water. He brought one of the big helicopters down to the Gulf of Aqaba; he and I jumped in that—he's a great pilot also—and we'd lower this cable down on an electric winch and hook up a ski rope to it and pull the gals up the Gulf. That was quite a sight."[49]

Lynn Novakofski said the king passed on his love of Cypress Gardens to his son Prince Abdullah, now King Abdullah. But what was most interesting to Lynn was finding himself hanging out with someone who was "one of the key players in international politics. One of my memories is that one year I was there, several of King Hussein's friends were there. Juan Carlos of Spain was there, somebody from Egypt, and one of the entourage was this tall guy with a mustache. We all shook hands, and I've always felt that was King Hussein of Iraq, but I've never found out for sure. But at the time in the 1980s, Hussein of Iraq was a friend of Hussein of Jordan. When I was there a couple of times, a lot of military equipment was going through Jordan up to Iraq. At the time, the United States was

Richard Johnson taught King Hussein how to fly one of the Cypress Gardens kites that Johnson built himself, circa 1960s. By permission of Cypress Gardens.

helping supply that equipment, and Hussein of Iraq was our friend."[50]

That wasn't the only time the skiers from Winter Haven found themselves in the midst of world-class politics. Once when the skiers were in Aqaba helping the king to put on a "Florida-type water carnival," a couple of Israeli pilots flew in low to check the festivities out, then disappeared before the Jordanian air force could chase them away.[51]

Elvis Sighting

A 1965 issue of the *Cypress Gardens News Real* mentioned two notable stories. One was that "there are strong possibilities that Joe Pasternak of MGM studio may bring Elvis to the Gardens to film a new musical," and the other was that O.J., a frog fed on Florida orange juice, traveled to California to compete in the Calaveras County Frog Jumping Contest. The frog lost.[52] And, as it turned out, Elvis never arrived at Cypress Gardens to make his musical. Dick Pope explained to a reporter why he dissed the King: "I didn't make a picture because I didn't like him. Ed Sullivan was one of my very close friends. When he ran Elvis, remember he ran the shot from here up? (motions to waistline.) I had a chance to get

At one point it was rumored that Elvis was going to make a film at Cypress Gardens, but it never came to be. By permission of Cypress Gardens.

Elvis here, and his manager is one of my very close friends. I just wasn't going to do it."[53]

The Gardens does have a photograph of a swimsuit-clad Elvis on water skis, and not just from the waist up. But even with the photographic evidence, the visit itself has taken on the aura of one of those "Elvis sightings" that became popular after the King's death. Bob Kehoe said that even though Colonel Parker and Dick Pope were friends, and even though he's sure Elvis had been invited, he couldn't swear that Elvis had actually come to the Gardens.[54]

The real headliner of 1965 was that Dick Pope was appointed president of the Florida World's Fair Authority by Governor Haydon Burns, who phoned him saying, "Something must be done to improve the Florida exhibit." The previous year had been a dismal one, but Pope was going to change that. The fair would be another of his public-relations breakthroughs. The Fair Authority considered New York the "biggest center of tourism in the world; the hub of newspaper syndicates, television, radio networks, magazine publication, as well as center of distribution for Florida's citrus crop." Dick Pope was right at home. Working with Governor Burns and Robert Moses, head of the World's Fair, he got the State of Florida to invest $1 million, and he negotiated

Florida governor Haydon Burns appointed Dick Pope Sr. to head the Florida World's Fair Authority, 1965. By permission of Cypress Gardens.

a takeover of the Billy Rose Aquacade Amphitheater, which was right next to the Florida Building.

The Billy Rose Aquacade had been the center attraction of the 1939 World's Fair—it featured synchronized swimmers, high divers, and roller skaters—but in 1964 it had housed an expensive and failing exhibit that had been shut down. Pope got the New York World's Fair Authority to refurbish the Aquacade by building an oval-shaped "water track, 35 feet wide and four feet deep" around the Aquacade pool. It would cost $300,000 and would be the first of its kind.

In addition to building the track, the World's Fair Authority let Florida lease the building for free. Pope hired Tommy Bartlett and Dick Rowe of Silver Springs to stage the *Florida Citrus Ski Show* using Cypress Gardens' champion skiers, including Barbara Cooper Clack, five-time U.S. ski jump champion, and national champions Buster MacCalla and Joker Osborne. "Everything in water skiing except for the kite act will be on the program," Dick Rowe said. One of the headliners was the jumping boats from the film *This Is Cinerama*. Miami Seaquarium provided a porpoise show—the highlight came when the porpoise tossed plastic oranges into the audience.[55]

Pope also commissioned musician Gram Parsons and the Shilos to write a song for the fair to promote "inland surfing" at the Gardens. Parsons was the grandson of John Snively, the citrus pioneer who'd helped Dick Pope start the Gardens. After his father, Coon Dog Parsons, killed himself in 1958, Gram moved to Winter Haven to live with his mother, Avis. He grew up around the Gardens, and at age thirteen even had a girlfriend who worked as a southern belle. According to his biographer, Ben Fong-Torres, Parsons and the belle used to sit on one of the benches in the Gardens and make out in full view of the tourists. Julie would not have been amused. For the fair, Parsons came up with "Surfinanny," a remake of "Gonna Raise a Ruckus Tonight." Pope sent the band to Chicago to make a recording, and although the song wasn't actually used at the fair, it became the unofficial Cypress Gardens theme song.[56]

Pope's greatest innovation, though, was simply to make the exhibition entirely free to the public. "We're aiming at lines longer than those at Ford and General Motors," Pope said. "We'll be the biggest hit of the Fair." He wrote as much in a note to the City of New York, as Florida Fair Authority president:

"Congratulations, New York, from the state that's going all out to become the heart of the Fair."

And he was right. The Florida Exhibit drew double the number of spectators as it had the previous year—so many that the asphalt pavement surrounding the Florida Building sank eleven inches into the ground. Nine thousand spectators could take their seats in the amphitheater where they could "make pictures and movies of the fast moving show with the Florida orange grove background."[57] The famous photographer Weegee was on hand at the Florida Pavilion snapping kaleidoscopic images of the skiers.

In December 1965, decked out in a Santa Claus suit, Dick Pope headed to Tallahassee, Florida's state capital, to present a giant check for $206,917 to Governor Burns. This check represented the money the exhibit earned after starting off with a deficit.[58] There was more to come. "A white elephant was turned into the most single [*sic*] productive promotional program for the state," Governor Burns told a reporter in 1966, when he was presented another installment check for $140,000 from the Florida World's Fair Authority.[59]

Coincidentally, while Dick Pope was in New York promoting Florida, someone had been sneaking around the state, buying up more than 26,000 acres of land in southeast Orlando. On November 15, 1965, just months after Pope's big splash at the World's Fair, Governor Burns held a press conference in Orlando to reveal the mystery buyer. "This is the most significant day in the history of Florida," Burns said in introducing the culprits, Walt Disney and his brother Roy. "We decided on Florida because of its year-round mild climate and the fact that it already has a large tourist volume," the Disney brothers told reporters. The purchase of so much land was necessary, Walt Disney said, in order to prevent the East Coast Disneyland from being tainted by "an influx of honkytonk attractions and other undesirable businesses," and he estimated it would "cost $100 million to get the show on the road." Because it would take at least four thousand employees to run the project, Disney said he was planning to construct a couple of communities for the workers—one would be called "Yesterday," and it would feature some of the "better things of the past," and the other would be called "Tomorrow," the "city of the future." Disney explained that he didn't want to simply replicate Disneyland: "We want this to be a family-style entertainment, as Disneyland in California is. It will not merely be a copy of what we have there,

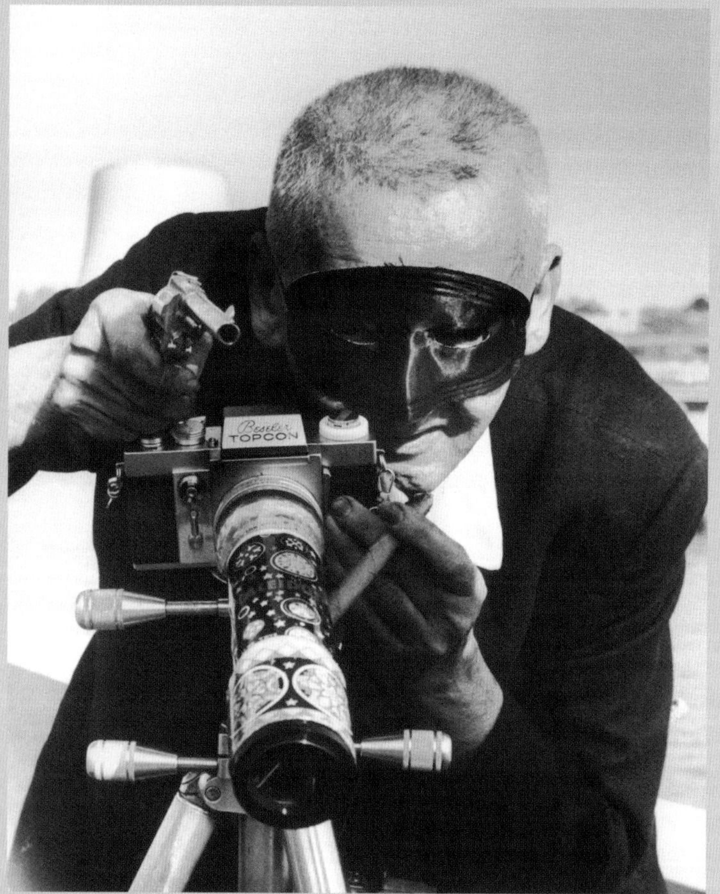

Above: Famous photographer Weegee (Arthur Fellig), shown here brandishing a cigar and a pistol, made a series of kaleidoscopic photos of the Cypress Gardens skiers at the 1965 World's Fair in New York, where this photo was taken on May 24, 1965. By permission of Bettman/CORBIS.

Right: Weegee made this kaleidoscopic photo of the skiers at the Florida Pavilion at the World's Fair in New York, 1965. By permission of Cypress Gardens.

although we may bring to Florida some of the things that have proved to be of great interest to our visitors in California. Of course we have to make money to stay alive, but making money is the furthest from our thoughts in this new enterprise. I mean it. We want it to be a labor of love."

Governor Burns said he expected the new attraction—coupled with an information center to be constructed at Cape Kennedy—to bring about a 50 to 100 percent increase in tourists as well as a huge increase in tax revenues.[60] Dick Pope responded to the news by putting "Disney Heads" on himself and his staff. Literally. Wearing a Donald Duck head above his usual flowered suit, and surrounded by staffers disguised as the Three Little Pigs, a rabbit and a couple of mice, he presided over a meeting, "Disney Style." The *Cypress Gardens News Real* explained Pope's reaction to Disney beneath the photo:

> Disneyland of the South, Disneyland East, or Walt Disney's City of Tomorrow—no matter what it's called, it's being hailed as the biggest and best thing that's ever happened to Florida. When Governor Haydon Burns announced that Walt Disney was the "mystery buyer" and planned to develop a greater attraction than Disneyland on 30,000 acres of land in Orange and Osceola, no one was more enthusiastic than Dick Pope. He said that he was confident that anything Disney builds will be good and will attract millions of people to the state. Mr. Pope also joined with other officials of the various Florida attractions to predict that with the new Disneyland venture in Florida to draw crowds, all other attractions in the state would benefit attendancewise.[61]

At a news conference in 1965, Florida governor Haydon Burns revealed the "mystery buyers" who had been sneaking around the Orlando area: Walt and Roy Disney. Courtesy of the State Archives of Florida.

Dick Pope Sr. did not waste any time getting into the spirit of Disney; wearing a Donald Duck head, he presides over a meeting at Cypress Gardens, circa 1960s. By permission of Cypress Gardens.

Seemingly in response to the news of the coming of Disney, in a sort of preemptive attack, the *Lakeland Ledger* saw fit to catalogue Polk County's charms in an article titled "From Eskimos to Headhunters, All Visit Polk's Attractions." In addition to the headhunters and Eskimos cited in the title (apparently an Eskimo named Puppygitwok-Koopauk visited the Gardens at one point. 'Water shoeing much fun," he said after a stint on skis), the article mentioned celebrities Esther Williams, Arnold Palmer, and Jimmy Dean. "Two million people visit here every year? Why?" the article asked, then answered: "Maybe they like warm weather, friendly people and a relaxing atmosphere. Maybe they crave good fishing or a tough game of shuffleboard." A tough game of shuffleboard? Then the article cited the main reason people come to Polk County: the large number of attractions in the area, including the "top tourist getter in the state," Cypress Gardens. Then there's the orange-painted Florida Citrus Showcase Dome, Slocum Gardens, Taylor's Citrus Candy Factory, the Singing Tower, the Black Hills Passion Play, Chalet Suzanne, the Phosphate Museum, and Frostproof, where "the sun shines 360 days or more per year." That's pretty incredible, when you consider there are only 365 days in a year. "And," the article ends, "Walt Disney's proposed 'world of tomorrow' is only 35 miles from Winter Haven."[62]

Over in Marion County, Lamar Mitchell, president of Rainbow Springs, was taking his own preemptive action: he announced a multimillion-dollar makeover at the attraction that would include a monorail with leaf-shaped carriers, a Seminole village, a quarter horse farm, a bird sanctuary, and a two-hundred-room hotel. Asked if Rainbow Springs would become another "monument to crass commercialism," Mitchell said: "No! An emphatic no. Every effort will be made to prevent a commercial appearance. We will enhance nature where we can and protect her in any case."[63]

Cypress Gardens was far from feeling the effects of Disney in February 1967—so far in fact, that along with Silver Springs, Weeki Wachee, Marineland, and Busch Gardens, Dick Pope signed a proclamation that read:

> Be It Known That . . . THE STATE OF FLORIDA ROLLS OUT THE ORANGE CARPET AND EXTENDS A WELCOME AS WARM AS THE FLORIDA SUN TO THE DISNEY ORGANIZATION. . . . Hurrah! for Disney World. We believe you're the greatest thing that's happened to Florida since Sunshine.[64]

Not only had the Gardens been attracting over 1 million visitors a year up to 1967, they were about to host the most popular show on television.[65] The *Mike Douglas Show* came to Cypress Gardens at the behest of the Florida Citrus Commission, the Cypress Gardens Association, and the Florida Development Commission. All three supplied funds to foot the bill for transporting the show from Philadelphia. It would be the first time the show was filmed in color, and it would be the first time an entire week's worth of shows were filmed outdoors.[66]

The crew was supposed to stay at the recently built Cypress Gardens Sheraton. Neither Dick Pope nor Cypress Gardens were financially tied to the hotel, although Dick Pope said he had been involved with the project for three years. "I'm terribly interested in making Polk County a resort area, not just a drive-in, drive-out area for tourists," he told a reporter, "but I have no interest in the hotel other than that." Malcolm Pope, Dick's half brother, was one of the stockholders, along with Bill Rutland and John Snively Jr.[67]

However, the hotel wasn't quite finished when Douglas and his crew arrived. "I remember when the hotel opened," said Brenda Mitchell, a former skier and belle. "It was supposed to have been finished way before, and Mike Douglas was coming with all these people, and Mrs. Pope said, 'I don't know what we're going to do, where we're going to put these people.' And I said, 'Is the water on over there?' and she said, 'Yes, but we don't have a certificate of occupancy.' So she said, 'We're going to Belk's,' and we bought dozens of sheets and towels, and she's throwing them in the basket, and she's getting pillows." Certificate of occupancy be damned; Mrs. Pope was going to see that her guests had a place to stay.

These guests included comedienne Totie Fields, Joey Heatherton, Muhammad Ali, and Dumbo the Elephant of the Clyde Beatty–Cole Brothers Circus. Dumbo was painted grapefruit

The famous talk-show host Mike Douglas brought his show to Cypress Gardens in 1967 and took a ride on Dumbo. By permission of Cypress Gardens.

Muhammad Ali sparred with Mike Douglas then visited the Florence Villa neighborhood in Winter Haven. By permission of Cypress Gardens.

yellow for her star turn drinking orange juice given to her by former Citrus Queen Pat Westphal.

Van Johnson, who had starred in *Easy to Love* at the Gardens back in 1953, was Douglas's co-host. Brenda remembered skiing around the lake in the actor's arms for a live shot. "Well, normally you would step a certain way, then throw your leg over the guy's arm and he would scoop you up—and here you are a babe in arms. Of course, he had no idea how to do this—I had to wiggle my way in. We practiced and everything was fine, and when we came around, some drivers in boats, trying to get away quickly, created huge wakes. So he said, 'so and so people, blankety blankety blank.' I'd never heard words like that. Then he realized we were in camera range, so he began smiling and grinning."[68]

Bob Kehoe remembered walking down into the Gardens to watch Muhammad Ali spar in the ring with Mike Douglas. "Muhammad Ali looked huge—he was a good-size fellow, and was really a gracious person. Well, of course, we paired him up with Sylvester. I was in Mr. Pope's office, and Sylvester comes in and says, 'I hope you don't mind Mr. Pope, but Muhammad Ali called the airport and booked another flight two hours later, and I'm going to take him down to Florence Villa and introduce him to some people that want to meet him.' And he took Muhammad Ali down to Florence Villa, and they walked the streets and Sylvester, who knew everybody, introduced Muhammad Ali around down there. Unbelievable."[69]

Not long after the Mike Douglas show packed up and left, Dick Pope was faced with the devastating news that his brother Malcolm was dead, apparently from a self-inflicted gunshot. The newspaper reported that Malcolm was at his bar, the Cloud Nine Nightspot, when he called the manager of his orange groves and asked him to come over. After speaking with him for a few minutes, Malcolm supposedly walked into the alley behind Cloud Nine and shot himself. Dick and Julie Pope were in New York at the time, about to fly to London for the Chelsea Flower Show. They came home immediately. Malcolm's wife, Mimi, was convinced that he had been murdered because he was an undercover FBI agent "investigating 'communist infiltration of the citrus and phosphate industries in the Tampa Bay Area.'" To corroborate this story, Sharon Rehling, Malcolm's former assistant, brought forth a letter she said had been sent to FBI Director J. Edgar Hoover a couple of days before Malcolm's death. The letter essentially informed Hoover that Malcolm was ending his twelve-year association with the FBI. No one at the FBI would comment.[70]

To this day, the family is unsure of what actually transpired, but they are fairly sure Malcolm would have never committed suicide. He was not a despondent man and, in fact, had a lifetime of success behind him. "Supposedly he had been a friend of Mel Purvis," said Margaret Chase Parry, "an FBI agent. Melvin Purvis also died of 'suicide' by gunshot."

Purvis, also known as "Little Mel," is the FBI special agent best remembered not only for tracking down Pretty Boy Floyd and Baby Face Nelson, but also for taking down John Dillinger. "When Mel Purvis was down in Miami," said Margaret, "Uncle Malcolm was gone during all that time. I think Aunt Mimi fully believed that Purvis was connected with the CIA or the FBI and that Uncle Malcolm was too. Whether it was suicide or not, I don't know." She added another thought: "He was vibrant. The odd thing was he was killed with a Luger that wasn't his, apparently; he was shot on the left side, and he was right-handed. What happened was when the coroner came—he took the Luger over to Aunt Mimi's and stuck it in a holster and said, 'yep, it was suicide.' That was a horrible time."[71]

Six months after Malcolm's death, attorney Francis Whitehair was able to persuade the court to rehear the case. Deputy Buddy Crews told the court that no fingerprints were found on the gun, and no traces of gunpowder were found on Malcolm's hands. The judge ruled that the case be reopened, stating: "It is established that death occurred by external means and that, at this

Johnny Carson filmed his first color show and his only "special" away from the studio at Cypress Gardens in 1968. Author's collection.

time, the person who fired the fatal shot is unknown."[72] The case remains unsolved.

As with any form of entertainment, the show must go on no matter what happens, and in the Gardens' case, the upcoming show was quite big. Apparently, spurred by the success of the shows Mike Douglas taped at Cypress Gardens, Johnny Carson decided he, too, would film an outdoor show at the attraction. *Johnny Carson Discovers Cypress Gardens* would be the star's first color show, and, as it turned out, his only "special" away from the studio. Carson told reporters he was excited about coming down to the Gardens and said he planned to do all his own stunts. He meant it.

According to *Ski News,* just minutes after Carson arrived in Winter Haven he dove into the water, literally, then shimmied onto a rocking chair attached to a water toboggan. With the camera crew following him on the *Miss Cover Girl* 5 photo boat, he took hold of a microphone and introduced the Cypress Gardens skiers as they glided past him. That particular segment of the show took over an hour and nearly 26 miles of skiing to film.[73]

Carson was making television history, and not just because he was sitting on a floating rocking chair. The shots were made with a hand-held

Norelco color camera being used for the first time. The cameraman, and the rest of the twenty-five-member crew, were able to film Carson's every move from the deck of the *Miss Cover Girl 5*, a brand-new 41-foot catamaran photo boat developed just for Cypress Gardens by Correct Craft. Apparently this had never been done before. The show wouldn't have been possible without both pieces of equipment.[74]

The next day Carson went at it again. He headed out to the Tropical Isles of Movieland, where he performed a stunt that caught the attention of *Time* magazine when the show aired in September.

> Let it not be thought that Johnny Carson is too cheap to buy water skis. It's just that his producers thought the gimmick of using two guys instead of two skis was too good to pass up. Which explains what Johnny was doing skimming around on the rib cages of two skiing champs, Dave Dershimer and Joe Powroznik, while filming his first TV special, *Johnny Carson Discovers Cypress Gardens.* The great Carsoni, who has not been water-skiing for nearly twelve years, even did his opening monologue riding around the lake on the shoulders of two skiers before

Johnny Carson rides a toboggan in this proof sheet from a photo shoot for *Johnny Carson Discovers Cypress Gardens*. By permission of Cypress Gardens.

they dumped him unceremoniously on the beach. Said Johnny: "The ride wasn't too bad, but you guys really oughta practice your landing."[75]

Dave Dershimer, former Cypress Gardens skier and former mayor of Winter Haven, resisted revealing how he and Joe Powroznik performed as human skis. "That's a trade secret," he said.

Johnny Carson used Joe Powroznik and Dave Dershimer as human skis for a scene on his show. By permission of Cypress Gardens.

"Actually Johnny was on the side of the boat, and Joe and I were on a short rope on a boom beside the photo boat, and once Joe and I got up on our backs for a little bit, Johnny stepped down on us and they filmed us for about thirty seconds and used about eight seconds of it in the show.

Asked if being a human ski was exciting, he laughs. "I think it was pretty exciting for Johnny," he said. "Joe and I were familiar with doing all kinds of silly things, skiing on the water with our bare feet, carrying girls on our shoulders, and building human pyramids while water-skiing, and Johnny Carson was a special addition to our act, but the act itself was something we were pretty capable of doing. Johnny was never at any risk—he was pretty valuable cargo."[76]

After skiing around on top of Joe and Dave, Carson climbed aboard an orange inner tube and was dragged behind a boat, swinging over the wake at 50 miles per hour. "That's the wildest ride I've ever taken," he told the driver when they stopped, "but when do I get the feeling in my toes back?" After a midafternoon break, he headed over to the Aquarama Pool, where he cavorted underwater in front of the Wetbacks, the politically incorrect name of the all-wet Polk Junior College band. When he emerged from the pool, he told producer Chester Feldman he wanted to put on some clothes: "I've been naked for two days, can't I put something on?"

"No," Feldman said, "you look fine the way you are."[77]

Carson was about to strap on a Delta kite and take to the air, and luckily for him, the kite had a harness. The Cypress Gardens skiers originally just hung onto the kites with their hands. Richard Johnson gave Carson a short lesson. "The network set aside the better part of three days to get him trained so he could safely execute this stunt," said Johnson. "He was so agile, we knocked it out in about four hours."[78]

"It was the old-style kite that I did Johnny Carson's instruction on," said Richard. "You hung onto it, too, but you had a harness that supported your weight. It was a great experience. He was an interesting person to be around. He was quite a sport."[79]

When the news got around that Carson was going to fly the kite after one brief lesson, the camera crew got real nervous. But Carson took off, and after gaining 50 feet of altitude, he glided to the shore for a brief moment and then took off again. He finally landed, and one of the crew asked him, "Did you hear us shouting and cheering for you?"

Johnny Carson performed underwater in the Aquarama Pool with the Polk Junior College band. By permission of Cypress Gardens.

Carson replied, "No, I couldn't hear you over my prayers."[80]

At least he didn't have to fly the Gyro-boat, or the Heli-boat, as it was also called. That job fell to Red McGuire. The Gyro-boat had been introduced to the Gardens in the late 1950s by Igor Bensen, a Russian immigrant who had managed General Electric's rotary-wing program during

Red McGuire flew Igor Bensen's Gyro-boat for a "Man from Glad" commercial, circa 1970s. By permission of Red McGuire.

World War II, and who had gone on to found his own aircraft company.[81] Like a lot of other inventors, Bensen knew the best place to launch a new idea was at Cypress Gardens:

> The place to go tell the world about a new watersport, of course, was the one and only incomparable Florida Cypress Gardens. Dick Pope and his bevy of beautiful aquamaids and daring waterski athletes have made an international name for themselves as the world's Mecca of watersports. It was at Cypress Gardens where I went to announce to the world the first Hydro-glider and the first Gyro-boat.[82]

"I had a boat that Igor Bensen built, a Gyro-boat, and I flew that for shows and special events," said Red McGuire. "Igor Bensen built several different models, and every time he came out with a new design, he brought it to the Gardens, and we'd get the publicity for him. Then the boat came, and that was one of a kind. After Igor flew it, Dick Pope Jr. flew it, and then I took over. I still have it, as a matter of fact." Red later flew the Gyro-boat in one of those cheesy 1970s "Man from Glad" commercials.[83]

Quite a few of the skiers at Cypress Gardens got in on the action with Johnny Carson. After posing as a mermaid with the film crew, Brenda Mitchell got her legs back and demonstrated "boat surfing" with Joker Osborne. Dick Pope Sr. had created "America's newest sport" a few years earlier—towing a surfboard behind a boat while the surfer rode the wake. It was sort of a reprise of the jitterboard Willa McGuire Cook rode back in the 1950s. At any rate, the press Pope got with "boat surfing" demonstrated that the man could make anything look exciting. The Cypress Gardens skiers not only "boat surfed" for Johnny, they skied on their hands, did handstands on chairs while skiing, and skied barefoot on one foot. Donna White Geurin one-upped Johnny on the kite. Wearing a tutu and water skis, she swung from a trapeze dangling from the kite that Don Seyez was flying.

More than 68 million viewers tuned in to watch the show when it aired in September—right before the 1968 Miss America Pageant—making it one of the highest-rated specials of the year.

Mike Douglas must have been watching because less than four months later he came back to the Gardens to film yet another week's worth of shows. This time Duke Ellington and his seventeen-piece band were guests,

The Cypress Gardens' skiers did their best to promote boat surfing as a sport. Author's collection.

along with opera star Roberta Peters, Johnny Weissmuller, and Gentle Ben, the OJ-guzzling grizzly bear.

Dubie Baxter wondered what all those stars like Johnny Carson, go-go dancer Joey Heatherton, and comedienne Totie Fields thought of their visits to Cypress Gardens: "The stars probably got a laugh out of Winter Haven; they were probably looking at us as if we were the original Beverly Hillbillies, but because of Dick Pope's personality and his ability to pull this off, they were probably in awe of him in some respects because he had the number-one tourist attraction in the world."[84]

And he was right. In the program put out by Johnny Carson for his special, Carson more or

Mike Douglas returned to Cypress Gardens for a second round of shows in 1968. By permission of Brenda Mitchell.

Mike Douglas drove an orange-studded car during his second visit to the Gardens in 1968. By permission of Cypress Gardens.

less wrote a mash note to the Gardens: "Bring on some more orange juice. I want to sit here and recap my visit to beautiful Cypress Gardens. Maybe next time I come here, the General and the Pope will let me stay a little longer than a week. You really do need more time to discover Cypress Gardens.[85]

Despite the success of such television shows, Dick Pope Jr., now president of Cypress Gardens, was keenly aware of the Disney empire taking shape outside of Orlando. In anticipation of the opening of Disney World in 1971, when the tourist population was projected to increase by the millions, the Cypress Gardens Association bought 30 more acres on Lake Eloise, including the mansion built by John Snively Jr. The Snivelys would continue to live in the mansion for the next five years according to the contract. Dick Pope Jr. said the purchase was made to allow for enlarging the attraction, and he added that the Popes planned to invest millions of dollars in additional improvements to the Gardens.[86]

Later that year, to celebrate the installation of its 750,000th telephone, General Telephone installed a one-of-a-kind contraption known as the Chatterbox in the Gardens. More than one hundred dignitaries showed up for the dedication of the unique phone booth. Fred Learey, president of GT, told the crowd why he'd chosen the Gardens as the site for his 750,000th telephone:

> Since tourism has played such an important role in the growth of Florida, it is only fitting this special booth be placed in Cypress Gardens, one of the most renowned tourist attractions in the country. Over a million persons visited these beautiful gardens last year. We are proud of this historical achievement and want the people who visit this attraction to share this historical milestone with us.

The Chatterbox, which had slanted glass windows and overlooked Lake Eloise, was designed so that a whole family could climb inside, mash a button, patch a call through an operator, then speak through a microphone. This was considered revolutionary because no coins were involved. The call would be charged to the speaker's home telephone or to her credit card.

Dick Pope stepped into the Chatterbox to make the first call. Ironically, the first person he called was Roy Disney, who was sitting in his office at Walt Disney Productions in California.[87] No one knows what he said.

6

The 1970s

Dick Welcomes Mickey

"Out of the muck and matted tangle of cypress and palmetto trees . . ." So began an article in the December 1970 *New York Times*. It could have been the opening to yet another puff piece on how the Maharajah of the Muck dug Cypress Gardens out of a swamp on Lake Eloise back in the 1930s, but it wasn't. It was something entirely different. Just how different became clear as the article continued: "the stately spires of Cinderella's castle spring into the Florida sky, waiting to welcome a storybook princess and 10 million visitors a year." Walt Disney World had arrived. In a photograph accompanying the article, Mickey Mouse literally stood by overseeing the construction of Cinderella's castle, hard hat in hand.[1]

Dick Pope Sr. greeted Disney World with open arms. Here he visits Cinderella's Castle, circa 1970. By permission of Julie Dantzler Pope.

The similarities between Disney World and Cypress Gardens began and ended at the swamp. Dick Pope looked at the cypress swamp on the edge of Lake Eloise and saw a haunting backdrop

Cypress Gardens' colorful flowers provide a nice contrast with the cypress swamp. Author's collection.

for the colorful Gardens he envisioned. Walt Disney looked at the cypress swamp on the edge of a "black lagoon" and said, "Can you change it?" Then, before you could say Donald Duck, as Florida historian Gary Mormino wrote in *Land of Sunshine, State of Dreams*, "his engineers would uproot the cypress trees and dredge the ancient tea-colored lakes, replacing them with imported white sand and lagoons of blue-tinted water."[2]

Forget those shovels Dick Pope borrowed from Carroll Smith's hardware store to dig out his gardens; forget the WPA crew men working for a dollar a day, the plants the Popes cadged off friends. The coming of Disney wasn't measured in how many cartfuls of muck the men hauled out; it was much bigger than that. According to Mormino, "In the history of tourism, Disney World represents the Biggest Bang."[3] Disney wouldn't just change the swamp; it would change the entire state. And this transformation called for big guns. The Corps of Engineers drained Disney's swamps in 1967, and "Disney crews dredged, blasted, constructed, and raised 40 miles of canals, 18 miles of levees, more than a dozen flood control structures, and 8 million cubic yards of earth."[4]

To handle the expected influx of tourists, the State of Florida funded a massive road-construction program, and then, in 1968, the Florida legislature voted to establish the Reedy Creek Improvement District, "a quasi-governmental body" that gave an unbelievable amount of power to Disney. Essentially, as Richard Fogelson, author of *Married to the Mouse* put it, Disney became "a sort of Vatican with Mouse ears with powers and immunities that exceed nearby Orlando's."[5] Dick Pope might have referred to his own office at the Gardens as the "little Vatican," but his tiny city-state could not compare with Disney's.

Walt Disney might have been able to speak to power, but one thing he couldn't control was the development at the periphery of his city-state. Just as he had predicted, new attractions sprung up at the edge of the Disney Empire. They weren't quite the honky-tonks that Walt had expressed an aversion to, but it's doubtful he would have approved. Johnny Weissmuller of *Tarzan* fame bought into a failed "western and jungle themed attraction" called "Florida Wonderland" over in Kissimmee that featured, among other flora and fauna, peacocks, performing porpoises, palm trees, and western shootouts. Before Weissmuller came aboard, the place was best known for the death of Wanda, an elephant who had broken her chains and bolted from the attraction only to be run over by a semi-truck on U.S. 1.[6] Weissmuller and his partner, Ben Whitehouse Jr., renamed the park "Tropical Wonderland" and added a petting zoo and a serpentarium. On opening day in June 1971, Weissmuller, decked out in a safari suit, greeted reporters. "I'm a spacefan," he said incongruously, perhaps referring to nearby Kennedy Space Center, which was also aiming to become a tourist attraction. Tropical Wonderland didn't last long—by 1972, Weissmuller was outta there, citing cruelty to animals. Years after the park closed, people complained of being harassed by packs of mischievous monkeys that had escaped from the park.[7]

Johnny Weissmuller tried to cash in on the arrival of Disney in 1971 with Tropical Wonderland. By permission of Tim Hollis.

An unlikely beneficiary of Disney World's impending arrival was Cassadaga, a small spiritualist community located between Daytona and Orlando that boasted one store, a beauty parlor, a post office, one pay phone, a couple of bars, and a lot of psychics. "People come to Cassadaga for one of three reasons," reported the *New York Times*: "They believe in the Spiritualist Church, they are curious about mediums and psychic experiences or they have discovered that the hotel here is an inexpensive headquarters for seeing the sights in Orlando (future home of Disney World)."[8]

A different sort of spiritual group descended on Cypress Gardens. *Day of Discovery,* the television offshoot of the *Radio Bible Class,* a nondenominational Christian organization, began filming weekly shows in Cypress Gardens in 1970. The show, which billed itself as the "largest syndicated television program in the world," set up shop on the shores of Lake Eloise. The Day of Discovery Singers positioned themselves on the Gazebo, where they lip-synched as water-skiers glided by toting flags that spelled out the name of the show.[9] The show must have provided Pope with some solace as he faced the Disney onslaught. Each episode opened with the camera panning over the cypress trees that edged Lake Eloise, then swooping up for an aerial view of the entire Gardens. *Day of Discovery* might have been a religious show, but that certainly didn't stop it from being a textbook example of "OPM squared."

Meanwhile, not even a medium from Cassadaga could have predicted the effect Disney would have on Florida. In the year before it opened, three-quarters of a million people visited the "Walt Disney World Preview Center," where they gazed at a 30-square-foot replica of the real thing and watched a twelve-minute-long slideshow. Before leaving, they could buy souvenirs: twelve-dollar Mickey Mouse wristwatches, dollar ashtrays, and buck-twenty-five baby bibs.[10] All that activity was making some Miami Beach resort owners nervous; they worried about the "Mickey Mouse Curtain" that "will halt the southward flow of visitors at Orlando, clean out their pockets and send them back home." Others were more optimistic, including Morris Lansburgh of the Eden Roc Hotel, and Ben Novack, owner of the Fontainebleau Hotel, where Dick Pope once staged a ski show in the swimming pool. Both men felt that Disney would "promote Florida and bring millions of first-time visitors to the state; ergo, Disney World must help, not harm Miami Beach." They were echoing sentiments

By 1978, the famed Fontainebleau Hotel, where Cypress Gardens skiers once performed in the pool, had been sold in bankruptcy. By permission of Cypress Gardens.

Dick Pope had long held: what's good for Florida is good for us. The reporter concluded the same, after detailing the immense road construction taking place to ferry tourists around the state: "A profitable spillover thus seems inevitable."[11]

However, by 1978, *Time* magazine described Miami Beach as "a seedy backwater of debt-ridden hotels, gaudy condominiums, and decaying apartments." Its inhabitants were "so old that lifeguards spend more time assisting heart-attack victims on the sand than pulling foundering swimmers out of the surf." Both the Fontainebleau—which the magazine noted had little "aesthetic sense" when it was built—and the Eden Roc Hotel had been sold in bankruptcy proceedings, in part because of popular resorts in Hawaii and Las Vegas; in part because of cruises headed to the Caribbean. The biggest culprit by far, though, was Disney World, by that time the most popular tourist spot in the world. "We were cut off at the pass by Disney World," the vice president of the Miami Chamber of Commerce told *Time*.[12]

The article infuriated Harold Gardner, vice president of marketing at the Fontainebleau, who wrote the editor:

> TIME describes the Fontainebleau as "a semicircular rococo monument . . . [with] little esthetic sense." Fontainebleau was built

Dressed in a Superman costume, Ed McMahon took to the air in 1971 for his own television special, *Ed McMahon and His Friends Discover Wet at Cypress Gardens.* By permission of Cypress Gardens.

> by Ben Novack, a man of great vision who deliberately created a fantasy-land designed to lift the general public from its humdrum existence and provide a memorable two-week vacation. I sincerely believe the Fontainebleau to be as esthetic as Disney World.[13]

In the spring of 1971, though, Disney's "esthetic" hadn't yet engulfed Florida. All was still well in Cypress Gardens; the attraction was even beginning to inspire a bit of nostalgia, as a reporter for *Motor Boating and Sailing* pointed out, recalling the days when, for a dime, a kid could watch a movie, a travelogue, and a newsreel: "We . . . can also remember that *The Eyes and Ears of the World* took us much too frequently down there to Cypress Gardens, Florida. Skidding around the cypress stumps. Zapping over the mudbars. Interminable. Inevitable."

Probably without meaning to, she documents another change that was already beginning to creep into American society as television supplanted the newsreels: boredom with actual experience:

> When the hot flash came through Johnson Motors that they were doing a one hour TV special based in good old C.G. the first weary reaction was sort of Ohmigod. Since then I've seen the film. . . . The whole original scene is there—the bronzed young bodies, exotic tropical foliage, knobby cypress knees, dimpled girly knees, *but it's the cameras, folks, that take it out of the banal and into the beautiful.* You get a watersnake's eye view, a gulls's eye view . . . cameras were mounted on boats, and airplanes. . . . For the first time ever . . . a sound camera was mounted on a delta wing kite so that you can not only come fly with the kite rider, but hear his voice through the whistling wind. Ed McMahon is your host and properly genial. Catch it on the Tube.[14]

With the words, "it's the cameras, folks, that take it out of the banal and into the beautiful," the writer hints at a world yet to come—a world where a virtual experience is preferable to a real one, a Disneyfied world.

On May 15, 1971, "Disneyfication" hadn't made it into dictionaries yet—that would happen in 1982—and Winter Haven was decked out like a Springtime Whoville, unaware that a real Grinch lay in wait in Orlando. The Havenites were celebrating "Dick Pope Day" with a parade and ball. More than four hundred people showed up at the Florida Citrus Showcase in Winter Haven to wish him well. Governor Reubin Askew called Pope "Florida's number one showman," and cited his ability to "[turn] disaster into cash." Johnny Weissmuller, now a bleached blond; former governor Claude Kirk; and Joan Crawford attended the ball that evening. Vice President Spiro Agnew telegrammed his congratulations. Ever the optimist, Dick Pope took advantage of the event to push his "Friendly Floridian" program, noting that Walt Disney World was "the greatest thing that could happen to Florida—a perpetual world's fair. Disney will do its part," he said; "but when people leave that place they will need to meet friendly Floridians to maintain the state's reputation for hospitality."

General Joe Potter, vice president of Walt Disney World, presented Pope with a plaque from the Council of 100. "[Dick's] the greatest guy I've ever known. I have no dearer friend," Potter told the audience, then added that Disney was hoping to "take some of Dick's overflow from Cypress Gardens."[15]

All joking aside, Dick Pope really was banking on his deeply felt notion that what was good for Florida was good for Cypress Gardens. Unfortunately, he was basing that optimism on a time when Florida attractions were equal, give or take an alligator or a parrot or two. "I just can't wait 'til [Disney] gets here, he told a group of businesspeople in Brevard County. "We're spending some 3.5 million on land and improvements at Cypress Gardens, based on the confidence we have in what Disney will mean to this part of Florida."[16] He told another reporter that he expected the number of tourists visiting Cypress Gardens to double once Mickey Mouse arrived.[17]

Pope wasn't alone in his expectation that Disney would share the wealth. George Turner Jr. of Sunken Gardens in St. Petersburg told reporters

Dick Pope Sr. created the Friendly Floridian program as a way of enticing tourists to return again and again to the Sunshine State. By permission of Adrienne Pope Watkins.

Dick Pope Sr. fought to get State Road 540 realigned so tourists could simply turn right off Highway 27 and head to Winter Haven. By permission of Cypress Gardens.

at a meeting of the Florida Attractions Association that "I have always thought all good attractions help one another. Only bad amusement operations hurt the business. There's no question, Disney World is first rate.[18]

On the eve of Walt Disney World's opening day, Dick Pope placed a full-page ad in the *Orlando Sentinel*:

> Cypress Gardens Welcomes THE MAGIC KINGDOM OF DISNEY. Today is THE day that all Florida has awaited for five years. It is our belief that the coming of Walt Disney World is the greatest thing that has happened to our state of Florida since sunshine. . . . Today [the dream] is a reality right in the center of the Holiday Highlands of Central Florida. This area today becomes the travel center of the world and surely this whirlpool of excitement will spread over the entire state of Florida.[19]

Disney World might have been located in the "center of the Holiday Highlands of Central Florida," as Pope wrote, but it certainly didn't offer tourists Florida the way Pope's Gardens always had. Russell Kay, writing on the day after Christmas in 1936, encouraged readers to go to the newly opened Cypress Gardens to see this "fairyland. . . . You make your way through tropical plantings of all manner of rare and beautiful plants, shrubs, trees and flowers by jungle path. Furry rabbits peek out at you from the heavy underbrush; frisky squirrels scamper about among trees while birds are everywhere."[20]

In contrast, a week after Disney opened in 1971, William Honan, the *New York Times* travel editor, wrote that as he made his way to the Magic Kingdom, he realized why American soldiers had used the term "Mickey Mouse" to "describe the performance of those meaningless rituals of which the authoritarian personality is inordinately fond." He went on to describe his Mickey Mouse tour through a Disney "jungle":

> There were huge plastic butterflies, and their wings flapped; plastic frogs opened their mouths and croaked; plastic crocodiles slithered and snapped; plastic hippopotamuses rose up out of the water and swam toward our boat. . . . Through it all, our guide recited a memorized spiel as thick as jungle growth with bad jokes. . . . What was particularly distressing about the Jungle Cruise was the squandering of so much effort and technical ingenuity on cheap tricks and an inane script.[21]

Jim Gormley, member of a Lakeland-based photography club, snapped this photo of a friend on a trip to Cypress Gardens in 1948. Photo by Jim Gormley. By permission of Fred Clark Jr.

Sounds like the guide could've used a few tips from some of Cypress Gardens' old boat drivers, like Spider Bell, who delivered his spiel to the tourists with the singsong cadence of a comedian: *On the left here is the catchiput malice malicaluca rhododendron—it looks like a palm tree; the leaves stay on but the bark comes off.*

There was certainly nothing Mickey Mouse about Cypress Gardens. Maybe Dick Pope had something when he told a reporter the secret to the Gardens' success: "We never had enough

Cypress Gardens boat drivers Barry Kaufman (*left*) and "Shorty" wait for tourists to arrive. By permission of Don "Spider" Bell.

money to spoil the natural beauty." Disney it seems, had a bit too much. In 1972, when Dick Pope walked through Cypress Gardens with Disney World executives Card Walker and Donn Tatum, they passed a banyan tree more than 150 feet in diameter. Disney World, of course, had its own banyan tree, a 50-foot round one they built for the Swiss Family Robinson attraction at a cost of about $3 million. That's about nine bucks apiece for each of its 330,000 polyethylene leaves. The Disney execs asked Pope how much his tree cost. "I wheeled it in here in 1932 in a wheelbarrow and it cost $3.50 . . . but yours is taller than mine," he said, trying to soften the blow. "Yours is wider," they replied.[22]

Florida citizens weighed in on the Disney aesthetic. In a letter to the *St. Petersburg Times*, one unhappy visitor condemned Disney for being a "direct threat to what the people of Florida enjoy—Florida's quiet unspoiled beauty. . . . Man-made beauty(?) replaced Mother Nature's. A false, 'plastic' world was created. One that gives nothing in return when the rain falls on it."[23] Right below this letter was another one defending Disney:

> Thank you Walt Disney that your wholesome entertainment gives us respite from real people who wage war, commit rape and robbery, corrupt politicians, clutter the television with idiotic commercials and programming, overwhelm us with nudity, sex and other kinds of filth, polluters of this earth. We are grateful that we don't have to push or take drugs to take a trip, we can go to Disney World.[24]

It seems most people agreed with the second writer. You didn't have to take drugs—you could just go to Disney World. So many did that two months after Disney World opened that the secretaries at Cypress Gardens found themselves dealing with overflow from the Mut-Tel, Cypress Gardens' kennels. It was the first time in the park's history that the Mut-tel had to turn dogs away. "The dogs were leashed to the secretary's desk," the local paper reported. "A beagle was sent to the front office manager and a bulldog to receiving and shipping." The reason for the overflow of dogs was that Disney World was experiencing its own overflow. It had closed its parking lot, turning visitors away. Dick Pope must have been thrilled because not only did Cypress Gardens have a record turnout of dogs; it also had a record turnout of tourists—over 26,000 showed up that day.[25]

In August 1972, Dick Pope Sr., enjoying a 40 percent increase in tourists since Disney World opened, called a press conference to announce a five-year expansion plan for the park that would include Florida's first "moving sidewalks" to transport tourists through the new Gardens of the World. He also planned to build a new stadium for the ski shows, a new entrance to the park, and a new photo center. That wasn't all. He said that the Gardens would also add a Chinese junk to ferry tourists over the lake, and it would build a housing complex that would feature "underwater boat rides."[26] By November, those plans included a "park tram, a monorail and overhead chair lift."[27]

Dick Pope Sr. wheeled this banyan tree into the Gardens in a wheelbarrow in 1932. Photo by Lu Vickers.

The optimism spread. Banking on Shamu's ability to take on Mickey Mouse, SeaWorld Incorporated purchased land for a new marine animal park just a few miles south of Orlando in the spring of 1971. The following year, Ringling Brothers announced they were putting their money on Barnum City, soon to be home to a tiny man named Michu, who at 33 inches tall was nearly a foot shorter than Tom Thumb. The

Cypress Gardens' Mut-tel was filled to overflowing in the early days when Disney World's crowds forced it to close its gates. By permission of Cypress Gardens.

Ringling Brothers initially planned to build a 19-story-tall elephant with an elevator in its leg as the centerpiece of its Circus World attraction in Haines City. Author's collection.

centerpiece of the attraction would be a nineteen-story-high jewel-studded elephant with an elevator in its leg.[28] Talk about tempting fate. But at the time, Barnum City seemed like a good idea. As one reporter speculated, the circus "may even steal some of the show from nearby Disney World which has held the center ring in this area's boom."[29]

Ironically, Cypress Gardens began its expansion in September 1972 with the demolition of the former Hundred Lakes Yacht Club through which almost 30 million tourists had passed since Cypress Gardens opened in 1936. The Spanish-style clubhouse with its pecky-cypress interior symbolized both the Florida boom, when Dick Pope was rear commodore of the yacht club, and the crash, when the club was boarded up and abandoned. But it also symbolized Pope's faith in his Gardens. Against the advice of practically everyone in 1930s Winter Haven, he bought both the yacht club and the swamp surrounding it.

A reporter from the *Winter Haven News Chief* was on hand the day of the demolition to document the dawning of the "new era." A group of tearful southern belles gathered on the terrace waving white hankies. Pope visited his office one last time before the wrecking crew came in. A photo shows him looking over his shoulder, one hand on the banister, one foot on the stairs heading down.

The Hundred Lakes Yacht Club was demolished in 1972 to make way for an expansion of the park. Author's collection.

Outside, a "sad quietness lay over the crowd" that had gathered on the shores of Lake Eloise to watch the landmark tumble to the ground. In one photo, John Snively Jr., son of the John Snively who'd built the Yacht Club, sat next to his grandson John Snively IV and watched the demolition. In another photograph, workmen walk through the wreckage. The photographs taken that day epitomized a truth, not just about

Dick Pope Sr. created his own Florida seal to advertise Florida attractions. By permission of Cypress Gardens.

Cypress Gardens, but about Florida. The look on Dick Pope's face said it all—there was no turning back.[30] With the coming of Disney World, the genie had been let out of the bottle.

Cypress Gardens got a taste of what setting the genie loose meant when Disney unveiled its *Wonderful World of Water* ski show after saying they had no plans to compete with Cypress Gardens. Corky and Corkette were replaced by Pluto, Donald Duck, and Goofy. The *Lakeland Ledger* reporter couldn't hide her disdain for the spectacle, writing that the show "began with seven water skiers . . . each carrying a Disney flag on a pole in the best Cypress Gardens' tradition. The performers skied to Walt Disney World music but the announcer sounded just like the one at Cypress Gardens." When asked what he thought about the ski show, Dick Pope Jr., ever the gentleman, said: "It's a free enterprise system. We've had water-ski shows daily since 1947 and will continue to have one of the best ski shows in the world."[31]

To help finance its multimillion-dollar upgrade to the park, in October 1972 Cypress Gardens went public, offering shares of stock between ten to twelve dollars per share. Bob Kehoe, chief financial officer at the time, explained what going public meant to the Gardens. The days of Dick Pope Sr.'s outlandish promotions were over. There would be no more free gardenias, no more Florida-shaped pools or Aquaramas. "In the public company world, you want your shareholders to get a 4 or 5 percent return every year. Once they went public, a decision like building the Aquarama Pool would've been questioned. You needed to go out and get a couple of bids, because you're using shareholder money.

An idea or two might have been passed by that Mr. Pope would've jumped on in the old days."

Like buying two thousand pairs of red socks to hand out at a ballgame. "The Boston Red Sox team came to Winter Haven to stay for their annual spring and summer training," said Bob. "Our new stadium had four thousand seats, so Mr. Pope found two thousand pairs of inexpensive red socks, and on opening day, everyone in the stands, courtesy of Dick Pope and Cypress Gardens, had a red sock to wave. And it was that kind of expense he would pay for personally and then a little later somehow work it in to be reimbursed. The pictures would roll in across America, the red socks being waved in the stands courtesy of Cypress Gardens, so Cypress Gardens got mentioned throughout America in all the press releases. So it must be expense, so we'd reimburse it. We subscribed to several press clipping services, and they would clip newspaper articles out of newspapers across America and put a little tag on them as to how big the circulation was and send them to the Gardens, and [Dick Pope] could look at piles and piles of those to see whether the picture we sent out was broadcasted well, and judge what to do."[32]

Going public also had ramifications for the folks who worked at the Gardens, like Dubie Baxter, whose family ran the Palm Terrace Restaurant: "That was the end of our family's tie. They were only given two weeks to get out of the Gardens because they were on a handshake not a contract. So they hired a corporation to come in and run the restaurant concession; it was a concession now, not a dining room or a Palm Terrace. I think they were doing it to avoid paying retirement. It was never the same old place again. You never had to stop working out there if you didn't want to. I never saw anybody retire—I don't know what happened to them after 1972."[33]

Despite Disney's magnetic pull on tourists, Ringling Brothers went ahead with plans to open Circus World and to create Barnum City, their own little town. Writers had a field day: "The old saying that elephants are afraid of mice doesn't hold true in Polk County," wrote one. And under the auspicious headline "Disney Fighting to Keep Spotlight," another writer described the Tom and Jerry matchup: "The next sound you hear to the north will be Walt Disney Officials trying to get Circus World on a string. Followed closely behind by a mouse squealing as the ring master makes a grab for his tail."[34]

The ground-breaking ceremony took place in April 1973. The reporter on hand wrote that Ringling Brothers had every intention of

Cypress Gardens unveiled its "Gardens of the World" in 1974; Dick Pope Sr. poses with a gold-painted Buddha. By permission of Adrienne Pope Watkins.

"getting in on the action" brought to the area by Disney—that, or "die trying."[35] They would die trying, only to be reincarnated later as Boardwalk and Baseball, only to die again.

Later that year, SeaWorld flew a doped-up Shamu, along with doped-up harbor seals, barking sea lions, and an elephant seal christened El Google, to Orlando where they would take up residence in the nearly completed SeaWorld located "near the giant Walt Disney World complex." SeaWorld survived.[36]

However, for every new attraction spawned by Disney, another older one seemed to fall. In 1974, citing the fuel crisis and the "staggering drop in attendance," Rainbow Springs closed after fifty years.[37] It wasn't surprising. Contrary to Walt Disney's assertion that Disney World was a "labor of love" and was not about making money, the fact is, as *New York Times* reporter William Honan pointed out, Disney set out to make as much as money as it possibly could from the very beginning. After surveying its supply of tourists at Disneyland in 1965, Disney statisticians determined that 74 percent of them arrived from west of the Mississippi. The second thing they determined—a fact that "profoundly irked Disney and his colleagues"—was that tourists spent more than $500 million just outside the doors of Disneyland, more than twice what they had spent inside the park. The solution to these problems was to build Disney World, then "surround it with hotels, motels and restaurants controlled by the parent organization, so that when the fatted wallet of the tourist was sliced into, the coins would not go rolling over the countryside to be snapped up by the Big Bad Wolves not franchised by Walt Disney Productions, Inc."[38]

Cypress Gardens unveiled its "Gardens of the World" in 1974, and Dick Pope reminisced with a reporter about the 1930s, when he'd gotten the idea to build the original gardens. "I decided that this was the best thing I could do—to have something beautiful that would make people come and look at Florida," he told her. "I was selling Florida." But, he said, he knew flowers were not enough—"you've got to have action to go with the flowers." And that came in the form of water-skiers. "When Disney came in, we knew we had it made," he said, as if his struggle to attract tourists were finally over.

As he took the reporter on a tour of the new Gardens—the Mediterranean Falls, the Dutch Windmill, A Little Bit of Ireland, and the Italian Fountains, he couldn't help but point out the "real Florida" that he'd fallen in love with as boy. When they passed the shore of Lake Eloise, he said: "Now this is the real Florida ecology. Look at that—ducks and birds and cypresses growing out of the water. And that big Palm tree there—I didn't plant that, or the fern that's growing out of the side of it. Isn't it amazing? If you tried to find something like this, it would be impossible."

Then he added, as if being jerked back to a Disney state of mind: "Eventually, we plan to have a sort of Taj Mahal right here on the shore of the lake. . . . And there will be moving sidewalks all through the gardens, so people won't have to walk. Many of our visitors are elderly." As they drove back to his office, past the Snively mansion, Pope pointed out a couple of trees that had probably been in the Gardens back in the 1930s: "Look at those two tremendous magnolia trees at each side. They're the real thing."[39]

Later that year, despite its additions, Cypress Gardens really began feeling the pinch of Disney World as well as the effects of rising inflation and gas shortages. In the "Message to the Stockholders," the Popes wrote that park attendance had decreased by 18 percent and that revenues were down 12 percent.[40] But Cypress Gardens still had its devotees. Frank Deford, writing in

Cypress Gardens celebrated the Bicentennial with this living birthday cake. Author's collection.

Sports Illustrated, reminded his readers: Before Disney World, there was Cypress Gardens. As he wrote in "An Honest Travel Story":

> People rave at what Disney wrought, and properly so, but the mistake is to suggest that his two places are American. Not so, not so at all. They are mechanical and nonsectarian, belonging to the world at large. . . . Cypress Gardens, though, is American to the core. If you could show a foreigner only one of each thing in America—one natural splendor, one historical site, one downtown, one national park—Cypress Gardens is what I would choose as the one American amusement, over a baseball game or a football game, over a state fair, over Disney World.[41]

Where else but Cypress Gardens could you see a Bicentennial celebration honoring the Battle of Lexington and Concord with a fife corps "showing the weariness and scars of a recent battle" as they water-skied past the tourists in the stadium?[42]

Bert Lacey was working at the Gardens then and recalled the brainstorming meetings the staff had with Dick Pope for the year-long event: "In 1976, when we were celebrating the bicentennial, he said, 'All of you get together—we'll have a meeting tomorrow morning, and I want you to have all your ideas about what to do for the Bicentennial.' This was '75, I guess. I had a big list of stuff. The horticulture guy started off first, and he said, 'I'm going to build a giant 40-foot-high birthday cake out of flowers and plants,' and I just threw my stuff in the trash. End of meeting. We got publicity all over the world on that."[43]

Ironically, the day after the Bicentennial, the *St. Petersburg Times* reported that McKee Jungle Gardens, which began its life in 1929 as a bit of the tropics next to the Indian River, had closed. "Can it be true?" the reporter asked, noting that the Disney years had been the "most profitable in Florida tourism history." How could anyone fail to make a buck off all of those tourists swarming to the state? The answer, according to Arthur McKee Latta, grandson of Arthur G. McKee, who founded the Gardens along with Waldo Sexton, was that McKee Gardens didn't "keep up with the times," as other attractions had. Silver Springs had "modernized its grounds"; Sarasota Jungle Gardens had tapped Ross Allen to perform his reptile show; Tiki Gardens served liquor in its restaurant; Marineland brought in trick-performing dolphins; Weeki Wachee hired a trick diver who set himself on fire. McKee Jungle Gardens owned the "world's largest table," a nearly 36-foot-long table made from a single piece of mahogany, and it had Amazonian waterlilies big enough for a small child to sit on. It was also

The Cypress Gardens skiers celebrated the Bicentennial with this four-tier pyramid, 1976. By permission of Cypress Gardens.

Arthur McKee Latta, whose grandfather cofounded McKee Jungle Gardens, wanted to keep the coastal hammock pristine. By permission of State Archives of Florida.

home to some of the world's rarest orchids and a quirky "Hall of Giants," a Robinson Crusoe–style building built with heart pine and driftwood. But these oddities weren't enough. Even the spider monkeys and rainbow lorikeets the Lattas added later weren't enough. "[Staying the same] was our downfall, no doubt about it," Latta said. "But it was my grandfather's greatest fear that this original part of Florida coastal hammock would get bulldozed over. . . . I could not in good faith . . . I WOULD not put monorails or Snow White or mechanical monkeys or a high dive tiger act on these precious grounds."

Don Meikeljohn, president of the Florida Attractions Association, said the closing was all McKee's fault. "[The Gardens] dropped membership in our association, [and] didn't promote itself. . . . It is ridiculous to say that it is impossible to survive as a completely natural attraction in this state, or as a family run attraction. It takes hustle and bustle."

Jerome Scherr, owner of Parrot Jungle, agreed, but with a caveat: "An attraction run just as a gardens can't hardly make it anymore. . . . People seem to prefer theme parks now. It's not so much competing with Disney—no one can do that. It's keeping up with the times. McKee never developed a bird show. They never expanded, improved. . . . The gardens, per se, just doesn't hack it anymore."[44]

Jerome Scherr's Parrot Jungle expanded and improved so much over the years that it no longer exists—at least not in name. Scherr's children sold Parrot Jungle to veterinarian Bern Levine in 1988, hoping he would keep the park "safe from developers."[45] Four years later, unable to expand due to protests from his neighbors, Levine decided to move the park out of the lush green spot it had inhabited since 1936 to manmade Watson Island in Biscayne Bay. He renamed the attraction Parrot Jungle Island. "We'll lose some of the charm of something that's going to be small and old," said Levine.[46]

In 2007, Levine erased "parrot" from the park's sign. Literally. Parrot Jungle is now "Jungle Island." At a press conference, workers showed off a menagerie of exotic animals: a chimp, an orangutan, and a kangaroo. No parrots were in sight. Levine's partner explained the name change. "Parrot Jungle just doesn't say it. A lot of people weren't interested in coming to an all-bird park. But when they heard we had a tiger and a crocodile . . . they became more interested."[47] Pinky, the bicycle-riding cockatoo who served as Parrot Jungle's mascot, was no longer the star of the show.

Parrot Jungle's Pinky the Cockatoo is no longer the star of the show at Jungle Island, but she still rides her bicycle. By permission of the State Archives of Florida.

Arthur McKee Latta, for his part, was unapologetic about maintaining his family's gardens as they'd been for the past forty-four years: "I'm somewhat disgusted with humanity, I guess. People no longer want to feel like Thoreau. They want things thrown up at them. . . . They don't want to walk the Appalachian Trail, they want to ride it. People don't want to sit under the oak tree and think anymore. They want to have someone think for them. They want the oak tree to talk and shed plastic leaves."[48]

The tourists may well have wanted talking oak trees with plastic leaves, but when those weren't available, when Disney closed its doors to overflow, they would make a beeline for Cypress

Gardens—at least for a while. Bert Lacey worked in public relations at the Gardens from 1974 to 1977: "I was talking to an assistant I had the other day, and he said, 'you know we were there during the best years.' All the hard work had been done; we were just kind of coasting on Mr. Pope's coattails at that time. Disney was not nearly as big as they are now, and lots of time they would shut their gates at 10 a.m. because they would be full. When they did that, the tourists would come pouring down to our place."[49]

Dave Dershimer, former skier and former mayor of Winter Haven, also thought that the 1960s and early 1970s were the Gardens' heyday, "if you want to judge success by revenue and popularity." He added, "In Polk County in the mid-1960s, as far as I knew there were only three attractions—Bok Tower, Masterpiece Gardens, and Cypress Gardens. And it was funny to see how they competed against each other when that was the right thing to do, and then they worked together when that was the right thing to do. Pope was smart enough to be the best in his industry. But he was smart enough not to leave the competition behind, so he was involved in organizations like the Florida Attractions Association. I can remember telling somebody at school in the early 1970s that I wished Disney luck but they'd never have any success competing against Cypress Gardens. Whoops. I think I was a little bit wrong in that. But you know, the Gardens did okay. Pope did welcome Disney with open arms, but he probably didn't know the length and breadth of their impact at the time. And the Gardens didn't expand into the Gardens of the World and their little shopping village until after Disney was pretty much up and running. So as time went on, a lot of people said that the Garden's response to Disney was maybe too little and too late."[50]

He was right. The years immediately following the arrival of Disney World were good for Cypress Gardens. In 1976, the Gardens broke its attendance record, pulling in nearly 1.7 million tourists. But by the end of 1977, that number had dropped to 1.3 million, largely due to the recession and a particularly harsh winter on top of Disney.[51] Bert Lacey remembered that year: "In 1977, I got a call from a horticulturist at 3:00 a.m., and he said, 'there's a blizzard here,' and I said, 'you're kidding me,' and I went outside and it had actually snowed, and it stayed until nine or ten the next morning. Mr. Pope was out there, and I told one of the photographers, 'Go have Mr. Pope write on one of the benches, 'Would you believe it' in the snow and we'll get a picture of that and send it out and get some publicity. He misspelled 'believe,' killed the whole shot."[52] Luckily, Dick Pope's success never rested on his spelling ability.

One of the things Pope's success did rest on was the ingenuity of the skiers who supplied the "action" at Cypress Gardens. People like Betty Bonifay. She was unhappy with the performance of her swivel ski, a Cypress Gardens specialty since Willa McGuire Cook had invented it and introduced it at the 1950 World Tournament with her trademark "swivel swan."

After being banned at tournaments for being a "gadget not readily available to all," the swivel soon became a fixture in ski shows. But it would only swivel 180 degrees, and that irked Betty. She wanted to go full circle. So one day in 1976, as she drove home from a show, she stopped at a gas station and asked one of the guys if he would "knock a peg" off the binding on her ski. The gas station guy messed around with it, and by the time she drove away, she was toting a 360-degree swivel ski. Over the year, she and fellow skier Sally Winter practiced using the ski while the others skiers looked on skeptically. "At that time, Betty was like everybody else, except for one thing—she had such tremendous drive," Nancy Zarza Daley told Kevin Wells of *WaterSki*

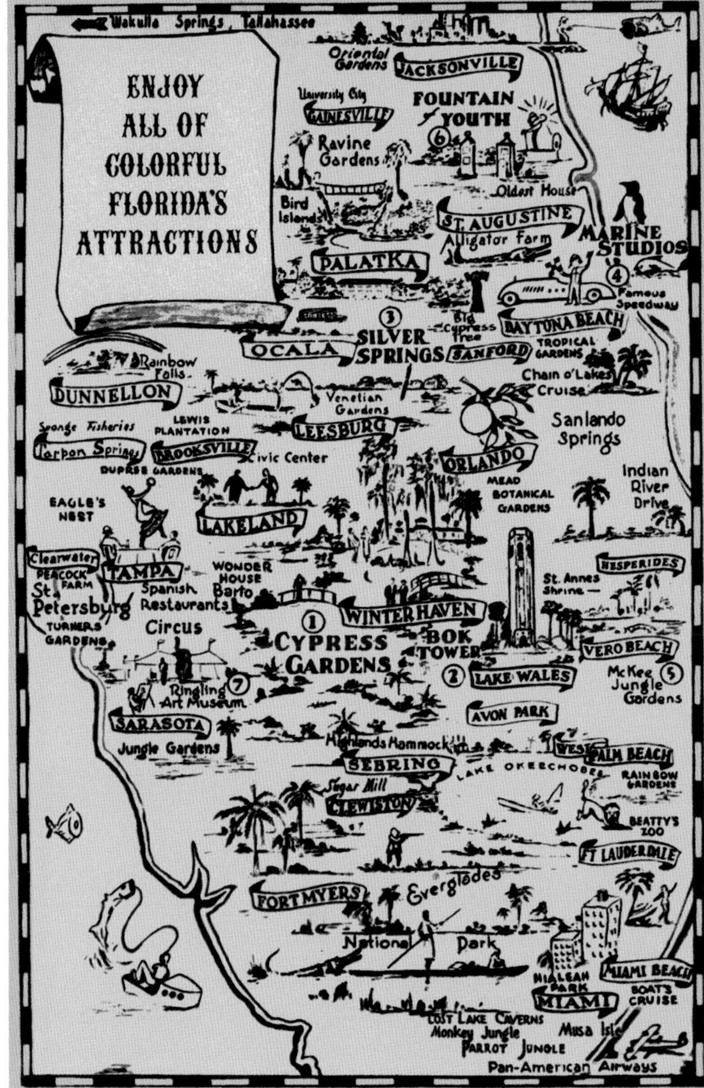

A page from an early Cypress Gardens brochure touts all of Florida attractions. By permission of Cypress Gardens.

LITTLE COLONEL'S CORNER — What a thrill for youngsters on the first-ever kite ride, the Delta Dip, and a miniature parachute drop, the Fundangler! Children also delight at operating tiny autos at Down the Pike around a 500-foot winding course past an animated lion, alligator, elephant and turtle.

The Little Colonels' Corner was part of Cypress Gardens' expansion in the late 1970s. By permission of Cypress Gardens.

Magazine. "She was so driven to become the very best. I remember the ones who had been around for a long time didn't want to bother with the 360."

Betty Bonifay kept right on going until she was ready to show the naysayers what she'd done. She waited until the Cypress Gardens' Super Show of 1977 to debut her new move, a swivel swan that rotated into a full 360. "A lot of skiers at that time just wanted to stick to their routines," she told the magazine. "They thought the 360 was trick skiing. They stayed back and wanted to see what would happen. But that just made me want to do it more." And, as Wells wrote, "She did, and a new era began."[53]

It was also a new era for the Gardens. In 1978, Dick Pope Jr. announced that Cypress Gardens was yet again expanding—this time to the tune of $5.5 million. The goal of this expansion was to appeal to more families and to double the time they visited, while maintaining the original concept of the Gardens. He explained that great care had been taken in designing the expansion because "We were proud of the reputation we have earned as one of the world's great gardens. We didn't want to do anything that would conflict with that image." Brenda Stevens, communications director at the Gardens, agreed, "We want to keep our reputation as 'the best blooming attraction in the world.'"

The improvements would include a kiddie-sized amusement park, a replica of a small southern town called "Southern Crossroads," an Aquadome, a "Gadgetorium," a baby shark exhibit, skeeball, and an "alligator demonstration." They would even be bringing in performing cockatoos. The changes were seen as necessary, Dick Pope Jr. said, not only because of Disney itself but also because Disney spawned "the proliferation of new attractions which began to have a dilutive effect on our business."[54]

All those other "worlds" were taking their toll—and it wasn't just Circus World and Sea-World. The Mystery Fun House, Wet 'n Wild, and Fun'n Wheels all opened about the same time just outside the doors of Disney. Disney itself was expanding, shifting down from worlds to lands: Fantasyland, Frontierland, Tomorrow-Land—all competing for the tourist dollars. In 1979, in what the *Winter Haven News Chief* billed as the "story of the year," the Gardens announced that its $5.5 million expansion—the biggest ever—would be opening in six weeks. The headline said it all: "Cypress Gardens Puts $5.5 Million on Polk's Tourist Future." The county was clearly counting on Dick Pope Sr. to work his magic: "Just as lightning can strike the same place twice," the reporter wrote, "the 'Swami' is about to strike again." Harking back to the Gardens' earliest days, when Dick Pope Sr. and Malcolm Pope used to rule the lakes and the newsreels with their motorboating antics, the

Cypress Gardens always prided itself on being distinctly Floridian; an early sign bets tourists will feel the same way. By permission of Cypress Gardens.

proposed Garden Cinema would show a film highlighting Florida water sports.[55]

The Cypress Gardens press release that was sent out to announce the opening emphasized the attraction's Florida roots: "There's a new Cypress Gardens! And it's not just in Florida . . . it IS Florida." Visitors could stop in the Garden Cinema and "command a speeding airboat through the Everglades" or, better yet, drive "fast-paced jump boats through the winding canals of Cypress Gardens." At Little Colonel's Corner, children could "control Delta kites" just like the skiers do. While the expansion included a lot of bells and whistles, it also included some more laid-back entertainment, like the Magic Lantern Theater and the Aquatube (formerly referred to as the Aquadome), which featured "marine-life indigenous to Florida." Over and over again, the press release emphasized Florida, Florida, Florida, ending with this boast: "Located 30 minutes from Walt Disney World near Winter Haven, Cypress Gardens is open daily year-round and is the only major attraction in Florida that couldn't have been built anywhere else in the world."[56]

The decade closed with a celebration of Cypress Gardens' fifty-thousandth ski show. Cornelia Wallace, the former wife of the late Alabama governor George Wallace—reprised her role as a 1960s skier. Naturally, she wore a white tutu, a crown, and long white gloves as she skied across Lake Eloise in the cold November air.

7 The 1980s and 1990s

Fighting Back against the "Worlds"

In 1980, when Dick Pope Sr. and Dick Pope Jr. unveiled their multimillion-dollar expansion of the park—which included, as an anodyne, a roller-skating parrot and a pair of Sicilian donkeys,[1] a local reporter wrote:

> A dream came to life Sunday. It was a dream that began more than 40 years ago and had its seeds in the muck around Lake Eloise; a dream that sprouted its first shoots when the "Swami of the Swamp," Dick Pope began clawing about that muck attempting to create a botanical wonderland. The dream? An attraction to rival the various "worlds" that sprang up through Central Florida. A dream called Cypress Gardens.

Dick Pope Sr. crosses his fingers for good luck as he poses with a pair of Sicilian donkeys in 1980. By permission of Adrienne Pope Watkins.

It seems the reporter didn't realize that Cypress Gardens hadn't been a dream for quite some time, that it had already been there and done that. The Gardens had bloomed into reality

A postcard scene of the original Gardens reveals a tropical beauty, circa 1930s. Author's collection.

in 1936, back when those citrus queens cut a ribbon strung over a walkway of pecky-cypress wood blocks, back when Mickey Mouse was just eight years old, a black-and-white drawing who possessed neither a land nor a world.

At the dedication ceremony for Cypress Gardens' expansion, Lietuenant Governor Wayne Mixon echoed words governors had been saying throughout the last four decades: "Despite the millions of dollars, and all the things the state has done to attract tourists to Florida, we have not yet begun to match what Dick Pope has done for tourism."[2] Still, despite Lieutenant Governor Mixon's words, it couldn't have been lost on the readers that Cypress Gardens, the epicenter of Florida tourism—indeed, once the nation's top attraction—was no longer first fiddle. It was described as being "located 30 minutes from Walt Disney World, near Winter Haven." In the old days, attractions like Parrot Jungle and Florida Wonderland had measured their distance from Cypress Gardens.[3]

Lucy Chambliss recalled the days when central Florida was not synonymous with a mouse but with Cypress Gardens: "I traveled around to sixteen states shooting, and people would say, 'Oh, you live in Winter Haven; Cypress Gardens is in Winter Haven.' Yep, Cypress Gardens is in Winter Haven."[4]

By April 1980, the Gardens' new roller-skating parrot was joined by a water-skiing scarlet macaw named Mr. Mo Bebee. After two months of training, the macaw perched on a tiny pair of skis pulled behind a two-foot-long boat with a toy motor. The motor didn't actually work—the boat was attached to a track that pulled it forward; still, the sight was pretty amusing. "He tried to get off [the skis] once and learned pretty fast that macaws don't swim," his trainer said.[5]

Months after Mo made his debut on water skis, Dick Pope Sr. celebrated his eightieth birthday. He was beginning to show signs of Alzheimer's, but he had lost none of his enthusiasm for the Gardens, wrote Miller Davis of the *Lakeland Ledger*: "Richard Downing Pope, Sr., the little giant, stood on the spot where it all began. He clapped, clapped, clapped like a kid seeing his first clown. But there wasn't a clown in sight. This mite of a man was applauding beauty. 'Look at all those trees, look at those flowers,'" Pope told Davis. "Some of them were here when the cows were here, when me and the Snively kids played here . . . oh . . oh . . . we had fun . . . fishing and swimming . . . chasing the cows." He thought he was celebrating his ninetieth birthday, and when he saw a poster that read "Happy 80th Boss!" he said: "Beautiful people. I love 'em. But they don't know I'm 90." Katy Turner Leifheit, his longtime secretary, winked at the reporter: "O.K. If he wants to be 90, let him be 90."

Surrounded by southern belles, Pope reminisced about serving in the Army Signal Corps, digging holes and planting telephone poles, a job he put to good use when he came back to the Gardens after the war. When the reporter pointed out to Pope that nearly a million and a half visitors had come to Cypress Garden in 1979 and

Dick Pope Sr. poses with some of his cameras that helped to make Cypress Gardens world-famous, circa 1950s. By permission of Cypress Gardens.

that the attraction had cleared almost a million and a half dollars, Pope clapped his hands again and said, "That's pretty good. But look, look at those trees and all those flowers." When the interview ended, Sylvester Denmark, Pope's longtime employee and friend, arrived. "Come on, Mister Pope," said Katy Leifheit. "Sylvester says it's time to go." Sylvester took his elbow, leading him to the door. "Mrs. Pope is waiting in the car, Mister Pope. We don't want to keep her waiting." As he passed the receptionist, she told him he looked good. "Everybody looks good today," he told her. "I love everybody."[6]

Julie Pope Dantzler said it was hard to tell when her grandfather starting developing Alzheimer's because of his creativity and spontaneity. "You had nothing to compare his behavior to; there was no baseline of some kind of 'normal,'" she said. "There was no 'normal' with him, so it took a while to figure out. One of the things he started doing when he had dementia was giving away their possessions—but he'd always done things like that. I mean if one of us started doing it, it'd be pretty obvious, but for him, it was just normal."

"By the time I came onto the scene," said Rick Dantzler, "he was already affected by dementia, or so it seemed, but it was hard to tell. I had seen him before in audiences when he might just stand up and start clapping. This was before he was experiencing dementia, so I was never sure."[7]

Those "trees and all those flowers" Dick Pope Sr. applauded on his birthday were still holding

Mick Haggerty, famous graphic designer and music video director, turned to Cypress Gardens when he designed the album cover and the video for the Go-Go's 1982 *Vacation* album. By permission of Mick Haggerty.

their own ten years after Disney World opened. As the *Boston Globe* reported in March 1981, "Despite the formidable competition emanating from the Disney-dominated hub of Orlando, one of Central Florida's most popular attractions continues to be an improved swamp." The reporter compared the Cypress Gardens Aqua Maids to the Radio City Music Hall Rockettes, noting that the skiers had become a "Florida institution" and had entered the "national consciousnesss."[8]

Proof of Cypress Gardens' persistent presence in the national consciousness came from an unlikely source: the Go-Gos, an all-girl punk band that got its start in L.A. in the late 1970s in punk rock clubs like Whisky A Go-Go and the Masque. Mick Haggerty, an artist who'd designed album covers for the Police and David Bowie, among others, was tapped to work with the Go-Gos on their 1982 album *Vacation.*

> [Ginger Canzoneri, the Go-Gos manager, and I] were both saturated in kitsch and Americana and both loved movies in which singers were filmed against obvious rear projections—like Elvis singing while he was surfing. . . . I researched the world of water skiing shows and soon found out that Cypress Gardens in Florida was known as 'the best.' . . . [T]he deal was sealed when I found out they had a camera boat I could use.

Haggerty's plan was to photograph and film a group of Cypress Gardens skiers, then superimpose the Go-Gos' heads onto their bodies. No one at the Gardens knew who the Go-Gos were, Haggerty said, but they knew "OPM squared" when they saw it, so management lined up about sixty skiers for Haggerty to choose from. He got out his measuring tape and went to work. He needed skiers whose bodies would match those of the Go-Gos: "I sheepishly got out my tape measure and ended up with a very odd choice of five girls, and the rest must have thought I was completely nuts. Luckily, the weather was fine, the sky was blue and we shot it all in one day, completing the rest of the shoot with the band on the West coast at the Charlie Chaplin stage at A&M."

Haggerty projected the film he'd shot of the skiers onto a screen and filmed the Go-Gos in front, "hamming it up in swimsuits and doing their best at lip synching." In between takes, he recalled that the singers would head outside to

Tourists sit in the grass next to the Palm Terrace to watch a ski show, circa 1950s. Author's collection.

smoke on Sunset Boulevard, still wearing their tiaras and tutus. "This being Los Angeles," he said, "no one seemed to notice—just a few more weirdos in Hollywood." The photo shoot resulted in an album cover featuring the Go-Gos as Cypress Gardens Aqua Maids, and a music video featuring the pop rockers "skiing."[9]

The band broke up a few years later, then reunited in 2001. Speaking to a reporter about their return to the stage in 2008, Jane Weidlin, cofounder of the group with Belinda Carlisle, revealed just how much the musical landscape had changed since the Go-Gos had donned their tutus and skied Cypress Gardens: "I think Radio Disney plays us a lot, so there is a whole new generation of music lovers that are discovering our music."[10]

Radio Disney was just a particle in the cloud the Disney empire cast over the national landscape, a cloud that was thickest over Florida. Like a mushroom emitting spores, Disney World, Florida's number-one attraction, spawned more and more "bigger, shinier, and more exciting attractions," and slowly started to erode the popularity of Cypress Gardens. David Nyhan, a *Boston Globe* reporter, had the audacity to call Disney World, "the Sunbelt's best example of the development ethic—creating wealth out of raw land and nothing else but sun, sand and water."[11] Sounds like Cypress Gardens redux. But you could walk through Dick Pope's Gardens and smell actual flowers, get close to actual skiers, and snap photos of girls in hoop skirts. Visitors to Disney World found a very different Florida, one that presented "artificial products to be consumed in the very places where the real thing is free as air."[12] Nyhan seconded that description:

> From the ticket pavilion you ride the famous circle-route monorail or take a large ferry

> across a huge manmade lagoon. . . . There is artful landscaping, but the peaceful lagoon, with its crescent of white, sandy beach is scrupulously bare of people. . . . Places to go off a bit and get away from the crush are for looking, not walking. . . . The flora and fauna . . . are all imitation, as they would have to be. Animals are statues, the sound effects and visuals are all out of a Hollywood set. Not til you get back to your car . . . is it quiet and peaceful. Your identity was stripped on the way in, you get it back when you leave.[13]

Disney officials had assured Florida's other attractions that they were "not trying to build a wall around Disney World. There's so much to see in Florida. We know that if people are pleased, they'll come back."[14] And they were right. But many of the tourists came back and came back and came back to Disney World, like Frank Frazzano of Orange, New Jersey. On his sixth visit to the Magic Kingdom, Frazzano "[sat] in an oversized teacup about to be spun and jerked around like socks in a wash cycle."[15]

It wasn't just Disney proper draining tourists away from Dick Pope's swamp. Florida's place in the national consciousness as a "dream" lush with palm trees and lagoons was undergoing a sea change as well. The *Boston Globe* reported that Floridians got what they asked for: "tourists . . . industry . . . a massive highway system. . . . Now they have to live with it. . . . The Florida that many dream of is gone."[16] The new highways bypassed some of the older roadside attractions, including Cypress Gardens, and the 1970s energy crisis put a damper on travel. Those developments, combined with the Mariel boat lifts of the late 1970s, the Liberty City riots of the 1980s, and an increase in crime, caused a decline in tourism even at Disney World.[17] But Disney still had Epcot to unveil, and Disney officials were counting on that new attraction to bring in an additional 7 million tourists.[18]

At the end of the fiscal year in October 1981, Cypress Gardens' earnings per share had fallen nearly 50 percent and attendance was down 11 percent. Still, the folks at Cypress Gardens were optimistic. "We're writing it off as a bad year," said Hal Hunt, company controller. "Nobody's panicking around here." He chalked up the decline to bad weather and a weak economy. A spokesman for Dean Witter Reynolds, Inc., which managed Cypress Gardens' move to go public, agreed, adding that the drop in tourism throughout the whole state also contributed.

Science-fiction writer Ray Bradbury helped design Spaceship Earth, the centerpiece of Disney's Experimental Prototype Community of Tomorrow. By permission of the State Archives of Florida.

Cypress Gardens added the one-of-a-kind Kodak Island in the Sky in 1983. By permission of Cypress Gardens.

"They should benefit directly from the opening of Epcot," he said.[19]

Epcot opened in October 1982, and it wasn't really anything like the city of "Tomorrow" that Walt had envisioned back in the 1960s when he was secretly buying up the land around Orlando. No one lived there except for the audio-animatronic cavemen and other historical figures that populated the dioramas tourists were whisked by. Disney imagineers concocted chemical smells to go with the animatronic figures, so tourists would get a whiff of a swamp when they passed the caveman scratching on his wall. Features like these made Epcot the most expensive private project ever undertaken.[20]

Faced with the prospect of even more tourists, one Orlando man told reporters: "God Almighty, this area will be a megalopolis from Orlando to Daytona Beach. It used to be so beautiful ecologically. But I haven't seen a hummingbird in years."[21]

In February 1983, the Gardens seemed to be banking on its roots as a photographer's paradise to attract more tourists. This approach had certainly worked in the past. Dick Pope Jr. announced a $2 million expansion that included a "picture-taking attraction" called "Island in the Sky." Kodak's Island in the Sky was a platform that would hoist about one hundred tourists 150 feet into the sky, where they could snap photos of the lake and the orange groves that still surrounded the Gardens.[22]

Longtime Gardens employee Fred Gaffney remembered when Dick Pope Sr. called Publix founder George Jenkins to tell him about the new attraction: "He called him and said, 'George I'm going to put an island in the sky.' He said, 'Well, I tell you what Dick. If you put an island in the sky, I'll put a cake in the sky.' You could see all the way to Bartow. You could see where they'd be digging that phosphate."[23]

The day after the announcement about the Island in the Sky, the Gardens reported that the company had recorded a first-quarter loss. By 1983, more and more tourists were foregoing the old-fashioned road trip to Florida where they crisscrossed the state in the family station wagon, hitting nearly a dozen cities, and staying with kinfolk. Now they were flying in, hopping into rental cars, and driving straight to Disney World for a week of "carefully packaged entertainment—often with a hotel room as part of the price." However, Cypress Gardens seemed to be holding its own; it still made the list of top tourist destinations; it was number five, following Disney, SeaWorld, Busch Gardens, and the Kennedy Space Center.[24]

One of the acts that kept Cypress Gardens on the list was Pepper, the famous boat-driving dog: "I went to SeaWorld, and Joel Slavin, Shamu's trainer, taught me how to train animals," said Donnie Croft, a boat driver who started working at the Gardens in 1972: "I picked out Pepper. I trained him from sit, stay, heel, speak, to 'drive the boat.'" Donnie and Pepper trained on a boat specially built by Mastercraft. Little windows had been installed in the bow of the boat right at the waterline, along with a throttle and a steering wheel, where Donnie could lie down and reach them. "There'd be a guy pretending to be a driver sitting in the driver's seat," said Donnie. "But I was driving the boat, and I'd pull up on the beach. The fake driver would see a knot in the rope, and when he stood up to untie the knot, he would tell this dog to drive. The dog would get into driver's seat and put his paws on the steering wheel, and when the line was tight, the guy would yell 'hit it!' and I'd just take off with the boat. A lot of people just didn't know how we did it."[25] Pepper was a hit, but, as one reporter wrote: "some would say the dog has it easy. She is, after all, the only performer in the Cypress Gardens Water Ski Revue who doesn't have to don skis, grab a tow rope and risk injury daily to earn her chow."[26]

The water-skiers were the reason Cypress Gardens was known as the Water Ski Capital of the World. Not surprisingly, when the Water Ski Hall of Fame inducted its first Hall of Famers in 1982, two of them were from Cypress Gardens: Dick Pope Sr. and Willa McGuire Cook, the Gardens' prima ballerina, eight-time overall national champion and three-time overall world champion. The Hall of Fame noted Dick Pope's contributions to the sport: "No single person has done more to make the world aware of the glamour and fun of water skiing than Dick Pope, and few, if any, have contributed more to the encouragement of tournament skiing."[27]

Willa McGuire Cook was inducted into the American Water Ski Hall of Fame in 1982. Author's collection.

The accolades continued. The 1983 Cypress Gardens ski show focused completely on waterskiing and its history at the Gardens, paying tribute to skiers like Willa; Charlene Wellborn, the first woman barefooter (1950); and Barbara Cooper Clack, who broke the world record for long-distance jumping thirteen times. The program also paid tribute to male barefooter and kite flyer Mark Voisard and to kite flyer Ken Tibado, who designed the first flat-wing kite to be flown at the Gardens. There was no indication that the Cypress Gardens ski show was hurting.

By 1984, though, said Lynn Novakofski, there wasn't much of a future in waterskiing, a situation that is even worse now. "The audience has gotten more sophisticated," he said. "We've kind of reached a plateau there as to the spectacular things we can do, and at the same time, there are more attractions in the area." Not only that, he said, but the cost to produce shows had gotten out of hand: "SeaWorld was spending $1 million producing a water ski show in the 1990s when I was out there in California, and over in Vegas they were spending $90 million producing some of the big shows over there. Maybe if somebody had $90 million to spend on a ski show we could come up with the spectacular acts and showcase them the way that would draw audiences—much like they do in Vegas, but money and inspiration and imagination don't get applied to water-ski shows anymore."[28]

Throw the interstate and the Florida turnpike into the mix, and it's even harder to get tourists to drive 40 miles from Disney World to Cypress Gardens to see a ski show. Both of those roads seemed to have a one-way track on them—one-way to Disney World. Although nearly 70 percent of the tourists who visited the Gardens also visited Disney World, less than 15 percent of Disney's guests returned the favor. An exasperated Dick Pope Jr. told a reporter in 1984, "Let's face it, we're off the beaten path."[29]

The irony, of course, is that Cypress Gardens was always off the beaten path. One of the twists of the modern psyche is that the time it takes to drive the 40 miles from Disney World seems an eternity, when in the old days—pre-Disney—people used to drive down from New York *just* to see Cypress Gardens. Of course, those were the days when natural Florida charmed the Yankees. Days when "genuine Florida alligators" were "flown to New York by airplane" to compete in

Lynn Novakofski, former Cypress Gardens' ski-show director, holds skier Brenda Mitchell aloft. By permission of Brenda Mitchell.

races in fancy hotels. Like the 1933 alligator race in the Grand Ballroom at the Waldorf Astoria in New York. The occasion? The Miami-Biltmore Fashion Show. "They will be the fastest obtainable," the *New York Times* said of the reptiles, "as time trials are being held at present on many large alligator farms in Florida. Alligators are not gifted with a strong sense of direction so the course has been arranged that the most distance covered in the least time will determine the winner."[30]

Those gators sound a bit like modern tourists—they have no sense of direction and whoever covers the most distance in the least time gets the prize, even if they run in circles. That might explain why they never leave the dog run of the Disney Compound.

Dick Pope Jr. seemed to take this sensibility into account when he described the park's new strategy, which was not to compete with Disney, but to lure Disney-goers over to Cypress Gardens, where they could enjoy more human-scaled entertainments like the water-ski shows and the petting zoo. He planned to accomplish this by advertising more in central Florida.[31]

The Cypress Gardens ski show was still a big draw in the 1980s. By permission of Cypress Gardens.

In another attempt to draw tourists to Winter Haven, Cypress Gardens' general manager Bill Sims negotiated a deal with Sears, Roebuck for a series of promotions that featured a trip to Cypress Gardens as a "first-place prize." It was quite similar to Dick Pope Sr.'s "OPM squared" strategy. An earlier promotion with the department store featured Cypress Gardens models and the Gardens themselves in nearly seventy pages of the Sears catalogue.[32] Dick Pope Sr. would've been proud.

Despite Cypress Gardens' makeover, in late May 1984, Harold Lieberman, a shareholder of the company, began a campaign to seize control of the company, arguing that the park needed some high-tech sizzle to compete with Disney. Bob Kehoe was chief financial officer at that time: "Harold Lieberman deliberately bought just a few shares of Cypress Gardens stock and then started beating up on us in the press questioning these things; we weren't doing anything wrong, but we were getting some bad publicity."[33]

Lieberman took out an advertisement in a local newspaper asserting that "The Gardens haven't kept up with the times," and suggesting that some "thrill rides" might be in order. The *Miami Herald* mocked his criticisms, noting that he thought Cypress Gardens was a "drag. . . . All those tacky old flowers and trees. And that water ski show! And this Chairman Dick Pope, Jr., the only guy who likes this dump the way it is, let's send him up on the big ski-kite and point that towboat out to sea." The editorial went on to explain why Cypress Gardens was perfect just as it was:

> The big draws at Cypress Gardens may not seem like much to the Lucas/Spielberg/MTV generation: There's a quiet boat ride . . . mossy old trees and babes in frilly 'Southern Belle' get ups. There's that water ski show, the epitome of tackiness, with the same weird acrobatics and bad jokes that made people groan in the 50s. And since last year, there's the "Island in the Sky" ride—sort of like standing on a huge pancake while a giant with a spatula picks it way up in the air. . . . It ain't no Space Mountain. But, praise God and Dick Pope, Cypress Gardens ain't no Disney World. . . . Trade your Cypress Gardens stock for Disney, please sir.[34]

Still, no matter how beloved the old-fashioned park was, neither it nor countless other small tourist attractions could hold their own against Disney. Six Gun Territory over in Ocala closed, and so did the Miami Wax Museum and the

Tom Gaskins opened the Cypress Knee Museum in Palmdale, Florida, in 1934. By permission of the State Archives of Florida.

Miami Serpentarium. Cypress Gardens was hanging in there, though, even as Dick Pope Jr. lamented that the corporate parks have "the big bucks and more resources to work with." Rick Norton, a researcher with a firm that served as a consultant to Disney World, put it more bluntly: "The corporate entity runs like a big business. Maybe it is a little impersonal. But they've got the marketing bucks . . . and they just blow family operations off the map."[35]

One person didn't seem to care about being blown off the map, and that was Tom Gaskins Sr., a self-described South Florida Cracker born in Tampa and raised in Arcadia. After he married the former Virginia Bible, his mother-in-law asked him to go out in the swamp and cut her a cypress knee—she thought it would make a nice vase. Gaskins did, and since it was during the Depression, he got the idea that selling objects made out of cypress could put food on the table. Tom Gaskins Jr. said that somehow Dick Pope heard of Gaskins's creations and drove down to Arcadia: "Dad showed him what he had, and Dick Pope bought cypress knees from him." In 1936, Tom Gaskins and his wife moved to Palmdale next to Fisheating Creek, where he began making "flower fountains," birdhouses, lamps, vases, and tables—and collecting cypress knees. By 1951, he had enough to open the Cypress Knee Museum, a squat structure on Highway 27 that he filled with cypress knees that looked like Quasimodo and Eleanor Roosevelt. The most famous of these was the 5.5-foot-tall "lady hippo in the Carmen Miranda hat."[36]

"When they put in these I-75s and things like that, it took away the traffic," Gaskins told a reporter. He was seventy-seven years old then and had been collecting cypress knees for most of his life, long enough to see that not many people travelled down Highway 27 anymore: "Don't mind about the business. The business is all right. I'll be here." Gaskins's handmade signs still hung in the trees along 27 then: *Come see Tom's knees*, and *Lady if he won't stop, hit him on head with shoe*. After his father finally retired, Tom Jr. told a reporter: "This place is real Florida. It's not a plastic mouse show. I'm a Florida Cracker, a piney woods rooter. I know how to survive on acorns. It'll be a long time before anyone ever shuts us down."[37]

In August 1985, after months of negotiations, an era of Florida history officially came to an end. Shareholders of Cypress Gardens stock agreed to a merger with publisher Harcourt Brace and Jovanovich, okaying a stock swap worth $23 million. The deal ended the Pope family's fifty-year-old Garden dynasty. Rick Dantzler recalled those difficult days when Dick Pope Jr. had to make the decision to sell the Gardens: "There had been a hostile takeover attempt, and Dick had the wisdom to see that things were changing and that he and his friends and his board and his contacts didn't have the resources to compete in this new environment that was emerging, so he made the decision to sell the Gardens, which I always viewed as a great act of love. A lot of people saw it as betrayal, but it was exactly the opposite of that; it was a way to allow the Gardens to continue. I think in his mind he knew he did the right thing, but it was still a time of great stress. He never gave me a reason to believe he doubted what he had done, but I always wondered if it tugged at him some."[38]

Dick Pope Sr. (*left front*), Julie Pope (*left rear*), Adrienne Pope Watkins (*right rear*), and Dick Pope Jr. (*right front*) pose for a family photo in the late 1940s. By permission of Julie Pope Dantzler.

Julie Pope Dantzler recalled her father's struggle to keep the Gardens going in the face of Disney and the heightened expectations of tourists: "My father always thought a great deal about the Gardens' employees and their families. So the sale of the Gardens was not a time when he worried about what other people thought as

Aquacade '85 featured the "snow-flyers," a group of daredevil skiers who shot down the "Showstopper," a 200-foot-long snow jump, before somersaulting into the Aquarama Pool. By permission of Cypress Gardens.

much as it was about his concern for whether the employees would fare well under the new ownership."[39]

Harcourt Brace Jovanovich (HBJ), which also owned SeaWorld in Orlando, was optimistic that it could pull in local crowds by investing $5 million to rejuvenate "some dead areas that needed to be livened up," said Jan Schultz, a senior vice president of marketing for HBJ's three SeaWorlds. Those "dead areas" included the Aquarama Pool that Pope Sr. had built for Esther Williams's television "spectacular" back in the 1960s. The HBJ team decided to create "Aquacade '85," a new water show that would feature a 100-foot diving tower and world-class high divers, including one who set himself on fire before plunging into the pool. They also added a steep snow-ski ramp that required skiers to rocket downhill before launching themselves head over heels into the pool.[40]

Some of the acts were throwbacks to the old days when Dick Pope Sr. ruled the place: a water-skier was towed across the Aquarama Pool with a winch, and then there were the "shocking pink clad synchronized swimmers who paddle the pool's turquoise depths." They could have "stepped out of a Vintage Florida postcard," mused one reporter. Bob Brown, a 1984 Olympic silver medalist, summed up the new program. "This is like an old-time Esther Williams' production with an 80s flair."[41]

Lynn Novakofski was on hand for the Aquacade. He commented on one of the more unlikely acts: the ski ramp with artificial snow. "We came down and did flips and stuff," he said. "We got that idea from a couple of snow fliers, because they'd been doing it out in Colorado and Utah. In the summer, they'd land in the water to practice these snow-flying routines, and that's where the idea came from; it was spectacular in Florida."

HBJ hired a crew of skiers from outside to do the stunts. "A few of us tried it," said Lynn, "but it was real different from waterskiing, and it was dangerous because the water was real shallow, so you really had to know what you were doing. If it'd been 10 foot of water, we would've encouraged the water-skiers to do it, but there was only about 5 foot of water."[42]

The ski ramp with the artificial snow wasn't the only winterlike touch added to the Gardens. The new owners remodeled a 750-seat theater and added what they billed as Florida's only permanent ice-skating show. *Southern Nights*, as the show was called, was a hit. It was a strange mishmash of Gardens history:

The plot of the show is that Jackie Frost (Jack's capricious sister) decides to freeze the South. There are wind sound effects and suddenly a snow-covered Southern Mansion slide appears on the stage. Brrrrrrrr. The skaters glide on stage with woolens on, bundled in scarves and mittens. . . . During the finale the female skaters change into hot spangle costumes cut like bikinis.[43]

Attendance soon increased, and not just because of the new shows. HBJ was able to lure 35 percent of the Gardens' daytime visitors to stay after dark with a series of shows called *Cypress Nights*, an innovation that apparently had been rejected by Dick Pope Sr. for years. Legend has it that when asked by tourists why they couldn't see the park at night, Pope would tell them, "Because you can see it in the daytime."

Harcourt Brace Jovanovich added an ice-skating rink to the Gardens in 1986. Victor Grantham and Robin Fenton performed in the 1989 "Ice Planet Fantasy" complete with lasers and dancing fountains. By permission of Cypress Gardens.

"We flew the kite every night for a hundred nights, and the guys there had a spot on the beach," said Lynn Novakofski. "There's a take-off dock about 10 feet square, and with all the conditions, dark at night and everything, those guys never missed that landing area. It was incredible."[44]

The year 1986 was notable for more than HBJ's innovations; it also marked a series of anniversaries. Cypress Gardens celebrated its fiftieth. More than 35 million tourists had walked through the paths, watched the ski shows, and snapped photos of the belles since the park opened in 1936. To celebrate their provenance as one of the "longest continually running productions in America," the skiers performed *The Golden Years*, a look back at the history of waterskiing as it developed at the Gardens. "We did a lot of research coming in here and found a world of history, a bit of Americana, that wasn't being told," said Ken McCabe. That history included skiing ballerinas and a "penchant for putting anything on skis, from hobby-horses to hot-rodding dogs."[45]

Three-year-old Parks Bonifay played a slightly older Dick Pope Jr. The tyke was an old pro—he started skiing when he was six months old. That's right. Six months. "He could've done it at 4 months," said his mother, Betty, the Cypress Gardens Aqua Maid who'd invented the 360 swivel ski. "But he did it at six months and five days. It took three weeks to make him a life jacket that floated him face up. You know the life jackets with the little bib on the back; we invented that."

Betty said that after Parks was born, instead of hanging a a typical baby mobile over his bed, she hung ski handles she got from the ski factory. "At three months he could sit," she said. She and her husband gave him a pair of Cypress Gardens skis designed for a three-year-old. Within a month. he was skiing behind the lawn mower.[46]

Parks made it into the *Guinness Book of World Records*, and soon after, the television cameras came trolling after him. Sort of a typical Cypress Gardens story. At the time, Betty said of her son: "Parks thinks to ski he needs a pair of skis, a life vest, a boat and a camera crew."[47] The kid was on to something. These days Parks, aka P Diddy, is considered the greatest free-riding wakeboarder in the world.[48] In 1997, *Time* magazine called him the "Tiger Woods" of wake boarding.[49]

Parrot Jungle also celebrated its fiftieth anniversary in 1986, serving up "Yellow Bird" cocktails to more than seven hundred guests, even though the park had seen a 50 percent drop in attendance over the last half decade. "We just do what we know how to do, and we've never lost money. Sometimes, we resist some things that could make us money," said Jerome Scherr, son of Franz, who opened the park back in 1936. Unlike a lot of attractions, Parrot Jungle never had one of those Mold-A-Ramas that squeezed out hollow plastic parrots on the premises for a quarter. The real ones were enough:

> The birds will be in full finery. There'll be roseate cockatoos decorous as ladies at lunch in their pearly mauves and grays, lories like hussies in drop-dead red and hyacinth macaws cloaked in imperious purple-blue. . . . Humans—confined to red and yellow, black and white—may wear their faded madras shorts. No one will be looking at them.[50]

Parrot Jungle's hussified lories and hyacinth macaws were certainly a bodacious come-on, but the crowd they drew—a measly seven hundred—paled beside the five to seven thousand

Long before *Time* magazine dubbed him the "Tiger Woods" of wake boarding, world-famous wakeboarder Parks Bonifay made the *Guinness Book of World Records* when he strapped on a pair of skis at Cypress Gardens. He was six months old. By permission of the American Water Ski Educational Foundation Museum.

Parrot Jungle's hyacinth macaws entertained guests at the attraction's fiftieth anniversary in 1986. By permission of the State Archives of Florida.

media reps invited to the bash of all bashes—the fifteenth anniversary of Disney World. Of course, Disney World paid for all their expenses, and then some. Dick Pope Sr. would've laughed at the thought of paying reporters for the privilege of covering Cypress Gardens, but Disney execs thought they got a bargain at $8 million for the three-day event.[51]

The event led one reporter to muse: "Mirror, mirror on the wall, who's the fairest, most powerful company of all? The Walt Disney Company of course."[52] The late Mike Royko of the *Chicago Tribune* wrote, "Whoever thought that Mickey Mouse would act like a Chicago alderman?[53]

Perhaps no one was as disgusted by the event as Carl Hiaasen, *Miami Herald* columnist and author of numerous Florida-based novels, as well as the nonfiction *Team Rodent: How Disney Devoured the World*, who was sent to Disney World by the *Miami Herald* to cover "the world's largest press party." Hiaasen, an unapologetic Disney-hater who wrote that "his dream is to be banned forever from Disney World," said that the anniversary party was the "last time I set foot in the Magic Kingdom." He turned down the discounted hotel room, and fought back a couple of Disney reps who tried to make him take a bag of Disney swag. "Team Rodent couldn't have hijacked the culture without enlisting the press," Hiaasen wrote, noting that the *Orlando Sentinel* had held the news back that Disney was secretly buying land around Orlando until after the job was complete. The sight of journalists scooping up Disney freebies and paying bargain-basement prices for pricey hotel rooms nearly sent him into apoplexy.[54]

Except for the swag, Disney execs did seem to take a page out of Dick Pope's playbook. They knew that the fifteenth anniversary wasn't big enough to garner the sort of press they wanted—no matter how many reporters they paid to show up—so they created a "hard-news edge" by linking their event with the Bicentennial of the U.S. Constitution. Initially, Disney's attempt to woo the Bicentennial Commission didn't go well. Thomas Elrod, Disney's vice president of marketing, said: "These were a group of intellectuals who had never, perhaps, gone to a Disney movie. There was a somewhat reluctant attitude. What they found was that Disney was a slice of America."[55]

In the end, the commission provided Disney with a "theme" for the event and sent along Chief Justice of the Supreme Court Warren Burger as a featured speaker. But the real coup of the evening was the arrival of Nicholas Daniloff, a correspondent with *U.S. News and World Report* who'd just been released from a prison in Soviet Russia. He'd been arrested on September 2, 1986, by the KGB in retaliation for the arrest of a Soviet UN employee in New York days earlier.

On the evening of the Disney anniversary, Daniloff proceeded to give his speech, his first since returning to American soil. He spoke emotionally of his "brother journalist" Terry Anderson, the AP bureau chief in Beirut who'd been kidnapped by Islamic jihadists in Lebanon in March 1985.[56] (Anderson was finally released in December 1991.)

The audience gave Daniloff a standing ovation. Disney reps couldn't have been happier. Then they sent Mickey onstage for a photo op. Daniloff was not amused. Prior to agreeing to do the speech, he had extracted a promise from Disney reps that he would not "be thrust face to face with Disney Characters."

"There was Mickey Mouse, lurching backward and forward with his hand out," Daniloff told a reporter later. His wife, Ruth, saw what was happening and shouted at the Disney folk to "Get that [bleeping] mouse off the stage." Daniloff was able to scoot past Mickey without being hugged as his wife shouted: "After one month of dealing with the KGB, now we have to be set up by Mickey Mouse?"

Mickey Mouse shows former Florida governor Bob Graham a model of Disney Studios in 1985. By permission of the State Archives of Florida.

Charles Ridgway, director of public relations at Disney, was insulted by Daniloff's refusal to shake hands with Mickey. "I'm sorry that they feel they're above that sort of thing," he said. "Mickey Mouse is a very well respected personality in this country. We're very careful about who he appears with as well."[57] However, they couldn't keep tabs on the mouse all the time.

Shortly after the dustup with Daniloff, Disney was sued by a woman who claimed a drunk man in a Mickey Mouse suit pushed her son against a fence near Cinderella's Castle after the kid yanked his tail.[58]

Luckily for Disney, there was no love lost between Mickey and the rest of the tourists. Of course, it didn't hurt that Disney's anniversary celebration would last one whole year and would include over one million prizes—one every fifteen minutes—including one Chevrolet Cavalier per day.[59]

As a result of Disney's media blitz, central Florida's smaller parks, such as Gatorland Zoo, Weeki Wachee, and Silver Springs, saw surges in attendance. "We'll have to give Disney credit," said Melvin Gentry, manager of Gatorland, where the top draw is the Gator Jumparoo Show, which features an alligator lurching out of the water to chomp down on a store-bought chicken. "There is no question that Disney's ad campaign and its promotions have made more people aware of Central Florida." More tourists *were* coming to central Florida, and more parks were seeing spillover, although the farther away they were from Disney, the smaller the spill.[60]

Cypress Gardens wasn't just relying on spillover from Disney, though. Using a bit of overkill, HBJ officials announced a "Holiday Magic Yuletide Package" that would combine "The greatness of nature's beauty . . . with the best that man can offer in modern technology." This "modern technology" was an ice-skating rink filled with that modern marvel—glice, or fake ice—and a laser show that featured the "marvel of laser technology" so audiences could watch as a "delta wing kite pilot rescues the electronically imprisoned 'good wizard' Gizmo, slicing right through the night sky's laser rays on a brightly lit kite." It was a show guaranteed to "beckon to the young and adventurous" and to appeal to "even the most jaded couch potatoes."[61]

Just one month later, Dick Pope Sr. died at home in Winter Haven. He was eighty-seven years old. The *New York Times* remembered him for passing out Florida-shaped pins and begging weather forecasters to say it was "partly sunny" instead of "partly cloudy." Former Florida governor Bob Graham, a U.S. senator at the time, said, "Dick Pope was the embodiment of Florida tourism." Jo Farmer, a Florida tourism official, said: "He set the stage for the exposure of Florida worldwide. There wasn't any place in the world you could go and not hear about Florida. He pretty much wrote the book."[62]

The Winter Haven newspapers were filled

with headlines touting his contributions: "Dick Pope: 'Mr. Water Ski,' A Showman, a Pioneer, a Man Loved"; "Pope Was Loved by Employees"; "Pope Was a Visionary"; "Tourism Leaders Credit Pope for Their Careers"; "Pope's Call to Dreamers." Dick Nunis, president of Disney Attractions, said: "He will always be known as 'Mr. Florida.' He will be truly missed by the people and will be remembered as one of the entertainment pioneers of this century."[63]

On a lighter note, his friends recalled their encounters with him over the years. Hart McKillop, Pope's lawyer, remembered slogging through the cypress swamp on the edge of Lake Eloise, looking for the boundary marker of the land that would become Cypress Gardens.[64] Donnie Terrell, head of wardrobe at the Gardens for more than thirteen years, remembered the time Dick Pope called her and asked her to make him a dress. "The men were having a fashion show as a fundraiser for St. Matthew's Church," she recalled. She made him a blue ball gown trimmed with ruffles. "He even wore the pantaloons I made him and a brown wig. If we had more like him, the world would really be a better place."[65]

Just ten weeks later, Dick Pope's wife and business partner, Julie, died. They had been married sixty-two years. The local papers recounted her contributions to the Gardens, how she inaugurated the ski show back in 1943 when her husband was away in the Signal Corps installing telephone poles and peeling potatoes. How after a freeze devastated the flame vines near the entrance to the park in 1940, she whipped out an antebellum hoop skirt and asked the secretary to put it on and stand by the front gate. Employees at the Gardens remembered that if Mrs. Pope wore a certain pair of red shoes, it was time to scoot.

"It isn't often that, when a man marries, he gets a new right and left hand, as well as a wonderful companion, but that's what my wife Julie has been for me," wrote Dick Pope Sr. when he dedicated his book *Water Skiing* to Julie. The Popes were married for sixty-two years. They pose next to a floral clock on their fiftieth wedding anniversary; the clock was made in England by the same company that made Big Ben. Author's collection.

Julie Dantzler, the Popes' granddaughter, wasn't surprised to hear about the shoes. She said her grandmother "was a belle, but she was tough as nails, and she didn't mince words. If you were in trouble with her, you knew it. She was tough on staff." And, added Margaret Chase Parry, Dick Pope Sr.'s niece, "She was generous to a fault; they both were."

Julie agreed: "She was. If I spent the night with them, there were a couple of things I could count on. I had a room that I stayed in, and we always knelt down to say prayers at bedtime. The magic that existed at the Gardens was present for me when I stayed at their house as a little girl. I could have breakfast in bed—always pancakes and guava jelly—served on a plate with a silver dome cover. It seems so surreal now to think of it, but that was just the way it was."

Rick Dantzler said Mrs. Pope's high expectations were reflected in other ways—"even the way she drove." he said. "I heard she ran red lights, stop signs, honking all the time . . . honking the horn as she went through the intersection."

For all of her imperiousness—which for all intents and purposes she developed in response to her husband's devil-may-care flamboyance, Julie Pope was generous. Margaret recalled how the Popes helped the man she would later marry, Bill Parry. His father had died when he was a child, his mother was extremely ill, and he had recently returned from serving in Vietnam. He was both working full-time and going to school. "Aunt Julie met him and knew he was studying ornamental horticulture at the University of Florida and asked him, 'What do you need?'"

He reluctantly told her that he could use the book *Exotica*, a pricey horticulture guide, and she immediately said, "You tell me how much that book is and go buy it." And then Margaret said: "She wanted his address, and they even sent him money for tuition. You have no idea how much that meant to him. He telephoned her to thank her and asked, 'What can I do for you, Aunt Julie?' She quickly replied, 'Just do the same thing for someone else.'"[66]

Julie Pope's generosity wasn't reserved just for family members. "The Popes had the Dick and Julie Pope Foundation, which they used to help underprivileged families or organizations any way they could," said Alvin Denmark, a Polk County lieutenant sheriff whose father worked at the Gardens for thirty-six years. "My dad and mom really didn't have the funds to support me fully in college as far as staying on campus and school supplies, but through the Dick and Julie

Pope Foundation I was able to go to Albany State College in Georgia. All my books and room and board were paid for by the Popes." He added that the Popes helped his family in other ways: "When we were growing up we lived in a small wood-frame house with two bedrooms and an outdoor toilet. I think there were five of us in one room with two beds. When I was around nine or ten years old, we were blessed with a new home, and today I know that the Popes had a lot to do with us moving to a new lakefront house. My dad never mentioned it to me, but I know that he couldn't have done it without some help from the Popes. So Cypress Gardens has been real good not only to my family but to others."[67]

Margaret recalled that Mrs. Pope gave flowers away as well: "She had this big florist's cooler in the garage, and she would go out with a basket everyday and cut the flowers and store them, and she would take them to people who were sick."

"That is a strong memory for me, too," said Julie. "There was a florist here in town, and the owner knew how much I loved just to stand in the cooler with all those flowers because it reminded me of the cooler Nana had at home."[68]

Harcourt Brace and Jovanovich continued adding attractions to the Gardens to keep the crowds coming. In June 1988, they added "Air Dancing," featuring break dancing and wire-walking, and they refurbished Whistle Stop, USA, the world's largest model-train exhibit. They also employed "furry critters" to walk around Mickey Mouse style, greeting guests and posing for photo ops. The promotions seemed to be working—nearly 1.5 million visitors pushed through the turnstiles in 1988. However, those

Dick Pope Sr. stands next to a 1950s-era sign. By permission of the State Archives of Florida.

numbers actually represented a downturn, and by June 1989, HBJ made the decision to put Cypress Gardens up for sale along with Boardwalk and Baseball and its four SeaWorlds. The decision was attributed to an overall decline in the region's tourist market, and to the "growing dominance" of Disney.[69]

Observers speculated that one of the many potential buyers might well be Disney World, who—if the parks were sold as a package deal—would like to "get its hands on the baby whale known as Shamu for its invaluable marketing potential."[70] Tim O'Brien of *Amusement Business* magazine noted that Shamu wasn't the only pretty face in town: "I think Cypress Gardens is one of the greatest parks in the country. . . . Who in the world has never heard of Cypress Gardens? It would be a feather in anyone's cap to own that park."[71]

After months of negotiations, the company that decided it wanted that feather in its cap wasn't Disney; they were content with the addition of the Disney–MGM Studio and their purchase of the rights to the Muppets characters. The buyer was the king of beers, Anheuser-Busch, a company already invested in theme parks, including Busch Gardens. If the deal went through, Anheuser-Busch would become the number-two theme-park operator in the country, just behind Disney.[72]

Anheuser-Busch finally closed the deal in September, buying the Gardens, along with Boardwalk and Baseball, and four other parks. Polk County business leaders applauded the deal, as did Gardens employees. Cypress Gardens' spokesperson Louise Murtaugh said, "Anheuser Busch is a top notch company, and we're happy to be part of it."[73] Both Cypress Gardens and Boardwalk and Baseball opened for business under the new ownership on December 1, 1989. Cypress Gardens celebrated the Christmas season with a skiing Santa and a four-tiered "living Christmas tree." However, despite the optimism expressed by the new owners, park attendance at both Cypress Gardens and Boardwalk and Baseball declined, largely because Disney World opened its MGM Studio theme park, enticing tourists to spend even more of their time at the Disney complex.

Just six weeks after purchasing the theme parks, W. Randolph Baker, president of Busch Entertainment Corp., announced that the company would be closing Boardwalk and Baseball. "There's so much to do in Central Florida. Time is the enemy," said Ken Howard, Boardwalk's president.[74] The reality was that Disney World, which was drawing more than 24 million visitors a year, had a stranglehold on tourists, many of whom never left the Disney premises the entire time they were in Florida. And that number included Floridians who have visited the park each year since it opened, and the eighty-year-old man who went to Disney more than five hundred times, popping in a couple of times a week.[75] Tourists ate at Disney restaurants, shopped at Disney stores and slept in Disney hotels. "You don't just visit a Walt Disney World resort," said one reporter. "You go on what Disney calls a "themed resort adventure."[76] Dale Stafford, the manager of Disney's Port Orleans Resort, explained: "Our resorts are an extension of our theme parks. We take a theme and "Disney-ize it."[77] At Port Orleans, that meant jazz-playing alligators and pool slides disguised as sea serpents.

Despite Disney's incredible hold on tourists, Anheuser-Busch was optimistic about Cypress Gardens' future; Cypress Gardens spokesperson Louise Murtaugh said the Gardens' fifty-year history provided the park with stability and name recognition. The president of Cypress Gardens, Ken Smith, said, "Busch has said they see a future for us."[78]

Banana George Blair, a barefoot skier named for the bananas he handed out by the truckload, must have been relieved to hear that the Gardens had a future. Lynn Novakofski said Blair reminded him of Dick Pope Jr., who became the first person to barefoot back in 1948, and he credited Blair with reviving that piece of Cypress Gardens' history. A statue of a barefooting Banana George stands just inside the Water Ski Museum on Holy Cow Road.

Banana George Blair didn't learn to ski until he was forty years old. Once he learned, though, he became a fixture at the Gardens, where, outfitted in yellow, he'd hand out bananas and ski barefoot across the lake. Just a couple of weeks after Boardwalk and Baseball closed, he celebrated his seventy-fifth birthday at the Gardens clad in a neon yellow body glove, barefooting across Lake Eloise for a noon audience. The Cypress Gardens skiers paid tribute to him as the "ambassador of barefoot skiing."[79]

Blair has barefooted on all seven continents, including Antarctica, where he skimmed across the surface of Whalers Bay barefoot for about fifteen seconds. "I met Banana George in 1969," said Lynn. "He'd been to the Gardens a few times before that. When he was in his sixties, his barefooting wasn't spectacular, but when he got into his seventies it was a big deal—a seventy-year-old guy barefooting. So I encouraged him

Banana George skied barefoot on all seven continents. By permission of Cypress Gardens.

to come out a lot, and I gave him a starring role whenever he was there. Of course, George loved to perform in front of an audience, and he loved to sign autographs so it was kind of a mutual admiration. I was watching some videotape the other day, from fifteen years ago, and it's amazing, fifteen years ago. We're talking about this incredibly old guy barefooting, and here he is fifteen years later, ninety-two years old, still barefooting."[80]

Just weeks after Banana George's seventy-fifth birthday party, Bill Reynolds, Cypress Gardens' manager for two months, eliminated some of the park's exhibits and laid off eighty employees. He cited the recession and the decline in attendance, blaming that decline in part on the Gardens' "out of the way location."[81] The layoffs and the elimination of the animal shows were supposed to help the company reestablish the Gardens as a "lush Florida paradise of yesteryear where Southern belles wander flower lined brick roads in hoop skirts, carrying parasols."[82]

Lynn Novakofski was one of the people laid off, and he wasn't happy about it: "I got there in September 1969, and Bill Reynolds in his infinite wisdom laid me off in April of 1991." Lynn had been connected with Cypress Gardens since he was a kid back in Minocqua, Wisconsin, where he saw a group of Cypress Gardens skiers at a national ski tournament. He'd recently learned to ski and was impressed with what he saw. "The Cypress Gardens skiers would come up and bring the boats, and they always had an experienced crew to help out," he said. "Pope used that tournament team to publicize Cypress Gardens. In the 1950s, not many people came to Florida in the summer so he would send skiers off to the nationals, to different fairs. Big world's fairs always had the Cypress Garden's skiers."

Skiing at Cypress Gardens was "something I dreamed about," he said. He grew up and joined the army, and when he got home from Vietnam, he got stationed in Miami and started skiing down there: "I beat a couple of guys from the Gardens in a tournament, and they found out I was getting out of the army and said, 'hey, why don't you come ski up at the Gardens?' It was a dream come true."

Over his twenty-two years at the Gardens, he saw a lot of changes, from HBJ putting a great deal of money into the park via new shows and advertising, to Anheuser-Busch cutting back. "Waterskiing is like anything else," he said; "the basic principle is that you have to have a new and improved product, and you have to tell people about it. That's one thing Pope Sr. did;

he advertised and advertised. Most of the time I was there he had six to eight staff photographers, and their main job was to take photos and make movies and send them out; get them on TV; get them in the newspapers. People would see a picture of a girl skiing at Cypress Gardens in the middle of the winter up in Detroit and say, 'Oh, gee, let's go down there and warm up for a couple of days.' Pope was pretty astute. A lot of people would use the word 'genius'; he certainly knew how to use that OPM formula to his advantage."[83]

Over his years at the Gardens, Lynn helped develop new tricks, including the world's first four-tier pyramid. "The emphasis during the 1950s and 1960s was on the daring-do," he says. "Just do it well enough to get a photo. When I came, my emphasis was on doing it over and over."[84] He said the skiers would practice stunts like the four-tier pyramid repeatedly on land before trying it out on water. "When we did it the first time, somebody said, 'when are you going to do a five-tier?' and I said, 'after we do this a few thousand times.' The first guy out doing a gainer on two skis took forever and a day, but after he figured out how to do it and started training other people, the training time was really shortened." Lynn built on the helicopters or upright

Cypress Gardens skiers performed the first five-tier pyramid in the world. By permission of Cypress Gardens.

360s the skiers had always done, adding flips and gainers. "Eventually the guys started doing something called the 'mobius,' which is a combination of a helicopter and a gainer. A lot of the tricks evolved just because we were so focused on the athletic components. We had the 360 ballet on the water, then they wanted to add more turns. We had the guys out there doing the adagio with the girls, and soon it wasn't enough just to hold a girl above your head—you had to start moving them around, spinning. And soon on the 360 swivel ski, it wasn't just enough to turn around. It was a friendly competition among the skiers to see how many times they could turn and in what direction and how they could pass the rope."

One thing Lynn continued doing that the Popes had always done was announce how many champions they had on board. "It was bragging rights." He said. "Cypress Gardens was The Place."[85]

Don Buffa, the ski-show director in 2009, said one of the reasons Cypress Gardens was "The Place" for the best skiers was because of all the international travel opportunities the Gardens offered skiers: "I started twenty years ago basically as a part-time skier, because they had a road show." He said his wife, Linda, got hired in 1988, and that spring they went abroad together: "We went to twenty-four different cities in about twenty-six days. At that time, a skier could go to SeaWorld, Marine World, many different places, but the Gardens had that lure of international travel."[86]

The Cypress Gardens skiers had been going abroad since 1949, when Dick Pope Jr. and Willa McGuire Cook competed in the first world tournament in Juan-les-Pins, France. Pope hosted the 1950 and 1957 world championships at the Gardens. For the 1957 championships, he chartered a DC-6 airplane to ensure the arrival of the best skiers in the world—seventy-eight from twenty-eight different countries.[87]

When Anheuser-Busch bought the park, Don said they quit doing the international road shows because they didn't see any value in them. "But there was value for the skiers themselves," he said. "So in 1990 they were still getting phone calls for international trips, and that's when I started my company, Stars of Florida; if the Gardens wasn't going to do it, then I was going to do it. Our first trip was a show to Japan, and we've done fifty-five international trips since then."[88]

Lynn Novakofski and Don Buffa weren't the only people thinking about Cypress Gardens' place in history. In June 1991, under the direction of David Woods and general manager Reynolds, Cypress Gardens opened Cypress Roots, a museum dedicated to exhibiting the park's fifty-five-year history. Some of the artifacts had been pulled from the trash by employees after Harcourt Brace and Jovanovich had ordered a massive housecleaning. Just a few years earlier, poking around storage rooms and closets, Woods himself had come across a stash of old cameras that had belonged to Dick Pope Sr. and arranged them in a display case. He then thumbed through the massive archive of negatives Pope and his battalion of photographers had left behind. Almost 300,000 negatives, documenting everything from Pope's first ski jump in the late 1920s to the *Esther Williams at Cypress Gardens* special, were stored in cabinets. Giant albums contained clippings from practically every newspaper or magazine article that had been written about the Gardens. Woods seemed surprised to discover the variety of queens Pope

David Woods, former manager of photographic services, assembled material for the Cypress Roots Museum not long after he discovered Dick Pope's stash of negatives for photos like this one of Esther Williams wading into Lake Eloise during the filming of *On an Island with You.* By permission of Cypress Gardens.

Cypress Gardens Aqua Maids ski through the clouds on this 1950s-era postcard. Author's collection.

had crowned over the years: "You had Christmas holly queens. We had azalea queens. For almost every type of flower, we had a queen."

One night, he came across a stack of old scrapbooks in which he found the very first brochure advertising the Gardens, a 1936 brochure touting the thirty-five-cent admission and featuring a romantic photo of a beautiful woman resting against a cypress tree—"Gail Armour, famous danseuse as 'The Spirit of Cypress Gardens.'"

Once employees heard about the museum, they showed up with artifacts they'd collected through the years. Woods added video footage from the *Ed Sullivan* and *Mike Douglas* shows along with clips from the Esther Williams television special. On one wall, Woods hung photos of the celebrities who had visited the park over the years: Carol Burnett, Betty Grable, Duke Ellington, Tiny Tim, Elsie the Cow, the Duke and Duchess of Windsor, Elvis. Photographer Dennis Hallinan, who had worked at the Gardens for eleven years, visited the museum. While looking over the photos from the past, he commented on the differences in the park: "It's changed quite a bit. It's much more of a business. It was a more family type place. And Dick Pope was very photo-minded. That was in his blood."[89]

In the 1990s, nostalgia seemed to be the catchword at Cypress Gardens. After figuring out that animal antics, ice capades, water ballet, or even magic tricks couldn't transform Cypress Gardens into a crowded amusement park, Bill Reynolds said the park would return to what it had always done best: "Cypress Gardens is known as the world famous botanical garden and is also known as the ski capital of the world. It's that uniqueness that sets us apart. We want to get back to the basics and we want to refine

Carol Burnett didn't limit herself to toting tackle at Cypress Gardens; she also skied and boated. By permission of Cypress Gardens.

them and do them better."[90] He didn't mention how firing veteran skier and show director Lynn Novakofski would help in realizing that goal.

However, Cypress Gardens added another first to its ski show in the summer of 1990, when it hired two African American skiers, Odis and Alicia Wilson, a brother and sister from Lake Wales. Odis said being the first African American to join the ski team at Cypress Gardens wasn't a big deal: "I'm just one of the guys." Mark Voisard, who had taken over as ski-show director, told a reporter that in the Gardens' fifty-five-year history no African Americans had ever sought a tryout before. "Odis and Alicia came to us as barefooters," he said, "and are now capable of doing every act in the show." Not bad for a couple of kids who started skiing before they even knew how to swim. Their father, Odis Wilson Sr., taught them, pulling them behind his boat on Lake Wailes when Odis was twelve and Alicia five. A couple of years later, they saw former world champion Ron Scarpa barefooting in an exhibition on the lake. "I thought I could ski until I saw those guys," Odis said.[91] Within a week of seeing Scarpa, Odis was barefooting behind his father's boat; Alicia was up after a month and a half. She kept going even after she had a run-in with a gator early one morning on the lake: "It was foggy

Nine-year-old Alicia Wilson, the Junior Girls 1985 Overall Champion, practices her barefooting skills. She and her brother Odis became Cypress Gardens' first African American skiers in 1990. By permission of USA Water Ski.

A paper doily from the Palm Terrace Restaurant advertises the ski show. By permission of the Winter Haven Historical Museum.

and the lake was glassy. We couldn't see anything." Then she saw the gator: "I skied over it. I was crying and screaming." She hit the gator and fell. "I didn't ski for a couple of weeks," she said. Apparently that little hiccup in her training didn't slow her down.

Both she and her brother took barefooting classes with Scarpa, and went on to win national championships before realizing their dream of joining the ski team at Cypress Gardens. In 1995, Scotty Clack, the Cypress Gardens production manager and a champion skier himself, described the two as "trendsetters." Duke Waldrop, executive director of the American Water Ski Association, agreed: "They are just outstanding athletes and ambassadors and champions for the sport."[92]

Despite adding another first to the ski show, it turned out that getting back to the basics really meant concentrating on the botanical side of the Gardens. Reynolds announced that the Gardens would begin building a multimillion-dollar butterfly aviary in August 1992 to house almost fifty species of butterflies from all over the world. Plans also included the "Plantation Gardens," a new exhibit that would feature a butterfly garden, a fruit and vegetable garden, a rose garden, and a herb garden.

"We see this as a catalyst which will keep the momentum of Cypress Gardens going as to attendance," he said. "There's no way this is not going to propel us into the future."[93] Like some of the other older Florida attractions, such as Gatorland and Weeki Wachee, the Gardens also planned to turn to niche advertising to draw new visitors. Older folks, said Reynolds, "are our best demographic group, and we're not ashamed of that. It's one of the fastest-growing demographic groups in the country." However, the Gardens wasn't about to give up on its youth market, either, and the ads would also remind people that Cypress Gardens was the "Water Ski Capital of the World." The most successful parks, predicted Ady Millman, director of the Dick Pope, Sr. Institute for Tourism Studies at the University of Central Florida, will be the ones who are able to connect with the tourists' nostalgia for the Florida of yesteryear. He admitted this wasn't a "big market," but he added: "It's out there. The same people who love Miami Beach's Art Deco hotels will want to see Weeki Wachee's mermaid theater."[94]

Whether they would want to drive to Cypress Gardens to see Wings of Wonder, the new butterfly exhibit that opened in January 1993, was another question. The butterflies certainly traveled a great distance; they were shipped in pupae form from an Amazonian rain forest in Ecuador, and once they reached the Gardens, were pinned onto foam boards, where they would emerge within a couple of weeks. Unfortunately, shortly after the Wings of Wonder conservatory opened, nearly a third of the one thousand butterflies died. Cypress Gardens quickly took action to figure out what went wrong. As it turned out, the butterflies had succumbed to small amounts of pesticide that were found on the plants. Within a couple of months, the staff weeded out all of the glitches, and the butterflies grew accustomed to their new environment. "We see them mating and behaving as they do in nature," said Richard Hesterberg, Cypress Gardens' lepidopterist.[95] Importing the butterflies wasn't cheap; it cost thousands of bucks every month to keep the conservatory stocked—in a perfect world, butterflies live for only two to four weeks. Hesterberg said he hoped to begin breeding butterflies on-site within a couple of years.

The bigger question on management's mind, though—bigger than whether they could breed butterflies on-site—was, "Will these butterflies attract tourists?" Apparently so. As one reporter wrote, "the ancient business of making money on wild animals is roaring into the 21st century with a new twist—cut-throat competition." And while butterflies certainly aren't "animals," they are "wild." When the Cypress Gardens butterfly exhibit opened, some SeaWorld executives were on hand at the moment a tiger swallowtail touched down on a child's fingertip: "'You can't do that with Shamu,' they muttered."[96]

Cypress Gardens wasn't alone in trying to reach new audiences with its hands-on wildlife

The ramp masters celebrate Cypress Gardens' fiftieth anniversary. By permission of Cypress Gardens.

exhibit. Nationwide, the money spent on aquariums and zoos had quadrupled since the late 1980s, and this interest in wildlife carried over to television. Jim Boyle of the Discovery Channel said the numbers of viewers doubles when "shark week" comes around: "If the animals can eat you, ratings go through the roof." The explanation? Clever marketing. As *USA Today* reported, Cypress Gardens didn't need to import killer bees to attract a crowd; blue morphos would do the trick: "From the new 'Wings of Wonder' 1,000 butterfly conservatory in Cypress Gardens, Fla. to gorilla tracking vacations in Rwanda . . . nothing but sex sells like wildlife."[97]

In 1993, Cypress Gardens celebrated fifty years of water-ski history with a water-ski reunion. Famous skiers from the past descended on the park: Willa McGuire Cook, Nancy Rideout Robinson, Buster MacCalla, and others. For the event, the park brought back some of Pope's more outlandish stunts like towing a baby grand piano across the lake, along with the old standbys like trick and jump skiing, kite flying, and Corky the Clown. The ski show had changed quite a bit from its inception back in 1943, when Julie Pope summoned her children, Adrienne and Dick, home from school to put on a show for servicemen. The human pyramid was taller and the jumps riskier. For the new show, the Ramp Masters, a group of Gardens skiers, created a "four man Serpentine jump," a stunt that set Cypress Garden's fifty-first skiing record. Robyn DeRidder, public-relations person for the Gardens, emphasized that "with our new ski show and other additions, like new botanical gardens and the Wings of Wonder Conservatory, we feel we're getting back to what Dick Pope would have liked."[98]

But nostalgia for the halcyon days of Dick Pope wasn't enough to persuade Anheuser-Busch to hang on to Cypress Gardens. Just one year after the anniversary, they announced plans to sell Cypress Gardens to the park's management team, a move some people found heartening. "These people can maybe focus it much better, operate it on a smaller scale, on a smaller budget and try to see it for what it really is," said Abraham Pizam, a professor or tourism management at the University of Central Florida. "It's not a Busch Gardens, it's not a Sea World. If it operates on a smaller scale, it can be very successful." The impending purchase by the management team, headed by Bill Reynolds, would also mean "a return to local control after two corporate owners."[99]

In April 1995, the sale became official, and in a press release, Reynolds wrote, "Cypress Gardens is a world-famous Florida landmark and we are committed to continuing the positive growth and expansion in areas that are most appealing to our guests."[100] It turns out that what appealed to the guests, most of whom were older, were flowers, so the park doubled the number of flower festivals. "In lieu of a roller coaster, in lieu of a simulator ride, these flower festivals create special event time periods," Reynolds told a reporter. "Forty-five million people have come to Cypress Gardens since it opened. We have to convince them to come back. Because we're so old, they have the impression that they've been there, done that. That's the obstacle we have to overcome."

Other parks, established during a time when a Florida vacation meant ogling flowers, feeding alligators, and eating saltwater taffy, were also fighting the tide. Some of them looked to the past for inspiration. Sunken Gardens added an alligator wrestler named Kachunga; Gator Jungle brought in the world's oldest alligator; Silver Springs decided to bring in a show featuring how Johnny Weissmuller's *Tarzan* movies were filmed back in 1930s and 1940s. Weeki Wachee seemed to be looking to Disney for inspiration, merging two Disney films into one production—*Pocahontas and the Little Mermaid*.

Bob Sehlinger, author of *The Unofficial Guide to Disney World*, said that although these parks, with their palm trees, springs, alligators, and mermaids, helped establish Florida as a vacation spot, they were now nearly anachronistic. Museum pieces. "Many of these places fall into the genre of a curiosity more than a bonafide attraction," he said. Bill Reynolds seemed to agree:

Cypress Gardens had its first Rose Festival in 1979; "Floral Magic," the 1985 mum festival, featured the largest collection of chrysanthemums in Florida. By permission of Cypress Gardens.

"We appeal to an older group and to people who are interested in what Florida used to be like. . . . We are not so hustle and bustle."[101]

Bert Lacey worked at the Gardens from 1974 to 1977, returning to the park in 1995. He said working at the Gardens in the 1970s was "like working with a family," and that feeling persisted even after the park had gone corporate, largely because of employees who knew the original Gardens and loved it: "It was still pretty much that way when I was there from 1995 to 2001, but it was going downhill. Everybody worked hard, and there were people like Nancy Daley. Nancy skied in the ski show, and she was the seamstress for the belles, and I was walking through the park one evening, and I hear somebody on a pontoon boat taking a tour out, and it was Nancy. Everybody just did what they needed to do to keep the thing going as much as possible. Like I said, we felt pretty much like a family."[102]

In 1996, amid rumors that the park was going to shut down, Cypress Gardens celebrated sixty years worth of water-ski shows, southern belles, and flowers. To acknowledge the Gardens' long history and perhaps to cast a vote of confidence in the park, Winter Haven's city commissioners decided to pay homage to the attraction in a distinctly southern way; they painted a southern belle, the Gardens' logo, on one of the city's water towers.[103]

"There are water towers painted to look like ears of corn, shaped like ketchup bottles, clad in Gothic stonework or advertised as 'the world's tallest Corinthian column,' wrote a *New York Times* reporter. Southern author Donna Tartt explained why: "I think that water towers occupy such a striking place in the Southern imagination because the landscape is so flat—especially in the Delta, where I was born."[104]

Despite that show of confidence in the Gardens, Bill Reynolds said the rumors of the park's demise drove him nuts: "The product must be pretty doggone enduring to have stood the test of time. We're not deviating from what we've been doing for the first 60 years. We're building on it."[105]

One of the ways Reynolds planned to build on the Gardens' history was to add a "Scriptural Garden" that would feature plants mentioned in the Bible. The announcement came at a time when the Southern Baptists were considering a boycott against Disney for what they perceived as a shift from "wholesome family entertainment." They were upset by two things: R-rated movies made by Miramax, a Disney company, and Disney policies that eliminated discrimination against gay people. "The Scripture is the . . . infallible word of God," said the Rev. Wiley Drake. "Disney needs to use it as their corporate policy."[106] Reynolds said the new garden was unrelated to Disney's woes.[107]

The park also inaugurated another feature it hoped would bring tourists back: the Junior Belle program. For $24.95, a girl aged three to twelve would get to dress up, have her hair done, then stroll around the park for a couple of hours

The southern belle has always been a fixture at Cypress Gardens. By permission of Cypress Gardens.

toting a parasol.[108] "The Southern Belles were a signature role," said Bert Lacey, "and I had a hard time getting the owners to keep as many belles in the gardens as they needed. You need to have a presence." He said the Junior Belle program was the brainchild of Scotty Clack, the park's events coordinator and a former skier: "It made lots of money for us, and I think it enhanced the image of the southern belles. There was another way of getting more than three or four belles in the garden that we didn't have money for."[109]

The Biblical Garden opened in February 1997. Planted on a plot of land "the same size as the floor of a suburban house," the garden contained lettuce, fig trees, and apple trees.[110] A *St. Petersburg Times* reporter seemed a bit dubious about its drawing power:

> In the corporate culture that is roller-coaster, runaway train, souvenir-sappy theme parks, creating a solemn place for meditation on biblical scripture and plants is not exactly a money maker. Definitely not a screaming must-see event that will pull you off the highway—and away from Orlando.[111]

Of course, this was two years before Marvin Rosenthal of Zion's Hope announced that his group would be building a theme park called the Holy Land Experience, complete with recreations of Noah's ark and Jesus' tomb, not to mention daily reenactments of the crucifixion. "If Jesus was going to have his own theme park," wrote Twila Decker of the *St. Petersburg Times*, "It was bound to happen here, where killer whales do flips 50 miles from the nearest ocean and Cinderella's Castle towers in the middle of the Florida scrub."[112]

Bill Reynolds seemed to take the Biblical Gardens to heart, telling reporters: "This is a natural addition to what God has given us here. So many people have made the quote to me that Cypress Gardens is as close to heaven as you can get on Earth." Six days after Cypress Gardens' Bible garden opened, a cold front came through Winter Haven, and park officials were forced to drag out the electric heaters to keep the plants from freezing. While Dick Pope may have felt Cypress Gardens was heaven on Earth, he was a bit more irreverent than Reynolds. When Pope fought off a freeze back in the 1960s, and his minister told him the Lord was looking out for him, he told his minister, "We put our faith in the Lord, put oil in the pots and fired to beat the Devil."

The only problem with using the Bible to create a garden, said Joe Freeman, the Gardens' chief horticulturalist, was that "the people who wrote the Bible were not horticulturalists." Tim O'Brien, an editor of *Amusement Business*, said that the Biblical Garden "may help solidify Cypress Gardens' niche in the world of theme parks. . . . They are doing what they know best. . . . And they are trying something new. I think that's cool."[113]

Cypress Gardens wasn't alone in trying to save itself from the "fate of drive-in movie theaters and eight track tapes." Or from the fate of Marineland, a sixty-year-old Florida classic that closed its doors in November 1998, unable to keep up with the megaparks. "Gatorland has added killer crocodiles," wrote Lesly Clark of the *Orlando Sentinel*, "At Silver Springs, country and western singers belt out tunes from the front steps of a faux antebellum mansion. Sunken Gardens in St. Petersburg is flirting with the notion of becoming a nudist colony."[114]

Like Dick Pope Sr., George Turner, the founder of Sunken Gardens, lived through the collapse of the Florida boom, only to find himself broke, but with a piece of land. The difference was that the piece of land Dick Pope acquired had a lake on it; Turner's piece of land used to *be* a lake. He'd drained it back in 1903 or so when he bought it so he could grow bananas and papayas in the fertile sinkhole left behind. Like Pope, Turner didn't cry about his bad luck when the Florida boom collapsed; he continued growing fruits and "eye-popping flora: coffee trees, tea plants, breadfruit and sausage trees." A classified ad in a 1934 *St. Petersburg Times* reads, "Turner's Papaya Farm and Sunken Gardens; Visitors Welcome, Papaya Fruit and Plants, Palms and cut roses, nice ripe tomatoes."[115] Turner finally started charging folks to walk through his garden. One visitor noted that "Mr. Turner deserves great credit for his grit and determination and the hard work he has done to make a beauty spot of what was just a tract of muck land."[116]

Turner sold his attraction to his sons George and Ralph in 1952; George sold his shares to Ralph in 1972; and Ralph sold the Gardens to his sons in 1979. By then, Disney World had decimated the park's attendance. In 1989, Turner's three grandsons put the Gardens up for sale, but found no takers until 1999. That's when the real-estate firm Titan Marketing Group came along with plans to buy the park and turn it into a nudist resort. "We want to retire," said Tom Turner, one of the grandsons. "It just isn't as good a business as it used to be," he said, referring to the days when a couple of thousand people per day would walk through

Sunken Gardens almost became a nudist camp in 1999; the City of St. Petersburg bought the attraction after that deal fell through. By permission of the State Archives of Florida.

the Gardens, shopping at the "World's Largest Gift Shop," and checking out the flamingos.

"The only thing that can save Sunken Gardens at this point is a niche market," said Galen Ballard, president of Titan. "[Nudism] is ideal because these are people looking for privacy and a place to go. The beauty of Sunken Gardens is those 14 foot high walls, bougainvillea dripping over them. You've got total seclusion." The group planned to call the nudist resort Gardens of Eden.[117] One can only wonder what Dick and Julie Pope would have made of that.

8 Defying Gravity and Hurricanes

That Cypress Gardens survived from 1936 all the way to the twenty-first century is remarkable, given the dramatic change in tourists' expectations. The Florida that entranced visitors from Ponce de Leon to William Bartram to Esther Williams is no longer the main attraction. Consider William Bartram's description of his encounter with an alligator on the St. Johns River: "Behold him rushing forth from the flags and reeds. His enormous body swells. His plaited tail brandished high, floats upon the lake. The waters like a cataract descend from his opening jaws. Clouds of smoke issue from his dilated nostrils. The earth trembles with his thunder."[1]

Now *that* is an alligator you will not find at Disney's Animal Kingdom.

Ken Breslauer, author of *Roadside Paradise: The Golden Age of Florida's Tourist Attractions,* said that even wrestling alligators doesn't tremble the earth anymore. "The 'video game' generation wants entertainment thrown at them, and they don't seem to have an appreciation of the real Florida, which is a shame."[2]

And yet, Cypress Gardens has hung in there, alligators or not. Over the years, the attraction expanded from its original 37 acres on the shores of Lake Eloise to 200 acres. From its initial

Florida's alligators have always loomed large (and larger than life) in some visitors' minds. Jacques LeMoyne drew images of the Timucua attacking 40-foot-long alligators after his visit to La Florida in the 1590s. Theodor de Bry later used LeMoyne's drawings to make engravings. Courtesy of the Library of Congress.

Cypress Gardens introduced topiaries in the early 1990s; each one took about twelve weeks to create. By permission of Cypress Gardens.

offerings of ski shows, southern belles, and canal cruises through the Gardens, it added, among other attractions, a few kiddie rides, laser-light shows, ice skating, and a bird show with a water-skiing macaw. It added the Gardens of the World and giant topiary bunnies and swans. And that had been enough to continue to attract its loyal clientele, many of whom came year after year with their children, then their grandchildren, then their great-grandchildren.

Then came September 11, 2001. The events of 9/11 not only changed the lives of the people intimately connected with the terrorist attacks, they also changed the lives of everyone else in the country. Some changes were immediate. Airlines, which transport over 50 percent of Florida's tourists, were arriving in the state half full. Hotels and motels stood empty, and all of those theme parks that dot the Florida landscape had to cut back on hours. Floridians were left wondering if the state had invested too much in tourism. "Tourism is wonderful," said state senator Daryl Jones, "but we need to have more diversity so we can survive these types of hits. The September 11 event and the fallout from that shows us that we need to take stronger action to diversify our sources of income."[3]

Surprisingly, six weeks after the attacks, tourists were ready to travel again, although many were still afraid to fly. They were also wary of going to Orlando's "mega-attractions." "A number of people decided to come to what we call 'Old Florida,'" said Scott Guthman of the Hernando County Tourist Development Commission. "So, in some sort of warped sense, it kind of benefited us. There were a number of people who mentioned to me rather than go to Universal or Disney, they decided to go to places they haven't been in years, such as Weeki Wachee and Cypress Gardens."[4] Two of those people were *Palm Beach Post* reporters:

> Forty miles southwest of Orlando and 30 years back in time, this theme park town that used to be resides forgotten in Florida's attic like Polaroids of vacations past. There's Mom in her straw hat and Jackie O glasses, purse stuffed with Coppertone, Teaberry gum and a AAA Trip Tik. There's Dad in a luau shirt and sandals, puffing a Viceroy and toting a 20-pound camera around his neck. And there you are, pink-skinned and sticky, streaked with sno-cone and raising welts on your little sister with the tail of your rubber

gator. Ah, those were the days! And those are the days in Winter Haven. . . . We went for a two-day respite from our noisy, busy, 21st-century lives. . . . But since we weren't going to stumble into a mystic portal back to 1970, we settled for Winter Haven.[5]

Although there were short-term gains for some of Florida's smaller attractions after 9/11, the reality was that the threat of another terrorist attack and the war in Iraq, coupled with the ongoing competition from Disney World and the other big attractions, finally took their toll on Florida's first theme park. On April 10, 2003, Bill Reynolds, CEO of Cypress Gardens, announced that the attraction would be closing its doors for good on April 13. He cited 9/11 as "part of the decision to close," adding that "attendance, the park's major source of revenue, has never rebounded from this event."[6]

After 9/11, a lot of tourists preferred visiting smaller attractions that represented "Old Florida." Author's collection.

The reality was that in 2003, fifty thousand fewer tourists walked through the turnstiles. Bert Lacey said the decline was predictable given some of the decisions the owners made: "They did like every bad businessman does—the first thing they cut was advertising and publicity. When I left, there were no billboards. Mr. Pope had billboards all over the country. That's what happened. I could see it was going to go down, and I didn't want to be there. I left in August, and they closed in April of the next year."[7]

Tom Flanigan, a spokesman for Visit Florida, confirmed Bert's thoughts on Cypress Gardens, noting that Florida tourism had declined in 2001 because of the terrorist attacks, but he pointed out that the industry was on the rebound. The state hosted a record number of tourists in 2002. "I know that some attractions have been impacted more severely than others," he said. "Everyone is trying desperately to get a piece of the pie." He added that tourists seemed interested in "Americana attractions, places that represent the quirkiness of their locale. . . . People think, 'Well darn it, if we're going to have a vacation, let's make it a really worthwhile family endeavor, instead of just dumping the kids off at a theme park.' This is the real Florida. Suddenly you're back in the '50s or '60s." One of the things that had changed at the Gardens, he noted, was the lack of advertising, which "has kept it off travelers' radar."[8] Dick Pope would not have liked that one bit—in 1954, an average of over 100 newspapers a day carried a photo taken at Cypress Gardens—and those were freebies.

The announcement to close the park came as a surprise to everyone close to it, including Dick Pope Jr. "I'm just glad my father and mother aren't living to see something like this," he told one reporter. "It's very sad. But there's been an awful lot of competition down the road. And we don't have a highway coming by the place. We did pretty good with it, though, for a very long time."

Dick Pope Jr. was president of the park from 1962 to 1985; he'd seen Cypress Gardens through some of its toughest years—the arrival of Disney World and a parade of other theme parks: Circus World, SeaWorld, Universal Studios. He spoke of the changes that had taken place in the tourism industry, one of which was that it wasn't always an industry run by anonymous corporations.[9] Dick Pope Sr. was anything but anonymous in his flamboyant flowery suits. As Dubie Baxter said, Dick Pope Sr. was psychedelic before there was psychedelic. You noticed the man.

A southern belle graces one of Cypress Gardens' road signs. By permission of the Winter Haven Historical Museum.

The reality was that over the last few years leading up to this moment, over 90 percent of

Dick Pope Sr. was known for his colorful haberdashery; here he is at the *Easy to Love* luau with Julie, Dick Pope Jr., and Frances Pope. By permission of Cypress Gardens.

the tourists who came to the Gardens were retirees. Steve Baker, president of Baker Leisure Group, a consulting firm, added that the Gardens' location was its biggest problem: "It was hard to get there," he said.[10] One employee was upset because she said the owners had just "let [the park] go" over the past few months: "They knew it was coming. They've been letting the park go down, down, down."[11]

Nick Jackson, a second-generation skier, remembered the days when the stadiums were full of spectators, especially on the days the park had concerts. Toward the end, that all changed: "There was nobody here. The owners were from around here; I still see them around. I think they were just pulling money out once they knew what was going on, and there was nothing they could do about it. Basically we came out on a Friday, and they said, 'Sorry, but we're shutting down on Sunday,' and that was it. I'm surprised they didn't get out of town."[12]

Other people in the Polk County area wondered about the effects of the closing on nearby attractions, such as Silver Springs and Bok Tower. "There are a lot of similarities in the natural experience you find at Cypress Gardens and Silver Springs, so their closing must cause concerns for Silver Springs," said Bob Taylor, a Winter Haven native and Ocala businessman. "How long can they hold out and compete against the electronic rides of Disney?"

Apparently, Silver Springs wasn't quaking in its boots, but it was pulling out its wallet. After expressing dismay over the news, Bob Gallagher, general manager of Silver Springs, said the attraction was moving right along. The Springs had recently been purchased by Palace

Entertainment, which planned on giving the attraction a multimillion-dollar makeover.[13]

Over at Historic Bok Sanctuary, staff members were handling frantic phone calls from brides looking for a place to have their weddings now that the Gazebo at Cypress Gardens was no longer available. Angel Novikov and Wolfgang Jank were the last couple to take their vows in the Gazebo. "We were shocked," she said, explaining that she heard the news during her rehearsal earlier in the week.[14]

But the bad news was good news of a sort to the Sanctuary, which was ironic, given that Dick Pope Sr. almost always advertised Bok Tower for free on his early postcards. But the Sanctuary wasn't as dependent on tourists; Bok left a trust fund behind that would carry the Sanctuary over in hard times. Still, after 9/11, people actually came to Bok seeking refuge, said Cindy Turner, marketing director.[15]

Bob Gernert, executive director of the Winter Haven Chamber of Commerce, wasn't giving up on Cypress Gardens' legacy as a Florida icon, even though he'd been in touch with Reynolds almost a year before the announcement, worried that the Gardens might not make it in a post-9/11 world. After spending the day handling phone calls and e-mails "that would make you cry," he told a reporter: "Many, many people are interested in exploring the feasibility of preserving the original botanical gardens of Cypress Gardens as a park. To be sure, its historic value to our city, county, and state [is] immeasurable." Essentially, Gernert said, Cypress Gardens put Florida and Winter Haven on the map.[16] What would happen if it disappeared off that map, the way it had literally back in 1957?

Cypress Gardens' 2003 closing meant more tourists visited Bok Tower. Author's collection.

Cypress Gardens' 1950s-era menu featured Amelia Newland's pecan pie: 1 cup chopped pecans, 3 eggs beaten, 1 cup dark brown sugar, 1 cup light corn syrup, ¼ teaspoon salt, 3 tablespoons milk, 1 teaspoon vanilla, 1 unbaked pastry shell. Place pecans in bottom of unbaked pie shell. Blend together remaining ingredients. Pour the mixture into the pie shell and bake at 450° for 10 minutes, then reduce oven heat to 325° for approximately 40 minutes. Author's collection.

"That's a good question," he said, "and not the kind of question I like to hear. But it's something we have to face." He also acknowledged that the Chamber of Commerce and others in the community had been aware of Cypress Gardens' troubles, and they had discussed the possibility of it closing. Just like the folks over at Bok Tower, the Winter Haven contingent had already begun looking for solutions, focusing on the Chain of Lakes and its series of canals and bridges that had been developed right about the time Dick Pope Sr. was digging his own canals. "We're looking for a totally new marketing outlook for the chain," he said. "It's something we've just taken for granted. But now we have to think like Dick Pope Sr. and find all the good that we can in our lakes. . . . We certainly don't want to diminish the impact of Cypress Gardens closing because it is heartbreaking, but we aren't out of the race yet."[17]

The local newspaper published letters from people who'd fallen in love at Cypress Gardens or with Cypress Gardens. Raymond MacCalla wrote in about Buster and Betty, who'd met at the Gardens as skiers and married. Louella and Merle Stevens wrote that they'd come to Florida on their honeymoon, had toured Parrot Jungle, Monkey Jungle, and Cypress Gardens. Thirty years later, they moved to Florida; Louella still had the 1952 menu from Cypress Gardens.[18]

On the Gardens' last day, more than fifteen thousand people showed up, including Burma Davis Posey of Orlando. A former Miss Georgia, she stood at the gates passing out "Save Cypress Gardens" fliers, urging patrons to call or write Florida governor Jeb Bush to encourage the state to step in.[19] She wasn't alone. The Cypress Gardens skiers put on their final performance that afternoon. Jaclyn LeDoux had been hired the week before, but she already felt the pain of losing her family. "When you're a water skier, you want to be at Cypress Gardens," she said. "It really is a family. We've been crying non-stop." Michelle Miller, who worked as an Aqua Maid for twenty-two years, agreed: "It's very emotional. We're trying to hold back the tears." But like a true performer, she said the skiers had put together a final routine that would wow the audience: "It should be the best show ever." Stacey Brinkerhoff, a skier who met and married her skiing husband at the Gardens, seemed to speak for everyone: "It was part of our identity. We had heard it was going downhill but we always thought it would be there."[20]

Within days of the closing, Polk County legislators were meeting to discuss the possibility of convincing the state to use monies from a land-preservation account to preserve the original Gardens. Jeb Bush had already asked the Department of Environmental Protection to look into ways of preserving the property. The Florida Forever program was one possibility. "The fund is available for environmentally sensitive land . . . or land that has historical and recreational value, and Cypress Gardens certainly fits into that criteria," said DEP spokesperson Kathalyn Gaither.[21]

Bob Gernert went to Tallahassee with a group to plead Cypress Gardens' case. Dick Pope Jr. who had become a pilot as a marine in the 1950s, volunteered to fly them up. "I watched Dick as we worked to save the Gardens," said Bob. "He went to the hearings,and he spoke, and he was eloquent, and he chose his words carefully. I mean, he could say more in two sentences than some people could say in an hour. I have tremendous respect for Dick Pope Jr. And he got more and more involved. Rick Dantzler, his son-in-law, was much more the front man for this, but Dick was wonderful. The governor wanted to meet him; people making the decisions saw the heir apparent sitting in the audience, and I think it really had a great effect on the deliberations to see him there."[22]

Dick Pope Jr. played down his role in saving the Gardens, crediting a group of skiers and belles and other park employees for getting Bush's attention. "I'm a peon not an icon," he told a reporter for *WaterSki Magazine,* undercutting his own and his family's iconic status in the world of waterskiing. Struck by his humility, the reporter wrote that "it would be difficult to name anyone else with as great an influence on American water skiing as Dick Pope, Jr. and his late father."[23]

Luckily, within a month of the closing, two interested buyers came to town. One was Kent Buescher, owner of the Wild Adventures Theme Park in Valdosta, Georgia, and the other was an Orlando real-estate developer, David Siegel. Buescher's plan included investing about $30 million not just to preserve the original site, but also to add roller coasters and other rides in order to draw younger crowds. Dick Pope Jr. was impressed with Buescher's plans: "He's hit on something with not enough younger people coming here. I just hope the Gardens go on forever." Siegel, on the other hand, had no plans for major changes, other than to rejuvenate the Gardens. He suggested the park might be known as the "Smithsonian of the South." Burma Davis Posey, who had organized the Friends of Cypress

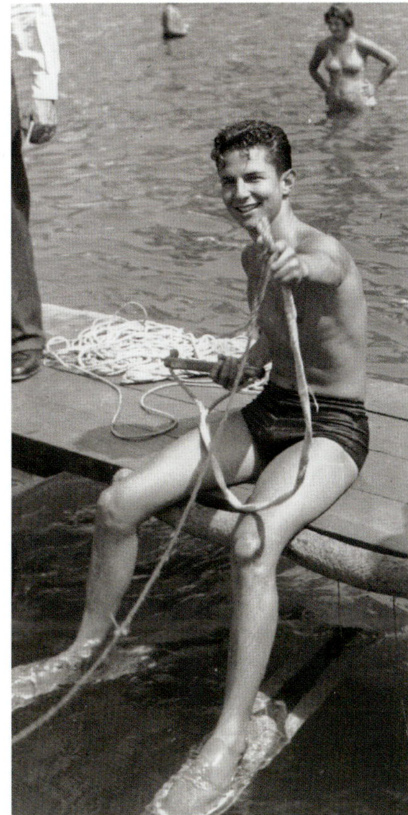

WaterSki Magazine recognized Dick Pope Jr. for his influence on American waterskiing. By permission of Cypress Gardens.

In this 1970s-era photo, southern belles frolic in the "original" Gardens, which were determined to be "culturally significant" to the State of Florida. Author's collection.

Gardens, apparently supported Siegel's low-impact plans for the Gardens. "Mr. Buescher is not the only option," she said.[24]

By June 2003, Florida's Acquisition and Restoration Council voted to add Cypress Gardens to the list of properties to be acquired through the state's land-conservation program, Florida Forever. David Struhs, secretary of the Department of Environmental Protection, said: "When a piece of property becomes a cultural icon, it is important to preserve it. . . . Cypress Gardens is a piece of Florida's modern history."[25]

Hearings were set for August 20 and 26, and the Friends of Cypress Gardens began organizing supporters, including out-of-work southern belles, for the journey to Tallahassee. "We're going to throw all the possible solutions against the wall because we really don't know which ones might stick," said Rick Dantzler, who headed up a Winter Haven Chamber of Commerce task force. "I'm hoping that whatever we do, we create the kind of flexibility the [state] will need to try to cobble together a deal."[26]

Meanwhile, the Gardens themselves were going to seed, literally. After four months without care, the topiary bunnies and swans were dying off, and the grounds were looking a bit ragged. But the magic was still there. "Like an elegant dowager caught in the rain," one reporter wrote, "Cypress Gardens looks shabby and disheveled but her charm still shines through."[27] The Trust for Public Land was bombarded with calls from people wanting to help clean up the Gardens. Bob Gernert was excited about the interest, but cautious. He seemed to be channeling the voice of Julie Pope, who'd traveled all over the world with her husband in search of plants for the Gardens: "What we surely need is people there who can coordinate the volunteers so we don't remove exotic plants. The right way to prune the plants is going to be a big issue."[28]

After the initial hearing, Rob Lovern, assistant director of the Division of State Lands, said the state was considering a "conservation easement" that would allow a third party to buy the Gardens, at which point the state would purchase the original Gardens with the stipulation that the new owner would preserve and then maintain the entire attraction. "We're not in the theme park business, and we shouldn't be," said Lovern. State historians were called in; they determined that about 60 acres were "culturally significant," and included the Florida pool, the original Gardens, and the waterskiing areas. "At the very least, we have to make sure we preserve the heart and soul of what has been so much a part of Florida's history for all these years," said Rick Dantzler.[29]

By the following week, the Trust for Public Land, a national nonprofit land-conservation group, had stepped in, saying they would like to purchase 107 acres of the park, a plan that frustrated the Friends of Cypress Gardens, who wanted the entire property purchased. They argued that the park was actually 225 acres, while the owners said the park was 174 acres. The Trust

Ballerina Gail Armour rests against a cypress tree in this 1930s-era "Study in Knees." Author's collection.

for Public Land would not keep the property; they would simply resell it to a party who would agree to preserve it.[30]

On August 26, to the delight of a group of hoop-skirted southern belles and costumed water-skiers, Governor Bush formally announced that Cypress Gardens would be listed along with other properties the state wanted to preserve. "Cypress Gardens is an important part of Florida's heritage," the governor said. "I am hopeful we can preserve this environmental and cultural treasure for years to come." This meant that the state was putting 176 acres worth of Cypress Gardens on the list, quite a bit more than the 107 acres the Trust for Public Land was willing to buy. "One hundred seven acres is not adequate to take the park and make it into a viable entity," said Kent Buescher. The problem was that the current owners still possessed a portion of the property, and getting them to sell was going to be difficult since they had already gotten a contract to sell 10 acres for about $5.5 million.[31]

By September, some people were questioning whether or not the state's preservation funds should be spent to save yet another failed tourist attraction. "Cypress Gardens has no known special environmental attributes," said John Ryan of the Polk County chapter of the Sierra Club. "Golf courses have as much environmental resources as Cypress Gardens does, and nobody's proposing to preserve old golf courses." Eric Draper of Florida Audubon agreed: "You could protect panthers and manatees and black bears and springs, which are probably the most endangered natural resources in our state. Instead, we're buying a fairly insignificant little landscape that's fairly artificial." Still, despite their misgivings, the Polk County Sierra Club was not protesting the purchase, stating that a buyout by the state was preferable to development.[32]

In the end, the Trust for Public Land decided to go ahead and purchase 142 acres, a deal that included the original Gardens, the water-ski area, Southern Crossroads, the butterfly conservatory, the entertainment arena, and the old Snively mansion. They would have until February 2004 to come up with the money, but they would immediately take over maintenance of the grounds. The deal was confusing, not just to outsiders but to insiders as well, from local government all the way to the governor. The acreage at stake kept going up and down. "I've got to look at it," said Governor Bush. "It wasn't the full property, as I understand it. We have to look at that to see if this means that Cypress Gardens can continue on as an ongoing concern."[33]

The acreage wasn't the only thing shifting around. The number of players kept changing as well. One thing was clear. It took a group effort to save Cypress Gardens. Three different entities submitted bids to the Trust: Kent Buescher, the theme park owner; David Siegel, time-share operator; and America's Choice, a company that wanted to turn Cypress Gardens into an indoor snow-ski facility. Initially, all three bids were declined. Greg Chelius, director of the Trust for Public Land, said the snow-ski idea was "difficult to take . . . seriously," but the Trust was still working with the other two bidders.[34]

In the end, Buescher won out. Polk County and the City of Winter Haven purchased the 30 acres that made up the original botanical gardens, and Buescher purchased the 120 acres surrounding the gardens. The State of Florida paid $11 million for development rights to the entire 150-acre parcel, a move that would protect the park from development. Dick Pope Jr. said the deal was "super": "I've been hoping this will take place." Lynn Novakofski, ski-show director at the Gardens for twenty-two years, also thought the deal was good: "A lot of people will complain about a roller coaster, but it will get the Gardens open."[35]

The southern belles couldn't wait to get back to work when Kent Buescher bought Cypress Gardens. By permission of Cypress Gardens.

Dick Pope Jr. shakes Kent Buescher's hand at a press conference. By permission of Bob Gernert.

Not everyone was pleased with Buescher's winning bid. Burma Davis Posey, the person who had initiated the Save Cypress Gardens effort, was one of his most outspoken critics. "I thoroughly believe that someone going in with thrill rides isn't going to be successful," she said, adding that the rides would disrupt the peacefulness at the Gardens. "It would just rape the land."[36]

Buescher saw his purchase of Cypress Gardens differently: "Today we took another step forward to rejuvenate and reopen this beloved jewel of Florida history and Florida tourism." He said he planned to invest close to $40 million in upgrades and renovations, adding a water park and roller coasters. He hoped for a Memorial Day opening. Some of the southern belles were right there with him. Carolina Beleut, former head belle, busied herself sewing hoop-skirted gowns because almost all of the Gardens' dresses had been sold when the park closed.[37] Jodi Stringer recalled her glory days as a belle, when people would walk right up to her and tell her she was beautiful, then take a picture of her. "You'd be in thousands of people's photo albums and family videos," she said. "It boosted your self-esteem." Many of the former belles found that their experiences at Cypress Gardens weren't quite what the outside workforce was looking for. Crystal Jernigan became a waitress and then a substitute teacher. "The preconceptions about being a Belle were hard to overcome," she said. "You had to convince people that we didn't just sit there and wave." But Annie Ruiz said that's what she liked about being a belle—the sitting and waving. She got a job at Walgreens. "You always heard positive things as a Belle," she said. At Walgreen's, you don't hear 'Oh, you're so pretty.' People yell and cuss you out." Still, she wasn't sure she wanted to return to the ease of belledom. "I'd love to go back. . . . [Y]ou get to sit and relax and stare out to the lake and just think. But I get $2 more an hour at Walgreen's."[38]

A little over a year after Cypress Gardens closed, Kent Buescher's roller coasters were sitting in storage in Orlando, which meant that he wouldn't be able to open the park by Memorial Day as he hoped. "If I can't open with all the roller coasters and water rides, I won't open," he said.[39]

Ironically, while Buescher was waiting for the first shipment of coaster tracks to arrive, another Florida attraction was biting the dust, or sand, over at Panama City Beach. Buddy Wilkes, manager of the Miracle Strip Amusement Park, announced that after forty-one years, the Miracle Strip would be shutting down on

Labor Day weekend.[40] The park opened in 1963 in the dunes off the Gulf of Mexico, with one ride, the Starliner, Florida's first major wooden roller coaster. It quickly grew into a full-blown amusement park—"a touch of Coney Island in Dixie"—with rides like the Abominable Snowman and Dante's Inferno. Val Valentine, a commercial artist famed for creating the outsized sculptures that became Panama City Beach's signature, designed a lot of the sets fronting the Miracle Strip's rides, including the giant red devil head leering in front of Dante's Inferno. "We had to make this one big," he said. "We didn't want anyone to hit their head on the Devil's tongue." As for the demise of the park, Valentine simply said, "There's a beginning and an end to everything."[41]

Faced with buildings in worse condition than he expected, as well as an international shortage of concrete, Buescher was forced to postpone the opening of the revamped Cypress Gardens until October. Unfortunately, this meant that he would lose out on the lucrative summer season, but he remained optimistic. He could have just bulldozed the trees and poured concrete, but he wanted the walkways to twist and turn beneath a canopy of oaks. "Trying to keep so many trees added two or three weeks to the design process," he said. "We lost some precious time, but the final product is going to be worth it."[42]

Kent Buescher christened one of Cypress Gardens' new coasters the Triple Hurricane after a trio of storms in 2004 damaged the park. Photo by John Finkbiner. By permission of John Finkbiner.

Two hundred of those trees came down anyway, despite Buescher's efforts. On August 13, 2004, Hurricane Charley tore through Polk County, decimating the gardens Frederick Law Olmsted designed over at Bok Sanctuary and blowing the windows out of the tower. One of the biggest and oldest trees at the Sanctuary fell across the reflecting pool that Dick Pope Sr. had featured on so many of his old postcards.

Cypress Gardens was hit hard as well. "It was absolutely devastating on Saturday morning," said spokesperson Alyson Gernert of damage to the park. "You can't get back 50-year-old trees that have been uprooted."[43]

Kent Buescher issued a press release, saying he was devastated as well by what he saw when he arrived at the park after the storm. He cried when he saw the debris: "We had spent so much time restoring and rejuvenating the park that it was heartbreaking to see six months of hard work disappear overnight."[44] He figured the storm did about $3.5 million worth of damage. Randy Diamond, a business writer for the *Tampa Tribune*, pointed out that the "stakes were high even before damage from Hurricane Charley" delayed the park's opening yet again, but he applauded Buescher's optimism and willingness to "[roll] the dice big," by investing $50 million to preserve a part of Florida history. "No one can accuse the new owner of Cypress Gardens Adventure park of being skittish about risk," Diamond wrote.[45] But the worst was yet to come. Less than three weeks later, Hurricane Frances blew across Polk County, and although she didn't do a whole lot of damage to the Gardens, she certainly didn't help, adding another hundred grand to the bill for cleanup.

Unbelievably, the rout wasn't over. Hurricane Jeanne struck the Gardens on September 25, knocking down even more trees and damaging the boat docks and ski-show area to the tune of about a million. She also blew down forty of the billboards Buescher had planted along the highways. Altogether, Buescher estimated the storms did close to $7 million worth of damage. Now the park's grand opening was pushed back to the first week in December.[46]

Meanwhile, Buescher was dealing with the insurance companies, who, not surprisingly, lowballed their assessments of the damage, putting it at $2.5 million; Buescher argued that it was closer to $8 million. "This has been the most insane time you could ever imagine," he said, but he was thrilled that people were lining up to buy annual passes.[47]

The gates to Cypress Gardens Adventure Park finally had a "soft opening" the day after Thanksgiving, just two months after the last hurricane. A thousand people showed up at 10 a.m., eager to be the first to see the new park. Before the weekend was over, thirty thousand people swarmed through the Gardens, including William Beatty, seventy-four, of Ft. Lauderdale, a former Cypress Gardens skier who'd had a bit part in *Easy to Love*, the Esther Williams film made back in 1953. "I have to go see the Florida pool and videotape it," he said. He also took a ride on the Triple Hurricane, a coaster Buescher named after the onslaught of the storms.[48]

Some longtime visitors worried that the tranquility of the Gardens would be compromised by the addition of the amusement park. However, Buescher's design took those concerns into consideration; the Gardens were separated from both sight and sound of the noisy amusement park area by a buffer of trees and plants. Visitor JoAnn Hamilton said of the design: "They did it right. . . . Now there's something for everyone."[49]

Of course, a southern belle was on hand to greet everyone. Kim Tucker, seventeen, had been coming to the Gardens for practically her whole life. At the opening, she wore a red, white, and blue belle gown and stood by the entrance waving and smiling. "It's awesome to meet a lot of people," she said. "And you get to dress up and be pretty. If Mr. Buescher never came, this would all be condos. It's awesome to have it back."[50]

"I know I was quoted at least once in the papers saying, 'Roller coasters on Cypress Gardens Boulevard; I'm not sure they're gonna take that,' but this was early on," said Bob Gernert. "We had no idea that someone would come in and do that." Bob soon changed his mind. "As beautiful as Cypress Gardens was as a gardens and ski show, there wasn't a teenager in the country who ever wanted to go there because there wasn't a thing for them to do. So Kent's plan was kind of the best of both worlds. If you wanted the Original Cypress Gardens experience, it was there for you. But if you had kids and wanted to go to Splash Island and ride rides, then you'd go the other way. For the most part, I would say the majority of people would tell you they're glad we still have the Gardens."[51]

The park officially opened on December 9, 2004. Lieutenant Governor Toni Jennings was on hand to give a speech, and Banana George performed in the grand-opening ski show wearing a yellow suit and yellow skis while a yellow plane buzzed overhead. Dick Pope Jr. was there as well, and he approved of what he saw. "People can't help but love it," he said. Asked what he thought his parents' reaction would be, he said, "I think they would be pleased." Jamie and Tim Potter were certainly pleased. The couple was clearly bonkers over Cypress Gardens—they had married in the Gazebo in 1996 and named their first daughter Cypress. At the opening, both Cypress and her little sister wore belle gowns. Jamie had joined Friends of Cypress Gardens after the park closed and had gone to Tallahassee

In 2005, Cypress Gardens acquired Tarzan, a seventy-five-year-old alligator who had starred with Johnny Weissmuller in the original *Tarzan* films. By permission of Cypress Gardens.

to tell Jeb Bush just how important the Gardens were. She said she'd been waiting patiently for the opening: "Nothing would have stopped us from being here."[52]

Still, despite all of the optimism and the huge crowds; despite the addition of the Swamp Thing, and Pharoah's Fury; despite the excitement of the Triple Hurricane; and despite the success of Wild Adventures in Valdosta, some observers thought Buescher was nuts. "Logic would say they're going to struggle a bit because they're near the biggest and best in Walt Disney World," said Bill Cullen, president of an Orlando-based theme-park consulting firm. "He sure picked a tough place to try it. It's a radically different environment from Valdosta."[53]

Abraham Pizam, dean of the Rosen College of Hospitality Management at the University of Central Florida, agreed: "It's not that the park is not attractive. It's not that it's not beautiful." What was at stake was whether or not the park could attract twenty-first-century tourists who beelined their way to the oversized attractions in Tampa and Orlando. "Realistically," Pizam said, "looking at it from the outside, I'm afraid they might fail."[54]

Comments such as these might have made the hair on most entrepreneurs' heads stand up, but Buescher remained unruffled, a feat that was particularly impressive after what he'd gone through with the wham, bam, thank you ma'am trifecta of hurricanes. As he'd told his detractors all along, he wasn't trying to compete with Disney World. He simply wanted to create an affordable source of entertainment for central Florida families. And he succeeded. As Bill Vanderford of the *Forsyth County News* wrote: "Though I had seen the show more than 40 years ago, the precision of youthful athletes performing gravity-defying tricks on and above the placid surface of a natural, Florida lake had me spellbound. . . . Kent Buescher and his group have woven a beautiful tapestry of old and new so that Cypress Gardens now has something for every taste. I think that Dick and Julie Pope would again be proud of how their dream has been reborn."[55]

By the spring of 2005, Buescher was so optimistic about the future of Cypress Gardens that he brought in an animal exhibit featuring a jaguar, a couple of crocodiles, and a seventy-five-year-old alligator named Tarzan that had starred with Johnny Weissmuller in the original *Tarzan* films.[56] Maybe he thought the alligator would bring him luck. As writer Fred Grimm observed: "What refugees from the scientifically planned, computerized, super-thrill modern theme parks

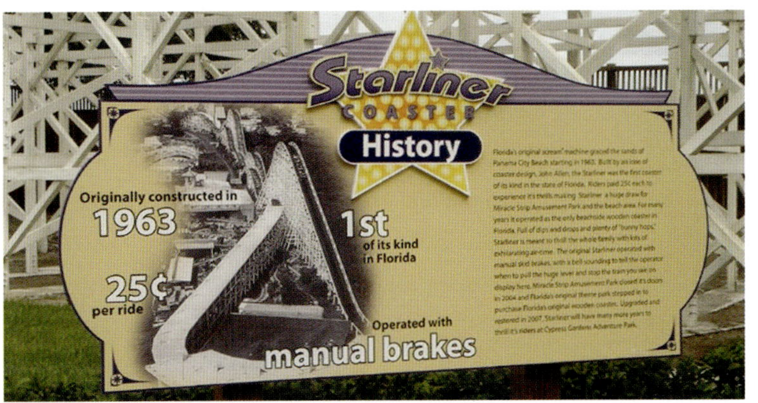

The Starliner was Florida's first major roller coaster. Photo by Robb Alvey. By permission of Robb Alvey, www.themeparkreview.com.

cherish, as they run screaming from the traffic and long lines . . . is a little old-fashioned hokey. They need alligators. . . . Every decent roadside 'gator attraction has a giant 'gator—often the world's largest—as its climactic exhibit."[57] The bigger and the meaner, the better.

Apparently, Buescher wasn't banking on his gator's power—Tarzan was in his seventies after all, not quite up to the Jumparoo featured at Gatorland—so he also bought the Starliner, the old wooden coaster that had been the main attraction at the ill-fated Miracle Strip Amusement Park. He wasn't sure if he would ship the coaster to Wild Adventures in Valdosta, or bring it to Cypress Gardens. Buddy Wilkes, former manager of the Miracle Strip, said he hoped Buescher would pick the Gardens as the Starliner's final resting

Colorful Dizzy Dragons have the Gardens as a backdrop. Photo by John Finkbiner. By permission of John Finkbiner.

place. "Cypress Gardens was Florida's first theme park," he said. "[The Starliner] was the first major coaster in Florida. We're hoping it stays in Florida."[58]

Just eight months after the Gardens reopened in December, more than 800,000 people had visited the park, compared to the 500,000 that had visited during its entire last year.[59] However, that was simply not enough. The park was successful, but the insurance companies refused to pay Buescher's claims for damages caused by the storms. He filed for nearly $25 million in both insured and uninsured losses, but Landmark American Insurance of Oklahoma paid only $7 million before closing the case. Buescher filed a lawsuit, and two years later, he still had not received a favorable ruling from the court.

On September 11, 2006, Buescher filed for Chapter 11 bankruptcy, even though nearly 1.5 million people were projected to come to the park by the end of the year. "The park has been successful," he said. "It's still going to be. This is a pledge I made. I have to honor it. This is a bump in the road. That's all." Bob Gernert stressed the economic impact made by Buescher's revitalization of Cypress Gardens: "[It] is more important to our economy now, than when it closed three and a half years ago. Few would dispute that he had brought a renaissance to our historic theme park."[60]

One year later, the company was still in bankruptcy, the lawsuit over the insurance claims still unresolved. Still, Buescher remained uncannily optimistic. He decided to pay $5 million to ship the Miracle Strip's famed Starliner Roller Coaster to Cypress Gardens, but in the end, neither the roller coaster nor the alligator could save Cypress Gardens.[61]

As former state senator Rick Dantzler said: "He put it all on the line. Then was hit by this perfect storm of misfortune." Just days after headlines like "Promotions, New Rides Help Attraction Mount Comeback," Buescher announced that he would be putting both Cypress Gardens Adventure Park and Wild Adventure, in Valdosta, up for sale in the hope that he could save both of them "for many years to come."

Burma Davis Posey of the Friends of Cypress Gardens admitted that Buescher hadn't been the organization's first choice for a buyer: "We didn't think roller coasters would attract enough people to compete with Disney and Universal in Orlando," she said. "But after he came in, we supported him 200 percent and became good friends. We are crushed this was not a success for Kent."[62]

Bob Kehoe said he had held his breath when Kent took over: "I talked to him briefly a couple of times, and went to several press conferences, and he seemed to know what he was talking about, and he had a great rapport with the public. But all along I wondered how you were going to get the number of people in to support the financial costs he kept pouring in there. Not having the inside, I could only say, 'I wish him luck and hope it comes out well.' He bought Cypress Gardens, except for the botanical gardens for $7 million, and there was an opportunity to put another $3 or $4 million into it, and then you could run with a smaller attendance base, make some good money, put it back into it and grow. But he didn't do that. He brought rides in and added the water park like he'd done at Valdosta and jump-started too big, I think."[63]

"What happened to Kent has been one of the most heartbreaking things I've ever seen as far as losing everything," said Bob Gernert, who became good friends with Buescher. "But what a godsend it was; without someone that would've taken that risk, we wouldn't have the Gardens; there was no one else on the horizon that had any credibility or vision to do this. The only other people who were looking at the park wanted to make it a series of museums—a museum of former beauty pageant dresses was one of the ideas, and we just didn't think that would generate a lot of traffic."[64]

As before, when the park closed, letters of support poured into newspapers across the state. Robert Bowden, director of Leu Gardens in Orlando, wrote that a visit to Cypress Gardens back when he was a child was like "[traveling] to another planet. We would bring home postcards (to the envy of our snow-bound neighbors) of water skiers standing atop one another in a pyramid and images of "ferocious" alligators. [Cypress Gardens] certainly had an impact on my life and . . . added to a bank of gardens and museums I visited as a child . . . ultimately led me

Visitors to Cypress Gardens were greeted by a poem. By permission of the State Archives of Florida.

to a career in horticulture and managing public gardens. Cypress Gardens is an American treasure and I hope that whomever ultimately buys it understands the impact that such magnificent gardens has had and can have on the guests that visit."[65]

With those words, Bowden echoed Dick Pope Sr., who had placed the following poem at the gates of his famous park:

If you'd have a mind at peace
A heart that cannot harden
Go find a door that opens wide
Upon a beautiful garden
Welcome to Cypress Gardens

Apparently, Bowden needn't have worried about the Gardens' demise. Days before the September 25, 2007, auction, a Mulberry, Florida–based investment group, Land South Holdings LLC, entered a bid of almost $17 million for the park.[66] On the day of the auction, a U.S. district judge approved the sale of both the Valdosta property and Cypress Gardens, much to the dismay of creditors who lost millions. Herschend Entertainment Group bought Wild Adventures, and Land South walked away with Cypress Gardens. Apparently, the only other bidder for Cypress Gardens besides Land South was Miami millionaire, William Beach, a former Cypress Gardens skier, however, Beach pulled out at the last moment.

Not everyone was relieved by the deal in spite of Land South's assurances. The company had a reputation for buying properties at low prices then subdividing them and reselling them for big profits. "We can now focus on the bright future of Cypress Gardens," said Brian Philpot, the manager of Land South, adding that the company "[relishes] the thought of being part of this park's storied history and ensuring that the park remains an integral part of Central Florida's landscape." As part of the deal, Buescher would stay on as president of Cypress Gardens.[67]

Some people felt like Land South really did walk away with the property. "Here they sit now, owning the park and owing less than was paid for the park when the State of Florida became involved," said Bob Gernert, referring to the original deal with Buescher back in 2003. Shortly after the deal went through, Bob said he was pleased with the new owners. "I have to be optimistic," he said. "The alternative is not something I want to contend with. They've grown up here; they both know what Cypress Gardens is; they both have children who love the park, and the more I hear and talk to them, the more I feel like the park is growing on them, and they're becoming emotionally involved with it, too. They're hard-nosed businessmen; there's no doubt about it. They're not going to go $60 million in debt—that's not going to happen. So I'm hopeful that the numbers will be good, and the traffic will be good, and it will produce enough revenue that they will want to keep it."[68]

In January 2008, Philpot and Harper made a tough decision regarding Cypress Gardens. They let Kent Buescher go and replaced him with Baker Leisure Group, a theme-park management team headed by Steve Baker, who'd worked for Disney for more than twenty years before forming his own company. Baker saw the opportunity as a challenge: "I don't want my name to be associated as being the company that operated Cypress Gardens when it closed."[69]

On November 11, 2007, Dick Pope Jr. passed away at home. "He was the best, he was number one, but he wanted to help everyone get better," his former Rollins College roommate Pete Fay told a reporter. The two attended college together in the 1940s. When they graduated, Pope Jr. went back to the Gardens, where he introduced barefoot skiing and became not only a world champion skier but also a champion skeet shooter before taking over as president of the Gardens. Fay, a senior judge in the U.S. Court of Appeals in Atlanta, Georgia, said Dick Pope Jr. "would help someone who would later ski a tournament against him. . . . He was the best, but he never mentioned it, he never talked about it."

Rick Dantzler, Pope Jr.'s son-in-law, agreed: "He cared about the employees deeply. He saw the Gardens as a family and maintained this relationship to the very end."[70] It's no small wonder, given that he lived more than half his life in the service of the Gardens. "My mother and father built that place," he told a reporter in 2003.

Dick Pope Jr. poses with some elephant ears at Cypress Gardens, circa 1940. By permission of Cypress Gardens.

"I made a lot of friends there. The thing I miss most is the people—I was there for 49 years."[71]

Back at the Gardens, skier Don Buffa was kept on by the new owners to oversee the nearly seventy-year-old ski show. All the recent shake-ups had taken their toll; gone were the ballet lines featuring twenty Aqua Maids, gone were the four-tier pyramids requiring twelve skiers. The skiers had one foot in the past, and one foot in an uncertain future. "You just missed Randy Rabe," Don said, as if the famous skier from 1961 had just stepped out to look over the lake. "He was the first back barefooter; he died last year. The story has it they used to hide him; he would go to a part of the lake that no one could see, no photographers, no reporters, and he'd actually get up on his ski backward and then step off backward. He had the monopoly on back barefooting, and as soon as people knew how he got there, how he started, then he would no longer have the glory of being the only guy who knew how to do it."

The story of back barefooter Randy Rabe is the sort of history that guided Don as he choreographed the new show. "There's a mystery about the place," he said. "It's not a SeaWorld that's only been around for twenty years. A day doesn't go by that somebody comes in and says, 'Hey, I used to know somebody who skied here,' or 'I skied here back in . . .'" Don would like the ski show to reflect the human-scaled history that had its beginnings in the late 1920s, when Dick Pope strapped on a pair of clunky Akwa-Skees at Miami Beach. "When you walk up these stairs," he said, referring to the stadium, "it needs to tell you that this is the Water Ski Capital of the World. That's important because people need to connect. If this is the Water Ski Capital of the World, what makes it that? Where are the pictures with Elvis? Where are the pictures with Johnny Carson? They should be all over the stadiums. That history lures people back in and hooks them into the what-it's-all-about."

He would also like to see the Gardens begin hosting tournaments and sending skiers overseas the way Dick Pope did starting in the 1950s: "They would say, 'Here's Jim Cassata who just came back two days ago from performing for King Hussein,' and the audience would say, 'Wow . . . Jordan?' We can still do that, even though King Hussein's not around. Abdullah's around. . . . [H]e learned to ski here."[72]

Whether or not King Abdullah could be lured to the Gardens for a shot at skiing across Lake Eloise again wasn't clear, even though King

Don Buffa carries skier Shaune Stoskopf during a show. By permission of David Laurie.

Left: Audiences still appreciate the pyramid of skiers at Cypress Gardens. Circa 2008. Photo by Gary Coates. By permission of Gary Coates.

Above: Cypress Gardens had four first-place winners on the 1955 U.S. men's ski team. *From left*: Red McGuire, Dick Binette, Scotty Scott, and Alfredo Mendoza. By permission of Cypress Gardens.

Abdullah told an interviewer in 2007 that one of his fondest memories was visiting Florida in the early 1970s with his father: "I went for a summer holiday on the East Coast—Washington and Florida. My late father, His Majesty King Hussein, was an avid water-skier and loved Cypress Gardens. So my first introduction to the United States was amazing." Ironically, the royal family also visited Disney World—"pretty impressive for a boy 10 or 11 years old," he added.[73]

The question is, with today's celebrity-saturated culture, would a water-skiing King Abdullah even register? Dick Pope Sr. didn't have that problem. Still, not even Paris Hilton could save Weeki Wachee when she showed up at the spring in 2004 to film *The Simple Life*, her reality TV show. By 2008, Weeki Wachee was on the brink of extinction when the state bought it and turned it into a state park.

Don reflected on Cypress Gardens' heyday when Dick Pope insisted the show go on whether there were ten or ten thousand people in the audience, the days when he would push the skiers to try new tricks, then "Boom! A press release would go out." It doesn't matter that times have changed, that newspapers themselves are endangered; Don believes in Cypress Gardens. "Like I said, Cypress Gardens gets its hooks in you and you can't get out. I'm forty-eight, and I can't get out."[74]

Boat driver Donnie Croft is another person who got snared by the heydays when the skiers broke world records nearly every year: "I pulled world records, like the nine-man flip jump. I pulled Zane Schwenk—he's a rep now for Mastercraft, but he did the first double flip off a ramp here. The first one in the world." It's been a while since the Gardens had enough skiers to perform the four-tier pyramids that were routine in years past. "Now we get standing ovations on this little 3, 2, 1 pyramid," said Donnie. "People are just glad to see us back, to see the show back. I think Cypress Gardens is going to come back and be Cypress Gardens again."[75]

The Aqua Maids may not don tiaras and tutus and cavort across magazine covers and through newsreels the way they did in the 1950s, but they are still basically the same after more than sixty-five years. Some things never change, said Shaune Stoskopf, who has performed ballet on water skis for nearly twenty years. "We're expected to be pretty all the time, to have our toes pointed and be nice and graceful and little. We still strive for the perfection of following each other in the ballet line." And over the years, she

Cypress Gardens skiers set a standard worldwide at the Water Ski Capital of the World. Author's collection.

Water Ski Hall of Famer Willa McGuire Cook is an inspiration to aspiring young skiers. By permission of Willa McGuire Cook.

said, she and her sister skiers did what Aqua Maids had always done; they would go and "belle" between shows. But skiing was her first love: "We'll keep going; we just need some water in the lake."[76]

Lyndsey Roma arrived at the Gardens in the footsteps of her sister in 1994, when the skiers were putting on their fiftieth-anniversary show. There was the "piano pulling," the "little boat that looked like a car," "Corky the Clown jumping out of a big fake birthday cake on the front dock." The Aqua Maids skied a twenty-four-girl ballet line that required two boats. "They had eight kites in the air," she said, "and they all came in *land land land,* and they had the nine-man jump act; it was really cool."

What was even cooler, Lyndsey said, was that one day she was surprised when watching TV to come across a scene that looked awfully familiar: "I said, 'hey, that looks like the Gardens; that's our shoreline.'" She'd found Esther Williams's film *Easy to Love* and ended up watching the whole movie, amazed at the scene with forty-eight skiers and eight boats. "That many people and that many boats on the lake took a lot of coordinating," she said, "because if one person falls, you've got to bring everybody back in, roll up all the ropes."[77]

All the skiers seemed to be connected to the past.

Jaclyn Ledoux grew up daydreaming about being a Cypress Gardens skier: "When they closed I was pretty heartbroken, so thank God, I got to come back." She started skiing in a club in Portland, Oregon, a hop, skip, and a jump from Lake Oswego, where Willa McGuire Cook got her start. "All of us idolized the Cypress Gardens skiers," she said. "Cypress Gardens represents the golden era of tourism and Florida's heyday. It's kind of an emblem of all that's good and pure, of how Florida came to be before all that other wonky stuff came along. When you walk through the Gardens, you can see the ski show, and it's evolved, but it hasn't grown out of the good parts. It's still a good reminder of the heyday.[78]

Another reminder of the heyday are the southern belles, but the new belles seem a bit tentative, not like the vintage belles, the ones who flirted with soldiers or played tricks on the tourists or turned cartwheels in the grass, grateful for their pantaloons. It turns out that most of these belles are new hires. Megan has only been a belle for two weeks. Her mother sits next to her, leaning in close as if to hear her daughter's answer to the question, "Why did you want to be a belle?"

"I'm very old-fashioned, and I love dressing up," Megan says. "I'd rather wear this than tight jeans—that's just me."

Megan explains the rules for belles: "Don't fall in the dress; don't run in the dress; be polite to visitors; be gracious when they ask you for your picture; smile. We go by the waterfalls to take pictures. I just greet the visitors in the morning and stand by the waterfall later. In the brochure, they say 'charming southern belles,' and there was a couple from England who said I was charming. I just love this. I haven't heard the history of the park yet."[79]

Brittany crosses one of the Gardens' bridges. She has been a belle for three days: "I wanted to be a southern belle because of the beauty in it, the history." She added that the new hires were going to take a class on the Gardens' history so they would know what to say when "guests ask, 'How did this start?' 'When did this start?' 'What became of it?'—the whole package. I know that in the '40s there was a frost in the winter, and the flowers decayed pretty much, and the lady who owned the park actually came up with the idea of ladies dressed in beautiful dresses sitting in the soil as flowers. I just learned this yesterday from my friend Whitney—we're actually the flowers of the Gardens."[80]

Joanna Baber became a southern belle in 2006. New York–based photographer Fiona Gardner made this photo of Joanna holding a Cypress Gardens fan for a series of photos based on the Cypress Gardens southern belle. By permission of Fiona Gardner.

The most interesting character at the Gardens has to be the African American southern belle, Samantha Williford. She's a wearing a pretty yellow dress and is sitting beneath an oak tree fanning herself near the stage where the remaining Temptations are singing. When asked how she became a belle, she said: "First I was in rides; then they transferred me to a belle, about two months ago. At first I didn't even know what a belle was, and when the belle supervisor asked me if I would like to be a belle, I said, 'Oh my gosh,' and I went around asking people what a belle was, and they told me, 'Oh they wear big dresses; they go down in history,' so I went on the Web site, and I was checking it out and said, 'Sure.'"[81]

What Samantha found on the Web site, of course, was not the *Gone with the Wind* version of belledom, but the history of Cypress Gardens belledom: the frozen flame vine, Julie Pope's quick decision to dress a secretary in a belle dress to lure the tourists past the wilted flowers, the subsequent use of the belle as photographic subject and marketing tool. In other words, the Cypress Gardens southern belle is no closer to Scarlett O'Hara than Jill Conner Brown, the self-described "fallen Southern Belle" and best-selling author who created the Sweet Potato

Queens. As Brown said: "Smiling and waving. That's what I got here with."[82]

"It was a kind of finishing school, modeling lesson and sex-ed class all rolled into one" wrote former belle Kimberly Moore of the Gardens when the park closed in 2003. "I learned more about sex from the other belles than I ever heard about from mom—or even read about in *Cosmopolitan*. And I worked hard to get the 'wave' down."

"It's like washing a window," a sister belle told her one day when they sat next to the Big Lagoon hiding out from the tourists.[83]

Samantha confirmed that chatting up the tourists is still a major part of the job: "I've never smiled and said 'Hi' so many times ever in my life. My friends are happy; they say, "I want to be a belle; I wanna be a belle,' and I say, 'you should come out here; maybe they will hire you.' I think we're supposed to be getting another black belle."[84]

Betty Doles was certainly surprised to find out that there was an African American southern belle at the Gardens. She said she'd been down at Polk Works, a local career center, right after Kent Buescher bought the park when someone asked her if she wanted to work at Cypress Gardens. "I said, 'yeah, if I can go as a southern belle,' and everybody thought that was so funny. When you think back, there wasn't no such thing as a black southern belle. A southern belle was a rich little girl around here on those plantations. I said I should apply and see what happens."

She waited a moment, then said: "Well, you couldn't have a black belle because there wasn't such a thing. You didn't have a plantation with your daughters running around in those dresses. Where would you find a rich black that owned a plantation?"[85]

It's probably safe to think of the Cypress Gardens southern belles not as the mint julep–drinking prima donnas who represent the antebellum southern aristocracy, but as flowers, as that novice belle did: *We're actually the flowers of the Gardens*. In Cypress Gardens mythology, the belle did act as a stand-in for that frozen flame vine. Gail Conner, the former entertainment manager at Cypress Gardens, said race wasn't an issue when determining who would make a good southern belle; the Gardens has hired African Americans and Hispanics, as well as girls from other countries. "Southern belle means southern beauty," she said. "I looked for girls who fit the description: happy, smiling people."[86]

Whether or not embracing the Cypress Gardens mythology can save the Gardens remains to

Although Cypress Gardens southern belles have that *Gone with the Wind* look, both literally and figuratively, in the Cypress Gardens mythology, they actually represent flowers. Author's collection.

be seen. Some folks think only Cypress Gardens can save Cypress Gardens; they would like to see the Gardens go back to its quasi-natural state. Lucy Chambliss thinks something was lost the day Cypress Gardens tried to become a "little Disney World."

"I wonder what would happen if they went in there and took out everything—the roller coasters, all that, what I call junk, and maybe even tried, if they've got the money, to build another Spanish-type clubhouse and then put the electric boats back in there, and make the Gardens as beautiful as they were. It used to be the clubhouse, the ski show, the nice place down there for people to use their cameras, and the rest was natural. They built that swimming pool for Esther Williams. But maybe they can't put it back the way it was. They need to go in there and redig those canals and then make the gardens beautiful around them. It would be expensive. But they spent millions on roller coasters."[87]

Oh, Lucy, if only. If only we could undo what has happened to all of Florida, roll history

Above: Southern belle and former skier Nance Stilley Hains poses as a bloom for this Cypress Gardens postcard. Author's collection.

Below: In this photo, a photographer captures another photographer making the shot. By permission of Cypress Gardens.

backward like a film. Cinderella's Castle would crumble into dust to be reclaimed by blackwater swamp, cypress trees, and alligators; the jerking robots in the Small, Small World would bore the tourists, who would then ooh and aah again over the sight of a great blue heron stalking fish at the edge of a lake. Tourists on Disney's Jungle Cruise would find themselves on the Jungle Cruise at Wakulla Springs instead, watching as tour guide Don Gavin points out the Suwannee cooters resting on a log: "Look at all those turtles on that log; it must be a Shell station." When a passenger asks for "more gators," Gavin will tell him God's honest truth: "Don't worry, this is nooooooo Disney. You'll see the gators when they're ready to see you."

Florida's springs would be crystal-clear again, instead of cloudy with algae, and looking deep into their "fathomless depths" would transport jaded tourists the way it did one early twentieth-century writer who gazed into the spring at Wakulla and "[lost] all sense of the earth." The sprawling highways would coil up like rattlesnakes and slither away through the longleaf pines that spring back up; the miles and miles and miles of cookie-cut subdivisions would be overtaken by the orange groves they replaced, and the air would fill with the scent of blossoms.

Cypress Gardens planned to go back to the basics in the twenty-first century. Photo by Lu Vickers.

The Cypress Knee Museum would have its glass cases replaced, and the thieves who made off with Tom Gaskins's best cypress knees would return them. Gaskins's handmade signs would hang in the trees again: "Forget Disney." Parrot Jungle would move back to its original spot and bring back Pinky, the bicycle-riding cockatoo. The abandoned fruit stands along Highway 27 would fill with oranges and grapefruit, and rental cars would be replaced with station wagons filled with screaming children wanting Pop to follow that sign to Cypress Gardens, where they would be awed by bougainvillea, one big banyan tree, a pyramid of water-skiers, and a bevy of waving belles. And Dick Pope, wearing a loud flowery suit, would stroll out of the old Hundred Lakes Yacht club, whip out an uncut sheet of ten-dollar bills, and polish the windshield of his Lincoln while tourists snapped away. He would then pass out free gardenias to all.

All we can do now is wait and see if Cypress Gardens will continue with its own gravity-defying tricks. "I don't know if anyone can divine the future of tourism," said Gary Mormino, co-director of the Florida Studies program at the University of South Florida in St. Petersburg. "Tourism has been really flat if not in decline for some time now. This started in the 1990s. Each generation creates its own Cypress Gardens. One generation may find it fuddy duddy, but who knows, maybe the baby boomers will take their grandkids there to try to re-create the romance they saw when they were kids. It's in some ways tied in to the future of Florida. I don't know if anyone knows the future of Florida—there are so many questions about whether baby boomers will even come here in the same fashion as their parents did."[88]

After just over a year of owning the Gardens, Brian Philpot and Rob Harper announced they would be closing the park temporarily on November 17, 2008. It's as though they heard Lucy's wish. They planned to take out all the rides and roller coasters and move the entrance back to where it was when Dick and Julie Pope opened the Gardens in 1936. "The last thing we want to do is jeopardize the history and long-term future of this storied park with elements that do not promote what made Cypress Gardens what it is today—a beautiful botanical garden," said Brian Philpot.[89]

Philpot and Harper looked to the past, hiring Bill Sims, who worked for Dick Pope Sr. from 1971 to 1985. Sims had been working for the City of Winter Haven when Pope asked him to lunch one day; over the course of the meal, Pope offered him a job. When Sims told him he was unfamiliar with the Gardens' business, Pope said he would teach him. By 1985, Sims was executive vice president.

When the Gardens sold, Sims became an owner of Silver Springs, holding onto the property for about fourteen years before selling it to the State of Florida, then leasing it back, something that had never been done before. He sold the lease after three or four years and fished for a couple of months, running his two Ripley's Believe It or Not Museums on the side. "And then I got a call from Brian and Rob and met with them at the end of last year."

Sims had big plans for the Gardens, plans that would have made the Popes happy. He hoped to revive the ski show but pointed out that it might not be as easy as it sounds since there simply aren't the number of professional skiers there were in the past. Still, he recognized the skiers' iconic status and, according to the executive director of USA Water Ski, enlisted the help of former Cypress Gardens ski-show director Lynn Novakofski to look into ways of bringing back the "glory years when huge show presentations were the hallmark of Cypress Gardens."[90]

Sims also wanted to rejuvenate the electric boats that used to glide through the canals, and he planned to bring the old "palm bowl" parking lot back. "We'll park beneath the oak trees just like we used to," he said, "and it will be a lot shorter walk to the Gardens."

He was banking on people like Lucy to come back for events Dick Pope Sr. used to have like the Mum Festival and the Poinsettia Festival. He reeled off a list of possible festivals: blueberry, watermelon, jazz. It's clear that Sims had paid a lot of attention to Dick Pope Sr.: "He taught me that the important thing really is to get people to come to the state of Florida and you'll get your fair share of them." Sims should know: He started Visit Florida, the official tourism marketing corporation for the state that was created by the legislature in 1996 as a public/private venture.[91]

Cypress Gardens planned to revive Dick Pope Sr.'s award-winning "Palm Bowl Parking Lot." Author's collection.

The Gardens opened again in late March 2009 with a new name denoting its two parks: Cypress Gardens and Splash Island Water Park. Each park had a separate entrance, and patrons could buy passes for either or both parks. The Starliner Roller Coaster and about a dozen other amusement-park rides still sat unsold on the property. The electric boats weren't running, and the "palm bowl" parking lot hadn't been restored to its former glory. Reviews were mixed. Some folks were pleased by the reduced prices but unhappy that there weren't more rides in the water park. Some were thrilled they could bypass the water park and head straight for the original Gardens. One woman wrote a rave in the local newspaper cheering Sims on: "Cypress Gardens is on the edge of returning to its golden age! . . . Bill Sims is the magic man in this restoration, but he needs believers in the program. Let it be you."[92]

Despite this call to dreamers, by June, a spokesperson for the Gardens said Sims was no longer at the park on a daily basis; by July, it was reported that he was "coordinating decisions on events and promotions" with the Gardens' new general manager, Justin Hardin.[93] By August, employees spotted survey crews eyeing the property, and guests complained that the park was not being kept up. Rumors began circulating that Merlin Entertainments Group—"second only to Walt Disney World Corporation, in the theme park market share"—was considering locating a Legoland in central Florida, perhaps at Cypress Gardens.[94]

Even though it seemed inevitable, no one was prepared when, on September 23, 2009, Cypress Gardens shut its doors yet again. This time, there was no advance notice. There were no last-day crowds jostling for a brush with Florida history; there was no ski-show finale, no time for a last stroll beneath Dick Pope's famous banyan tree, no time for that one last photo with a smiling belle. Philpot and Harper issued a press release stating that they were "in the process of negotiating with several potential purchasers" and didn't feel it was fair to employees or visitors to "continue operations . . . with the future of the property in flux." Rick Dantzler, representing Land South Holdings, said the owners were hoping to find a buyer who would continue operating the Gardens as a theme park.[95]

An editorial lauded Philpot and Harper for taking a chance on reviving the Gardens, adding that there were 16.9 reasons they should be "given a good portion of respect," alluding to the $16.9 million they had forked over to buy the park in 2007.[96] "It's disappointing," said Rick Dantzler of the closure, "but the world is changing and we're struggling to find a configuration that works in today's marketplace."[97] The *Tampa Tribune* editorialized that Dantzler might be right, that "the world is not the same as it was thirty or forty years ago," concluding that "Cypress Gardens is not meant to be a commercial enterprise. Its fate may lie as a state and county park."[98]

In mid-December 2009, Mark Jackson, a former Cypress Gardens skier who is now executive director of Polk County Tourism and Sports Marketing announced "something formal will happen in the next two weeks." He remained vague, citing confidentiality agreements, but Legoland was on some folks' minds.[99]

On January 21, 2010, Nick Varney, the chief executive officer of Merlin Entertainments Group, stood on the patio in front of the old Snively Mansion at Cypress Gardens behind a podium shaped like a giant Lego block. Greeting Florida Governor Charlie Crist, state Senator J. D. Alexander, Polk County Commissioner Bob English, and a gathering of other elected officials and the press, Varney revealed, in a soft British accent, what he called "Florida's worst kept secret": that Cypress Gardens would indeed become Legoland Florida. After workers unveiled a backdrop featuring scenes from "Legoland Florida," Varney turned to the audience: "You know," he said, "Walt Disney once famously remarked to one of his executives, 'Remember guys, this all began with a mouse.'"

Varney might have been referring to that moment, the moment that Cypress Gardens ceased to exist in name as an attraction almost 75 years to the day after it first opened, 82 years after Mickey Mouse was created, 39 years after Disney World arrived and Florida's family owned attractions began to disappear. But as Varney continued speaking, it was clear he wasn't referring to Cypress Gardens' demise at all; he was referring to the Legoland story, how it, too, started small, "with a humble Lego brick back in 1949."[100]

Like the creations of Walt Disney and Dick Pope, Legoland had its origins in the Depression era. In 1929, a Danish carpenter named Ole Kirk Christiansen started feeling the effects of the failing economy. To ward off bankruptcy, in 1932, he began building wooden pull toys for children. He named his toy company Lego, after the Danish phrase *leg godt,* or "play well." After meeting with some success, he bought the first plastic molding machine in Denmark and began cranking out the "Automatic Binding Blocks" that would later be known as Legos.

By 1960, at the factory in Billund, workers—including Ole Christiansen's niece, Dagny Holm—began creating large Lego models for display in department stores and toy shows. Before long, the factory was besieged by visitors curious to see the models.

Godtfried Christiansen, Ole Kirk's son, and by this time the sole owner of LEGO, decided to divert visitors from the factory by setting up models outside. "What I had in mind first," Godtfried told a reporter in 1980, "was something in the way of a large open-air show . . . where a pensioner couple could sell tickets and perhaps run a small cafeteria." By the time he and his collaborators began designing the displays on paper, they realized they had something bigger on their hands: a Lego theme park. And like the experience of a certain Dick Pope, once Christiansen announced his plans, he found no shortage of detractors. "Just about everybody shook their heads," he said. "It was a utopian notion to think that you could set up a tourist attraction in the middle of the bleak Jutland moors, where people had no desire to come. But I've inherited a good chunk of my father's obstinacy." Godtfried soon hired a designer from Copenhagen to help him develop Legoland, and within two years, the park expanded to nearly ten times its original size.[101]

Given that history, it seemed logical that Merlin Entertainments would want to build a Legoland at Cypress Gardens. Varney said that Merlin considered other locations nearer to Orlando, but Cypress Gardens had that something special: "warm welcoming friendly people," the infrastructure, and the Gardens themselves. He took pains to describe some of Merlin Entertainments' other parks in Europe, emphasizing their natural elements. Alton Towers, the United Kingdom's number one theme park has "at its heart" beautiful gardens that are over two hundred years old. Gardaland, Italy's number one theme park, is situated next to a lake, and it, too, features gardens. Legoland Windsor sits amidst protected forests, just a couple of miles from Windsor Castle, where the Queen of England resides. "We celebrate that something special," Varney said, adding that in 2008 when he first set foot in the Gardens, "the hairs on the back of my neck stood up. It was evocative; it was beautiful; it was unique; it was love at first sight and that was exactly what all of my colleagues felt as well. . . . The botanical gardens will always be one of the compelling reasons why people should come here." He said, "I can assure any of you who were concerned that the gardens of Cypress Gardens are very, very safe in our hands."

When asked whether Legoland Florida would retain the world famous ski shows, Varney said he imagined they would keep the show, after putting a "Lego-twist" on it. Several reporters asked if there was a chance Legoland Florida might be called Legoland Cypress Gardens. "The botanical gardens will retain the name," he said. "People will come to Legoland Florida to see Cypress Gardens."[102]

At least a couple of newspapers missed that point, penning headlines like "Legoland to Brick over Cypress Gardens" and "Legoland to Replace Cypress Gardens." The gardens aren't going anywhere; Polk County owns the original 30 acres containing the botanical gardens Dick Pope started with, and it will lease them to Merlin.

Alton Towers, Merlin Entertainments' British theme park, although not a Legoland, is perhaps the best model Cypress Gardens' fans can hope for. It began its life in 1000 BC as an iron age fort and by AD 700 was a fortress for a Saxon king. Sir John Talbot, who later became the First Earl of Shrewsbury, took ownership in 1406. Four hundred years later, in 1811, Charles Talbot, the 15th Earl of Shrewsbury, transformed a former hunting lodge on the site into a house, and then turned his attention to the adjacent sandstone valley where he would create some of Britain's most luxurious gardens, no small feat since the valley was not exactly prime property. Like Dick Pope 120 years later, Talbot had to dig canals and divert water into ponds before he could fulfill his vision. Over the next two decades, he would add Dutch and Italian gardens, a Chinese Pagoda fountain, and a miniature Stonehenge. By the 1860s Alton Towers began offering "grand fetes" with performers such as "tightrope walkers, strong men, acrobats, trapeze artists, freaks, clowns and various other show people." During the early 1920s, having passed from earl to earl, the gardens and the estate languished. A private company bought the site in 1924, restored it and began operating it as a full-scale tourist attraction. When World War II began, Alton Towers was commissioned to house soldiers, not to be reopened to the public until 1952.[103]

The first amusements offered to the public in the 1950s were "motor events" featuring motor cycle races and steam engine rallies. Throughout the 1960s Alton Towers added more attractions including a zoo, a fairground, and a miniature railway. In the 1970s the park began hosting "Mirror Days," sponsored by the *Daily Mirror* newspaper, and featuring such events as "Welly Wanging," a British version of Florida's mullet toss—they tossed a Wellington boot instead of a fish.

By far, the most-popular events at Mirror Days were the beauty pageants featuring the Mirror Belles. Despite the popularity of Mirror Days though, attendance began falling. The directors of Alton Towers, realized they needed to

Merlin Entertainments, owner of the Legoland theme parks, is no stranger to famous gardens; the company runs Alton Towers, home to some of the most beautiful gardens in Britain. By permission of Merlin Entertainments.

modernize their park, but they wanted to do it in a way that would respect Alton Towers' "history and heritage."

In a set of notes, director Dennis Bagshaw wrote that "for the gardens and landscape park to continue," it was necessary for the attraction to step up its "competitiveness . . . in order to bring it into line with the best of the World's Leisure Parks." He'd like to do so, he wrote, "without the intensive plastic and concrete approach of Disneyland." To this end, the park added roller coasters, a pirate ship, and a bob sled ride, all without sacrificing the gardens.[104]

After a series of sales over the next 20 years, the park ended up in the hands of an investment firm who now lease it to Merlin Entertainments. The gardens remain one of the most attractive features of the park. As one theme park guide noted, "if it wasn't for the magnificent gardens and grounds that surround Alton Towers, then we probably wouldn't have a theme park here at all."[105]

The parallels are obvious.

Right now, it seems as though Cypress Gardens' new owners feel the same way, that they recognize the value in this old Florida attraction and will see fit to revive it.

At the press conference, John Jakobsen, managing director of Legoland parks, demonstrated that the company had already begun its study of Florida history, unveiling two Florida icons: the panther and a basketball-sized orange, both made of Legos. Could there be a Lego southern belle in the future? A Lego sculpture of Willa McGuire Cook jitterboarding in her tutu? Lego sculptures of Dick and Julie Pope? Perhaps. For now, though, the Cypress Gardens of the past exists only in a virtual world.

You can go to the Florida Archives and watch Dick Pope as he talks in his gruff voice about the World's Fair he staged for Florida. You can go to the Water Ski Museum on Holy Cow Road, where the dusty-rose costume Esther wore for the most-iconic scene of her motion-picture career hangs behind glass. Out in cyberspace, people have set up unofficial Cypress Gardens Web sites; they have uploaded vintage Cypress Gardens' photos along with recent ones on Flickr. You can hit up YouTube, where the glamorous Willa McGuire Cook skis on one foot wearing her tutu and tiara, where Malcolm jumps boats, and Dick aquaplanes in grainy black-and-white footage. There is footage of Dick Pope Jr. racing his boat through and up the sides of cypress trees. People have uploaded vintage home movies of vacations at the Gardens. There they are, preserved forever: the 1957 Aqua Maids and southern belles, the crowds of tourists sitting on the photo pier, the flame vine, the electric boats, and the proud voice of the narrator, "We arrived just in time to see the famous Aqua Maids."

In another video, Esther Williams skis across Lake Eloise in a clip from *Easy to Love,* easily Dick Pope's most lasting example of "OPM squared" and, as it turns out, a pinnacle in the careers of both choreographer Busby Berkeley and Esther Williams. As Vincent Canby noted in a review of *That's Entertainment II*, an anthology of MGM's biggest hits, Berkeley was "less of a choreographer than a sculptor, whose medium is live people":

> Berkeley was a Pop artist before anyone knew what Pop art was. The Cypress Gardens water ski ballet—the finale of *Easy to Love*—is one of the most breathtaking examples of pure cinematic invention ever realized and Esther Williams, on her own water skis, taking her own jumps, and finally, being hauled aloft by a helicopter, was the perfect Busby Berkeley star, magnificently formed, fair of face and apparently not to be perturbed by air, wind, fire or water. A goddess."[106]

Esther Williams skis across Lake Eloise in a scene from *Easy to Love*. By permission of Cypress Gardens.

In a move Dick Pope Sr. would have appreciated, John Jakobsen, managing director of Legoland Parks, oversees the cascade of 100,000 Lego bricks at Cypress Gardens. Photo by Bob Gernert.

But she was Dick Pope's goddess first, and *Easy to Love* was his "one hour and 36 minute Technicolor commercial on Florida and Cypress Gardens." There she is, skiing across Lake Eloise flanked by Cypress Gardens skiers decked out in black and yellow, followed by the forty-eight skiers who make up the giant *V*. On YouTube, someone has added a melancholy song to the clip, and as Esther skis past the Florida pool, through a grove of cypress trees, through the geysers, her rose-colored sash flying in the air behind her, both she and her costar—the Gardens—seem to sail into eternity. One can only hope Cypress Gardens persists in Legoland Florida, if for no other reason than to remind us there was a time when water-skiers and flowers were enough.

Someone in Cypress Gardens' advertising department had faith in the Gardens' staying power. By permission of Cypress Gardens.

Acknowledgments

A book like this one isn't written by one person; it is written by many—by the people who shared their stories, by the people who wrote about the Gardens way before I came along (literally, since work on the Gardens began in the 1930s), by the people who took photos, by the people who put together the enormous Cypress Gardens Archive, by the people who put together the Cypress Gardens articles at the Polk County Historical and Genealogical Library, by the people who read the manuscript and offered criticisms, and by Dick Pope Sr. himself.

First and foremost, I want to thank the Pope family, particularly Julie Pope Dantzler, Rick Dantzler, Margaret Chase Parry, and Adrienne and Jack Watkins. They kindly shared stories about Dick Pope Sr., their one-of-a-kind father, grandfather, and uncle. They also shared stories about Julie Pope, the proverbial woman behind the man. The more I got to know about Dick Pope Sr., the more remarkable I found his wife and business partner. Living with him must have been like living with a small cyclone.

Julie, Rick, and Margaret also gave me insight into Dick Pope Jr., who headed up the Gardens after his father stepped down. The stories they told about him echoed what I heard from everyone else: Dick Pope Jr. was the consummate southern gentleman, emphasis on gentle.

I couldn't have written the book without the help of the people at Cypress Gardens. I first went to the Gardens after Kent Buescher bought the attraction. I was waiting to get into the archives when a man wearing shorts offered to walk me over. On the way, I told him what I was up to, and he told me he'd ridden the Starliner Roller Coaster that morning and found the ride to be fairly smooth. We walked through the maintenance area, and when we arrived at the archive, I said, "Thanks. I'm afraid I didn't catch your name." He said, "Kent Buescher." Cypress Gardens was saved from oblivion by this unassuming man who put everything he had on the line. Thanks, Mr. Buescher.

Thanks also to Rob Harper and Brian Philpot, who bought the Gardens after Kent Buescher; they saved the Gardens yet again. They also made sure I had complete access to the archives.

Thanks to Alyson Gernert, Lynn Wright, Doug High, and Jennifer Mansfield, who helped facilitate my visits to the Gardens. A special thanks to Nancy Zarza Daley, who spent a couple of days in the archive with me and who shared her story. Thanks to the folks at the Admiral's Inn—the discount kept me from going entirely broke.

A special thanks goes to Dorinda Garrard, Dorothy Manley, and Gail Seger of the Polk County Historical and Genealogical Library in Bartow. They compiled volumes of clippings on Cypress Gardens—clippings that were indispensible for my research.

Thanks to Bob Gernert, executive director of the Winter Haven Chamber of Commerce. A Cypress Gardens enthusiast, Bob not only shared stories but opened the door of the Winter Haven Historical Museum.

Thanks to Fiona Gardner, James Cusick, and Adam Watson. When he isn't playing with his band, the Intoxicators, Adam is a photographic archivist extraordinaire. Thanks to Arlyn Hernandez of *WaterSki Magazine*.

Thanks to Carole Lowe and Lynn Novakofski, who allowed me access to materials at the American Water Ski Educational Foundation Museum on Holy Cow Road. Besides sharing his story, Lynn helped me understand the world of waterskiing.

Thanks to each and every person who shared their stories with me. Bob Kehoe, Dubie Baxter, Red McGuire, and Willa McGuire Cook were particularly helpful—Bob worked at the Gardens for fifty-two years, and Dubie practically grew up there. Red was a skier for seven years and a photographer for twenty-five; Willa was Cypress Gardens' prima ballerina. After speaking with folks like Lucy Chambliss, Bert Lacey, the Doles family, Billye-Mullins Smith, Brenda Mitchell, Bill Bell, Spider Bell, Don Buffa, Dallas Abercrombie, Betty Skelton Erde, Richard Johnson, Nancy Zarza Daley, Lynn Novakofski, Simon Khoury, Dave Dershimer, the southern belles, and the water-skiers, I could see why people said the water in Polk County tastes like cherry wine.

A posthumous thanks goes to Dick Pope Sr., who wrote about the Gardens before they were the Gardens, and who wrote a book on the history of the sport he helped popularize: *Water Skiing.* He was the architect of his own story—he documented the history of Cypress Gardens with about a half million photos and a zillion clippings—all saved in the Cypress Gardens Archive. It isn't often you come across a person universally loved, but that was the case with Dick Pope Sr., Mr. Florida.

A special thanks to Joy Wallace Dickinson and Tracy Revels. They read the manuscript and offered suggestions on how I could make it better. Thanks to Meredith Morris-Babb and John Byram, my editor, and to Michele Fiyak-Burkley, Larry Leshan, and Susan Murray. To Pam Ball, my dear friend, who never says no when I ask her to read something, thanks again. Thanks to Sue Gambil for proofreading the manuscript. Thanks to Jennifer, who read the manuscript and who gave me the most essential gift: time to write. Thanks to my boys, Jordan, Samuel, and Elias, who despite missing me when I was "on location," gave their total support. A writer couldn't get by without the support of friends, and I have some of the best—way too many to list here. You know who you are.

Notes

Chapter 1. Land of Sunshine and Roses

1. John E. Long, "Touring Florida's Ridge Country," *New York Times*, January 13, 1957, ProQuest Historical Newspapers, http://proquest.umi.com/login.

2. Cheryl Blackerby, "Down Florida's Spine: U.S. 27 Is Historic Foundation of State's Tourism Industry," *Austin-American Statesman*, December 14, 1997, Newsbank Newsfile Collection, http://infoweb.newsbank.com.

3. John E. Long, "Touring Florida's Ridge Country," *New York Times*, January 13, 1957, ProQuest Historical Newspapers, http://proquest.umi.com/login.

4. Ibid.

5. "Suncoast Is the Jumping Off Place for Dozens of Attractions," *St. Petersburg Times*, October 15, 1963.

6. Malvina Reynolds, "Little Boxes" (Berkeley, Calif.: Schroder Music Company, 1962, 1990).

7. "Citrus Yields to Subdivisions in West Orange and South Lake," *Orlando Sentinel*, December 17, 1999, Newsbank Newsfile Collection, http://infoweb.newsbank.com.

8. Carrie Alexander, "Sweet Slice of Florida Life: Roadside Stands Still Offer Bounties of Fruit at Open-Air Markets," *Orlando Sentinel*, January 8, 2006, Newsbank Newsfile Collection, http://infoweb.newsbank.com.

9. Parker Nash, "Fruit Vendors Standing Firm on Selling Out," *Orlando Sentinel*, January 10, 1998, Newsbank Newsfile Collection, http://infoweb.newsbank.com.

10. James Lilliefors, "In Search of Hidden Mickeys: Book Guide about Hunting of Camouflaged Mickeys Turns Disney World Trip into a Vacation Mission," *Naples Daily News*, July 13, 2003, Newsbank Newsfile Collection, http://infoweb.newsbank.com.

11. Dick Pope Sr., *Water Skiing* (Englewood Cliffs, N.J.: Prentice-Hall, 1958), 12; "Jockey Hartack Ends Year on Big Day," *Blythedale Courier News*, December 12, 1955, Newspaper Archive, http://www.newspaperarchive.com.

12. *Cypress Gardens News Real*, April 1, 1956, Cypress Gardens Archive.

13. Frank Deford, "An Honest Travel Story," *Sports Illustrated*, January 26, 1976, 32–34, 39–40.

14. Joe Guzior, "Dick Pope, Sr. 77 Years Young and Still Going Strong," *Gazette: The Voice of Cypress Gardens, Inc.*, October 1977, Cypress Gardens Archive.

15. William B. Furlong, "Babes in a Swampland," *Sports Illustrated*, October 21, 1963, 66–80.

16. William Bygrave and Art Sills, "Pope Rubbed Elbows with the Rich, Famous," *Winter Haven News Chief*, January 29, 1988.

17. Richard Field and Scott DeGarmo, "Little Mr. Big Ambition," *St. Petersburg Times*, July 5, 1970.

18. "Jottings," *St. Petersburg Times*, November 2, 1955, Google News Archive, http://www.news.google.com.

19. Zora Neale Hurston, *Mules and Men* (New York: HarperPerennial, 1990), 55.

20. "Winter Haven, The Future Prospects," September 19, 1890, Polk County Historical and Genealogical Library.

21. Kenneth Recker, *A History of the Winter Haven Lake Region Boat Course District* (Winter Haven, Fla.: Canal Commission, 1986), 13.

22. "Winter Haven, A Spot on God's Footstool That Is Incomparable," May 1, 1891," Polk County Historical and Genealogical Library.

23. GIM, "Winter Haven. Reminiscences of Polk Eight Years Ago. Another of GIM's Valuable Articles," February 19, 1891, Polk County Historical and Genealogical Library.

24. Russell Haas, "Winter Haven Offers Beauty and Riches in Its Unrivaled Site among Lakes," *Polk County Record*, September 5, 1924, Polk County Historical and Genealogical Library.

25. "Among the Lakes, Summer Joys in the Winter Haven Neighborhood," July 29, 18[?], Polk County Historical and Genealogical Library.

26. Margaret Chase Parry interview, February 18, 2008.

27. Julie Pope Dantzler interview, February 18, 2008.

28. Lillian Pope to J. Walker Pope, undated (courtesy of Julie Pope Dantzler).

29. Lillian Pope to J. Walker Pope, July 7, 1906 (courtesy of Julie Pope Dantzler).

30. Margaret Chase Parry interview.

31. Paul Ferguson, "Dick Pope . . . A Showman for All Seasons," *Jacksonville Times-Union and Journal*, January 28, 1973.

32. Dick Bothwell, "Mr. Cypress Gardens," October 9, 1960, Cypress Gardens Archive.

33. Undated clipping, Julie Pope Dantzler collection.

34. Sarah Stegall, "After 51 Years, Bill Bell Shuts the Door," *Lakeland Ledger*, November 21, 2006; "Addison Mizner, Resort Architect," *About.com*, http://architecture.about.com/od/architectsaz/p/mizner.htm.

35. Bill Bell interview, February 2008.

36. Dorothy Kaucher, *They Built a City* (Lake Wales, Fla., 1970), 48.

37. Janyce Barnwell Ahl, *Crown Jewel of the Florida Highlands, Lake Wales* (Lake Wales: Lake Wales Library Association, 1983), 17.

38. Jack Gurnett, "Oil May Add New Chapter to Career of 'Mr. Florida," *Orlando Star*, April 27, 1952, Cypress Gardens Archive.

39. Robert Pitts, "Dick Pope Sr. First Saw State's Beauty as a Boy," *Winter Haven News Chief*, January 29, 1988.

40. William R. Adams, *Historic Lake Wales* (St. Augustine, Fla.: Southern Heritage Press, 1992), 17.

41. Margot Ammidown, "Edens, Underworlds, and Shrines: Florida's Small Tourist Attractions," special Florida issue, *Journal of Decorative and Propaganda Arts* 23 (1998): 239–59.

42. Adams, *Historic Lake Wales*, 93.

43. Nixon Smiley, "Dick Pope: The Man Who Can't Stop Running," *Miami Herald*, Sunday magazine, February 5, 1967.

44. Canter Brown, *In the Midst of All That Makes Life Worth Living: Polk County, Florida to 1940* (Tallahassee: Sentry Press, 2001), 239.

45. Untitled clipping, August 10, 1915, Polk County Historical and Genealogical Library.

46. Hy Peskin and Norman Wood, "The Man Who Invented Florida," *Argosy*, June 1950, 29–31, 70.

47. Ceel Pasternak, "Profile of Dick Pope," *Spray: The Waterskiing Magazine*, July 1978, 22–25, 56–57, 60–61.

48. Kevin Desmond, *The Golden Age of Water-skiing* (St. Paul, Minn.: MBI, 2001), 26.

49. "Aquaplanes at Oyster Bay, Society Folk Thrilled by Play of Local Experts," *New York Times*, August 13, 1917, ProQuest Historical Newspapers, http://proquest.umi.com/login.

50. Aquaplaning Has Thrills," *Los Angeles Times*, July 22, 1919, Newspaper Archive, www.newspaperarchive.com.

51. "Aquaplane Wins Debut Stakes at Belmont and Igloo Completes Double for Coe," *New York Times*, May 21, 1929, ProQuest Historical Newspapers, http://proquest.umi.com/login.

52. Recker, *A History of the Winter Haven Lake Region Boat Course District*, 27.

53. "Largest Grove Sale Ever Made in Florida," *Florida Chief*, December 2, 1920 (courtesy of Adrienne Pope Watkins).

54. Quoted in Brown, *In the Midst of All That Makes Life Worth Living*, 289.

55. "Glimpses of Who's Who in the Haven-Villa Investment Company," *Lakeland Evening Register*, March 7, 1925.

56. "Winter Haven Captured by Dahlgrens," *Winter Haven News Chief*, July 7, 1999, www.polkonline.com.

57. "Glimpses of Who's Who in the Haven-Villa Investment Company."

58. Recker, *A History of the Winter Haven Lake Region Boat Course District*, 28.

59. Advertisement, *New York Times*, September 20, 1925, ProQuest Historical Newspapers, http://proquest.umi.com/login.

60. Harvey Snively interview, May 21, 2009.

61. D. Pope Sr., *Water Skiing*, 15.

62. Pasternak, "Profile: Dick Pope."

63. D. Pope Sr., *Water Skiing*, 16.

64. Margaret Chase Parry interview.

65. Brown, *In the Midst of All That Makes Life Worth Living*, 284.

66. Quoted in Kaucher, *They Built a City*, 176.

67. Adams, *Historic Lake Wales*, 25.

68. Lynn Phillips, "Dick Pope Sr.," *Orlando Sentinel Star*, Sunday magazine, April 22, 1979.

69. Ellen Scarborough, "Pope Home: 'We Just Live Relaxed Here,'" undated clipping, Cypress Gardens Archive.

70. "Downing-Pope Wedding Was a Brilliant Event of Wednesday," *Brewton Standard*, April [?], 1926 (courtesy of Adrienne Pope Watkins).

71. Walter Doles interview, February 2008.

72. Bert Lacey interview, February 2008.

73. Dubie Baxter interview, February 2008.

74. Pitts, "Dick Pope First Saw State's Beauty as a Boy."

75. Desmond, *The Golden Age of Water-skiing*, 42.

76. D. Pope Sr., *Water Skiing*, 15.

77. Muriel Murrell, *Miami: A Backward Glance* (Sarasota, Fla.: Pineapple Press, 2003), 140.

78. D. Pope Sr., *Water Skiing*, 15.

79. James Vincent, *Parting the Waters: How Vision and Faith Made Good Business* (Chicago: Moody Press, 1997), 28.

80. "Sea Cowboy Rides Bronc: In Thrilling Leap," *Decatur Illinois Daily Review*, February 12, 1928, Newspaper Archive, www.newspaperarchive.com.

81. "Rockets to Propel Boat," *New York Times*, December 12, 1929, ProQuest Historical Newspapers, www.linccweb.org.

82. Furlong, "Babes in a Swampland," 66–80.

83. D. Pope Sr., *Water Skiing*, 177.

84. Richard Pope, "Zip It's Motor Boating Time in Auburndale," *Florida Municipal Record*, April 1930, 8–9.

85. Dick Pope, "Ten Days on Location," *Outboard Motor Boating*, May 1930, 205–6, 232.

86. Pitts, "Dick Pope Sr. First Saw State's Beauty as a Boy."

Chapter 2. The 1930s: The Barnum of Botany

1. "The Gardens come to Life," *Cypress Gardens, 60th Anniversary: 1936–1996*, 12 (courtesy of Bob Gernert).

2. Norman Vincent Peale, "Confident Living," *The Progress Index* (Petersburg, Va., October 9, 1955), Cypress Gardens Archive.

3. Roy Bongartz, "The Superswamp: Cypress Gardens: Florida's Eighteen-Karat Illusion," *Saturday Evening Post*, November 26, 1963, 78–81.

4. Nancy Gurnett Hardy, "Personalities of the Week: Dick and Julie Pope," *Winter Haven Herald*, March 6, 1959, Cypress Gardens Archive.

5. Jack Gurnett, "Oil May Add New Chapter to Career of Mr. Florida," *Orlando Star*, April 27, 1952, Cypress Gardens Archive.

6. Kenneth Recker, *A History of the Winter Haven Lake Region Boat Course District* (Winter Haven, Fla.: Canal Commission), 2.

7. Robert Pitts, "Dick Pope, Sr. First Saw State's Beauty as a Boy," *Winter Haven News Chief*, January 29, 1988.

8. Nixon Smiley, "The Man Who Can't Stop Running," *Miami Herald*, Sunday magazine, February 5, 1967.

9. Lucy Chambliss interview, February 2008.

10. William Bygrave, "Pope Was a 'Visionary,' Lawyer Recalls," *Winter Haven News Chief*, January 29, 1988.

11. Quoted in James in Vincent, *Parting the Waters: How Vision and Faith Made Good Business* (Chicago: Moody Press, 1997), 39.

12. Nancy Gurnett Hardy, "Personalities of the Week: Dick and Julie Pope," *Winter Haven Herald*, March 6, 1959, Cypress Gardens Archive.

13. Pitts, "Dick Pope, Sr. First Saw State's Beauty as a Boy."

14. P. J. Brownlee, "'Where de Water Drink Lak Cherry Wine': The Importance of Zora Neale Hurston's Work in Polk County Florida," *Polk County Historical Quarterly* 27, no. 1 (June 2000): 1–3, 7.

15. Zora Neale Hurston, *Mules and Men* (New York: HarperPerennial, 1960), 59.

16. Zora Neale Hurston, *Dust Tracks on a Road* (New York: HarperPerennial, 1996), 147–48.

17. Zora Neale Hurston and Dorothy Waring, *Polk County: A Comedy of Negro Life on a Sawmill Camp with Authentic Negro Music in Three Acts*, Library of Congress, http://hdl.loc.gov/loc.rbc/mhurston.0301.

18. Paul Ferguson, "Dick Pope . . . A Showman for All Seasons," *Jacksonville Times-Union and Journal*, January 28, 1973.

19. Stephen Branch, "Florida with Flair, Dick Pope and the Making of Cypress Gardens," *Polk County Historical Quarterly* 30 (September 2003): 1, 4–5, 8–9, 12.

20. Adrienne Pope Watkins interview, February 2008.

21. "Everglades Wonder Gardens," www.sanybel.com/everglades_wonder_gardens.htm.

22. Dick Pope Sr., *Water Skiing* (Englewood Cliffs, N.J.: Prentice-Hall, 1958), 124.

23. Jack Jones, "Cashing in on Liquid Assets," *Florida Municipal Record*, January 1933, 23, 58.

24. Ibid.

25. Hy Peskin and Norton Wood, "The Man Who Invented Florida," *Argosy*, June 1950, 29, 30–31, 70.

26. Richard Pope, "Havenites Have Unique Program for Enhancing City's Beauty," *Florida Municipal Record*, January 1933, 20–21.

27. Ibid.

28. Ibid.

29. Lucy Chambliss interview.

30. Branch, "Florida with Flair, Dick Pope and the Making of Cypress Gardens."

31. Bygrave, "Pope Was a 'Visionary,' Lawyer Recalls."

32. Pitts, "Dick Pope, Sr. First Saw State's Beauty as a Boy."

33. Bob Driscoll, "Dick Pope: Host to 20 Million Americans," *St. Petersburg Evening Independent*, *Family Weekly*, June 18, 1961.

34. Jacqueline Doles Staton interview, February 2008.

35. Excerpt from Garnault Agassiz, "Florida in Tomorrow's Sun," *Suniland* 3, no. 2 (November 1925): 37–45; 88–94, 113–33, in "Exploring Florida" http://fcit.usf.edu/FLORIDA/docs/f/fruit.htm.

36. Canter Brown, *In the Midst of All That Makes Life Worth Living: Polk County, Florida, to 1940*, Polk County Historical Association (Tallahassee: Sentry Press, 2001), 164–65.

37. Betty Doles interview, February 2008.

38. Jacqueline Doles Staton interview.

39. Betty Doles interview.

40. "Winter Haven Captured by Dahlgrens," July 10, 1999, http://polkonline.com.

41. Bob Kehoe interview, February 2008.

42. D. Pope Sr., *Water Skiing*, 196.

43. Lucy Chambliss interview.

44. Bygrave, "Pope Was a 'Visionary,' Lawyer Recalls."

45. "Music Teacher Pushes for New State Song," *Naples News*, March 25, 2007, Newsbank Newsfile Collection, http://infoweb.newsbank.com.

46. "A Garden's Stroll down Memory Lane," January 19, 2006, http://polkonline.com.

47. Pitts, "Dick Pope, Sr. First Saw State's Beauty as a Boy."

48. "Publix Buys 49 Fla. Stores from Albertson's LLC," *Progressive Grocer*, June 10, 2008, www.progressivegrocer.com.

49. Mark Albright, "George Jenkins Jr. 1907–1996: Public Founder, Supermarket Pioneer Dies," *St. Petersburg Times*, April 10, 1996, Newsbank Newsfile Collection, http://infoweb.newsbank.com.

50. Joe Guzior, "A Pictorial View of Mr. Cypress Gardens: Dick Pope, Sr.," *Gazette*, October 1977.

51. Advertisement in *Florida Municipal Record*, July 1935.

52. "Governor Dave Sholtz Dedicates Cypress Gardens Here Thursday," *Winter Haven Herald*, January 25, 1935, Polk County Historical and Genealogical Library.

53. "Formal Opening of the Cypress Gardens Tonite," *Winter Haven Herald*, March 1, 1935, Polk County Historical and Genealogical Library.

54. "Water Sports at Cypress Gardens Sunday Afternoon," *Winter Haven Herald*, May 3, 1935, Polk County Historical and Genealogical Library.

55. "Section of Winding Cypress Garden Trail," *Winter Haven Herald*, December 20, 1935, Polk County Historical and Genealogical Library.

56. "World Famous Stunters to Stage Water Carnival Here in County-Wide Celebration," *Lake Wales News*, November 7, 1935.

57. Bert Lacey interview.

58. "Growing up at the Gardens," *Cypress Gardens, 60th Anniversary: 1936–1996*, 32 (courtesy of Bob Gernert).

59. "Formal Opening of Gardens 22nd," *Winter Haven Herald,* December 13, 1935, Polk County Historical and Genealogical Library.

60. "Cypress Gardens to Open Sunday P.M.," *Winter Haven Herald,* December 27, 1935, Polk County Historical and Genealogical Library.

61. "Cypress Gardens Are Dedicated As Bird Sanctuary," *Winter Haven Herald*, January 31, 1936, Polk County Historical and Genealogical Library.

62. "Queen Coronation to Highlight First Gardenia Festival," *Winter Haven Herald*, April 10, 1936, Polk County Historical and Genealogical Library.

63. Arthur Herzog, "The King of Beauty Queens," *Esquire*, September 1957, 120–28.

64. Nixon Smiley, "Men Who Make Florida," *All-Florida*, February 11, 1940.

65. "Gardens Stresses Hospitality Theme," *Winter Haven Daily News Chief*, June 20, 1948, Polk County Historical and Genealogical Library.

66. Cypress Gardens brochure, 1936, Cypress Gardens Archive.

67. William Furlong, "Babes in a Swampland," *Sports Illustrated*, October 21, 1963, 66–80.

68. Spider Bell interview.

69. Dubie Baxter interview, February 2008.

70. "Feature Length Sportlight to Be Made Here Soon, *Winter Haven Herald*, March 26, 1937, Polk County Historical and Genealogical Library.

71. "Local Talent Now Making Sportlight at Cypress Gardens," *Winter Haven Herald*, April 2, 1937, Polk County Historical and Genealogical Library.

72. "Aquabats, Filmed at Cypress Gardens, at Ritz Sat. to Mon," *Winter Haven Herald*, July 30, 1937, Polk County Historical and Genealogical Library.

73. Dubie Baxter interview.

74. "Cypress Gardens to Hold Open House for Havenites Sunday," *Winter Haven Herald*, November 5, 1937, Polk County Historical and Genealogical Library.

75. Quoted in Branch, "Florida with Flair, Dick Pope and the Making of Cypress Gardens."

76. *Florida: A Guide to the Southernmost State*, compiled and written by the Federal Writers' Project of the Works Progress Administration (1939; New York: Oxford University Press, 1956), 368.

Chapter 3. The 1940s: War, Water Skis, and Belles

1. *Statistical Report on the Pictorial Publicity Program of the Florida Citrus Commission*, undated document, Cypress Gardens Archive.

2. James A. Clendenin, "About Florida: What, No Oranges? Florida's Master Publicity Peddler Must Be Slipping," *Tampa Tribune*, undated clipping, Cypress Gardens Archive.

3. "Winter Haven Movie Will Be Shown at Exhibit," *Winter Haven Herald,* July 19, 1940, Polk County Historical and Genealogical Library.

4. "City Has Prominent Role at Big Fair," *St. Petersburg Evening Independent,* August 10, 1940, Cypress Gardens Archive.

5. Randy Wayne White, "Girls! Gators! Glitz!" *Southern Magazine*, August 1998, 46–51, 71–72.

6. "Men Who Make Florida," *All Florida*, February 11, 1940, Cypress Gardens Archive.

7. Bill Carter, "Rare Plants on Display in Open Showcase," *Winter Haven Daily News Chief*, June 20, 1948, Cypress Gardens Archive.

8. "Local Spot Is Often Called a Speedy Trek around the World," *Winter Haven Daily News Chief*, June 20, 1948, Cypress Gardens Archive.

9. Carter, "Rare Plants on Display in Open Showcase."

10. Ida Bailey Allen, "Let's Eat," *Middletown (N.Y.) Times Herald*, February 16, 1949, Newspaper Archive, www.newspaperarchive.com.

11. Margot Ammidown, "Edens, Underworlds, and Shrines: Florida's Small Tourist Attractions, special Florida issue, *Journal of Decorative and Propaganda Arts* 23 (1998): 239–59.

12. "Men Who Make Florida."

13. Bert Lacey interview, February 2008.

14. "Betty Grable," History Department, University of San Diego, http://history.sandiego.edu/gen/ww2Timeline/bettygrable.html.

15. "Movie Company Begins Cypress Gardens Scenes," *Winter Haven Herald,* February 21, 1941, Polk County Historical and Genealogical Library.

16. "Most Photographed Girl," *Pittsburgh Press*, "Roto" section, April 27, 1941, Cypress Gardens Archive.

17. "Blonde Double for Betty Grable Faces Battery of Cameramen at Gettysburg College," *Gettysburg Times*, October 22, 1941, Newspaper Archive, www.newspaperarchive.com.

18. Lucy Chambliss interview, February 2008.

19. Delee Perry interview, November 15, 2004.

20. Gallons of Oil Save Beauty Spot," *All-Florida*, February 11, 1940, Cypress Gardens Archive.

21. Nancy Gurnett Hardy, "Personalities of the Week," *Winter Haven Herald*, March 6, 1959, Cypress Gardens Archive.

22. Jack Gurnett, "Oil May Add New Chapter to Career of Mr. Florida," *Orlando Star*, April 27, 1952, Cypress Gardens Archive.

23. Nancy Zarza Daley interview, March 2008.

24. Amy Edwards, "Gardens Veterans Ride Waves of Memory: Former Water Skiers Who Made a Splash in the Park's Past Come Back to Celebrate Cypress Gardens' Revival," *Orlando Sentinel*, December 16, 2004, Newsbank Newsfile Collection, http://infoweb.newsbank.com.

25. Linda Florea, "Water-Skier Made a Splash in Cypress Gardens' Past: Nance Stilley Hains Is among 1,200 of the Attraction's Former Workers Invited to a Reunion over the Weekend," *Orlando Sentinel*, August 24, 2003, Newsbank Newsfile Collection, http://infoweb.newsbank.com.

26. Ibid.

27. Brenda Mitchell interview, February 2008.

28. Dorothy Clifford, "Bathing Belles: At Cypress Gardens in the 50s, the Water-Skiers Would Also Slip into Antebellum Gowns to Pose among the Flowers," *Tallahassee Democrat*, April 7, 2002, Newsbank Newsfile Collection, http://infoweb.newsbank.com.

29. Nancy Zarza Daley interview.

30. Olive Ann Burns, "Whee-e-e . . . Let's Ski!" undated article, Cypress Gardens Archive.

31. Panky Snow, "Locals Feel Saddened by Closing of Gardens," *Tampa Tribune*, April 19, 2003, Newsbank Newsfile Collection, http://infoweb.newsbank.com.

32. *Citrus Magazine*, April 1950.

33. Spider Bell interview, February 2008.

34. Nancy Zarza Daley interview.

35. Karen Haymon Long, "Surviving in a Disney World," *Tampa Tribune*, May 14, 2000, Newsbank Newsfile Collection, http://infoweb.newsbank.com.

36. Bert Lacey interview.

37. "Where Photographer Is King," *Panama City News-Herald,* November 4, 1956, Newspaper Archive, www.newspaperarchive.com.

38. Red McGuire interview, February 2008.

39. Willa McGuire Cook interview, February 2008.

40. "Where Photographer Is King."

41. Virginia Schmidt, "Treks," *Mountain Democrat Times,* Placerville, Calif., May 19, 1978, Newspaper Archive, www.newspaperarchive.com.

42. William Furlong, "Babes in a Swampland," *Sports Illustrated*, October 21, 1963, 66–80.

43. "Haven Girls Ride in Private Car with Duke and Duchess, Pictures Do Duchess an Injustice Cypress Gardens Queens Declare in Interview with Herald Reporter," *Winter Haven Herald*, November 7, 1941, Polk County Historical and Genealogical Library.

44. Betty Doles interview, February 2008.

45. Walter Doles interview, February 2008.

46. Betty Doles interview.

47. Jacqueline Doles Staton interview, February 2008.

48. Betty Doles interview.

49. Jacqueline Doles Staton interview.

50. Dubie Baxter interview, February 2008.

51. Bob Gernert interview, February 2008.

52. Walter Doles interview.

53. "Dick Pope, Sr. Adds Colorful History to Florida Cypress Gardens," November 1979 (clipping courtesy of Brenda Mitchell).

54. Pope family album (courtesy of Julie Pope Dantzler).

55. Ceel Pasternak, "Profile: Dick Pope," *Spray: The Waterskiing Magazine,* July 1978, 22–25, 56–57, 60–61.

56. Billye-Mullins Smith interview, February 2008.

57. Lucy Chambliss interview.

58. Press release, "By-Line Feature, A Special

Photo Story by International News Photos," New York, November 1, 1942, Cypress Gardens Archive.

59. Dick Pope Sr., *Water Skiing* (Englewood Cliffs, N.J.: Prentice-Hall, 1958), 126–27.

60. Adrienne Pope Watkins interview, February 2008.

61. "Cypress Gardens Founder Dick Pope Sr. Dies at 87," *Lakeland Ledger*, January 29, 1988 (courtesy of Adrienne Pope Watkins).

62. "Movietone News, Cameraman's Dope Sheet," Digital Collections, University of South Carolina, http://digital.tcl.sc.edu.

63. "Rounds out His Training," *New Castle Pa. News*, June 17, 1943, Newspaper Archive, www.newspaperarchive.com.

64. "Flowers, Not Birds," *Nebraska State Journal*, May 20, 1943, Newspaper Archive, www.newspaperarchive.com.

65. Quoted in Jim Frye, "A Family's Legacy: Remembering Cypress Gardens with Dick Pope, Jr.," *WaterSki Magazine*, July 2003, 27–28.

66. Adrienne Pope Watkins interview.

67. Lucy Chambliss interview.

68. "Dick Pope Sr. Adds Colorful History to Florida Cypress Gardens."

69. "Cypress Gardens Show Scheduled to Appear Here," *Winter Haven Herald*, April 16, 1943, Polk County Historical and Genealogical Library.

70. Billye-Mullins Smith interview.

71. Douglass Martin, "Hartzell Spence, 93, Dies; Pinup Pioneer," *New York Times*, May 25, 2001, Newsbank Newsfile Collection, http://infoweb.newsbank.com.

72. "Dick Pope Becomes Florida's Picture Taker," ca. 1949, Cypress Gardens Archive.

73. "Florida's New Cover Girl," clipping (courtesy of Lucy Chambliss).

74. Russell Kay, "Cypress Gardens Claims Nation's Most Beautiful and Charming Girls," *Hollywood Sun-Tattler*, February 4, 1944, Cypress Gardens Archive.

75. Roy Peter Clark, "Pretty As a Picture," *St. Petersburg Times*, July 1, 2001, Newsbank Newsfile Collection, http://infoweb.newsbank.com.

76. "Ace Picture Man Joins City Staff," *St. Petersburg Times*, September 14, 1944, Google News Archive, www.news.google.com January 23, 2009.

77. Ray Kendall Williams, letter to the editor, *St.Petersburg Times*, March 6, 1945, Google News Archive, www.news.google.com January 23, 2009.

78. "Early Park Photo Shoot," *Cypress Gardens 70th Celebration, Winter Haven News Chief*, January 21, 2006.

79. Mary Flekke, Sarah MacDonald, and Randall MacDonald, *Images of Cypress Gardens* (Charleston, S.C.: Arcadia, 2006), 26.

80. "Chamblisses Backed Park from the Start," *Cypress Gardens 70th Celebration, Winter Haven News Chief*, January 21, 2006.

81. Flekke, MacDonald, and MacDonald, *Images of Cypress Gardens*, 28.

82. "'Life' Makes Pictures Here: Magazine to Boost Cypress Gardens, Bok Tower in February," *Winter Haven Herald*, November 30, 1945, Polk County Historical and Genealogical Library.

83. "'Jitterboarding' at Cypress Gardens," *Winter Haven Herald*, December 14, 1945, Polk County Historical and Genealogical Library.

84. Willa McGuire Cook interview.

85. Lynn Novakofski interview, February 2008.

86. "Jitterboarding Is New Thrill," *Winter Haven Daily News Chief*, June 20, 1948, Polk County Historical and Genealogical Library.

87. "Speaking of Pictures . . . Champion Water Skier Shows Off Skill in Florida Sunshine," *Life*, February 17, 1947, 6–8.

88. James Clendenin, "About Florida: What, No Oranges?: Florida's Master Publicity Peddler Must Be Slipping," *Tampa Tribune*, undated clipping, Cypress Gardens Archive.

89. Esther Williams, *The Million Dollar Mermaid* (New York: Harvest Books, 2000), 117.

90. "Real Treat," *Winter Haven Herald*, June 20, 1948, Polk County Historical and Genealogical Library.

91. "Pope Handles Many Picture Accounts Now," *Winter Haven Daily News Chief*, June 20, 1948 (courtesy of Adrienne Pope Watkins).

92. "Gardens Head Changes Old Concepts," *Winter Haven Daily News Chief*, June 20, 1948 (courtesy of Adrienne Pope Watkins).

93. "Producers Use Florida Light to Advantage," *Winter Haven Daily News Chief*, June 20, 1948 (courtesy of Adrienne Pope Watkins).

94. "'Alone on an Island with You' Filmed in Florida," *Winter Haven Herald*, July 2, 1948 (courtesy of Adrienne Pope Watkins).

95. "City 'Went Hollywood' a Year Ago," *Winter Haven Daily News Chief*, June 20, 1948 (courtesy of Adrienne Pope Watkins).

96. "Hollywood Stars Draw Autograph Hunters Here," *Winter Haven Herald*, June 6, 1947.

97. "City 'Went Hollywood' a Year Ago."

98. William Bygrave and Art Sills, "Pope Rubbed Elbows with the Rich, Famous," *Winter Haven News Chief*, January 29, 1988.

99. "City 'Went Hollywood' a Year Ago."

100. Williams, *The Million Dollar Mermaid*, 160–61.

101. Lucy Chambliss interview.

102. "'Alone on an Island with You' Filmed in Florida."

103. "Miss Williams Became Co-Ed," *Winter Haven Daily News Chief*, June 20, 1948 (courtesy of Adrienne Pope Watkins).

104. Advertisement, *Winter Haven Daily News Chief*, June 20, 1948 (courtesy of Adrienne Pope Watkins).

105. "'On an Island with You' Has Premiere Here," *Winter Haven Daily News Chief*, June 20, 1948 (courtesy of Adrienne Pope Watkins).

106. Dale Wimbrow, "Ballyhoo Cheesecake and Glamour," *Indian River News*, May 12, 1948, Cypress Gardens Archive.

107. Hy Peskin and Norman Wood, "The Man Who Invented Florida," *Argosy*, June 1950, 29–31, 70.

108."Shutterbugs to Have Field Day in State," *Winter Haven Daily News Chief*, June 20, 1948 (courtesy of Adrienne Pope Watkins).

109. "Dick Pope Becomes Florida's Picture-Taker," *Tampa Tribune*, undated clipping, Cypress Gardens Archive.

110. Bill Bell interview.

111. Adrienne Pope Watkins interview.

112. Glenn Garvin, "Merv Griffin Reminisces on His 'Improbable Career,'" *Miami Herald*, April 21, 2006, Newsbank Newsfile Collection, http://infoweb.newsbank.com.

113. Bill Bell interview.

114. Cypress Gardens official program, 1983, Cypress Gardens Archive.

115. "Florida Steals Winter Interest," *Winter Haven Daily News Chief*, June 20, 1948 (courtesy of Adrienne Pope Watkins).

116. "Cypress Gardens Again Hits the Publicity Jackpot," *Winter Haven Herald*, February 11, 1949, Polk County Historical and Genealogical Library.

117. Willa McGuire Cook interview.

118. Paul Ferguson, "Dick Pope . . . A Showman for All Seasons," *Jacksonville Times Union and Journal*, January 28, 1973.

Chapter 4. The 1950s: The Man Who Invented Florida (and the Florida-Shaped Pool)

1. "Busy Boy: Girl Photos Bring Fame to Floridian," *Los Angeles Times*, ca. 1950, Cypress Gardens Archive.

2. "Speaking of Pictures . . . The Governor of Florida Applauds Promoters Pictures of Fruit and Girls," *Life*, 1948.

3. Hy Peskin and Norman Wood, "The Man Who Invented Florida," *Argosy*, June 1950, 29–31, 70.

4. "World Water Ski Champs of Eight Nations Come to Florida," *Orlando Sunday Sentinel*, November 19, 1950, Cypress Gardens Archive.

5. "The Evolution of the Gardens," *Cypress Gardens, 60th Anniversary: 1936–1996*, 22 (courtesy of Bob Gernert).

6. John Dillin of Public Relations at Marine Studio to Bob Eastman, August 1, 1951, Cypress Gardens Archive.

7. "Ray" to Dick Pope, August 10, 1951, Cypress Gardens Archive.

8. Bert Lacey interview, February 2008.

9. "Timeline," *Jantzen*, www.jantzen.com/timeline.asp.

10. "Self-Propelled Surfboard," *Mechanics Illustrated*, April 1950, 74–75, *Modern Mechanix*, http://blog.modernmechanix.com/2006/08/30/self-propelled-surfboard/.

11. Charlie Wadsworth, "Presenting Dick Pope," *Orlando Sentinel*, March 30 1952, Cypress Gardens Archive.

12. Betty Skelton Erde interview, July 2009.

13. "Cypress Gardens," *Water Skier*, October 1951, Water Ski Hall of Fame.

14. "Growing up at the Gardens," *Cypress Gardens, 60th Anniversary: 1936–1996*, 32 (courtesy of Bob Gernert).

15. Dick Pope Sr., *Water Skiing* (Englewood Cliffs, N.J.: Prentice-Hall, 1958), 198–99.

16. Katherine Preble, "Reaching for the Mendoza Line: The Former Water Ski Champion Passes along the Skills He Mastered More Than 40 Years Ago at Cypress Gardens," *Tampa Tribune*, August 23, 1995, Newsbank Newsfile Collection, http://infoweb.newsbank.com.

17. Dubie Baxter interview, February 2008.

18. John Clayton, "Binette Soared into Nonexistent Hall of Fame," *New Hampshire Sunday News*, April 18, 2004, Newsbank Newsfile Collection, http://infoweb.newsbank.com.

19. D. Pope Sr., *Water Skiing*, 53–54.

20. Tyler Treadway, "Port Lucie Man Recalls His Day as World-Champion Ski Jumper: Remembering Life at the Gardens," *Stuart News/Port Lucie News*, April 26, 2003, Newsbank Newsfile Collection, http://infoweb.newsbank.com.

21. Willa McGuire Cook interview, February 2008.

22. Brenda Mitchell interview, February 2008.

23. Red Hurd, "Willa's a Wizard on Water," *Sunday Oregonian*, September 4, 1955, Cypress Gardens Archive.

24. Willa McGuire Cook interview.

25. Ceel Pasternak, "Profile: Dick Pope," *Spray: The Waterskiing Magazine*, July 1978, 22–25, 56–57, 60–61.

26. "Hollywood Dope by Pope," *Cypress Gardens News Real, Published Occasionally Hot from the Coffee Table*, November 1951, Cypress Gardens Archive.

27. Bill Stern, "Dancing on the Waves," *American Weekly*, June 29, 1952, Cypress Gardens Archive.

28. Lynn Novakofski interview, February 2008.

29. Willa McGuire Cook interview.

30. *This Is Cinerama* (author's collection).

31. “Cinerama Pioneers Bios,” Cinerama Adventure, August 3, 2007, www.cineramaadventure.com/pioneers.htm?

32. D. Pope Sr., *Water Skiing*, 12.

33. Red McGuire interview, February 2008.

34. *This Is Cinerama*.

35. Michael Coate, “Remembering Cinerama,” Cinerama Treasures, http://cinematreasures.org/news/19645_0_1_0_C/.

36. Billye-Mullins Smith interview, February 2008.

37. Richard Kleiner, “New Cinerama Called Aesthetic Atomic Bomb,” *Alton (Ill.) Evening Telegraph*, October 16, 1952, Newspaper Archive, www.newspaperarcive.com.

38. Hedda Hopper, “Cinerama Will Amaze You,” *Chicago Daily Tribune*, December 21, 1952, Newspaper Archive, www.newspaperarcive.com.

39. John Lotz, “The Suffix–rama,” *American Speech* 29, no. 2 (May 1954): 156–58, JSTOR, TCC Library, www.jstor.org.

40. D. Pope Sr., *Water Skiing*, 12.

41. Susan Mason, “They Loved Us in New York,” *St. Petersburg Times*, September 7, 1952, Cypress Gardens Archive.

42. Red McGuire interview.

43. Quoted in Dick Bothwell, “Mr. Cypress Gardens,” October 9, 1960, Cypress Gardens Archive.

44. Joe Pasternak, as told to David Chandler, *Easy the Hard Way* (London: W. H. Allen, 1956), 189.

45. Bill Bell interview, February 2008.

46. D. Pope Sr., *Water Skiing*, 192–93.

47. Tony Thomas and Jim Terry, *The Busby Berkeley Book*, with Busby Berkeley (Greenwich, Ct.: New York Graphic Society, 1973), 177.

48. Spider Bell interview.

49. Paul Thompson, “Movie Star Esther Williams Begins Ski-reer at Gardens,” *Orlando Sunday Sentinel Star*, February 1, 1953.

50. Bothwell, “Mr. Cypress Gardens.”

51. Thompson, “Movie Star Esther Williams Begins Ski-reer at Gardens.”

52. Thomas and Terry, *The Busby Berkeley Book*, 178.

53. Red McGuire interview.

54. William Bygrave and William Sills, “Pope Rubbed Elbows with the Rich, Famous,” *Winter Haven News Chief*, January 29, 1988.

55. “Swimming Pool Built in a Lake,” *Popular Mechanics*, July 1953, 107.

56. Bob Kehoe interview, February 2008.

57. “Cypress Gardens in State of Confusion: Movie in the Making,” *Winter Haven Herald*, February 13, 1953, Polk County Historical and Genealogical Library.

58. “Full Cast in Winter Haven for Cypress Gardens Film,” *Winter Haven Herald*, February 13, 1953, Polk County Historical and Genealogical Library.

59. Esther Williams, *Million Dollar Mermaid* (New York: Harvest Books, 2000), 219–20, 170, 245.

60. Gertrude Vredeveld, “Cypress Gardens Goes Hollywood,” *Water Skier*, February 1953, 2, American Water Ski Educational Foundation Museum.

61. Willa McGuire Cook interview.

62. “Esther Williams’ Hubby Takes Bows,” *Orlando Morning Sentinel*, February 4, 1953.

63. Williams, *Million Dollar Mermaid*, 246–47.

64. D. Pope Sr., *Water Skiing*, 195.

65. “Esther Williams Too Busy for Public Appearances,” *Winter Haven Herald*, February 6, 1953, Polk County Historical and Genealogical Library.

66. “Cypress Gardens in State of Confusion; Movie in the Making,” *Winter Haven Herald*, February 13, 1953, Polk County Historical and Genealogical Library.

67. Edee Green, “Florida and Dick Pope Grab Hits on Broadway,” *Orlando Sentinel*, December 6, 1953, Cypress Gardens Archive.

68. Williams, *Million Dollar Mermaid*, 247.

69. Ernie Shier, quoted in Thomas and Terry, *The Busby Berkeley Book*, 178.

70. Red McGuire interview.

71. Bob Kehoe interview.

72. Williams, *Million Dollar Mermaid*, 248–49.

73. “Hollywood Notables Finish Scenes at Cypress Gardens,” *Winter Haven Herald*, February 27, 1953, Polk County Historical and Genealogical Library.

74. Willa McGuire Cook interview.

75. Williams, *Million Dollar Mermaid*, 251.

76. Thomas and Terry, *The Busby Berkeley Book*, 178.

77. Red McGuire interview.

78. Willa McGuire Cook interview.

79. Dallas Abercrombie interview, February 2008.

80. Dubie Baxter interview.

81. Betty Doles interview, February 2008.

82. Nick Christy interview, March 2008.

83. Bill Bell interview.

84. “New Motion Picture Is Called Technicolor Commercial of Florida,” *Winter Haven Herald*, November 13, 1953, Polk County Historical and Genealogical Library.

85. D. Pope Sr., *Waterskiing*, 193-94.

86. Edee Greene, “Florida and Dick Pope Grab Hits on Broadway,” *Orlando Sentinel*, *Florida Magazine*, December 6, 1953, Cypress Gardens Archive.

87. “Easy To Love,” *Newsweek*, November 30, 1953, 104–5.

88. John McCarten, “Current Cinema,” *New Yorker*, December 19, 1953, 97.

89. "SR Goes to the Movies," *Saturday Review*, December 19, 1953, 30.

90. Willa McGuire Cook interview.

91. Richard Johnson interview, February 2008.

92. Mike Markowitz interview, March 2008.

93. Lynn Novakofski interview.

94. Lenz, Stephanie. "So Anyway . . ." http://piggyhawk.wordpress.com/2005/09/13/embarrassing-photo-night/.

95. Paul Wilder, "The Fabulous Mr. Pope: Florida's Human Buzz Saw," *Tampa Sunday Tribune*, May 9, 1954, Cypress Gardens Archive.

96. Richard Thruelsen, "Fanciest Frolic on Water," *Saturday Evening Post*, April 3, 1954, 24.

97. Wilder, "The Fabulous Mr. Pope."

98. "Extremely Bracing Weather," *Atchison (Kans.) Daily Globe*, March 29, 1958, Google News Archive, http://news.google.com.

99. Bob Kehoe interview.

100. William Furlong, "Babes in a Swampland," *Sports Illustrated*, October 21, 1964, 66–80.

101. Spider Bell interview.

102. Arthur Herzog, "The King of Beauty Queens," *Esquire*, September 1957, 120–28.

103. Bob Kehoe interview.

104. Jack Gurnett, "Tom Moore Is Florida's Ambassador of Good Will," *Orlando Sunday Sentinel Star, Florida Magazine,* February 1, 1953.

105. Willa McGuire Cook interview.

106. "The Shah by the Seashore," *Life*, February 14, 1955, 60–61.

107. "His Royal Iranian Highness Beds in Winter Haven Hotel," undated article (courtesy of Lucy Chambliss).

108. Lucy Chambliss interview, February 2008.

109. "His Royal Iranian Highness Beds in Winter Haven Hotel," undated article (courtesy of Lucy Chambliss).

110. Pasternak, "Profile: Dick Pope," *Spray: The Waterskiing Magazine*, July 1978.

111. Willa McGuire Cook interview.

112. "McFayden Wins, Is Named Shah," *Cypress Gardens News Real*, 1955, Cypress Gardens Archive.

113. "Dick Pope Resigns from State Post," *Winter Haven Herald*, January 21, 1955, Polk County Historical and Genealogical Library.

114. Betty Skelton Erde interview.

115. "Courtesy of Dick Pope," *Ocala Star-Banner,* June 22, 1955, Cypress Gardens Archive.

116. Loyal Frisbie, "Off My Chest . . ." *Polk County Democrat*, June 21, 1955, Cypress Gardens Archive.

117. Norman Vincent Peale, "Your Situation Could Be Better," *Anderson (S.C.) Independent*, undated article, Cypress Gardens Archive.

118. "Dick Pope: Sermon Topic," July 23, 1955, clipping, Cypress Gardens Archive.

119. Joe Rukenbrod, "Dick Pope Subject of Sermon," reprinted in undated *Cypress Gardens News Real,* Cypress Gardens Archive.

120. Bob Bartlett, "Four Million Dollar Sunshine Springs Opens as Tourist Attraction," *St. Petersburg Times*, December 4, 1955.

121. Tim Hollis, *Glass Bottom Boats and Mermaid Tails* (Mechanicsburg, Pa.: Stackpole Books, 2006), 140.

122. Merrill Folsom, "Florida Diversions Ashore and Afloat," *New York Times*, March 17, 1957, ProQuest Historical Newspapers, http://proquest.umi.com/login.

123. Calvin Sands, "Mr. Sands Says Water Skiing Elephant May Breed Bigger Stunts," *St. Petersburg Times*, March 25, 1956, Google News Archive, www.news.google.com.

124. Merrill Folsom, "Florida Diversions Ashore and Afloat, *New York Times*, March 17, 1957, ProQuest Historical Newspapers, http://proquest.umi.com/login.

125. Simon Khoury interview, July 2009.

126. "Sudden Breeze Troubles Florida's 'Human Kite,' *Berkshire Eagle*, July 7, 1956, Newspaper Archive, www.newspaperarchive.com.

127. Simon Khoury interview.

128. D. Pope Sr., *Water Skiing*, 205.

129. "Cyclops Opens Eyes," letter from Dick Pope to *Business Week*, March 31, 1956.

130. "Television: New Cyclops," *Business Week*, March 10, 1956, 76–104.

131. Dorothy Singer and Jerome Singer, *Handbook of Children and the Media* (Thousand Oaks, Calif.: Sage, 2001), 224.

132. John Corry, "T.V. Review: Bill Moyers Studies Old Newsreels," *New York Times*, February 22, 1984.

133. Donald Freeman, "Newsreels Bring Old, Old Friends," *San Diego Union*, September 25, 1955.

134. Jack Gurnett, "Officials Mum on Proposal," *Orlando Sentinel*, ca. March 1956, Cypress Gardens Archives.

135. Williams, *Million Dollar Mermaid*, 314.

136. Clipping from *Cypress Gardens News Real*, 1955, Cypress Gardens Archive.

137. "Cypress Gardens' Tropical Isles of Movieland," Polk County Historical and Genealogical Library.

138. Lisa Nees, "Cypress Gardens: The Beauty Queens Playground," *Pageantry Magazine* (2000), www.pageantrymagazine.com.

139. Red McGuire interview.

140. Dubie Baxter interview.

141. Gary White, "Our Beauty Queen," *Lakeland*

Ledger, January 25, 2007, Polk County Historical and Genealogical Library.

142. Lisa Nees, "Cypress Gardens The Beauty Queens Playground," *Pageantry Magazine* (2000), www.pageantrymagazine.com.

143. Jim Halbe, "Dick Pope Suggests Canal for Turnpike," *Orlando Sentinel*, March 5, 1957, Cypress Gardens Archive.

144. Mike Morgan, "Moment with Morgan," *Tampa Daily Times*, February 19, 1957, Cypress Gardens Archive.

145. Cypress Gardens brochure, State of Florida Archives.

146. Arthur Herzog, "The King of Beauty Queens," *Esquire*, September 1957, 120–28.

147. "King Saud Visits Polk County," June 26, 1957, clipping, Cypress Gardens Archives.

148. Dubie Baxter interview.

149. "Post Office for Cypress Gardens Plan," *Winter Haven Herald*, July 26, 1957, Polk County Historical and Genealogical Library.

150. "Pope Is Getting a Sub-Postoffice!" *Tampa Sunday Tribune*, October 6, 1957, Cypress Gardens Archives.

151. "W-GTO Airs First Cypress Gardens Show," *Winter Haven Herald*, August 23, 1957, Polk County Historical and Genealogical Library.

152. "Plain Talk: Governor Collins," December 1957, clipping, Cypress Gardens Archives.

153. Bob Kehoe interview.

154. "The Gardens Back on Map," undated article, Cypress Gardens Archive.

155. "Pope to Be Judge of Miss America Contest," *Winter Haven Herald*, April 25, 1958, Cypress Gardens Archives.

156. Wilbur E. Garrett, "The Booming Sport of Waterskiing," *National Geographic*, November 1958, 700–711.

157. Donna Kelly, "Rollins Mourns Loss of Hall of Fame Skier Dick Pope, Jr.," *Lakeland Ledger*, November 11, 2007.

158. William Levesque, "Waterski Maker to Shut Down Haven Unit, *Lakeland Ledger*, June 15, 1991, Polk County Historical and Genealogical Library.

159. Garland Pollard, "Cypress Gardens' Skis, Please," *Brandland USA*, May 28, 2007, www.brandlandusa.com.

160. D. Pope Sr., *Water Skiing*, 113.

161. "There's Romance in Colony, Says Tourism Promoter," *Hong Kong Standard*, May 9, 1959, Cypress Gardens Archive.

162. "Publicising Glamour of Hong Kong: Florida Tourist Executive's View," *South China Morning Post*, May 9, 1959, Cypress Gardens Archive.

163. Margaret Chase Parry interview, February 18, 2008.

164. "Cordial Royalty Give Tourists Treat," undated article, Cypress Gardens Archive.

165. Roy Bongartz, "The Superswamp: Cypress Gardens: Florida's Eighteen-Karat Illusion," *Saturday Evening Post*, November 26, 1963, 78–81.

166. Betty Doles interview.

167. Christopher Gray, "Streetscapes: Kodak Colorama; The End of the Line for Grand Central's Big Picture," *New York Times*, June 18, 1989, Newsbank Newsfile Collection, http://infoweb.newsbank.com.

168. *Colorama: The World's Largest Photographs*, 2009, www.aperture.org/ August 14, 2008.

169. Advertisement in *Time* magazine, December 28, 1959, Cypress Gardens Archive.

170. "Pope Selected for Hall of Fame," Polk County Historical and Genealogical Library.

Chapter 5. The 1960s: Esther Williams, Mike Douglas, and Johnny Carson Come to Town

1. Dick Bothwell, "Mr. Cypress Gardens," October 9, 1960, Cypress Gardens Archive.

2. Esther Williams, *Million Dollar Mermaid* (New York: Harvest Books, 2000), 314–15.

3. Charles Witbeck, "Esther Performs in Dream Pool," *Charleston (W. Va.) Gazette Mail*, August 7, 1960, Newspaper Archive, www.newspaperarchive.com.

4. "For TV Spectacular: Head of Cypress Gardens Talks State Cabinet into Approving $5,000 Outlay," *Tampa Tribune*, June 22, 1960, Cypress Gardens Archive.

5. "TV Spectacular Cost Reported over 500,000," undated clipping, Cypress Gardens Archive.

6. Williams, *Million Dollar Mermaid*, 316.

7. Bill Bell interview, February 2008.

8. Williams, *Million Dollar Mermaid*, 315.

9. Claire Cox, "Television in Review," United Press International, August 8, 1960, Newspaper Archive, www.newspaperarchive.com.

10. Vernon Scott, "Esther Williams to Have TV's Biggest Splash This Summer," *Kittaning (Pa.) Leader Times*, August 4, 1960, Newspaper Archive, www.newspaperarchive.com.

11. Harris Powers, "Dick Pope Still Irrepressible," *Sarasota Journal*, September 21, 1960, Cypress Gardens Archive.

12. John P. Shanley, "Esther Williams Floats in Cypress Gardens," *New York Times*, August 9, 1960, ProQuest Historical Newspapers, http://proquest.umi.com/login.

13. William Furlong, "Babes in a Swampland," *Sports Illustrated*, October 21, 1963, 66–80.

14. Rick Dantzler interview, February 18, 2008.

15. Bob Kehoe interview, February 2008.

16. Susan Barbosa, "Big Syl," *Lakeland Ledger*, September 20, 1981.

17. Fred Gaffney interview, February 2008.

18. Dubie Baxter interview, February 2008.

19. Bob Kehoe interview.

20. Alvin Denmark interview, May 2009.

21. Barbosa, "Big Syl."

22. Bob Kehoe interview.

23. Barbosa, "Big Syl."

24. Furlong, "Babes in a Swampland."

25. "'Road's Tag' Creates Problem," undated clipping, Cypress Gardens Archive.

26. "Dick Pope Day Announced for Florida," *Winter Haven Herald*, November 25, 1960, Polk County Historical and Genealogical Library.

27. Hy Peskin and Norton Wood, "The Man Who Invented Florida, *Argosy*, June 1950, 29–31, 70.

28. "Cornelia: Determined to 'Make Do,'" *Time*, May 29, 1972, www.time.com.

29. Cornelia Wallace, *C'nelia* (Philadelphia: A. J. Holman, 1976), 212–14.

30. Dubie Baxter interview.

31. Mary Margaret McBride, "Where Water Skiers Come From," *Modesto Bee*, December 7, 1954, Newspaper Archive, www.newspaperarchive.com

32. Roy Bongartz, "The Superswamp: Cypress Gardens: Florida's Eighteen-Karat Illusion," *Saturday Evening Post*, November 26, 1963, 78–81.

33. Fred Gaffney interview.

34. Roy Bongartz, "The Superswamp: Cypress Gardens: Florida's Eighteen-Karat Illusion," *Saturday Evening Post*, November 26, 1963, 78–81.

35. Willa McGuire Cook interview, February 2008.

36. Red McGuire interview, February 2008.

37. Rick Dantzler interview.

38. Bob Kehoe interview.

39. Dubie Baxter interview.

40. Furlong, "Babes in a Swampland."

41. Dubie Baxter interview.

42. Simon Khoury interview, July 2009.

43. Hedrick Smith, "Hussein Confers with President," *New York Times,* April 15, 1964, ProQuest Historical Newspapers, http://proquest.umi.com/login.

44. "Hotel History," The Colony, Palm Beach, www.thecolonypalmbeach.com.

45. John Larosch, "Jordan King Pays Visit to Winter Haven," *Orlando Sentinel*, April 20, 1964, Cypress Gardens Archive.

46. Simon Khoury interview.

47. Mark Voisard interview, March 2008.

48. Virgninia Kraft, "His Majesty, The Leadfoot," *Sports Illustrated*, May 8, 1967, 42–48.

49. Richard Johnson interview, February 2008.

50. Lynn Novakofski interview, February 2008.

51. "People," *Sports Illustrated*, October 26, 1964.

52. "Jumping Frog Trained Here," *Cypress Gardens News Real,* undated, Cypress Gardens Archive.

53. Ceel Pasternak, "Profile: Dick Pope," *Spray: The Waterskiing Magazine*, July 1978, 22–25, 56–57, 60–61.

54. Bob Kehoe interview.

55. "Dick Pope to Run '65 Florida Show at Fair," *Winter Haven Daily News Chief*, February 21, 1965, Cypress Gardens Archive.

56. Ben Fong-Torres, *Hickory Wind: The Life and Times of Gram Parsons* (New York: St. Martin's Griffin, 1998), 27, 44–45.

57. William Tucker, "Florida Wins Fair Aquacade," *Miami News*, February 5, 1965, Cypress Gardens Archive.

58. "Florida World's Fair Santa Paying the State: Tallahassee, Florida," State Library and Archives of Florida, http://fpc.dos.state.fl.us/reference/gv024002.jpg.

59. "Governor Accepts Exhibit Installment," *St. Petersburg Times*, July 29, 1966, Cypress Gardens Archive.

60. C. E. Wright, "East-Coast Disneyland to Rise near Orlando," *New York Times*, November 21, 1965, ProQuest Historical Newspapers, http://proquest.umi.com/login.

61. "Cypress Gardens Staff Meeting—Disney Style," *Cypress Gardens News Real*, December 1965, Cypress Gardens Archive.

62. "From Eskimos to Headhunters, All Visit Polk's Attractions," *Lakeland Ledger*, March 26, 1966, Polk County Historical and Genealogical Library.

63. John Ryan, "Some Thoughtful Spring Cleaning," *St. Petersburg Times*, April 30, 1967, Google News Archive, www.news.google.com.

64. Advertisement, *Orlando Sentinel-Star*, February 2, 1967.

65. "More Than a Million Visit Cypress Gardens Annually," *Winter Haven Herald*, February 16, 1967, Polk County Historical and Genealogical Library.

66. Untitled article, *Winter Haven Herald*, February 16, 1967.

67. "Multi-Million Dollar Resort Hotel Planned near Cypress Gardens," undated article, Cypress Gardens Archive.

68. Brenda Mitchell interview, February 2008.

69. Bob Kehoe interview.

70. "Murder or Suicide? $130,000 Question," *St. Petersburg Times,* October 23, 1967, Google News Archive, http://news.google.com.

71. Margaret Chase Parry interview, February 18, 2009.

72. "Murder or Suicide? $130,000 Question."

73. "Johnny Carson Discovers Cypress Gardens," *Ski News*, Summer 1968, American Water Ski Educational Foundation Museum.

74. "Johnny Carson Discovers Cypress Gardens" (author's collection).

75. "People," *Time* magazine, September 6, 1968, www.time.com.

76. Dave Dershimer interview, February 2008.

77. "Carson Discovers Cypress Gardens," *Panama City News*, August 19, 1968, Google News Archive, http://news.google.com.

78. "Polk Friend Remembers Johnny Carson," Polkonline.com.

79. Richard Johnson interview, February 2008.

80. "Carson Discovers Cypress Gardens," *Panama City News*, August 19, 1968, Google News Archive, http://news.google.com.

81. "Bensen," http://daddybobphotos.com/Aircraft/Manufacturer/Bensen /pages/BEN-B6-Gyroglider-H.htm.

82. Igor Bensen, *A Dream of Flight* (Indianapolis: Abbott Company, 2003), 86.

83. Red McGuire interview.

84. Dubie Baxter interview.

85. "Johnny Carson Discovers Cypress Gardens" (author's collection).

86. "30 Acres on Lake Eloise Bought by Cypress Gardens," *Winter Haven Herald*, August 28, 1969.

87. "Gen-Tel Installs 750,000th Phone," *Bradenton Herald*, October 26, 1969, Cypress Gardens Archive.

Chapter 6. The 1970s: Dick Welcomes Mickey

1. Jon Nordheimer, "New Disney World Is Rising," *New York Times*, December 29, 1970, ProQuest Historical Newspapers, http://proquest.umi.com/login.

2. Gary Mormino, *Land of Sunshine, State of Dreams* (Gainesville: University Press of Florida, 2005), 119–20.

3. Ibid., 101.

4. Ibid. 103–4.

5. Richard Fogelsong, *Married to the Mouse: Walt Disney World and Orlando* (New Haven: Yale University Press, 2003), 5.

6. "Large Elephant Escapes Chains, Killed by Truck," *St. Petersburg Times*, April 13, 1966, Google News Archive, http://news.google.com.

7. Jaye Wright, "Florida Wonderland," *Florida Today*, August 8, 2002.

8. Nancy Beth Jackson, "In Florida's Cassadaga the Mediums Are the Message," *New York Times*, March 15, 1970, ProQuest Historical Newspapers, http://proquest.umi.com/login.

9. Ann Weldon, "They Gather Beside a Lake . . ." *St. Petersburg Evening Independent*, April 8, 1978, Google News Archive, http://news.google.com.

10. Paul J. C. Friedlander, "What Has Mickey Mouse Wrought?" *New York Times*, March 21, 1971, ProQuest Historical Newspapers, http://proquest.umi.com/login.

11. Paul J. C. Friedlander, "Miami: Worries about Disney World," *New York Times*, April 4, 1971, ProQuest Historical Newspapers, http://proquest.umi.com/login.

12. "Ebb Tide at Miami Beach," *Time*, December 19, 1977.

13. Harold Gardner, Letters to the Editor, *Time*, January 16, 1978.

14. Mary Ellen Slate, "Cypress Gardens Rides Again," *Motor Boating and Sailing*, March 1971.

15. Janice Miller and Kathy Hedge, "Notables Pay Honor to Pope on His Day," *Winter Haven Daily News*, May 17, 1971, Cypress Gardens Archive.

16. Phil Hevener, "Brevard Awaits Disney Spin-Off," *Florida Today*, undated article, Cypress Gardens Archive.

17. "'Plant Safari' Man Pleased with S.A.," undated article, Cypress Gardens Archive.

18. Tom Burke, "Disney World Wins Nod from 'Pros,'" *St. Petersburg Times*, May 2, 1971, Google News Archive, http://news.google.com/.

19. "Cypress Gardens Welcomes the Magic Kingdom of Disney," advertisement, *Orlando Sentinel*, October 2, 1971, Cypress Gardens Archive.

20. Russell Kay, "Too Late to Classify," *St. Petersburg Evening Independent*, December 26, 1936, Google News Archive, http://news.google.com/.

21. William Honan, "If you Gave Mickey Mouse $400 Million, Here's How He'd Spend It," *New York Times*, October 10, 1971, ProQuest Historical Newspapers, http://proquest.umi.com/login.

22. Paul Ferguson, "Dick Pope . . . A Showman for All Seasons," *Jacksonville Times-Union and Journal*, January 28, 1973, Cypress Gardens Archive.

23. Kurt Spitzer, letter to the editor, *St. Petersburg Times*, November 6, 1971, Google News Archive, http://news.google.com/.

24. Anne Massey, letter to the editor, *St. Petersburg Times*, November 6, 1971, Google News Archive, http://news.google.com/.

25. Charlie Wadsworth, "Hush Puppies," December 31, 1971, Cypress Gardens Archive.

26. Vance Johnston, "Booming Tourist Attractions Plan Expansion," *Tampa Tribune*, August 14, 1972, Cypress Gardens Archive.

27. M. J. Potter, untitled article, *Orlando Sentinel*, November 19, 1972, Polk County Historical and Genealogical Library.

28. Ron Wiggins, "Behind Curtain Life . . ." *St. Petersburg Times*, January 12, 1973, Google News Archive, http://news.google.com/.

29. David Langford, "Barnum City to Be Built in

Florida," *Bryan Times*, February 18, 1972, Newspaper Archive, www.newspaperarchive.com.

30. "Cypress Gardens Moves into a New Era," *Winter Haven News Chief*, September 13, 1972, Cypress Gardens Archive.

31. Wendy Domaingue, "Cypress Gardens' Competition?" *Lakeland Ledger*, undated clipping, Cypress Gardens Archive.

32. Bob Kehoe interview.

33. Dubie Baxter interview.

34. Lonnie Brown, "Disney Fighting to Keep Spotlight," *Lakeland Ledger*, April 25, 1973, Google News Archive, http://news.google.com/.

35. Dick Bothwell, "A Groundbreaking to Rival Disney's: It's Circus World," *St. Petersburg Times*, April 27, 1973, Google News Archive, http://news.google.com/.

36. David L. Langford, "A Far and Fishy Flight of Fancy," *St. Petersburg Times*, November 19, 1973, Google News Archive, http://news.google.com/.

37. "Gas Shortage to Close Rainbow Springs," *St. Petersburg Times*, February 16, 1974, Google News Archive, http://news.google.com/.

38. Honan, "If You Gave Mickey Mouse $400-Million, Here's How He'd Spend It."

39. John Cooper, "Gardens of the World," *Orlando-Land,* March 1974, Cypress Gardens Archive.

40. "Message to the Stockholders," December 19, 1974, Cypress Gardens Archive.

41. Frank Deford, "An Honest Travel Story," *Sports Illustrated*, January 26, 1976, 39–40.

42. "Ski Show to Salute America," *St. Petersburg Evening Independent*, July 1, 1975, Google News Archive, http://news.google.com/.

43. Bert Lacey interview, February 2008.

44. Peter R. Gallagher, "Natural Beauty No Longer Holds Tourists' Attention," *St. Petersburg Times*, July 5, 1976, Google News Archive, http://news.google.com/.

45. Karen Branch, "Parrot Jungle Sold, Will Remain Bird Haven," *Miami Herald*, October 2, 1988, Newsbank Newsfile Collection, http://infoweb.newsbank.com.

46. John Pain, "Big Move Is All the Talk at Parrot Jungle: Venerable Attraction Getting New Miami Location on an Island," *Miami Herald*, December 29, 2002, Newsbank Newsfile Collection, http://infoweb.newsbank.com.

47. Douglas Hanks, "The Parrot Has Left the Jungle . . ." *Miami Herald*, June 29, 2007, Newsbank Newsfile Collection, http://infoweb.newsbank.com.

48. Peter R. Gallagher, "Natural Beauty No Longer Holds Tourists' Attention," *St. Petersburg Times*, July 5, 1976, Google News Archive, http://news.google.com/.

49. Bert Lacey interview.

50. Dave Dershimer interview.

51. "Cypress Gardens Profit, Crowds Decline," *St. Petersburg Times*, December 21, 1977.

52. Bert Lacey interview.

53. Kevin Wells, "Middle of the Swarm," *WaterSki Magazine*, undated, www.waterskimag.com.

54. Larry Kieffer, "Cypress Gardens Expands," *Winter Haven News Chief*, undated article, Polk County Historical and Genealogical Library.

55. Rick Allen, "Another Score for the Swami, Cypress Gardens Puts $5.5 Million on Polk's Tourist Future," *Winter Haven News Chief,* October 28, 1979, Cypress Gardens Archive.

56. Cypress Gardens press release, October 1979, Cypress Gardens Archive.

Chapter 7. The 1980s and 1990s: Fighting Back against the "Worlds"

1. "News from Cypress Gardens," press release, ca. 1980, Cypress Gardens Archive.

2. Rick Allen, "Gardens' Dream a Reality," *Winter Haven News Herald*, January 14, 1980, Polk County Historical and Genealogical Library.

3. William Furlong, "Babes in a Swampland," *Sports Illustrated*, October 21, 1964, 66–80.

4. Lucy Chambliss interview, February 2008.

5. Walt Belcher, "Being the First Bird on Water Skis Doesn't Ruffle Mr. Mo's Feathers a Bit," *Tampa Tribune*, April 24, 1980, Cypress Gardens Archive.

6. Miller Davis, "The Little Giant, Dick Pope, Sr," *Lakeland Ledger*, February 8, 1981, Cypress Gardens Archive.

7. Julie Pope Dantzler and Rick Dantzler interview, February 18, 2008.

8. William A. Davis, "Cypress Gardens Endures, For 45 Years This Florida Park Has Lured Millions of Visitors," *Boston Globe*, March 22, 1981, Newsbank Newsfile Collection, http://infoweb.newsbank.com.

9. "Cover Story—the Go-Go's—'Vacation,' cover by Mick Haggerty," September 17, 2007, *Sugartune*, www.sugartune.com.

10. Steve Spears, "Go-Gos Enjoy Their 'Sedate' Phase," *St. Petersburg Times*, February 7, 2008, Newsbank Newsfile Collection, http://infoweb.newsbank.com.

11. David Nyhan, "Centerpiece: 'The Magic Kingdom Boot Camp' Courtesy of Big Brother Walt," *Boston Globe*, June 26, 1981, Newsbank Newsfile Collection, http://infoweb.newsbank.com.

12. Daniel Boorstin, *The Image: A Guide to Pseudo-Events in America* (New York: Vintage, 1992), 99.

13. Nyhan, "Centerpiece: 'The Magic Kingdom Boot Camp' Courtesy of Big Brother Walt."

14. Morris Rosenberg, "The Mouse That Roared," *Washington Post*, October 11, 1981, Newsbank Newsfile Collection, http://infoweb.newsbank.com.

15. Rick Sylvain, "No Famine of Fans in Disney World; EPCOT Has Heaps of Hype but the Magic Kingdom Keeps Its Fans," *Detroit Free Press*, December 5, 1982, Newsbank Newsfile Collection, http://infoweb.newsbank.com.

16. David Nyhan, "Sunny Florida Struggling with Rapid Growth, Success," *Boston Globe*, August 23, 1981, Newsbank Newsfile Collection, http://infoweb.newsbank.com.

17. Rosenberg, "The Mouse That Roared."

18. Charles Whited, "Epcot's Lure, Tourist Influx Have a Price," *Miami Herald*, October 3, 1982, Newsbank Newsfile Collection, http://infoweb.newsbank.com.

19. Lauren Ritchie, "Cypress Gardens Profits Plunge as Attendance Dips," *Orlando Sentinel-Star*, January 1982, Polk County Historical and Genealogical Library.

20. William Davis, "Enter a Future World with a Familiar Feel," *Boston Globe*, October 24, 1982, Newsbank Newsfile Collection, http://infoweb.newsbank.com.

21. Whited, Epcot's Lure, Tourist Influx Have a Price."

22. "Cypress Gardens, a Loss and a Lift," *St. Petersburg Times*, February 16, 1983, Newsbank Newsfile Collection, http://infoweb.newsbank.com.

23. Fred Gaffney interview, February 13, 2008.

24. Paul Anderson, "Changing Habits in Travel Leave Region Behind," *Miami Herald*, September 19, 1983, Newsbank Newsfile Collection, http://infoweb.newsbank.com.

25. Donnie Croft interview, February 2008.

26. Jennie Hess, "Getting into the Ski of Things: It's Showtime for Performers at Cypress Gardens," *Atlanta Constitution*, September 22, 1985, Newsbank Newsfile Collection, http://infoweb.newsbank.com.

27. "Richard D. Pope, Sr.," American Water Ski Educational Foundation, www.waterskihalloffame.com/home.htm.

28. Lynn Novakofski interview, February 2008.

29. Sam Jacobs, "Cypress Gardens Is Still a Natural," *Miami Herald*, May 20, 1984, Newsbank Newsfile Collection, http://infoweb.newsbank.com.

30. "Florida Setting to Mark Benefit," *New York Times*, December 3, 1933, ProQuest Historical Newspapers, http://proquest.umi.com/login.

31. Sam Jacobs, "Cypress Gardens Is Still a Natural," *Miami Herald*, May 20, 1984, Newsbank Newsfile Collection, http://infoweb.newsbank.com.

32. "Cypress Gardens Pins Its Hopes of Recovery on Ads with Sears," *St. Petersburg Times*, November 20, 1984, Google News Archive, http://news.google.com/.

33. Bob Kehoe interview, February 2008.

34. "Save Cypress Gardens," editorial, *Miami Herald*, November 29, 1984, Newsbank Newsfile Collection, http://infoweb.newsbank.com.

35. Joel Achenbach, "Parks' New Theme: Lure the Locals," *Miami Herald*, March 17, 1985, Newsbank Newsfile Collection, http://infoweb.newsbank.com.

36. Tom Gaskins Jr. interview, May 16, 2009.

37. "Gaskins Cypress Knee Museum—Closed," Roadside America, www.roadsideamerica.com/story/2061.

38. Rick Dantzler interview.

39. Julie Pope Dantzler interview.

40. Vicki Vaughan, "Cypress Gardens Spruces Up, Adds Shows Owner Harcourt Brace Pumps $5 Million into Improvements," *Orlando Sentinel*, December 2, 1985, Newsbank Newsfile Collection, http://infoweb.newsbank.com.

41. Lauren McFaul, "Tourist Traditional Cypress Gardens Show Is Pure Florida History," *Orlando Sentinel*, July 14, 1985, Newsbank Newsfile Collection, http://infoweb.newsbank.com.

42. Lynn Novakofski interview.

43. Janis Froelich, "Southern Belle Gets a Face Lift," *St. Petersburg Times*, March 4, 1986.

44. Lynn Novakofski interview.

45. McFaul, "Tourist Traditional Cypress Gardens' Show Is Pure Florida History."

46. Betty Bonifay interview, May 20, 2009.

47. Hess, "Getting in the Ski of Things."

48. "Parks Bonifay," Entertainment and Sports Programming Network, http://expn.go.com/athletes/bios/BONIFAY_PARKS.html.

49. "Wave of the Future," *Time*, May 26, 1997, www.time.com.

50. Cathy Lynn Grossman, "Parrot Jungle at 50," *Miami Herald*, October 18, 1986, Newsbank Newsfile Collection, http://infoweb.newsbank.com.

51. Vicki Vaughan, "Disney Bash Covers the Tab, Party Rakes in More Than Enough Exposure to Cover Costs," *Orlando Sentinel*, October 13, 1986, Newsbank Newsfile Collection, http://infoweb.newsbank.com.

52. Cynthia Campbell, "The Fairest of them All?" *Baton Rouge Advocate*, October 12, 1986, Newsbank Newsfile Collection, http://infoweb.newsbank.com.

53. John J. Goldman, "Journalists' Junket Was No Mickey Mouse Operation," *Albany (N.Y.) Times-Union*, November 16, 1986, Newsbank Newsfile Collection, http://infoweb.newsbank.com.

54. Carl Hiaasen, *Team Rodent* (New York: Random House, 1998), 58, 60, 61.

55. Goldman, "Journalists' Junket Was No Mickey Mouse Operation."

56. Ibid.

57. Lloyd Grove, "With Mikhail or Mickey, Daniloff Stands His Ground," *Seattle Times*, October 12, 1986, Newsbank Newsfile Collection, http://infoweb.newsbank.com.

58. Peter Carlson, "'86, The Year of Living Stupidly," *Washington Post*, December 26, 1986, Newsbank Newsfile Collection, http://infoweb.newsbank.com.

59. Cynthia Campbell, "The Fairest of Them All?" *Baton Rouge Advocate*, October 12, 1986, Newsbank Newsfile Collection, http://infoweb.newsbank.com.

60. Vicki Vaughan, "Small Attractions Prosper: More Tourists in General Mean Attendance Gains for Everyone," *Orlando Sentinel* July 5, 1987, Newsbank Newsfile Collection, http://infoweb.newsbank.com.

61. "Ice-Skating Rink at Cypress Gardens Latest Step in Its Metamorphosis," *Horizons*, December 17, 1987, Polk County Historical and Genealogical Library.

62. "Richard Downing Pope, 87, Dies; Promoter of Florida and Tourism," *New York Times*, January 30, 1988, Newsbank Newsfile Collection, http://infoweb.newsbank.com.

63. Anna Turner, "Tourism Leaders Credit Pope for Their Careers," *Winter Haven News Chief*, January 29, 1988.

64. William Bygrave, "Pope Was a 'Visionary,' Lawyer Recalls," *Winter Haven News Chief,* January 29, 1988.

65. Billie Ellis, "Pope Was Loved by Employees," *Winter Haven News Chief*, January 29, 1988.

66. Julie Pope Dantzler, Rick Dantzler, and Margaret Chase Parry interviews, February 18, 2008.

67. Alvin Denmark interview. May 21, 2009.

68. Julie Pope Dantzler and Margaret Chase Parry interviews.

69. Susan Bloodworth and Robert Pitts, "Workers Assured of Job Security," *Winter Haven News Chief*, June 21, 1989, Polk County Historical and Genealogical Library.

70. Susan Bloodworth, "Bargaining Delays Park's Sale," *Winter Haven News Chief*, August 15, 1989, Polk County Historical and Genealogical Library.

71. Robert Pitts, "Gardens Would Be Gem for Buyer, Expert Says," *Winter Haven News Chief*, June 23, 1989, Polk County Historical and Genealogical Library.

72. Randolph Picht, "Anheuser Busch to Purchase Harcourt Brace Theme Parks," *Philadelphia Inquirer*, September, 29, 1989, Newsbank Newsfile Collection, http://infoweb.newsbank.com.

73. Susan Bloodworth, untitled clipping, *Winter Haven News Chief*, September 29, 1989, Polk County Historical and Genealogical Library.

74. "Amusement Park Abruptly Closed," *Winter Haven News Chief*, January 18, 1990, Polk County Historical and Genealogical Library.

75. Georgann Koelin, "A World of Fun: From Its Glittering Kingdom in Central Florida, Walt Disney World Exerts a Powerful Pull on Kids from Dodge City to Dusseldorf," *St. Paul Pioneer Press*, December 23, 1990, Newsbank Newsfile Collection, http://infoweb.newsbank.com.

76. Jan Tuckwood, "Of Bygone Days by the Sea," *Palm Beach Post*, December 23, 1990, Newsbank Newsfile Collection, http://infoweb.newsbank.com.

77. "Disney's Port Orleans Recalls the Old South," *Palm Beach Post*, June 16, 1991, Newsbank Newsfile Collection, http://infoweb.newsbank.com.

78. "Amusement Park Abruptly Closed," *Winter Haven News Chief*, January 18, 1990, Polk County Historical and Genealogical Library.

79. Donna Lynch, "Barefoot Skier, 75, Goes Bananas over the Sport," *Winter Haven News Chief*, February 3, 1990, Polk County Historical and Genealogical Library.

80. Lynn Novakofski interview.

81. Susan Strother, "Cypress Gardens Cuts Work Force, Theme Park Trims 22% of Staff," *Orlando Sentinel*, April 30, 1991, Newsbank Newsfile Collection, http://infoweb.newsbank.com.

82. David Szymanski, "Cypress Gardens Cuts Staff, Closes Parts of Park," *Tampa Tribune*, April 30, 1991, Newsbank Newsfile Collection, http://infoweb.newsbank.com.

83. Lynn Novakofski interview.

84. Jim Frye, "The Legacy of Cypress Gardens," waterskimag.com.

85. Lynn Novakofski interview.

86. Don Buffa interview, March 2008.

87. "Richard D. Pope, Sr.," American Water Ski Educational Foundation, www.waterskihalloffame.com/home.htm.

88. Don Buffa interview.

89. Arthur McCune, "The Roots of Cypress Gardens," *Lakeland Ledger*, July 18, 1991, Polk County Historical and Genealogical Library.

90. Lisa Backman, "Cypress Gardens Returns to Established Features," *Ocala Star Banner*, August 2, 1991, Newsbank Newsfile Collection, http://infoweb.newsbank.com.

91. Susan Bloodworth, "Brother, Sister Team First Blacks at Gardens," *Lakeland Ledger*, August 15, 1991, Google News Archive, http://news.google.com/.

92. Lisa Coffey, "Siblings Grow up in Waterskiing Legacy," *Lakeland Ledger*, October 1, 1995, Google News Archive, http://news.google.com/.

93. Steve Newborn, "Cypress Gardens to Add Display of Butterflies," *Tampa Tribune*, July 14, 1992, Newsbank Newsfile Collection, http://infoweb.newsbank.com.

94. Vicki Vaughan, "Some Small Attractions Walking Tall, Tourist Stops Target Visitors with 'Natural' Bent, Little Time," *Orlando Sentinel*, September 20, 1992, Newsbank Newsfile Collection, http://infoweb.newsbank.com.

95. Susan Strother, "Park Finds Butterflies a Good Fit, Cypress Gardens Hopes Conservatory will Draw Visitors," *Orlando Sentinel*, March 15, 1993, Newsbank Newsfile Collection, http://infoweb.newsbank.com.

96. Marty Rosen, "Tiny Wings of Wonder Take Flight," *St. Petersburg Times*, January 16, 1993, Newsbank Newsfile Collection, http://infoweb.newsbank.com.

97. Del Jones, "Zoo World Meets Corporate Jungle: Wild Kingdom Competition Grows Fiercer," *USA Today*, August 10, 1993, Newsbank Newsfile Collection, http://infoweb.newsbank.com.

98. Caron Pappas, "Gardens Celebrates 50th Year of Skiing," *Tampa Tribune*, June 18, 1993, Newsbank Newsfile Collection, http://infoweb.newsbank.com.

99. Steve Newborn, "Veteran to Pilot Cypress Gardens," *Tampa Tribune*, February 24, 1995, Newsbank Newsfile Collection, http://infoweb.newsbank.com.

100. Steve Newborn, "Cypress Gardens Managers Buy Park from Anheuser-Busch," *Tampa Tribune*, April 4, 1995, Newsbank Newsfile Collection, http://infoweb.newsbank.com.

101. Lisa Backman, "Classic Florida: The State's Older Tourist Attractions Rely on Their Florida Roots and New Exhibits to Draw Visitors," *Tampa Tribune*, May 7, 1995, Newsbank Newsfile Collection, http://infoweb.newsbank.com.

102. Bert Lacey interview, February 2008.

103. Steve Newborn, "Cypress Gardens Turns 60: Attendance at the Park Peaked in 1976, but the CEO Plans for It to Be the Best of Its Kind by 2000," *Tampa Tribune*, January 29, 1996, Newsbank Newsfile Collection, http://infoweb.newsbank.com.

104. Shaila Dewan, "Seeking a Tribute to the Ordinary in a Water Tower," *New York Times*, February 9, 2009, Newsbank Newsfile Collection, http://infoweb.newsbank.com.

105. Jill Jorden Spitz, "Cypress Gardens Turns 60: Park's Past Plays Role in Future," *Orlando Sentinel*, February 18, 1996, Newsbank Newsfile Collection, http://infoweb.newsbank.com.

106. Mary Foster, "Longtime Pals Disney, Southern Baptists Hit Skids: Church Feels Mickey's Parent Has Strayed from Family Values," *Milwaukee Journal Sentinel*, June 29, 1996, Newsbank Newsfile Collection, http://infoweb.newsbank.com.

107. Leslie Doolittle, "Christianity to Take Root at Cypress Gardens' New Bible-Themed Exhibit," *Orlando Sentinel,* July 23, 1996, Newsbank Newsfile Collection, http://infoweb.newsbank.com.

108. Catherine Stengel, "That Face Rings a Belle," *Tampa Tribune*, September 2, 1996, Newsbank Newsfile Collection, http://infoweb.newsbank.com.

109. Bert Lacey interview.

110. Paul Power, "Park Adds Biblical Garden," *Tampa Tribune*, February 6, 1997, Newsbank Newsfile Collection, http://infoweb.newsbank.com.

111. Jennifer Stevenson, "Planting a New Eden," *St. Petersburg Times*, February 7, 1997, Newsbank Newsfile Collection, http://infoweb.newsbank.com.

112. Twila Decker, "A Religious Experience in Orlando," *St. Petersburg Times*, September 29, 1999, Newsbank Newsfile Collection, http://infoweb.newsbank.com.

113. Stevenson, "Planting a New Eden."

114. Lesly Clark, "Theme Is Survival: In Era of Megaparks, Old-Florida Attractions Must Adapt—or Die," *Orlando Sentinel*, November, 15, 1998, Newsbank Newsfile Collection, http://infoweb.newsbank.com.

115. Advertisement, *St. Petersburg Evening Independent*, February 22, 1934, Google News Archive, http://news.google.com/.

116. "The Rambler," *St. Petersburg Evening Independent*, March 28, 1938, Google News Archive, http://news.google.com/.

117. Lesley Clark, "Sunken Gardens to Turn over New Fig Leaf," *Orlando Sentinel*, January 2, 1999, Newsbank Newsfile Collection, http://infoweb.newsbank.com.

Chapter 8. Defying Gravity and Hurricanes

1. William Bartram, *Travels of William Bartram*, edited by Mark Van Doran (Athens: University of Georgia Press, 1998), 114.

2. Elliott Jones, "Florida's Old-Time Roadside Attractions," *Fort Pierce Tribune*, October 19, 2003, Newsbank Newsfile Collection, http://infoweb.newsbank.com.

3. Mike Schneider, "Terrorism Exposes Florida's Reliance on Tourism," *Post-Tribune*, October 7, 2001, Newsbank Newsfile Collection, http://infoweb.newsbank.com.

4. Teresa Burney, "After Attacks, Tourists Returned to 'Old Florida,'" *St. Petersburg Times*, February 13, 2002, Newsbank Newsfile Collection, http://infoweb.newsbank.com.

5. Dan Neal and Nicole Piscopo, "Welcome to a Colorful World Free of Focus, and Haste," *Palm Beach Post*, June 2, 2002, Newsbank Newsfile Collection, http://infoweb.newsbank.com.

6. Mary Toothman, "Cypress Gardens to Close Sunday," *Lakeland Ledger*, April 11, 2003, Polk County Historical and Genealogical Library.

7. Bert Lacey interview, February 2008.

8. Dave Simanoff, "Big Parks, Economy Weed out Old Player," *Tampa Tribune*, April 11, 2003, Newsbank Newsfile Collection, http://infoweb.newsbank.com.

9. Toothman, "Cypress Gardens to Close Sunday."

10. Mark Albright, "Cypress Gardens Bows Out," *St. Petersburg Times*, April 11, 2003, Newsbank Newsfile Collection, http://infoweb.newsbank.com.

11. Toothman, "Cypress Gardens to Close Sunday."

12. Nick Jackson interview, March 2008.

13. Harriet Daniels, "Reaction Similar from Ocala's Silver Springs," *Lakeland Ledger*, April 11, 2003, Polk County Historical and Genealogical Library.

14. Margarita Martin-Hidalgo, "The Final Wedding on a Perfect Day," *Lakeland Ledger*, April 13, 2003, Polk County Historical and Genealogical Library.

15. Bill Bair, "For Serenity, More Look to Bok Sanctuary," *Lakeland Ledger*, April 13, 2003, Polk County Historical and Genealogical Library.

16. Mary Toothman, "Park Chief Focusing on Dignified End," *Lakeland Ledger*, April 12, 2003, Polk County Historical and Genealogical Library.

17. Suzie Schottlekotte, "East Polk Looks beyond the Gardens," *Lakeland Ledger*, April 13, 2003, Polk County Historical and Genealogical Library.

18. "Park Patrons Recall Happy Times at the Attraction," *Lakeland Ledger*, April 13, 2003, Polk County Historical and Genealogical Library.

19. Eric Pera, "Thousands Sadly Jam Cypress Gardens on Its Last Day," *Lakeland Ledger*, April 14, 2003, Polk County Historical and Genealogical Library.

20. Amy Edwards, "For 60 Years, Water Skiing Shows Were a Staple at Cypress Gardens," *Lakeland Ledger*, April 14, 2003, Polk County Historical and Genealogical Library.

21. Bill Rufty, "State Leader to Discuss Saving Park," *Lakeland Ledger*, April 16, 2003, Polk County Historical and Genealogical Library.

22. Bob Gernert interview, February 2008.

23. Jim Frye, "A Family's Legacy: Remembering Cypress Gardens with Dick Pope, Jr.," *WaterSki Magazine*, July 2003.

24. John Chambliss, "Gardens Could Bloom," *Lakeland Ledger*, May 28, 2003, Polk County Historical and Genealogical Library.

25. "Cypress Gardens Named to State Priority List," *Polk County Democrat*, June 9, 2003, Polk County Historical and Genealogical Library.

26. Lloyd Dunkelberger, untitled article, *Lakeland Ledger*, August 17, 2003, Polk County Historical and Genealogical Library.

27. Bill Rufty, "Gardens Now Sit Shabby, But Beauty Peeks Through," *Lakeland Ledger*, August 17, 2003, Polk County Historical and Genealogical Library.

28. Joy Cochran, "Gardens' Next Step Involves Yardwork," *Lakeland Ledger*, August 28, 2003, Polk County Historical and Genealogical Library.

29. Lloyd Dunkelberger, "Cypress Gardens Options Laid Out," *Lakeland Ledger*, August 21, 2003, Polk County Historical and Genealogical Library.

30. Lloyd Dunkelberger and Bill Rufty, "Group Hopes to Preserve Gardens," *Lakeland Ledger*, August 26, 2003, Polk County Historical and Genealogical Library.

31. Gary Fineout, "State Agrees to Help Save Gardens," *Lakeland Ledger*, August 27, 2003, Polk County Historical and Genealogical Library.

32. Julie Hauserman, "Roadside Distraction?" *St. Petersburg Times*, September 15, 2003, Newsbank Newsfile Collection, http://infoweb.newsbank.com.

33. Bill Rufty, "Cypress Gardens Deal All But Done," *Lakeland Ledger*, September 26, 2003, Polk County Historical and Genealogical Library.

34. Christopher Sherman, "Icy Idea Melts at Cypress Gardens: 2 Proposals Remain to Buy Attraction," *Orlando Sentinel*, December 11, 2003, Newsbank Newsfile Collection, http://infoweb.newsbank.com.

35. Keith Kohn, "Now Cypress Gardens Fans Dare to Dream of a Future," *Orlando Sentinel*, December 25, 2003, Newsbank Newsfile Collection, http://infoweb.newsbank.com/.

36. Christopher Sherman, "New Boss Will Rev up Cypress Gardens," *Tallahassee Democrat*, January 4, 2004, Newsbank Newsfile Collection, http://infoweb.newsbank.com.

37. "New Owner Promises Rejuvenation for Florida's Cypress Gardens," *Washington (Pa.) Observer-Reporter*, May 16, 2004, Newsbank Newsfile Collection, http://infoweb.newsbank.com.

38. Cara Buckley, "Life's No Ball for Belles since Theme Park Closed," *Miami Herald*, July 11, 2004, Newsbank Newsfile Collection, http://infoweb.newsbank.com.

39. Christopher Sherman, "Cypress Gardens Postpones Date for Reopening," *Orlando Sentinel*, April 16, 2004, Newsbank Newsfile Collection, http://infoweb.newsbank.com.

40. Mark Hinson, "The Days of Miracle Are Numbered," *Tallahassee Democrat*, April 25, 2004, Newsbank Newsfile Collection, http://infoweb.newsbank.com.

41. Jim Auchmutey, "Coasting to a Close: Florida Beach Town's Old-Fashioned Amusement Park Takes Last Ride," *Atlanta Journal and Constitution*, September 3, 2004, Newsbank Newsfile Collection, http://infoweb.newsbank.com.

42. Christopher Sherman, "New Target: October—Cypress Gardens to Miss Out on Summer Crowds,"

Orlando Sentinel, June 15, 2004, Newsbank Newsfile Collection, http://infoweb.newsbank.com.

43. Keith Kohn, "Scenes of Loss and Survival: All across Polk, People Wept, Worked Hard," *Orlando Sentinel*, August 19, 2004, Newsbank Newsfile Collection, http://infoweb.newsbank.com.

44. Kelly Griffith, "Historic Cypress Gardens," *South Florida Sun,* April 10, 2005, www.southflorida.com.

45. Randy Diamond, "Risky Business," *Tampa Tribune,* August 23, 2004, Newsbank Newsfile Collection, http://infoweb.newsbank.com.

46. Christopher Sherman, "Park Sets Date for Opening: Cypress Gardens Will Have Several 'Soft Openings' before the Grand Opening Scheduled for Dec. 9," *Orlando Sentinel*, October 6, 2004, Newsbank Newsfile Collection, http://infoweb.newsbank.com.

47. Christopher Sherman, "Gardens Taking Shape: Cypress Gardens Adventure Park's Grand Opening Is Just Weeks Away, and the Attraction Has Already Sold Thousands of Annual Passes," *Orlando Sentinel*, November 6, 2004, Newsbank Newsfile Collection, http://infoweb.newsbank.com.

48. Joy Cochran, "Opening Jitters," *Lakeland Ledger*, November 27, 2004, Polk County Historical and Genealogical Library.

49. Julia Crouse, "Rides Are New, but Same Ol' Gardens," *Lakeland Ledger*, November 27, 2004, Polk County Historical and Genealogical Library.

50. Gayle White, "Cypress Saved: Ex-Miss Georgia's Zeal Moves Florida, Businessman to Rescue Landmark Amusement Park," *Atlanta Journal Constitution*, December 9, 2004, Newsbank Newsfile Collection, http://infoweb.newsbank.com.

51. Bob Gernert interview, February 2008.

52. Amy Edwards, "Visitors Thrilled by Revamped Park," *Orlando Sentinel*, December 10, 2004, Newsbank Newsfile Collection, http://infoweb.newsbank.com.

53. Joy Cochran, "Gardens Officially Reopens Today," *Lakeland Ledger*, December 9, 2004, Polk County Historical and Genealogical Library.

54. Christopher Elliot and Kari Haugeto, "Cypress Gardens Renews, Revs Up and Rebounds?" *Boston Globe*, December 12, 2004, Newsbank Newsfile Collection, http://infoweb.newsbank.com.

55. Bill Vanderford, "Cypress Gardens Reborn: Keeping Its History, Park Now Offers New Attractions," *Forsyth County News,* August 12, 2007, Newsbank Newsfile Collection, http://infoweb.newsbank.com.

56. Amy Edwards, "Attraction Gets Teeth: Today Cypress Gardens Adventure Park Opens Nature's Way, the Park's Redesigned Animal Exhibit," *Orlando Sentinel*, May 26, 2008, Newsbank Newsfile Collection, http://infoweb.newsbank.com.

57. Fred Grimm, "Give Me That Old-Time Florida," *Miami Herald*, June 8, 2003, Newsbank Newsfile Collection, http://infoweb.newsbank.com.

58. Amy Edwards, "Cypress Gardens Could Snag Coaster," *Orlando Sentinel*, March 28, 2005, Newsbank Newsfile Collection, http://infoweb.newsbank.com.

59. Mary Awosika, "Rebirth—Cypress Gardens, Once Slated for Closure, Is Attracting Visitors in Droves," *Sarasota Herald Tribune*, August 5, 2005, Newsbank Newsfile Collection, http://infoweb.newsbank.com.

60. Joy Cochran, "Cypress Gardens Files for Chapter 11," *Lakeland Ledger*, September 13, 2006, Polk County Historical and Genealogical Library.

61. Billy Townsend, "Cypress Gardens Grafts Fun, Thrills onto Beauty," *Tampa Tribune*, September 4, 2007, Newsbank Newsfile Collection, http://infoweb.newsbank.com.

62. Kumari Kelly, "Cypress Gardens Auction Is September 25," *Orlando Sentinel*, September 8, 2007, Newsbank Newsfile Collection, http://infoweb.newsbank.com.

63. Bob Kehoe interview, February 2008.

64. Bob Gernert interview, February 2008.

65. Kumari Kelly, "Readers E-mail Best Wishes for Cypress Gardens," *Orlando Sentinel*, September 16, 2007, Newsbank Newsfile Collection, http://infoweb.newsbank.com.

66. "First Suitor Makes Proposal for Theme Park," *St. Petersburg Times*, September 24, 2007, Newsbank Newsfile Collection, http://infoweb.newsbank.com.

67. Amy Edward, "New Owners, New Hope: Cypress Gardens' Sale to a Mulberry Investment Company Is Expected to Be Wrapped up in Mid-October," *Orlando Sentinel*, September 30, 2007, Newsbank Newsfile Collection, http://infoweb.newsbank.com.

68. Bob Gernert interview, February 2008.

69. Dan Ping, "Baker Leisure in, Buescher out at Cypress Gardens," *Orlando Business Journal*, January 2, 2008, Newsbank Newsfile Collection, http://infoweb.newsbank.com.

70. Donna Kelly, "Rollins Mourns Loss of Hall of Fame Skier, Dick Pope, Jr., *Lakeland Ledger*, November 11, 2007, www.rollinssports.com.

71. Jim Frye, "A Family's Legacy: Remembering Cypress Gardens with Dick Pope, Jr.," *WaterSki Magazine*, July 2003.

72. Don Buffa interview, March 2008.

73. Susan Hack, "A Conversation with Jordan's King Abdullah II," *Condé Nast Traveler*, January 2007, www.concierge.com/cntraveler/articles/10529?pageNumber=2.

74. Don Buffa interview.

75. Donnie Croft interview, March 2008.

76. Shaune Stoskopf interview, March 2008.

77. Lyndsey Roma interview, March 2008.

78. Jaclyn Ledoux interview, March 2008.

79. Megan interview, March 2008.

80. Britanny interview, March 2008.

81. Samantha Williford interview, March 2008.

82. Jill Conner Brown, *Official Web site of the Sweet Potato Queens*, www.sweetpotatoqueens.

83. Kimberly Moore, "Ex-Belle Bids Adieu to Cypress Gardens," *Florida Today*, April 13, 2003, Newsbank Newsfile Collection, http://infoweb.newsbank.com.

84. Samantha Williford interview.

85. Betty Doles interview.

86. Gail Conner interview, September 1, 2009.

87. Lucy Chambliss interview, February 2008.

88. Gary Mormino interview, July 2009.

89. Cypress Gardens press release.

90. Steven M. Locke, "USA Water Ski Executive Director's Report—Week of March 9, 2009," *USA Waterski*, skiowsa.com/component/option,com_docman/task,doc. . ./gid,104/.

91. Bill Sims interview, May 20, 2009.

92. Velma Seawell Daniels, "Readers' Rants and Raves," *Winter Haven News Chief*, April 27, 2009, www.newschief.com.

93. Merissa Green, "New Owners Still Trying to Transform Cypress Gardens," *Lakeland Ledger*, July 6, 2009, www.theledger.com.

94. Donna Kelly, "Positive Signs Seen for Cypress Gardens," *Winter Haven News Chief*, December 16, 2009, www.newschief.com.

95. Gary White and Kyle Kennedy, "Cypress Gardens Closes—Lawyer Says Owners Are Looking to Sell Property to Someone Who Will Reopen It as a Theme Park," *Lakeland Ledger*, September 24, 2009, www.theledger.com.

96. "Questions Aside, Gardens' Owners Took Risk with Park," *Winter Haven News Chief*, September 25, 2009, www.newschief.com.

97. White and Kennedy, "Cypress Gardens Closes."

98. "Time Passes Polk Treasure," *Tampa Tribune*, October 7, 2009, www2.tbo.com.

99. Donna Kelly, "Positive Signs Seen for Cypress Gardens," *Winter Haven News Chief*, December 16, 2009, www.newschief.com.

100. Legoland Florida Press Conference, Cypress Gardens, January 21, 2010.

101. Jim Hughes, "Building LEGOLAND," *Brick Journal* 5, vol. 1 (Summer 2006).

102. Legoland Florida Press Conference.

103. Gary J.Kelsall, "Alton Towers Heritage," January 28, 2010, http://www.altontowersheritage.com.

104. Ibid.

105. *Alton Towers Almanac*, "About This Area," February 7, 2010, http://www.towersalmanac.com.

106. Vincent Canby, "That's Entertainment II (1976): Magical Sequel to 'That's Entertainment,'" *New York Times*, May 17, 1976, ProQuest Historical Newspapers, http://proquest.umi.com/login.

Bibliography

Adams, William R. *Historic Lake Wales.* St. Augustine, Fla.: Southern Heritage Press, 1992.

Agassiz, Garnault. "Florida in Tomorrow's Sun." *Suniland* 3, no. 2 (November 1925): 37–45, 88–94, 113–33. *Exploring Florida,* http://fcit.usf.edu/FLORIDA/docs/f/fruit.htm.

Ahl, Janyce Barnwell. *Crown Jewel of the Florida Highlands, Lake Wales.* Lake Wales: Lake Wales Library Association, 1983.

Ammidown, Margot. "Edens, Underworlds, and Shrines: Florida's Small Tourist Attractions." Special Florida issue, *Journal of Decorative and Propaganda Arts* 23 (1998): 239–59.

Bartram, William. *Travels of William Bartram.* Edited by Mark Van Doren. Athens: University of Georgia Press, 1998.

Bensen, Igor. *A Dream of Flight.* Indianapolis: Abbott, 2003.

Bongartz, Roy. "The Superswamp: Cypress Gardens: Florida's Eighteen-Karat Illusion." *Saturday Evening Post,* November 26, 1963, 78–81.

Branch, Stephen. "Florida with Flair: Dick Pope and the Making of Cypress Gardens." *Polk County Historical Quarterly* 30 (September 2003): 1, 4–5, 8–9, 12.

Brown, Canter. *In the Midst of All That Makes Life Worth Living: Polk County, Florida to 1940.* Tallahassee: Sentry Press, 2001.

Brownlee, P. J. "'Where de Water Drink Lak Cherry Wine': The Importance of Zora Neale Hurston's Work in Polk County Florida." *Polk County Historical Quarterly* 27, no. 1 (June 2000): 1–3, 7.

"Cornelia: Determined to 'Make Do.'" *Time,* May 29, 1972.

Cypress Gardens 60th Anniversary: 1936–1996.

"Cypress Gardens." *Water Skier,* October 1951.

Deford, Frank. "An Honest Travel Story." *Sports Illustrated,* January 26, 1976, 32–34, 39–40.

Desmond, Kevin. *The Golden Age of Waterskiing.* St. Paul, Minn.: MBI, 2001.

"Easy To Love." *Newsweek,* November 30, 1953, 104–5.

"Ebb Tide at Miami Beach." *Time,* December 19, 1977. www.time.com.

Flekke, Mary, Sarah MacDonald, and Randall MacDonald. *Images of Cypress Gardens.* Charleston, S.C.: Arcadia, 2006.

Florida: A Guide to the Southernmost State. 1939. Compiled and written by the Federal Writers' Project of the Works Progress Administration. New York: Oxford University Press, 1956.

Foglesong, Richard. *Married to the Mouse: Walt Disney World and Orlando.* New Haven: Yale University Press, 2003.

Fong-Torres, Ben. *Hickory Wind: The Life and Times of Gram Parsons.* New York: St. Martins Griffin, 1998.

Frye, Jim. "A Family's Legacy: Remembering Cypress Gardens with Dick Pope, Jr." *WaterSki Magazine,* July 2003, 27–28.

———. "The Legacy of Cypress Gardens." waterskimag.com.

Furlong, William B. "Babes in a Swampland." *Sports Illustrated,* October 21, 1963, 66–80.

Garrett, Wilbur E. "The Booming Sport of Waterskiing." *National Geographic,* November 1958, 700–711.

Herzog, Arthur. "The King of Beauty Queens." *Esquire,* September 1957, 120–28.

Hiaasen, Carl. *Team Rodent.* New York: Random House, 1998.

Hollis, Tim. *Glass Bottom Boats and Mermaid Tails.* Mechanicsburg, Pa.: Stackpole Books, 2006.

Hurston, Zora Neale. *Dust Tracks on a Road.* New York: HarperPerennial, 1996.

———. *Mules and Men.* New York: HarperPerennial, 1990.

Hurston, Zora Neale, and Dorothy Waring. *Polk County: A Comedy of Negro Life on a Sawmill Camp with Authentic Negro Music in Three Acts.* Library of Congress. http://hdl.loc.gov/loc.rbc/mhurston.0301.

Jones, Jack. "Cashing in on Liquid Assets." *Florida Municipal Record,* January 1933, 23, 58.

Kaucher, Dorothy. *They Built a City.* Lake Wales, Fla., 1970.

Kraft, Virginia. "His Majesty, The Leadfoot." *Sports Illustrated,* May 8, 1967, 42–48.

Lotz, John. "The Suffix–rama." *American Speech* 29, no. 2 (May 1954): 156–58.

McCarten, John. "Current Cinema," *New Yorker*, December 19, 1953, 97.

Mormino, Gary. *Land of Sunshine, State of Dreams*. Gainesville: University Press of Florida, 2005.

Murrell, Muriel. *Miami: A Backward Glance*. Sarasota: Pineapple Press, 2003.

Nees, Lisa. "Cypress Gardens: The Beauty Queens' Playground." *Pageantry Magazine* (2000). www.pageantrymagazine.com.

Pasternak, Ceel. "Profile: Dick Pope." *Spray: The Waterskiing Magazine*, July 1978, 22–25, 56–57, 60–61.

Pasternak, Joe. *Easy the Hard Way*. As told to David Chandler. London: W. H. Allen, 1956.

Peskin, Hy, and Norton Wood. "The Man Who Invented Florida." *Argosy*, June 1950, 30–31, 70.

Pope, Dick, Sr. "Havenites Have Unique Program for Enhancing City's Beauty." *Florida Municipal Record*, January 1933.

———. "Ten Days on Location." *Outboard Motor Boating*, May 1930, 205–6, 232.

———. *Water Skiing*. Englewood Cliffs, N.J.: Prentice-Hall, 1958.

———. "Zip It's Motorboating Time in Auburndale. *Florida Municipal Record*, April 1930, 8–9.

Recker, Kenneth. *A History of the Winter Haven Lake Region Boat Course District*. Winter Haven, Fla.: Canal Commission, 1986.

"Self-Propelled Surfboard." *Mechanics Illustrated*, April 1950, 74–75, *Modern Mechanix*, http://blog.modernmechanix.com/2006/08/30/self-propelled-surfboard/.

"The Shah by the Seashore." *Life*, February 14, 1955, 60–61.

Singer, Dorothy, and Jerome Singer. *Handbook of Children and the Media*. Thousand Oaks, Calif.: Sage, 2001.

Slate, Mary Ellen. "Cypress Gardens Rides Again." *Motor Boating and Sailing*, March 1971.

"SR Goes to the Movies." *Saturday Review*, December 19, 1953, 30.

"Swimming Pool Built in a Lake." *Popular Mechanics*, July 1953, 107.

"Television: New Cyclops," *Business Week*, March 10, 1956, 76–104.

Thomas, Tony, and Jim Terry. *The Busby Berkeley Book*. With Busby Berkeley. Greenwich, Ct.: New York Graphic Society, 1973.

Thruelsen, Richard. "Fanciest Frolic on Water." *Saturday Evening Post*, April 3, 1954, 24.

Vincent, James. *Parting the Waters: How Vision and Faith Made Good Business*. Chicago: Moody Press, 1997

Vredeveld, Gertrude. "Cypress Gardens Goes Hollywood." *Water Skier*, February 1953.

Wallace, Cornelia. *C'nelia*. Philadelphia: A. J. Holman, 1976.

"Wave of the Future." *Time*, May 26, 1997, www.time.com.

Wells, Kevin. "Middle of the Swarm." *WaterSki Magazine*, undated, www.waterskimag.com.

White, Randy Wayne. "Girls! Gators! Glitz!" *Southern Magazine*, August 1998, 46–51, 71–72.

Williams, Esther. *The Million Dollar Mermaid*. New York: Harvest Books. 2000.

Index

Page numbers in italics refer to illustrations.

Lu Vickers has published numerous essays and short stories in magazines such as Salon.com and *Apalachee Review*, and she has received three Individual Artist's Grants for fiction from the Florida Division of Cultural Affairs. In 2007, she published the novel *Breathing Underwater* and *Weeki Wachee, City of Mermaids: A History of One of Florida's Oldest Roadside Attractions.* She is currently working on a second novel.